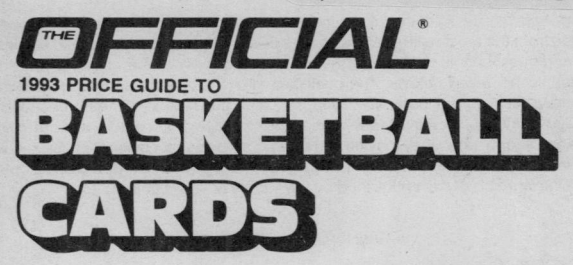

THE OFFICIAL
1993 PRICE GUIDE TO
BASKETBALL CARDS

**BY
DR. JAMES BECKETT**

SECOND EDITION

HOUSE OF COLLECTIBLES • NEW YORK

Sale of this book without a front cover may be unauthorized. If this book is coverless, it may have been reported to the publisher as "unsold or destroyed" and neither the author nor the publisher may have received payment for it.

Important Notice. All of the information, including valuations, in this book has been compiled from the most reliable sources, and every effort has been made to eliminate errors and questionable data. Nevertheless, the possibility of error in a work of such immense scope, always exists. The publisher will not be held responsible for losses which may occur in the purchase, sale, or other transaction of items because of information contained herein. Readers who feel they have discovered errors are invited to write and inform us, so they may be corrected in subsequent editions. Those seeking further information on the topics covered in this book are advised to refer to the complete line of *Official Price Guides* published by the House of Collectibles.

© 1992 by James Beckett III

HC This is a registered trademark of Random House, Inc.

All rights reserved under International and Pan-American Copyright Conventions.

Published by:
House of Collectibles
201 East 50th Street
New York, New York 10022

Distributed by Ballantine Books, a division of Random House, Inc., New York and simultaneously in Canada by Random House of Canada Limited, Toronto.

Manufactured in the United States of America

ISSN: 1062-6980

ISBN: 0-876-37896-3

Second Edition: November 1992

10 9 8 7 6 5 4 3 2 1

TABLE OF CONTENTS

Introduction 2
How to Collect 3
    Obtaining Cards 3
    Preserving Your Cards 4
    Collecting/Investing 5
Nomenclature 6
Glossary/Legend 7
Basketball Card History 12
Business of Sports Card Collecting 14
    Determining Value 14
    Regional Variation 15
    Set Prices 16
    Scarce Series 16
    Grading Your Cards 16
    Centering 17
    Corner Wear 17
    Creases 20
    Alterations 20
    Categorization of Defects 20
    Condition Guide 21
    Selling Your Cards 22
Interesting Notes 24
Advertising 25
Recommended Reading 26
Prices in this Guide 28
About the Author 29
Series:
    Bowman (1948) 30
    Classic Draft Picks (1991-1992) 33
    Courtside Draft Pix (1991) 41
    Fleer (1961-1962, 1986-1992) 44
    Front Row (1991-1992) 93
    Hoops (1989-1992) 108
    Sky Box (1990-1992) 159
    Star (1983-1986) 199
    Star Pics (1990-1991) 215
    Topps (1957-1958, 1969-1982) 222
    Upper Deck (1991-1992) 336
    Wild Cards (1991-1992) 352

PREFACE

Isn't it great? Every year this book gets bigger and bigger, packed with all the new sets coming out. But even more exciting is that every year there are more collectors, more shows, more stores, and more interest in the cards we love so much. This edition has been enhanced and expanded from the previous edition. The cards you collect — who they depict, what they look like, where they are from, and (most important to many of you) what their current values are — are enumerated within. Many of the features contained in the other Beckett Price Guides have been incorporated into this volume since condition grading, nomenclature, and many other aspects of collecting are common to the card hobby in general. We hope you find the book both interesting and useful in your collecting pursuits.

Everyone knows about the tremendous growth in interest in baseball cards, but basketball cards are quite popular as well. In fact, interest in basketball cards is currently at an all-time high. They are becoming increasingly visible at the nation's card shows and stores.

The reason for the emergence of these cards in particular is due in large part to the continuing and increasing popularity of the sport itself. This increased popularity has made basketball superstars well known to millions of fans who watch them during the winter and spring and read about them all year. Megastars such as Michael Jordan, Clyde Drexler and David Robinson are among the most famous and recognizeable athletes in the world. Finally, the comparatively high cost of premium baseball cards has persuaded many collectors to pursue cards of other sports as a more affordable means of pursuing the sports collectibles hobby. Nevertheless, as you can see from the prices in this book, basketball cards are valuable — and they are perceived by a growing number of collectors as being good values for their hobby dollar.

Basketball cards are also typically produced in smaller sets than baseball, football and hockey sets, making it easier for collectors to complete them. The small size of all except the most recent basketball card sets has another positive aspect: There are more star cards and fewer commons.

The Beckett Guide has been successful where other attempts have failed because it is complete, current, and valid. This Price Guide contains not just one, but three prices by condition for all the football cards listed. These account for almost every football card in existence. The prices were added to the card lists just prior to printing and reflect not the author's opinions or desires but the going retail prices for each card, based on the marketplace (sports memorabilia conventions and shows, sports card shops, hobby papers, current mail-order catalogs, computer trading networks, auction results, and other firsthand reportings of actual realized prices).

What is the best price guide on the market today? Of course card sellers will consider the price guide with the highest prices as the best — while card buyers will naturally prefer the one with the lowest prices. Accuracy, however, is the true test. Use the price guide used by more collectors and dealers than all the others combined. Look for the Beckett name. I won't put my name on anything I won't stake my reputation on. Not the lowest and not the highest — but the most accurate, with integrity.

To facilitate your use of this book, read the complete introductory section in the pages following before going to the pricing pages. Every collectible field has its own terminology; we've tried to capture most of these terms and definitions in our glossary. Please read carefully the section on grading and the condition of your cards, as you will not be able to determine which price column is appropriate for a given card without first assessing its condition.

Welcome to the world of basketball cards.

Sincerely, Dr. James Beckett

ACKNOWLEDGMENTS

A great deal of diligence, hard work, and dedicated effort went into this year's volume. However, the high standards to which we hold ourselves could not have been met without the expert input and generous time contributed by many people. Our sincere thanks are extended to each and every one of you.

I believe this year's Price Guide is our best yet. For that, you can thank all of the contributors nationwide (listed below) as well as our staff here in Dallas. Our company now boasts a substantial Technical Services team which has made (and is continuing to make) direct and important contributions to this work. Technical Services capably handled numerous technical details and provided able assistance in pricing for this edition of the annual guide. That effort was directed by Technical Services manager Pepper Hastings. He was assisted by Technical Services coordinator Mary Gregory, Price Guide analysts Theo Chen, Mike Hersh, Dan Hitt, Mary Huston, Rich Klein, Tom Layberger, Allan Muir, Grant Sandground, Dave Sliepka, and Steve Smith. Also contributing to our Technical Services functions were Scott Layton, Margaret Mall, Peter Tepp, and Jana Threatt, whose special assistance was invaluable in making this project a success. The price gathering and analytical talents of this fine group of hobbyists has helped make our Beckett team stronger, while making this guide and its companion monthly Price Guides more widely recognized as the hobby's most reliable and relied upon sources of pricing information.

Granted, the production of any book is a total staff effort. However, I owe special thanks to the members of our Book Team who demonstrated extraordinary contributions to this basketball book.

Scott Layton, our research associate, served as point man in the demanding area of new set entry and was a key person in the organization of both technological and people resources for the book. Margaret Mall and Kent Lawrence ensured the proper administration of our contributor price guide surveys. Pricing analysts Theo Chen, Rich Klein, and Grant Sandground track the basketball card market year round, and their baseline analysis and careful proofreading were key contributions to the accuracy of this annual.

Airey Baringer spent many late-night hours paginating and typesetting the text layout. Gayla Newberry was responsible for many of the card photos you see throughout the book. Maria Gonzalez-Davis again was meticulous in her work on the paste-up table. Wendy Kizer spent tireless hours on the phone attending to the wishes of our dealer advertisers. Once the ad specifications were delivered to our offices, John Marshall used his computer skills to turn raw copy into attractive display advertisements that were carefully proofed by Bruce Felps. Finally, Managing Editor of Special Projects, Susan K. Elliott, set up initial schedules and ensured that all deadlines were met.

My sincere thanks to everyone on our Book Team and to all at Beckett Publications, who are listed below, for another job well done.

It is very difficult to be "accurate" — one can only do one's best. But this job is especially difficult since we're shooting at a moving target: Prices are fluctuating all the time. Having several full-time pricing experts has definitely proven to be better than just one, and I thank all of them for working together to provide you, our readers, with the most accurate prices possible.

Those who have worked closely with us on this and many other books, have again proven themselves invaluable in every aspect of producing this book: Rich Altman, Mike Aronstein, Baseball Hobby News (Frank and Vivian Barning), Jerry Bell, Chris Benjamin, Sy Berger (Topps Chewing Gum), Mike Blaisdell, Bill Bossert (Mid-Atlantic Coin Exchange), Barry Colla, Mike Cramer (Pacific Trading Cards), Todd Crosner (California Sportscard Exchange), Bud Darland, Bill and Diane Dodge, Willie Erving, Gervise Ford, Steve Freedman, Larry and Jeff Fritsch, Steve Galletta, Tony Galovich, Jim Galusha, Dick Gariepy, Dick Gilkeson, Mike and Howard Gordon, George Grauer, John Greenwald, Wayne Grove, Bill Haber, Bill Henderson, George Henn, Jerry Hersh, Steve Johnson, Edward J. Kabala, Judy and Norman Kay, Alan Kaye (*Sports Card News*), Lesnik Public Relations (Timm Boyle and Bob Ibach), Robert Levin (The Star Company), Lew Lipset, Dave Lucey, Jim Macie, Paul Marchant, Brian Marcy (Scottsdale Baseball Cards), Dr. John McCue, Michael Moretto, Brian Morris, B.A. Murry, Jack Pollard, Tom Reid, Gavin Riley, Alan Rosen (Mr. Mint), John Rumierz, San Diego Sport Collectibles (Bill Goepner and Nacho Arredondo), Kevin Savage (Sports Gallery), Mike Schechter (MSA), Bill Shonscheck, John Spalding, Nigel Spill (Oldies and Goodies), Sports Collectors Store (Pat Quinn and Don Steinbach), Frank Steele, Murvin Sterling, Dan Stickney, Steve Taft, Ed Taylor, Paul S. Taylor, Lee Temanson, Bill Wesslund, Kit Young, Robert Zanze, and Bill Zimpleman.

Many other individuals have provided price input, illustrative material, checklist verifications, errata, and/or background information. At the risk of inadvertently overlooking or omitting these many contributors, we should like to personally thank Jerry Adamic, Tom Akins, Dennis Anderson, Ellis Anmuth, Arkansas Sports Distributing, Toni Axtell, Douglas Baker, Baseball Cards Plus, Josh Baver, Bay State Cards (Lenny DeAngelico), Chris Becirel, Klaus Becker, Darrell E. Benjamin Jr., Andy Bergman, Carl Bergstrom, Adrian Betts, Beulah Sports, Brian Bigelow (Candl), Walter Bird, Brian Black, Keith and Ryan Bonner, Gary Boyd, Michael Boyd, Terry Brock, Fritz Brogan, Scott Brondyke, Karen Sue Brown, Dan Bruner (The Card King), Buckhead Baseball Cards (Marc Spector), Shawn Burke, Zac Burke, Curtis H. Butler, California Card Co., Mark Cantin, Danny Cariseo, Phil Carpenter, Cee Tim's Cards, Dwight Chapin, Rich Chavez, Dennis Chin, Bradley Clark, Shane Cohen (Grand Slam), Aaron Cole, Matt Collett, Danny Collins, H. William Cook, Ben Coulter, Enrique Cuenca, Robert Curtis, Herb Dallas Jr., Kenneth Dean, Matt DeBrabant, David Diehl, Cliff Dolgins, Discount Dorothy, Bill Eckle, David Edwards, Robert Ehnert, Robin Emmerling, Ed Emmitt, Mark Enger, David Erickson, Jonathan R. Farmer, Andy Feinstein, James Fendley, Terry Fennell, L.V. Fischer (The Collectors Den), Steve Foster,

Doug French, Donny Frost, Dick Fuisz, Rob Gagnon, Robby Gantt, Steve Gerber, Michael R. Gionet, Steve Gold (AU Sports), Jeff Goldstein, Brandon Goodloe, Darin Goodwin, Gary W. Graber (Minden Games), David Grauf (Cards for the Connoisseur), Nick Grier, Erik Griggs, Don Guilbert, Hall's Nostalgia, Sean Hank, Chad Harris, Jacob Harrison, Lenny Helicer, Vaughn Hickman, Clay Hill, Alisa Hills, H.L.T. and T. Sports (Harold and Todd Nelkin), Will Ho, Russell Hoffman, Verdeen Hogan, Home Plate of Provo (Ken Edick), Keith Hora, Gene Horvath, Thomas James, Andy Jenkins, Kevin Jeu, Richard Johnson, Darryl Jordan, Tom Judd, Patricia Kaleihehana, Kevin Kamel, Bruce Kangas, Jay Kasper, Kim Kellogg, Joe Kelly, Dan Kent, Jeff Kluger, Roger Krafve, Paul Krasinkewicz, Mayank Keshaviah, Nicholas Krupke, Thomas Kunnecke, Vasin Laiteerapong, Ted Larkins (The Card Clubhouse), Dan Lavin, John F. Law, Stephen M. Lawson, A.B. Leo, Nathan Leon, Irv Lerner, Howie Levy of Blue Chip, Scott M. Lewandowski, Craig Lightcap, Dan Linroth, Jim Loeffler, Cody Lorance, R.J. Lyons, Jack Maiden, Larry Marks, Maurice Massey, Robert Matonis, Gary O. May, Jack Mayes, Leonard McClure, Anthony McCoy, Mike McDonald (Sports Page), Lou McDonough, Timothy McElroy, Erik McKenzie, Jay F. McLain, James McNaughton, Dale C. Meek, Steve Melnick, Blake Meyer, Darren Milbrandt, Alan Miller, Richard Mold, Sean Moody, William Moorhead, Joe Morano, Joe Morris, Paul Morrison, Jeff Mowers, David Mowett, Fred Muollo, Dave Murray, Funz Napolitano, Cory T. Neu, No Gum Just Cards, Brad Norwood, John O'Hara, Trace Ono, Jeremy Opperman, Paul Orlick, G. Michael Oyster, Ricky Parker, Clay Pasternack, Earl Petersen, Troy Peterson, Tom Pfirrmann, John Pollack, Darren Porter, Ben Powers, Jonathan Ramos, Josh Randall, Phil Regli, David Renshaw, Louis Rene Reyes, Emily Rice, Mark Risk, Juan Rivera, Richard Robinson, Chuck Roethel, Steven Roeglin, Barry J. Rossheim, Ted Russo, Terry Sack, Joe Sak, Garret Salomon, Arnold Sanchez, Ron Sanders, Michael Sang, Bob Santos, Nathan Schank, Michael Seaman, Sebring Sports, Steven Senft, Mark Shields, Terry C. Shook, Ryan D. Shrimplin, Glen Sidler, Darrin Silverman, Gail Smith, Raymond Smith, Ron Smith, Bob Snyder, Luke Somers, William Soung, Carl Specht, Sports Legends, Doug Stauduhar, Paul M. Stefani, Allen Stengel (Perfect Image), Cary Stephenson, Scott Stucki, Michael Stuy, Doug Such, Mark Tanaka (Front Row), Chris Tateosian, Robert Taylor, Steve Taylor, Nick Teresi, Craig Thomas, Melanie Thomas, Mike Thompson, Emerson Tongco, Jeffrey K. Tsai, Peter Tsang, Jessie Turner, Warren Utsunomiya, Mark Velger (Trade Mark SportsCards), Eric Ware, Matthew Waten, David Weber, Jennifer Wegner, Richard West, Gregory Wiggins, Bob Wilke (The Shoe Box), Brian Wilkie, Shawn Williacy, Jeff Williams, Mark Williams, Matt Winters, Mike Woods (The Dugout), World Series Cards (Neil Armstrong), Mike Yost, and Zards Cards.

Every year, we make active solicitations for expert input. We are particularly appreciative of help (however extensive or cursory) provided for this volume. We receive many inquiries, comments and questions regarding material within this book. In fact, each and every one is read and digested. Time constraints, however, prevent us from personally replying. But keep sharing your knowledge. Your letters and input are part of the "big picture" of hobby information we can pass along to readers in our books and magazines. Even though we cannot respond to each letter, you are making significant contributions to the hobby through your interest and comments.

In the years since this guide debuted, Beckett Publications has grown beyond any rational expectation. A great many talented and hard working individuals have been instrumental in this growth and success. Our whole team is to be congratulated for what we together have accomplished.

Our Beckett Publications team is led by Associate Publisher Claire Backus, Vice Presidents Joe Galindo and Fred Reed, and Director of Marketing Jeff Amano. They are ably assisted by Fernando Albieri, Theresa Anderson, Gena Andrews, Jeff Anthony, Airey Baringer II, Barbara Barry, Nancy Bassi, Therese Bellar, Louise Bird, Wendy Bird, Cathryn Black, Terry Bloom, Lisa Borden, Dianne Boudreaux, Amy Brougher, Anthony Brown, Chris Calandro, Emily Camp, Mary Campana, Renata Campos, Becky Cann, Sammy Cantrell, Susan Catka, Jose Chavez, Theo Chen, Lynne Chinn, Tommy Collins, Belinda Cross, Billy Culbert, Randy Cummings, Patrick Cunningham, Gail Docekal, Andrew Drago, Louise Ebaugh, Alejandro Egusquiza, Mila Egusquiza, Susan Elliott, Daniel Evans, Bruce Felps, Jorge Field, Sara Field, Jean Paul Figari, Jeany Finch, Robson Fonseca, Kim Ford, Jeannie Fulbright, Gayle Gasperin, Anita Gonzalez, Mary Gonzalez-Davis, Jeff Greer, Mary Gregory, Julie Grove, Marcio Guimaraes, Karen Hall, Carmen Harbour, Sabrina Harbour, Jim Harmeyer, Vivian Harmon, Patti Harris, Beth Harwell, Jenny Harwell, Mark Harwell, Pepper Hastings, Joanna Hayden, Cindy Herbert, Mike Hersh, Barbara Hinkle, Tracy Hinton, Dan Hitt, Heather Holland, E.J. Hradek, Rex Hudson, Mary Huston, Don James, Sara Jenks, Julia Jernigan, Wendy Jewell, Jay Johnson, Matt Keifer, Fran Keng, Monte King, Debbie Kingsbury, Amy Kirk, Sheri Kirk, Rudy Klancnik, Rich Klein, Frances Knight, John Knotts, Kent Lawrence, Tom Layberger, Jane Ann Layton, Scott Layton, Lori Lindsey, Cheryl Lingenfelter, Margaret Mall, Mark Manning, Louis Marroquin, John Marshall, Laura Massey, Kaki Matheson, Teri McGahey, Kirk McKinney, Mary McNertney, Omar Mediano, Edras Mendez, Sherry Monday, Robert Montenegro, Stephen Moore, Glen Morante, Elizabeth Morris, Daniel Moscoso, Daniel Moscoso Jr., Mike Moss, Randy Mosty, Allan Muir, Hugh Murphy, Shawn Murphy, Marie Neubauer, Wendy Neumann, Allen Neumann, Gayla Newberry, Rosanna Olaechea, Lisa O'Neill, Rich Olivieri, Abraham Pacheco, Guillermo Pacheco, Michael Patton, Mike Payne, Suzee Payton, Ronda Pearson, Julie Polomis, Tim Polzer, Reed Poole, Roberto Ramirez, Roger Randall, Nikki Renshaw, Patrick Richard, Cristina Riojas, Jamile Romero, Stephen Rueckhaus, Grant Sandground, Gary Santaniello, Gabriel Santos, Manuel Santos, Stacy Schreiner, Maggie Seward, Elaine Simmons, Carol Slawson, Steve Slawson, Dave Sliepka, Judi Smalling, Steve Smith, Lisa Spaight, Margaret Steele, Mark Stokes, Jason Stone, Cindy Struble, Doree Tate,

Peter Tepp, Jim Tereschuk, Christiann Thomas, Becky Thompson, Jana Threatt, Jason Todd, Brett Tulloss, Valerie Voigt, Steve Wilson, Carol Ann Wurster, and Robert Yearby. In addition, our consultants James and Sandi Beane and Dan Swanson performed several major system programming jobs for us again this year, to help us accomplish our work faster and more accurately. The whole Beckett Publications team has my thanks for jobs well done. Thank you, everyone.

I also thank my family, especially my wife, Patti, and daughters, Christina, Rebecca, and Melissa, for putting up with me again.

ERRATA

There are thousands of names, more than 100,000 prices, and untold other words in this book. There are going to be a few typographical errors, a few misspellings, and possibly, a number or three out of place. If you catch a blooper, drop me a note directly and we will fix it in next year's edition.

THE OFFICIAL
PRICE GUIDE TO
BASKETBALL CARDS

INTRODUCTION

Welcome to the exciting world of sports card collecting, America's fastest-growing avocation. You have made a good choice in buying this book, since it will open up to you the entire panorama of this field in the simplest, most concise way. Hundreds of thousands of different sports cards have been issued during the past century. And the number of total sports cards produced by all manufacturers last year has been estimated at several billion, with an initial wholesale value of more than $1 billion. Sales of older cards by dealers may account for an equal or greater amount. With all that cardboard available in the marketplace, it should be no surprise that several million sports fans like you collect sports cards today, and that number is growing each year.

The growth of Beckett Baseball Card Monthly, Beckett Basketball Monthly, Beckett Football Card Monthly, Beckett Hockey Monthly, and Beckett Focus on Future Stars is another indication of this rising crescendo of popularity for sports cards. Founded in 1984 by Dr. James Beckett, the author of this Price Guide, Beckett Baseball Card Monthly has reached the pinnacle of the sports card hobby, with nearly two million readers anxiously awaiting each enjoyable and informative issue. The other four magazines have met similar success, with hundreds of thousands of readers devoted to each publication.

So collecting sports cards — while still pursued as a hobby with youthful exuberance by kids in your neighborhood — has also taken on the trappings of an industry, with thousands of full- and part-time card dealers, as well as vendors of supplies, clubs and conventions. In fact, each year since 1980, thousands of hobbyists have assembled for a National Sports Collectors Convention, at which hundreds of dealers have displayed their wares, seminars have been conducted, autographs penned by sports notables, and millions of cards changed hands. These colossal affairs have been staged in Los Angeles, Detroit, St. Louis, Chicago, New York, Anaheim, Arlington (Texas), San Francisco, Atlantic City, Chicago, Arlington (Texas), Anaheim, and this year in Atlanta. So sports card collecting really is national in scope!

This increasing interest is reflected in card values. As more collectors compete for available supplies, card prices rise (especially for older premium-grade cards). A perusal of the prices in this book, compared to the figures in earlier editions of this Price Guide, will quickly confirm this. Which brings us back around to the book you have in your hands. It is the best guide available to the exciting world of your favorite sport's cards. Read it and use it. May your enjoyment and your card collection increase in the coming months and years.

HOW TO COLLECT

Each collection is personal and reflects the individuality of its owner. There are no set rules on how to collect cards. Since card collecting is a hobby or leisure pastime, what you collect, how much you collect, and how much time and money you spend collecting, are entirely up to you. The funds you have available for collecting and your own personal taste should determine how you collect. Information and ideas presented here are intended to help you get the most enjoyment from this hobby.

It is impossible to collect every card ever produced. Therefore, beginners as well as intermediate and advanced collectors usually specialize in some way. One of the most popular aspects of this hobby is that individual collectors can define and tailor their collecting methods to match their own tastes. To give you some ideas of the various approaches to collecting, we will list some of the more popular areas of specialization.

Many collectors select complete sets from particular years. For example, they may concentrate on assembling complete sets from all the years since their birth or since they became avid sports fans. They may try to collect a card for every player during that specified period of time. Many others wish to acquire only certain players. Usually such players are the superstars of the sport, but occasionally collectors will specialize in all the cards of players who attended a particular college or came from a certain town. Some collectors are only interested in the first cards or rookie cards of certain players.

Another fun way to collect cards is by team. Most fans have a favorite team, and it is natural for that loyalty to be translated into a desire for cards of the players on that favorite team. For most of the recent years, team sets (all the cards from a given team for that year) are readily available at a reasonable price. This concept can also be applied to your favorite college's products. For instance, Maryland collectors would pursue cards of Brad Davis, Albert King, Tom McMillen, John Lucas, Tony Massenburg, Jerrod Mustaf and Walt Williams — or Georgia Tech collectors would pursue cards of Mark Price, John Salley, Tom Hammonds, Dennis Scott, Kenny Anderson, etc.

Obtaining Cards

Several avenues are open to card collectors to seek their favorite issues. Cards can be purchased in the traditional way at the local candy, grocery, or drug stores, with the bubble gum or other products included. For many years, it has been possible to purchase complete sets of cards through mail-order advertisers found in traditional sports media publications, such as The Sporting News, Basketball Digest, Street & Smith yearbooks, and others. These sets are also advertised in card collecting periodicals. Many collectors will begin by subscribing

4 / How to Collect

to at least one of the hobby periodicals. In fact, subscription offers can be found in the advertising section of this book. In addition, a great variety of cards (typically from all eras and all sports) are available through the growing number of hobby retail stores dedicated to sports cards and memorabilia around the country.

Most serious card collectors obtain old (and new) cards from one or more of several main sources: (1) trading or buying from other collectors or dealers; (2) responding to buy, sell or auction ads in hobby publications; (3) buying at a local hobby store; and/or (4) attending sports collectibles shows or conventions. We advise that you try all four methods since each has its own distinct advantages: (1) trading is a great way to make new friends; (2) hobby periodicals help you keep up with what's going on in the hobby (including when and where the conventions are happening); (3) stores provide the opportunity for considering (any day of the week) a great diversity of material in a relaxed sports-oriented atmosphere most fans love; and (4) shows provide enjoyment and the opportunity to view thousands of collectibles under one roof, in addition to meeting some of the hundreds or even thousands of other collectors with similar interests, who also attend the shows.

Preserving Your Cards

Cards are fragile. They must be handled properly in order to retain their value. Careless handling can easily result in creased or bent cards. It is, however, not recommended that tweezers or tongs be used to pick up your cards since such utensils might mar or indent card surfaces and thus reduce those cards' conditions and values. In general, your cards should be handled directly as little as possible. This is sometimes easier to say than to do. Although there are many who use custom boxes, storage trays, or even shoe boxes, plastic sheets represent an inexpensive method to store and display cards. A collection stored in plastic pages in a three-ring album allows you to view your collection at any time without the need to touch the card itself. Cards can also be kept in single holders (of various types and thickness) designed for the enjoyment of each card individually. Most experienced collectors use a combination of the above methods. When purchasing plastic sheets for your cards, be sure that you find the pocket size that fits the cards snugly. Don't put your oversized 1969-70 Topps basketball cards in a sheet designed to fit standard 2 1/2" by 3 1/2" cards. Most hobby and collectibles shops and virtually all collectors' conventions will have these plastic pages available in quantity, or you can purchase them directly from the advertisers in this book. Also remember that pocket size isn't the only factor to consider when looking for plastic sheets. Some collectors concerned with long-term storage of their cards in plastic sheets are cautious to avoid sheets containing PVC and request non-PVC sheets from their dealer.

Damp, sunny and/or hot conditions — no, this is not a weather forecast — are three elements to avoid in extremes if you are interested in preserving your collection. Too much (or less frequently, too little) humidity can cause gradual deterioration of a card. Direct sunlight (or fluorescent light) will bleach out the color of a card. Extreme heat accelerates the decomposition of the card. On the other hand, many cards have lasted more than 50 years with minimal scientific intervention. So be cautious, even if the above factors typically present a problem only when present in the extreme. It never hurts to be prudent.

Collecting/Investing

Collecting individual players and collecting complete sets are both popular vehicles for investment and speculation. Most investors and speculators stock up on complete sets or on quantities of players they think have good investment potential.

There is obviously no guarantee in this book, or anywhere else for that matter, that cards will outperform the stock market or other investment alternatives in the future. After all, sports cards do not pay quarterly dividends and cards cannot be sold at their "current values" as easily as stocks or bonds.

Nevertheless, investors have noticed a favorable long-term trend in the past performance of many sports collectibles, and certain cards and sets have outperformed just about any other investment in some years. Many hobbyists maintain that the best investment is, and always will be, the building of a collection, which traditionally has held up better than outright speculation.

Some of the obvious questions are: Which cards? When to buy? When to sell? The best investment you can make is in your own education. The more you know about your collection, the hobby and the players depicted on the cards, the more informed the decisions you will be able to make. We're not selling investment tips. We're selling information about the current value of sports cards. It's up to you to use that information to your best advantage.

NOMENCLATURE

Basketball sets, generally having been produced in the modern era from 1948 to present, can be described and identified by their year, maker, type of issue, and any other distinguishing characteristic. Regional issues are usually referred to by year, maker, and sometimes by title or theme of the set.

The following abbreviations are used for identifying major basketball sets:

B - Bowman (1948)
F - Fleer (1961-62, 1986-87 to 1991-92)
H - NBA Hoops (1989-90 to 1991-92)
S - Star Company (1983-84 to 1985-86)
SB - SkyBox (1990-91 to 1991-92)
T - Topps (1957-58, 1969-70 to 1981-82)
UD - Upper Deck (1991-92)

GLOSSARY/LEGEND

Our glossary defines terms frequently used in the card collecting hobby. Many of these terms are also common to other types of sports memorabilia collecting. Some terms may have several meanings, depending on use and context.

ABA - American Basketball Association.
ACC - American Card Catalog.
AL - Active Leader.
ART - All-Rookie Team.
AS - All-Star card.
ALP - Alphabetical.
BRICK - A group of cards, usually 50 or more having common characteristics, that is intended to be bought, sold, or traded as a unit.
CBA - Continental Basketball Association.
CC - Classic Confrontations.
CHECKLIST - A list of the cards contained in a particular set. The list is always in numerical order if the cards are numbered. Some unnumbered sets are artificially numbered in alphabetical order, or by team and alphabetically within the team for convenience.
CL - Checklist card. A card that lists in order the cards and players in the set or series. Older checklist cards in Mint condition that have not been checked off are very desirable and command large premiums.
CO - Coach card.
COIN - A small disc of metal or plastic portraying a player in its center.
COLLECTOR - A person who engages in the hobby of collecting cards primarily for his own enjoyment, with any profit motive being secondary.
COLLECTOR ISSUE - A set produced for the sake of the card itself with no product or service sponsor. It derives its name from the fact that most of these sets are produced for sale directly to the hobby market.
COMBINATION CARD - A single card depicting two or more players (but not a team card).
COMMON CARD - The typical card of any set; it has no premium value accruing from subject matter, numerical scarcity, popular demand or anomaly.
CONVENTION ISSUE - A set produced in conjunction with a sports collectibles convention to commemorate or promote the show. Most recent convention issues could also be classified as promo sets.
COR - Corrected card. A version of an error card that was fixed by the manufacturer.
COUPON - See Tab.
DEALER - A person who engages in buying, selling, and trading sports

8 / Glossary/Legend

collectibles or supplies. A dealer may also be a collector, but as a dealer, he anticipates a profit.

DFO - Don't Foul Out.

DIE-CUT - A card with part of its stock partially cut, allowing one or more parts to be folded or removed. After removal or appropriate folding, the remaining part of the card can frequently be made to stand up.

DISC - A circular-shaped card.

DISPLAY CARD - A sheet, usually containing three to nine cards, that is printed and used by the manufacturer to advertise and/or display the packages containing his products and cards. The backs of display cards are blank or contain advertisements.

DISPLAY SHEET - A clear, plastic page that is punched for insertion into a binder (with standard three-ring spacing) containing pockets for displaying cards. Many different styles of sheets exist with pockets of varying sizes to hold the many differing card formats. The vast majority of current cards measure 2 1/2 by 3 1/2 inches and fit in nine-pocket sheets.

DP - Double-printed card. A card that is approximately twice as common as a regular card in the same set.

ERR - Error card. A card with erroneous information, spelling, or depiction on either side of the card. Most errors are never corrected by the producing card company.

FULL SHEET - A complete sheet of cards that has not been cut up into individual cards by the manufacturer. Also called an uncut sheet.

GQ - Gentleman's Quarterly.

HL - Highlight card.

HOF - Hall of Fame.

HOR - Horizontal pose on card as opposed to the standard vertical orientation found on most cards.

IA - In Action card. A special type of card depicting a player in an action photo, such as the 1982 Topps cards.

INSERT - A special card or other collectible (often a poster or sticker) contained and sold in the same package along with cards of a major set. Sometimes called a BONUS CARD.

IS - Inside Stuff.

ISSUE - Synonymous with set, but usually used in conjunction with a manufacturer, e.g., a Topps issue.

LEGITIMATE ISSUE - A set produced to promote or boost sales of a product or service, e.g., bubble gum, cereal, cigarettes, etc. Most collector issues are not legitimate issues in this sense.

LID - A circular-shaped card (possibly with tab) that forms the top of the container for the product being promoted.

LL - League leader card. A card depicting the leader or leaders in a specific statistical category form the previous season. Not to be confused with Team Leader (TL).

Glossary/Legend / 9

MAG - Magic of SkyBox card.

MAJOR SET - A set produced by a national manufacturer of cards containing a large number of cards. Usually 100 or more different cards comprise a major set.

MS - Milestone card.

MINI - A small card or stamp (the 1991-92 SkyBox Canadian set, for example).

MVP - Most Valuable Player.

NY - New York.

OBVERSE - The front, face, or pictured side of the card.

OLY - Olympic team card (1984-85 Star Company subset).

PANEL - An extended card composed of multiple individual cards. The most obvious basketball panels are found in the 1980-81 Topps set.

PERIPHERAL SET - A loosely defined term that applies to any non-regular issue set. This term is most often used to describe food issue, giveaway, regional or sendaway sets that contain a fairly small number of cards and are not accepted by the hobby as major sets.

PREMIUM - A card, sometimes on photographic stock, that is purchased or obtained in conjunction with (or redeemed for) another card or product. This term applies mainly to older products, as newer cards distributed in this manner are generally lumped together as peripheral sets.

PREMIUM CARDS - A class of products introduced recently that are intended to have higher quality card stock and photography than regular cards, but more limited production and higher cost. Defining what is and isn't a premium card is somewhat subjective.

PROMOTIONAL SET - A set, usually containing a small number of cards, issued by a national card producer and distributed in limited quantities or to a select group of people such as major show attendees or dealers with wholesale accounts. Presumably, the purpose of a promo set is to stir up demand for an upcoming set. Also called a preview, prototype or test set.

RARE - A card or series of cards of very limited availability. Unfortunately, "rare" is a subjective term sometimes used indiscriminately. Using the strict definitions, rare cards are harder to obtain than scarce cards.

RB - Record Breaker card.

RC - Rookie Card. A player's first appearance on a regular issue card from one of the major card companies. Each company has only one regular issue set per season, and that is the traditional set that is widely available. With a few exceptions, each player has only one RC in any given set. A Rookie Card cannot be an All-Star, Highlight, In Action, league leader, Super Action or team leader card. It can, however, be a coach card, draft pick or top prospect card.

REGIONAL - A card issued and distributed only in a limited geographical area of the country. The producer may or may not be a major, national producer of trading cards. The key is whether the set was distributed nationally in any form or not.

10 / Glossary/Legend

REVERSE - The back side of the card.

REV NEG - Reversed or flopped photo side of the card. This is a major type of error card, but only some are corrected.

RIS - Rising Star.

ROY - Rookie of the Year.

SA - Super Action.

SAL - SkyBox Salutes.

SASE - Self-addressed, stamped envelope.

SC - Supreme Court.

SCARCE - A card or series of cards of limited availability. This subjective term is sometimes used indiscriminately to promote or hype value. Using strict definitions, scarce cards are not as difficult to obtain as rare cards.

SD - Slam Dunk.

SERIES - The entire set of cards issued by a particular producer in a particular year, e.g., the 1978-79 Topps series. Also, within a particular set, series can refer to a group of (consecutively numbered) cards printed at the same time, e.g., the first series of the 1972-73 Topps set (#1 through #132).

SET - One each of the entire run of cards of the same type produced by a particular manufacturer during a single season. In other words, if you have a complete set of 1988-89 Fleer basketball cards, then you have every card from #1 up to and including #132; i.e., all the different cards that were produced.

SHOW - A large gathering of dealers and collectors at a single location for the purpose of buying, selling, and trading sorts cards and memorabilia. Conventions are open to the public and sometimes also feature autograph guests, door prizes, films, contests, etc.

SM - Sky Masters.

SMALL - Small School Sensation.

SP - Single or Short Print. A card which was printed in lesser quantity compared to the other cards in the same series (also see DP). This term can only be used in a relative sense and in reference to one particular set. For instance, the shortprinted 1989-90 Hoops Pistons Championship card (#353A) is less common than the other cards in that set, but it isn't necessarily scarcer than regular cards of any other set.

SPECIAL CARD - Generic term that applies to any card that portrays something other than a single player or team.

SS - Shooting Star.

STAR CARD - A card that portrays a player of some repute, usually determined by his ability, but sometimes referring to sheer popularity.

STAY - Stay in School.

STICKER - A card with a removable layer that can be affixed to another surface, for example the 1986-87 through 1989-90 Fleer bonus cards.

STOCK - The cardboard or paper on which the card is printed.

SUPERSTAR CARD - A card that portrays a superstar, e.g., a Hall of Fame

Glossary/Legend / 11

member or a player whose current performance likely will eventually warrant serious Hall of Fame consideration.

TC - Team checklist card.

TEAM CARD - A card that depicts or represents an entire team, notably the 1989-90 and 1990-91 NBA Hoops Detroit Pistons championship cards and the 1991-92 NBA Hoops subset.

TEST SET - A set, usually containing a small number of cards, issued by a national producer and distributed in a limited section of the country or to a select group of people. Presumably, the purpose of a test set is to measure market appeal for a particular type of card. Also called a promo or prototype set.

THEN - Then and Now.

TL - Team Leader card.

TP - Top Prospect.

TR - Traded card.

TW - Teamwork.

UER - Uncorrected error card.

USA - Team USA card.

VARIATION - One of two or more cards from the same series with the same number (or player with identical pose if the series is unnumbered) differing from one another in some aspect, including the printing, stock or other feature of the card. This is usually caused when the manufacturer becomes aware of an error or inconsistency in a particular card, fixes the mistake and resumes the print run. In this case there will be two variations of the same card. Sometimes one of the variations is relatively scarce. Variations can also result from accidental or deliberate design changes, information updates, photo substitutions, etc.

VERT - Vertical pose on a card.

XRC - Extended Rookie Card. A player's first appearance on a card, but issued in a limited distribution, major set not distributed nationally nor in packs. In basketball sets, this term refers only to 1983-84, 1984-85 and 1985-86 Star Company sets.

YB - Yearbook.

6M - Sixth Man.

BASKETBALL CARD HISTORY

Basketball cards have been produced on and off since 1948 with the scarce 72-card Bowman set of that year. However, one must skip ahead to 1957-58 to find the next basketball set, this time an 80-card set issued by Topps. Then skip ahead to 1961-62 to the 66-card Fleer issue. Finally in 1969, Topps began a 13-year run of producing basketball card sets which ended in 1981-82. Ironically, this was about the time the league's popularity had bottomed out and was about to begin its ascent to the lofty level it's at today.

Topps' run included several sets that are troublesome for today's collectors. The 1969-70, 1970-71 and 1976-77 sets are larger than standard size, thus making them hard to store and preserve. The 1980-81 set consists of standard-size panels containing three cards each. Completing and cataloging the 1980-81 set (which features the classic Larry Bird RC/Magic Johnson RC/Julius Erving panel) is challenging, to say the least.

In 1983, this basketball card void was filled by the Star Company, a small company which issued three attractive sets of basketball cards, along with a plethora of peripheral sets. Star's 1983-84 premiere offering was issued in four groups, with the first series (cards 1-100) very difficult to obtain, as many of the early team subsets were miscut and destroyed before release. The 1984-85 and 1985-86 sets were more widely and evenly distributed. Even so, players' initial appearances on any of the three Star Company sets are considered Extended Rookie Cards, not regular Rookie Cards, because of the relatively limited distribution. Chief among these is Michael Jordan's 1984-85 Star XRC, the most valuable sports card issued in a 1980s major set.

Then, in 1986, Fleer took over the rights to produce cards for the NBA. Their 1986-87, 1987-88 and 1988-89 sets each contain 132 attractive, colorful cards depicting mostly stars and superstars. They were sold in the familiar wax pack format (12 cards and one sticker per pack). Fleer increased its set size to 168 in 1989-90, and was joined by NBA Hoops, which produced a 300-card first series (containing David Robinson's only Rookie Card) and a 52-card second series. The demand for all three Star Company sets, along with the first four Fleer sets and the premiere NBA Hoops set, skyrocketed during the early part of 1990.

The basketball card market stabilized somewhat in 1990-91, with both Fleer and Hoops stepping up production tremendously. A new major set, SkyBox, also made a splash in the market with its unique "high-tech" cards featuring computer-generated backgrounds. Because of overproduction, none of the three major 1990-91 sets have experienced significant price growth, although the increased competition apparently has led to higher quality and more innovative products. Another milestone in 1990-91 was the first-time inclusion of current rookies in update sets (NBA Hoops and SkyBox Series II, Fleer Update). The NBA Hoops and SkyBox issues contain just the 11 lottery picks, while Fleer's 100-card boxed set includes all rookies of any significance. A small company called "Star Pics" (not to be confused with Star Company) tried to fill this niche by printing a 70-card set in late 1990, but because the set was not licensed by the NBA, it is not considered a major set by the majority of collectors. It does, however, contain the first nationally distributed cards of 1990-91 rookies such as Derrick Coleman, Kendall Gill, Dee Brown and others.

In 1991-92, the draft pick set market that Star Pics opened in 1990-91 now has expanded to include several competitors. More significantly, that season brought with it the three established NBA card brands plus Upper Deck, known throughout the hobby for its high quality card stock and photography in other sports. Upper Deck's first basketball set probably captured NBA action better than any previous set. But its value — like all other major 1990-91 and 1991-92 NBA sets — declined because of overproduction.

On the bright side, the historic entrance of NBA players to Olympic competition kept interest in basketball cards going long after the Chicago Bulls won their second straight NBA championship. So for at least one year, the basketball card market — probably the most seasonal of the four major team sports — remained in the spotlight for an extended period of time.

BUSINESS OF SPORTS CARD COLLECTING

Determining Value

Why are some cards more valuable than others? Obviously, the economic law of supply and demand is applicable to sports card collecting, just as it is to any other field where a commodity is bought, sold, or traded in a free, unregulated market.

Supply (the number of cards available on the market) is less than the total number of cards originally produced, since attrition diminishes that original quantity. Each year a percentage of cards is typically thrown away, destroyed, or otherwise lost to collectors. This percentage is much smaller today than it was in the past because more and more people have become increasingly aware of the value of sports cards.

For those who collect only Mint condition cards, the supply of older cards can be quite small indeed. Until recently, collectors were not so conscious of the need to preserve the condition of their cards. For this reason, it is difficult to know exactly how many 1948 Bowman basketball cards are currently available, Mint or otherwise. It is generally accepted that there are many fewer 1948 Bowmans available than 1969-70 Topps or 1987-88 Fleer basketball cards. If demand were equal for each of these sets, the law of supply and demand would increase the price for the least available sets. Demand, however, is never equal for all sets, so price correlations can be complicated.

The total number of cards produced for any given issue can only be approximated, as compared to other collectibles such as coins and stamps. The reason is simple: Card manufacturers are predominantly private companies which are not required to reveal such internal information, while governments are required to release figures regarding currency and postage stamp production. The demand for any given card is influenced by many factors. These include: (1) the age of the card; (2) the number of cards printed; (3) the player(s) portrayed on the card; (4) the attractiveness and popularity of the set; and perhaps most importantly, (5) the physical condition of the card.

In general, (1) the older the card, (2) the fewer the number of the cards printed, (3) the more famous the player, (4) the more attractive and popular the set, or (5) the better the condition of the card, the higher the value of the card will be. There are exceptions to all but one of these factors: the condition of the card. Given two cards similar in all respects except condition, the one in the best condition will always be valued higher.

While there are certain guidelines that help to establish the value of a card, the numerous exceptions and peculiarities make any simple, direct mathematical

Business of Sports Card Collecting / 15

formula to determine card values impossible.

One certainty in the sports card hobby is the high demand for Rookie Cards, specifically for RCs of superstar players. A Rookie Card is defined as the first card from a major set of a particular player. Because minor league baseball players have signed contracts and are therefore professionals, baseball Rookie Cards often are issued before or during a player's first major league season. These cards usually are designated "Future Stars," "Major League Prospects," "Rated Rookies," or something similar on the front.

Basketball Rookie Cards, on the other hand, cannot be issued when a player is still in college. They can only be printed once a player has no more collegiate eligibility. Therefore, until 1990-91, basketball Rookie Cards were generally released in the year after the player's first (or even second or third, for late bloomers) professional season. And until recently, the fronts of basketball Rookie Cards did not have any special notation. But in the 1990-91 NBA Hoops set, rookies of the previous year have "Rookie Star" designations on the fronts. Also in 1990-91, the three major NBA card manufacturers (Fleer, NBA Hoops and SkyBox) each issued RCs for current rookies. The 1990-91 and 1991-92 NBA Hoops and SkyBox Series II sets contain only the 11 lottery picks, while the Fleer Update sets from both seasons depict all 1990-91 rookies of any significance. Upper Deck's 1991-92 set was the first to include June's draftees in its first series set, which immediately set it apart from the competition.

Regional Variation

Two types of price variations exist among the sections of the country where a card is bought or sold. The first is the general price variation on all cards bought and sold in one geographical area as compared to another. Card prices are slightly higher on the East and West coasts, and slightly lower in the middle of the country. Although prices may vary from the East to the West, or from the Southwest to the Midwest, the prices listed in this guide are nonetheless presented as a consensus of all sections of this large and diverse country.

Still, prices for a particular player's cards are usually higher in his home team's area than in other regions. This represents the second type of regional price variation in which local players are favored over those from distant areas. For example, a John Havlicek card is valued higher in Boston than in Los Angeles because Havlicek played in Boston; therefore, the demand there for Havlicek cards is higher than it is in Los Angeles. On the other hand, a Jerry West card is priced higher in Los Angeles where he played and is still the Lakers general manager, than in Boston, for similar reasons. Frequently, even common player cards command such a premium from hometown collectors.

16 / Business of Sports Card Collecting

Set Prices

A somewhat paradoxical situation exists in the price of a complete set versus the combined cost of the individual cards in the set. In nearly every case, the sum of the prices for the individual cards is higher than the cost for the complete set. This is especially prevalent in the cards of the past few years. The reasons for this apparent anomaly stem from the habits of collectors, and from the carrying costs to dealers. Today, each card in a set is normally produced in the same quantity as all others in its set.

However, many collectors pick up only stars, superstars, and particular teams. As a result, the dealer is left with a shortage of certain player cards and an abundance of others. He therefore incurs an expense in simply "carrying" these less desirable cards in stock. On the other hand, if he sells a complete set, he gets rid of large numbers of cards at one time. For this reason, he is generally willing to receive less money for a complete set. By doing this, he recovers all of his costs and also makes a profit.

The disparity between the price of the complete set and that for the sum of the individual cards has also been influenced by the fact that some major manufacturers are now pre-collating card sets. To date, the only pre-collated basketball set produced was the 1991-92 Upper Deck factory set.

Set prices also do not include rare card varieties, unless specifically stated. Of course, the prices for sets do include one example of each type for the given set, but this is the least expensive variety.

Scarce Series

Only a select few basketball sets contain scarce series: 1948 Bowman, 1970-71 and 1972-73 Topps and 1983-84 Star Company. The 1948 Bowman set was printed on two 36-card sheets, the second of which was issued in significantly lower quantities. The two Topps scarce series are only marginally tougher than the set as a whole. The Star Company scarcity actually is for particular team sets (the 76ers, Lakers, Celtics, Bucks and Mavericks) which, to different extents, were less widely distributed.

Grading Your Cards

Each hobby has its own grading terminology — stamps, coins, comic books, beer cans, right down the line. Collectors of sports cards are no exception. The one invariable criterion for determining the value of a card is its condition. The better the condition of the card, the more valuable it is. However, condition grading is very subjective. Individual card dealers and collectors differ in the strictness of their grading, but the stated condition of a card should be determined without regard to whether it is being bought or sold.

Business of Sports Card Collecting / 17

The physical defects that lower the condition of a card are usually quite apparent, but each individual places his own estimation (negative value, in this case) on these defects. We present the condition guide for use in determining values listed in this Price Guide in the hopes that excess subjectivity can be minimized.

The defects listed in the condition guide below are those either created at the time of printing, such as uneven borders, or those defects that occur to a card under normal handling — corner sharpness, gloss, edge wear, light creases — and finally, environmental conditions, such as browning. Other defects to cards are caused by human carelessness, and in all cases should be noted separately and in addition to the condition grade. Among the more common alterations are tape, tape stains, heavy creases, rubber band marks, water damage, smoke damage, trimming, paste, tears, writing, pin or tack holes, any back damage, and missing parts (tabs, tops, coupons, backgrounds).

Centering

It is important to define in words and pictures what is meant by frequently used hobby terms relating to grading cards. The adjacent pictures portray various stages of centering. Centering can range from well-centered to slightly off-center to off-center to badly off-center to miscut.

Slightly Off-Center (60/40): A slightly off-center card is one which is found to have one border bigger than the opposite border. This degree once was only offensive to purists, but now some hobbyists try to avoid cards that are anything other than perfectly centered.

Off-Center (70/30): An off-center card has one border which is noticeably more than twice as wide as the opposite border.

Badly Off-Center (80/20 or worse): A badly off-center card has virtually no border on one side of the card.

Miscut: A miscut card actually shows part of the adjacent card in its larger border and consequently a corresponding amount of its card is cut off.

Corner Wear

Degrees of corner wear generate several common terms used to facilitate accurate grading. The wear on card corners can be expressed as fuzzy corners, corner wear or slightly rounded corners, rounded corners, or badly rounded corners.

Fuzzy Corners: Fuzzy corners still come to a right angle (to a point) but the point has begun to fray slightly.

Corner Wear or Slightly Rounded Corners: The slight fraying of corners has increased to where there is no longer a point to the corner. Nevertheless, the

18 / Business of Sports Card Collecting

CENTERING

SLIGHTLY OFF-CENTERED

OFF-CENTERED

Business of Sports Card Collecting / 19

BADLY OFF-CENTERED

MISCUT

corner is still reasonably sharp. There may be evidence of some slight loss of color in the corner also.

Rounded Corners: The corner is no longer sharp but is not badly rounded.

Badly Rounded Corners: The corner is rounded to an objectionable degree. Excessive wear and rough handling are evident.

Creases

A third common defect is the crease. The degree of creasing in a card is very difficult to show in a drawing or picture. On giving the specific condition of an expensive card for sale, the seller should note any creases additionally. Creases can be categorized as to severity according to the following scale.

Light Crease: A light crease is a crease which is barely noticeable on close inspection. In fact when cards are in plastic sheets or holders, a light crease may not be seen (until the card is taken out of the holder). A light crease on the front is much more serious than a light crease on the card back only.

Medium Crease: A medium crease is noticeable when held and studied at arm's length by the naked eye, but does not overly detract from the appearance of the card. It is an obvious crease, but not one that breaks the picture surface of the card.

Heavy Crease: A heavy crease is one which has torn or broken through the card's picture surface, e.g., puts a tear in the photo surface.

Alterations

Deceptive Trimming: This occurs when someone alters the card in order (1) to shave off edge wear, (2) to improve the sharpness of the corners, or (3) to improve centering — obviously their objective is to falsely increase the perceived value of the card to an unsuspecting buyer. The shrinkage is usually only evident if the trimmed card is compared to an adjacent full-sized card or if the trimmed card is itself measured.

Obvious Trimming: Obvious trimming is noticeable and unfortunate. It is usually performed by non-collectors who give no thought to the present or future value of their cards.

Deceptively Retouched Borders: This occurs when the borders (especially on those cards with dark borders) are touched up on the edges and corners with magic marker of appropriate color in order to make the card appear to be Mint.

Categorization of Defects

A "Micro Defect" would be fuzzy corners, slight off-centering, printers' lines, printers' spots, slightly out of focus, or slight loss of original gloss. A NrMt card

Business of Sports Card Collecting / 21

may have one micro defect. An ExMt card may have two or more micro defects.

A "Minor Defect" would be corner wear or slight rounding, off-centering, light crease on back, wax or gum stains on reverse, loss of original gloss, writing or tape marks on back, or rubber band marks. An Excellent card may have minor defects.

A "Major Defect" would be rounded corner(s), badly off-centering, crease(s), deceptive trimming, deceptively retouched borders, pin hole, staple hole, incidental writing or tape marks on front, severe warping, water stains, medium crease(s), or sun fading. A Vg card may have one major defect. A Good card may have two or more major defects.

A "Catastrophic Defect" is the worst kind of defect and would include such defects as badly rounded corner(s), miscutting, heavy crease(s), obvious trimming, punch hole, tack hole, tear(s), corner missing or clipped, destructive writing on front. A Fair card may have one catastrophic defect. A Poor card has two or more catastrophic defects.

Condition Guide

Mint (Mt) - A card with no defects. The card has sharp corners, even borders, original gloss or shine on the surface, sharp focus of the picture, smooth edges, no signs of wear, and white borders. A Mint card does NOT have printers' lines or other printing defects, or other serious quality control problems that should have been discovered by the card company before distribution. Note also that there is no allowance made for the age of the card.

Near Mint (NrMt) - A card with a micro defect. Any of the following would be sufficient to lower the grade of a card from Mint to the Near Mint category: layering at some of the corners (fuzzy corners), a very small amount of the original gloss lost, very minor wear on the edges, slightly off-center borders, slight wear visible only on close inspection, slight off-whiteness of the borders.

Excellent to Mint (ExMt) - A card with micro defects, but no minor defects. Two or three of the following would be sufficient to lower the grade of a card from Mint to the ExMt category: layering at some of the corners (fuzzy corners), a very small amount of the original gloss lost, minor wear on the edges, slightly off-center borders, slight wear visible only on close inspection, slight off-whiteness of the borders.

Excellent (Ex) - A card with minor defects. Any of the following would be sufficient to lower the grade of a card from Mint to the Excellent category: slight rounding at some of the corners, a small amount of the original gloss lost, minor wear on the edges, off-center borders, wear visible only on close inspection, off-whiteness of the borders.

Very Good (Vg) - A card that has been handled but not abused. Some rounding at all corners, slight layering or scuffing at one or two corners, slight notching on edges, gloss lost from the surface but not scuffed, borders might be somewhat uneven but some white is visible on all borders, noticeable yellowing or browning of borders, light crease(s), pictures may be slightly off focus.

Good (G) - A well-handled card, rounding and some layering at the corners, scuffing at the corners and minor scuffing on the face, borders noticeably uneven and browning, loss of gloss on the face, medium crease(s), notching on the edges.

Fair (F) - Round and layering corners, brown and dirty borders, frayed edges, noticeable scuffing on the face, white not visible on one or more borders, medium to heavy creases, cloudy focus.

Poor (P) - An abused card: The lowest grade of card, frequently some major physical alteration has been performed on the card, collectible only as a filler until a better-condition replacement can be obtained.

Categories between these major condition grades are frequently used, such as Very Good to Excellent (VgEx), Fair to Good (F-G), etc. Such grades indicate a card with all qualities at least in the lower of the two categories, but with several qualities in the higher of the two categories. In the case of ExMt, it essentially refers to a card which is halfway between Excellent and Mint.

Unopened packs, boxes and factory-collated sets are considered Mint in their unknown (and presumed perfect) state. However, once opened or broken out, each of these cards is graded (and valued) in its own right by taking into account any quality control defects (such as off-centering, printers' lines, machine creases, or gum stains) present in spite of the fact that the card has never been handled.

Cards before 1980 that are priced in the Price Guide in top condition of NrMt are obviously worth an additional premium when offered in strict Mint condition. This additional premium increases relative to the age and scarcity of the card. For example, Mint cards from the late 1970s may bring only a 10 percent premium for Mint (above NrMt), whereas high demand (or condition rarity) cards from early vintage sets can be sold for as much as double (and occasionally even more) the NrMt price when offered in strict Mint condition.

Selling Your Cards

Just about every collector sells cards or will sell cards eventually. Someday you may be interested in selling your duplicates or maybe even your whole collection. You may sell to other collectors, friends, or dealers. You may even sell cards you purchased from a certain dealer back to that same dealer. In any event, it helps to know some of the mechanics of the typical transaction between buyer and seller.

Dealers will buy cards in order to resell them to other collectors who are interested in the cards. Dealers will always pay a higher percentage for items which (in their opinion) can be resold quickly, and a much lower percentage for those items which are perceived as having low demand and hence are slow moving. In either case, dealers must buy at a price that allows for the expense of doing business and a margin for profit.

If you have cards for sale, the best advice we can give is that you get several offers for your cards — either from card shops or at a card show — and take the best offer, all things considered. Note, the "best" offer may not be the one for the highest amount. And remember, if a dealer really wants your cards, he won't let you get away without making his best competitive offer. Another alternative is to place your cards in an auction as one or several lots.

Many people think nothing of going into a department store and paying $15 for an item of clothing the store paid $5. But, if you were selling your $15 card to a dealer and he offered you only $5 for it, you might think his mark-up unreasonable. To complete the analogy: most department stores (and card dealers) that consistently pay $10 for $15 items eventually go out of business. An exception is when the dealer has a willing buyer for the item(s) you are attempting to sell lined up, or if the cards are so Hot that it's likely he'll only have to hold the cards for a short period of time.

In those cases, an offer of up to 75 percent of book value will still allow the dealer to make a reasonable profit considering the short time he will need to hold the merchandise. In general, however, most cards and collections will bring offers in the range of 25 to 50 percent of retail price. Also consider that most material from the past five to 10 years is very plentiful. If that's what you're selling, expect even less or no offer at all unless you have Hot cards that the dealer can move easily.

INTERESTING NOTES

The numerically first card of an issue is the single card most likely to obtain excessive wear. Consequently, you will typically find the price on the No. 1 card (in NrMt or Mint condition) somewhat higher than might otherwise be the case. Similarly, but to a lesser extent (because normally the less important, reverse side of the card is the one exposed), the numerically last card in an issue is also prone to abnormal wear. This extra wear and tear occurs because the first and last cards are exposed to the elements (human element included) more than any other cards. They are generally end cards in any brick formations, rubber bandings, stackings on wet surfaces, and like activities.

Sports cards have no intrinsic value. The value of a card, like the value of other collectibles, can only be determined by you and your enjoyment in viewing and possessing these cardboard swatches.

Remember, the buyer ultimately determines the price of each baseball card. You are the determining price factor because you have the ability to say "No" to the price of any card by not exchanging your hard-earned money for a given card. When the cost of a trading card exceeds the enjoyment you will receive from it, your answer should be "No." We assess and report the prices. You set them!

We are always interested in receiving the price input of collectors and dealers from around the country. We happily credit major contributors. We welcome your opinions, since your contributions assist us in ensuring a better guide each year. If you would like to join our survey list for the next editions of this book and others authored by Dr. Beckett, please send your name and address to Dr. James Beckett, 4887 Alpha Road, Suite 200, Dallas, Texas 75244.

ADVERTISING

Within this guide you will find advertisements for sports memorabilia material, mail order, and retail sports collectibles establishments. All advertisements were accepted in good faith based on the reputation of the advertiser; however, neither the author, the publisher, the distributors, nor the other advertisers in the Price Guide accept any responsibility for any particular advertiser not complying with the terms of his or her ad.

Readers should also be aware that prices in advertisements are subject to change over the annual period before a new edition of this volume is issued each fall. When replying to an advertisement late in the sporting year following the fall release of this volume, the reader should take this into account, and contact the dealer by phone or in writing for up-to-date price quotes and availability. Should you come into contact with any of the advertisers in this guide as a result of their advertisement herein, please mention to them this source as your contact.

RECOMMENDED READING

With the increase in popularity of the hobby in recent years, there has been a corresponding increase in available literature. Below is a list of the books and periodicals that receive our highest recommendation and that we hope will further your knowledge and enjoyment of our great hobby.

The Sport Americana Baseball Card Price Guide by Dr. James Beckett (Fourteenth Edition, $15.95, released 1992, published by Edgewater Book Company) — the most informative, up-to-date, and reliable Price Guide/checklist on its subject matter ever compiled. No serious hobbyist should be without it.

The Official Price Guide to Baseball Cards by Dr. James Beckett (Twelfth Edition, $5.99, released 1992, published by The House of Collectibles) — this work is an abridgment of *The Sport Americana Baseball Card Price Guide* immediately above, published in a convenient and economical pocket-size format and provides Dr. Beckett's pricing of the major baseball sets since 1948.

The Sport Americana Football Card Price Guide by Dr. James Beckett (Ninth Edition, $14.95, released 1992, published by Edgewater Book Company) — the most comprehensive price guide/checklist ever issued on football cards. No serious football card hobbyist should be without it.

The Official Price Guide to Football Cards by Dr. James Beckett (Twelfth Edition, $5.99, released 1992, published by The House of Collectibles) — an abridgment of *The Sport Americana Football Card Price Guide* listed above in a convenient and economical pocket-size format providing Dr. Beckett's pricing of the major football sets since 1948.

The Sport Americana Hockey Card Price Guide by Dr. James Beckett (Second Edition, $12.95, released 1992, published by Edgewater Book Company) — the most informative, up-to-date, and reliable Price Guide/checklist on its subject matter ever compiled. The introductory section is presented in both English and French. No serious hobbyist should be without it.

The Official Price Guide to Hockey Cards by Dr. James Beckett (Second Edition, $5.99, released 1992, published by The House of Collectibles) — this work is an abridgment of *The Sport Americana Hockey Card Price Guide* immediately above, published in a convenient and economical pocket-size format and provides Dr. Beckett's pricing of the major hockey sets since 1951. The introductory section and the set descriptions are presented in both English and French.

The Sport Americana Basketball Card Price Guide and Alphabetical Checklist by Dr. James Beckett (Second Edition, $12.95, released 1992, published by Edgewater Book Company) — the most informative, up-to-date, and reliable Price Guide/checklist on its subject matter ever compiled. No serious hobbyist should be without it.

The Sport Americana Price Guide to Baseball Collectibles by Dr. James Beckett (Second Edition, $12.95, released 1988, published by Edgewater Book Company) — the complete guide and checklist with up-to-date values for box cards, coins, decals, R-cards, bread labels, exhibits, discs, lids, fabric, pins,

Recommended Reading / 27

Canadian cards, stamps, stickers, and miscellaneous Topps issues.

The Sport Americana Baseball Card Alphabetical Checklist by Dr. James Beckett (Fifth Edition, $14.95, released 1992, published by Edgewater Book Company) — an alphabetical listing, by the last name of the player portrayed on the card. Virtually all major and minor league baseball cards produced through the 1991 major sets are listed.

The Sport Americana Price Guide to the Non-Sports Cards 1930-1960 by Christopher Benjamin and Dennis W. Eckes ($14.95, released 1991, published by Edgewater Book Company) — the definitive guide to virtually all popular non-sports American tobacco and bubblegum cards issued between 1930 and 1960. In addition to cards, illustrations and prices for wrappers are also included.

The Sport Americana Price Guide to the Non-Sports Cards by Christopher Benjamin (Fourth Edition, $14.95, released 1992, published by Edgewater Book Company) — the definitive guide to all popular non-sports American cards. In addition to cards, illustrations and prices for wrappers are also included. This volume covers non-sports cards from 1961 to 1992.

The Sport Americana Baseball Address List by Jack Smalling and Dennis W. Eckes (Sixth Edition, $12.95, released 1990, published by Edgewater Book Company) — the definitive guide for autograph hunters, giving addresses and deceased information for virtually all major league baseball players, managers, and even umpires, past and present.

The Sport Americana Team Baseball Card Checklist by Jeff Fritsch (Sixth Edition, $12.95, released 1992, published by Edgewater Book Company) — includes all Topps, Bowman, Fleer, Play Ball, Goudey, Upper Deck and Donruss cards, with the players portrayed on the cards listed by their team. The book is invaluable to the collector who specializes in an individual team because it is the most complete baseball card team checklist available.

The Sport Americana Team Football and Basketball Card Checklist by Jane Fritsch, Jeff Fritsch, and Dennis W. Eckes (First Edition, $10.95, released 1990, published by Edgewater Book Company) — The book is invaluable to the collector who specializes in an individual team because it is the most complete football and basketball card team checklist available.

Beckett Baseball Card Monthly, published and edited by Dr. James Beckett — contains the most extensive and accepted monthly Price Guide, collectible glossy superstar covers, colorful feature articles, "who's Hot and who's not" section, Convention Calendar, tips for beginners, "Readers Write" letters to and responses from the editor, information on errors and varieties, autograph collecting tips, and profiles of the sport's Hottest stars. Published every month, BBCM is the hobby's largest paid circulation periodical.

Beckett Football Card Monthly, *Beckett Basketball Monthly*, *Beckett Hockey Monthly*, and *Beckett Focus on Future Stars* were built on the success of BBCM. These other publications contain many of the same features as BBCM, and contain the most relied upon Price Guides to their respective segments of the sports card hobby.

PRICES IN THIS GUIDE

Prices found in this guide reflect current retail rates just prior to the printing of this book. They do not reflect the FOR SALE prices of the author, the publisher, the distributors, the advertisers, or any card dealers associated with this guide. No one is obligated in any way to buy, sell, or trade his or her cards based on these prices. The price listings were compiled by the author from actual buy/sell transactions at sports conventions, buy/sell advertisements in the hobby papers, for sale prices from dealer catalogs and price lists, and discussions with leading hobbyists in the U.S. and Canada. All prices are in U.S. dollars.

ABOUT THE AUTHOR

Dr. Jim Beckett, the leading authority on sport card values in the United States, maintains a wide range of activities in the world of sports. He possesses one of the finest collections of sports cards and autographs in the world, has made numerous appearances on radio and television, and frequently has been cited in many national publications. He was awarded the first "Special Achievement Award" for Contributions to the Hobby by the National Sports Collectors Convention in 1980, the "Jock-Jasperson Award" for Hobby Dedication in 1983, and the "Buck Barker, Spirit of the Hobby" Award in 1991.

Dr. Beckett is the author of *The Sport Americana Baseball Card Price Guide, The Official Price Guide to Baseball Cards, The Sport Americana Price Guide to Baseball Collectibles, The Sport Americana Baseball Memorabilia and Autograph Price Guide, The Sport Americana Football Card Price Guide, The Official Price Guide to Football Cards, The Sport Americana Hockey Card Price Guide, The Official Price Guide to Hockey Cards, The Sport Americana Basketball Card Price Guide and Alphabetical Checklist, The Official Price Guide to Basketball Cards*, and *The Sport Americana Baseball Card Alphabetical Checklist*. In addition, he is the founder, publisher, and editor of *Beckett Baseball Card Monthly, Beckett Basketball Monthly, Beckett Football Card Monthly, Beckett Hockey Monthly*, and *Beckett Focus on Future Stars*, magazines dedicated to advancing the card collecting hobby.

Jim Beckett received his Ph.D. in Statistics from Southern Methodist University in 1975. Prior to starting Beckett Publications in 1984, Dr. Beckett served as an Associate Professor of Statistics at Bowling Green State University and as a Vice President of a consulting firm in Dallas, Texas. He currently resides in Dallas with his wife Patti and their daughters, Christina, Rebecca, and Melissa.

30 / 1948 Bowman

1948 Bowman

The 1948 Bowman basketball card set of 72 cards was Bowman's only basketball issue. It was also the only major basketball issue until 1958. Cards in the set measure 2 1/16" by 2 1/2". The set is in color and features both player cards and diagram cards. The player cards in the second series are sometimes found without the red or blue printing on the card front, leaving only a gray background. These gray-front cards are more difficult to find, as they are printing errors where the printer apparently ran out of red or blue ink that was supposed to print on the player's uniform. The key rookie cards in this set are Joe Fulks, William "Red" Holzman, George Mikan, Jim Pollard, and Max Zaslofsky.

	NRMT	VG-E	GOOD
COMPLETE SET (72)	6000.00	2750.00	750.00
COMMON PLAYER (1-36)	36.00	18.00	3.60
COMMON PLAYER (37-72)	60.00	30.00	6.00
☐ 1 Ernie Calverley	100.00	30.00	6.00
Providence Steamrollers			
☐ 2 Ralph Hamilton	36.00	18.00	3.60
Ft. Wayne Pistons			
☐ 3 Gale Bishop	36.00	18.00	3.60
Philadelphia Warriors			
☐ 4 Fred Lewis CO	42.00	21.00	4.20
Indianapolis Jets			
☐ 5 Basketball Play	25.00	12.50	2.50
Single cut off post			
☐ 6 Bob Ferrick	45.00	22.50	4.50
Washington Capitols			
☐ 7 John Logan	36.00	18.00	3.60
St. Louis Bombers			
☐ 8 Mel Riebe	36.00	18.00	3.60
Boston Celtics			
☐ 9 Andy Phillip	80.00	40.00	8.00
Chicago Stags			
☐ 10 Bob Davies	80.00	40.00	8.00
Rochester Royals			

1948 Bowman / 31

☐ 11	Basketball Play	25.00	12.50	2.50
	Single cut with return pass to post			
☐ 12	Kenny Sailors	36.00	18.00	3.60
	Providence Steamrollers			
☐ 13	Paul Armstrong	36.00	18.00	3.60
	Ft. Wayne Pistons			
☐ 14	Howard Dallmar	45.00	22.50	4.50
	Philadelphia Warriors			
☐ 15	Bruce Hale	45.00	22.50	4.50
	Indianapolis Jets			
☐ 16	Sid Hertzberg	36.00	18.00	3.60
	Washington Capitols			
☐ 17	Basketball Play	25.00	12.50	2.50
	Single cut			
☐ 18	Red Rocha	36.00	18.00	3.60
	St. Louis Bombers			
☐ 19	Eddie Ehlers	36.00	18.00	3.60
	Boston Celtics			
☐ 20	Ellis(Gene) Vance	36.00	18.00	3.60
	Chicago Stags			
☐ 21	Andrew(Fuzzy) Levane	45.00	22.50	4.50
	Rochester Royals			
☐ 22	Earl Shannon	36.00	18.00	3.60
	Providence Steamrollers			
☐ 23	Basketball Play	25.00	12.50	2.50
	Double cut off post			
☐ 24	Leo(Crystal) Klier	36.00	18.00	3.60
	Ft. Wayne Pistons			
☐ 25	George Senesky	36.00	18.00	3.60
	Philadelphia Warriors			
☐ 26	Price Brookfield	36.00	18.00	3.60
	Indianapolis Jets			
☐ 27	John Norlander	36.00	18.00	3.60
	Washington Capitols			
☐ 28	Don Putman	36.00	18.00	3.60
	St. Louis Bombers			
☐ 29	Basketball Play	25.00	12.50	2.50
	Double post			
☐ 30	Jack Garfinkel	36.00	18.00	3.60
	Boston Celtics			
☐ 31	Chuck Gilmur	36.00	18.00	3.60
	Chicago Stags			
☐ 32	William Holzman	250.00	125.00	25.00
	Rochester Royals			
☐ 33	Jack Smiley	36.00	18.00	3.60
	Ft. Wayne Pistons			
☐ 34	Joe Fulks	225.00	110.00	22.00
	Philadelphia Warriors			
☐ 35	Basketball Play	25.00	12.50	2.50
	Screen play			
☐ 36	Hal Tidrick	36.00	18.00	3.60
	Indianapolis Jets			
☐ 37	Don(Swede) Carlson	60.00	30.00	6.00
	Minneapolis Lakers			
☐ 38	Buddy Jeanette CO	70.00	35.00	7.00
	Baltimore Bullets			

32 / 1948 Bowman

☐ 39	Ray Kuka New York Knicks	60.00	30.00	6.00
☐ 40	Stan Miasek Chicago Stags	60.00	30.00	6.00
☐ 41	Basketball Play Double screen	36.00	18.00	3.60
☐ 42	George Nostrand Providence Steamrollers	60.00	30.00	6.00
☐ 43	Chuck Halbert Boston Celtics	70.00	35.00	7.00
☐ 44	Arnie Johnson Rochester Royals	60.00	30.00	6.00
☐ 45	Bob Doll St. Louis Bombers	60.00	30.00	6.00
☐ 46	Horace McKinney Washington Capitols	85.00	42.50	8.50
☐ 47	Basketball Play Out of bounds	36.00	18.00	3.60
☐ 48	Ed Sadowski Philadelphia Warriors	60.00	30.00	6.00
☐ 49	Bob Kinney Ft. Wayne Pistons	60.00	30.00	6.00
☐ 50	Charles(Hawk) Black Indianapolis Jets	60.00	30.00	6.00
☐ 51	Jack Dwan Minneapolis Lakers	60.00	30.00	6.00
☐ 52	Cornelius Simmons Baltimore Bullets	60.00	30.00	6.00
☐ 53	Basketball Play Out of bounds	36.00	18.00	3.60
☐ 54	Bud Palmer New York Knicks	75.00	37.50	7.50
☐ 55	Max Zaslofsky Chicago Stags	180.00	90.00	18.00
☐ 56	Lee Roy Robbins Providence Steamrollers	60.00	30.00	6.00
☐ 57	Arthur Spector Boston Celtics	60.00	30.00	6.00
☐ 58	Arnie Risen Rochester Royals	75.00	37.50	7.50
☐ 59	Basketball Play Out of bounds play	36.00	18.00	3.60
☐ 60	Ariel Maughan St. Louis Bombers	60.00	30.00	6.00
☐ 61	Dick O'Keefe Washington Capitols	60.00	30.00	6.00
☐ 62	Herman Schaefer Minneapolis Lakers	60.00	30.00	6.00
☐ 63	John Mahnken Baltimore Bullets	60.00	30.00	6.00
☐ 64	Tommy Byrnes New York Knicks	60.00	30.00	6.00
☐ 65	Basketball Play Held ball	36.00	18.00	3.60
☐ 66	Jim Pollard Minneapolis Lakers	250.00	125.00	25.00
☐ 67	Lee Mogus Baltimore Bullets	60.00	30.00	6.00

1991 Classic Draft / 33

☐ 68	Lee Knorek	60.00	30.00	6.00
	New York Knicks			
☐ 69	George Mikan	3000.00	1250.00	400.00
	Minneapolis Lakers			
☐ 70	Walter Budko	60.00	30.00	6.00
	Baltimore Bullets			
☐ 71	Basketball Play	36.00	18.00	3.60
	Guards Play			
☐ 72	Carl Braun	125.00	40.00	8.00
	New York Knicks			

1991 Classic Draft

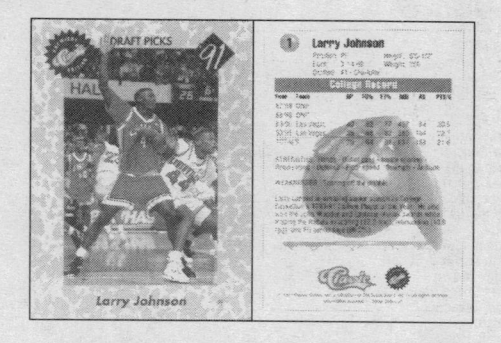

This 50-card set was produced by Classic Games, Inc. and features 48 players picked in the first two rounds of the 1991 NBA draft. A total of 450,000 sets were issued, and each set is accompanied by a letter of limited edition. The cards measure the standard size (2 1/2" by 3 1/2"). The fronts feature a glossy color action photo of each player. The backs have statistics and biographical information. Special cards included in the set are a commemorative number one draft choice card of Larry Johnson and a "One-on-One" card of Billy Owens slam-dunking over Johnson.

	MINT	EXC	G-VG
COMPLETE SET (50)	12.00	6.00	1.20
COMMON PLAYER (1-50)	.05	.02	.00
☐ 1 Larry Johnson	5.00	2.50	.50
UNLV			
☐ 2 Billy Owens	3.50	1.75	.35
Syracuse			
☐ 3 Dikembe Mutombo	2.50	1.25	.25
Georgetown			
☐ 4 Mark Macon	.35	.17	.03

34 / 1991 Classic Draft

	Temple		
☐ 5 Brian Williams	.60	.30	.06
	Arizona		
☐ 6 Terrell Brandon	.40	.20	.04
	Oregon		
☐ 7 Greg Anthony	.40	.20	.04
	UNLV		
☐ 8 Dale Davis	.35	.17	.03
	Clemson		
☐ 9 Anthony Avent	.20	.10	.02
	Seton Hall		
☐ 10 Chris Gatling	.40	.20	.04
	Old Dominion		
☐ 11 Victor Alexander	.30	.15	.03
	Iowa State		
☐ 12 Kevin Brooks	.15	.07	.01
	Southwest Louisiana		
☐ 13 Eric Murdock	.30	.15	.03
	Providence		
☐ 14 LeRon Ellis	.12	.06	.01
	Syracuse		
☐ 15 Stanley Roberts	1.00	.50	.10
	LSU		
☐ 16 Rick Fox	1.00	.50	.10
	North Carolina		
☐ 17 Pete Chilcutt	.20	.10	.02
	North Carolina		
☐ 18 Kevin Lynch	.15	.07	.01
	Minnesota		
☐ 19 George Ackles	.08	.04	.01
	UNLV		
☐ 20 Rodney Monroe	.35	.17	.03
	North Carolina State		
☐ 21 Randy Brown	.15	.07	.01
	New Mexico State		
☐ 22 Chad Gallagher	.08	.04	.01
	Creighton		
☐ 23 Donald Hodge	.35	.17	.03
	Temple		
☐ 24 Myron Brown	.10	.05	.01
	Slippery Rock		
☐ 25 Mike Iuzzolino	.35	.17	.03
	St. Francis		
☐ 26 Chris Corchiani	.15	.07	.01
	North Carolina State		
☐ 27 Elliott Perry UER	.15	.07	.01
	Memphis State		
☐ 28 Joe Wylie	.08	.04	.01
	Miami (FL)		
☐ 29 Jimmy Oliver	.20	.10	.02
	Purdue		
☐ 30 Doug Overton	.08	.04	.01
	LaSalle		
☐ 31 Sean Green	.15	.07	.01
	Iona		
☐ 32 Steve Hood	.10	.05	.01
	James Madison		
☐ 33 Lamont Strothers	.15	.07	.01

1992 Classic Draft Picks / 35

	Chris. Newport			
☐ 34	Alvaro Teheran	.05	.02	.00
	Houston			
☐ 35	Bobby Phills	.10	.05	.01
	Southern			
☐ 36	Richard Dumas	.08	.04	.01
	DNP (Spain/Okla.St.)			
☐ 37	Keith Hughes	.08	.04	.01
	Rutgers			
☐ 38	Isaac Austin	.15	.07	.01
	Arizona State			
☐ 39	Greg Sutton	.20	.10	.02
	Oral Roberts			
☐ 40	Joey Wright	.08	.04	.01
	Texas			
☐ 41	Anthony Jones	.05	.02	.00
	Oral Roberts			
☐ 42	Von McDade	.08	.04	.01
	Milwaukee/Wisconsin			
☐ 43	Marcus Kennedy	.08	.04	.01
	E. Michigan			
☐ 44	Larry Johnson	.75	.35	.07
	UNLV Top Pick			
☐ 45	Larry Johnson and	.75	.35	.07
	Billy Owens			
	UNLV and Syracuse			
☐ 46	Anderson Hunt	.10	.05	.01
	UNLV			
☐ 47	Darrin Chancellor	.08	.04	.01
	S. Mississippi			
☐ 48	Damon Lopez	.05	.02	.00
	Fordham			
☐ 49	Thomas Jordan	.05	.02	.00
	DNP (Spain/Okla.St.)			
☐ 50	Tony Farmer	.08	.04	.01
	Nebraska			

1992 Classic Draft Picks

The 1992 Classic Draft Pick set contains 100 standard-size (2 1/2" by 3 1/2") cards, including all 54 drafted players. The set features the only 1992 trading card of NBA first overall pick Shaquille O'Neal as well as the only draft cards of second pick Alonzo Mourning and fourth pick Jimmy Jackson. The set also includes a Flashback (95-98) subset. The fronts feature glossy color action photos bordered in white. The player's name appears in a silver stripe beneath the picture, which intersects the Classic logo at the lower left corner. The backs have a second color player photo and present biographical information, complete college statistics, and a scouting report. The cards are numbered on the back. Cards 61-100 were only available in foil packs as the blister sets contained only cards 1-60.

	MINT	EXC	G-VG
COMPLETE SET (100)	15.00	7.50	1.50
COMMON PLAYER (1-60)	.07	.03	.01

36 / 1992 Classic Draft Picks

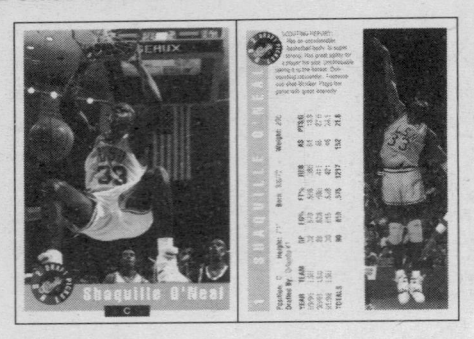

COMMON PLAYER (61-100)	.07	.03	.01
☐ 1 Shaquille O'Neal LSU	6.00	3.00	.60
☐ 2 Walt Williams Maryland	.50	.25	.05
☐ 3 Lee Mayberry Arkansas	.25	.12	.02
☐ 4 Tony Bennett Wisconsin (Green Bay)	.15	.07	.01
☐ 5 Litterial Green Georgia	.25	.12	.02
☐ 6 Chris Smith Connecticut	.20	.10	.02
☐ 7 Henry Williams NC (Charlotte)	.15	.07	.01
☐ 8 Terrell Lowery Loyola	.12	.06	.01
☐ 9 Radenko Dobras South Florida	.10	.05	.01
☐ 10 Curtis Blair Richmond	.15	.07	.01
☐ 11 Randy Woods La Salle	.25	.12	.02
☐ 12 Todd Day Arkansas	.60	.30	.06
☐ 13 Anthony Peeler Missouri	.40	.20	.04
☐ 14 Darin Archbold Butler	.07	.03	.01
☐ 15 Benford Williams Texas	.07	.03	.01
☐ 16 Terrence Lewis Washington State	.07	.03	.01
☐ 17 James McCoy Massachusetts	.07	.03	.01

1992 Classic Draft Picks / 37

☐ 18	Damon Patterson Oklahoma	.07	.03	.01
☐ 19	Bryant Stith Virginia	.30	.15	.03
☐ 20	Doug Christie Pepperdine	.25	.12	.02
☐ 21	Latrell Sprewell Alabama	.20	.10	.02
☐ 22	Hubert Davis North Carolina	.35	.17	.03
☐ 23	David Booth DePaul	.10	.05	.01
☐ 24	David Johnson Syracuse	.35	.17	.03
☐ 25	Jon Barry Georgia Tech	.35	.17	.03
☐ 26	Everick Sullivan Louisville	.10	.05	.01
☐ 27	Brian Davis Duke	.20	.10	.02
☐ 28	Clarence Weatherspoon Southern Mississippi	.40	.20	.04
☐ 29	Malik Sealy St. John's	.35	.17	.03
☐ 30	Matt Geiger Georgia Tech	.15	.07	.01
☐ 31	Jimmy Jackson Ohio State	1.50	.75	.15
☐ 32	Matt Steigenga Michigan State	.20	.10	.02
☐ 33	Robert Horry Alabama	.25	.12	.02
☐ 34	Marlon Maxey UTEP	.15	.07	.01
☐ 35	Reggie Slater Wyoming	.07	.03	.01
☐ 36	Lucius Davis Cal (Santa Barbara)	.07	.03	.01
☐ 37	Chris King Wake Forest	.15	.07	.01
☐ 38	Dexter Cambridge Texas	.07	.03	.01
☐ 39	Alonzo Jamison Kansas	.07	.03	.01
☐ 40	Anthony Tucker Wake Forest	.07	.03	.01
☐ 41	Tracy Murray UCLA	.35	.17	.03
☐ 42	Vernel Singleton LSU	.07	.03	.01
☐ 43	Christian Laettner Duke	1.25	.60	.12
☐ 44	Don MacLean UCLA	.35	.17	.03
☐ 45	Adam Keefe Stanford	.30	.15	.03
☐ 46	Tom Gugliotta North Carolina State	.35	.17	.03

38 / 1992 Classic Draft Picks

☐ 47	LaPhonso Ellis Notre Dame	.50	.25	.05
☐ 48	Byron Houston Oklahoma	.35	.17	.03
☐ 49	Oliver Miller Arkansas	.25	.12	.02
☐ 50	Ron "Popeye" Jones Murray State	.15	.07	.01
☐ 51	P.J. Brown Louisiana Tech	.15	.07	.01
☐ 52	Eric Anderson Indiana	.10	.05	.01
☐ 53	Darren Morningstar Pittsburgh	.20	.10	.02
☐ 54	Isaiah Morris Arkansas	.15	.07	.01
☐ 55	Stephen Howard DePaul	.07	.03	.01
☐ 56	Reggie Smith TCU	.20	.10	.02
☐ 57	Elmore Spencer UNLV	.20	.10	.02
☐ 58	Sean Rooks Arizona	.20	.10	.02
☐ 59	Robert Werdann St. John's	.15	.07	.01
☐ 60	Alonzo Mourning Georgetown	1.75	.85	.17
☐ 61	Steve Rogers Alabama State	.15	.07	.01
☐ 62	Tim Burroughs Jacksonville	.15	.07	.01
☐ 63	Ed Book Canisius	.07	.03	.01
☐ 64	Herb Jones Cincinnati	.10	.05	.01
☐ 65	Mik Kilgore Temple	.07	.03	.01
☐ 66	Ken Leeks Central Florida	.07	.03	.01
☐ 67	Sam Mack Houston	.07	.03	.01
☐ 68	Sean Miller Pittsburgh	.07	.03	.01
☐ 69	Craig Upchurch Houston	.07	.03	.01
☐ 70	Van Usher Tennessee Tech	.07	.03	.01
☐ 71	Corey Williams Oklahoma State	.20	.10	.02
☐ 72	Duane Cooper USC	.20	.10	.02
☐ 73	Brett Roberts Morehead State	.15	.07	.01
☐ 74	Elmer Bennett Notre Dame	.20	.10	.02
☐ 75	Brent Price Oklahoma	.20	.10	.02

1992 Classic Draft Picks / 39

☐ 76	Daimon Sweet .... .10 Notre Dame	.05	.01
☐ 77	Darrick Martin .... .10 UCLA	.05	.01
☐ 78	Gerald Madkins .... .10 UCLA	.05	.01
☐ 79	Jo Jo English .... .07 South Carolina	.03	.01
☐ 80	Alex Blackwell .... .07 Monmouth	.03	.01
☐ 81	Anthony Dade .... .07 Louisiana Tech	.03	.01
☐ 82	Matt Fish .... .15 NC (Wilmington)	.07	.01
☐ 83	Byron Tucker .... .07 George Mason	.03	.01
☐ 84	Harold Miner .... .60 USC	.30	.06
☐ 85	Greg Dennis .... .07 East Tennessee State	.03	.01
☐ 86	Jeff Roulston .... .07 South Carolina	.03	.01
☐ 87	Keir Rogers .... .07 Loyola (Illinois)	.03	.01
☐ 88	Billy Law .... .07 Colorado	.03	.01
☐ 89	Geoff Lear .... .07 Pepperdine	.03	.01
☐ 90	Lambert Shell .... .07 Bridgeport	.03	.01
☐ 91	Elbert Rogers .... .07 Alabama (Birmingham)	.03	.01
☐ 92	Ron Ellis .... .15 Louisiana Tech	.07	.01
☐ 93	Predrag Danilovic .... .15	.07	.01
☐ 94	Calvin Talford .... .07 East Tennessee State	.03	.01
☐ 95	Stacey Augmon .... .12 UNLV Flashback 1	.06	.01
☐ 96	Steve Smith .... .15 Michigan State Flashback 2	.07	.01
☐ 97	Billy Owens .... .25 Syracuse Flashback 3	.12	.02
☐ 98	Dikembe Mutombo .... .25 Georgetown Flashback 4	.12	.02
☐ 99	Checklist 1 (1-50) .... .07	.03	.01
☐ 100	Checklist 2 (51-100) .... .07	.03	.01
☐ BC	Christian Laettner .... 2.00 (Bonus Card)	1.00	.20

40 / 1992 Classic Draft Picks LP Inserts

1992 Classic Draft Picks LP Inserts

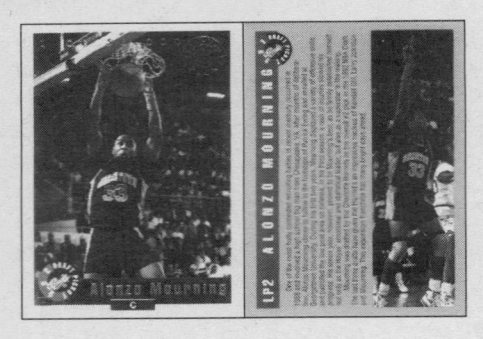

This 10-card set, subtitled "Top Ten Pick", features the top ten picks of the 1992 NBA Draft. These standard size (2 1/2" by 3 1/2") cards were inserted in 1992 Classic Draft Pick foil packs. The fronts feature glossy color action photos enclosed by white borders. The player's name appears in a silver foil stripe beneath the picture, which intersects the Classic logo at the lower left corner. The production figures "1 of 56,000" and the "Top Ten Pick" emblem at the card top are also silver foil. The horizontally oriented backs have a silver background and feature a second color player photo and player profile. The cards are numbered on the back with an LP (limited print) prefix.

	MINT	EXC	G-VG
COMPLETE SET (10)	45.00	22.50	4.50
COMMON PLAYER (1-10)	3.00	1.50	.30
☐ LP1 Shaquille O'Neal	18.00	9.00	1.80
LSU			
☐ LP2 Alonzo Mourning	8.00	4.00	.80
Georgetown			
☐ LP3 Christian Laettner	6.00	3.00	.60
Duke			
☐ LP4 Jimmy Jackson	7.00	3.50	.70
Ohio State			
☐ LP5 LaPhonso Ellis	4.00	2.00	.40
Notre Dame			
☐ LP6 Tom Gugliotta	3.00	1.50	.30
North Carolina State			
☐ LP7 Walt Williams	4.00	2.00	.40
Maryland			
☐ LP8 Todd Day	4.00	2.00	.40
Arkansas			
☐ LP9 Clarence Weatherspoon	3.00	1.50	.30
Southern Mississippi			
☐ LP10 Adam Keefe	3.00	1.50	.30
Stanford			

1991 Courtside Draft Pix

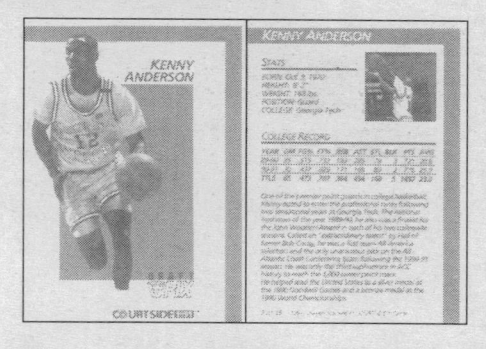

The 1991 Courtside Draft Pix basketball set consists of 45 cards measuring the standard size (2 1/2" by 3 1/2"). All 198,000 sets produced are numbered and distributed as complete sets in their own custom boxes each accompanied by a certificate with a unique serial number. It has also been reported that 30,000 autographed cards were randomly inserted in the 9,900 cases. The card front features a color action player photo. The design of the card fronts features a color rectangle (either pearlized red, blue, or green) on a pearlized white background, with two border stripes in the same color intersecting at the upper right corner. The player's name appears at the upper right corner of the card face, with the words "Courtside 1991" at the bottom. The backs reflect the color on the fronts and present stats (biographical), college record (year by year statistics), and player profile. The cards are numbered on the back. The unnumbered Larry Johnson sendaway card is not included in the complete set price below.

	MINT	EXC	G-VG
COMPLETE SET (45)	10.00	5.00	1.00
COMMON PLAYER (1-45)	.05	.02	.00
☐ 1 Larry Johnson First Draft Pick UNLV	2.00	1.00	.20
☐ 2 George Ackles UNLV	.08	.04	.01
☐ 3 Kenny Anderson Georgia Tech	1.50	.75	.15
☐ 4 Greg Anthony UNLV	.40	.20	.04
☐ 5 Anthony Avent Seton Hall	.20	.10	.02
☐ 6 Terrell Brandon Oregon	.40	.20	.04
☐ 7 Kevin Brooks Southwestern Louisiana	.15	.07	.01
☐ 8 Marc Brown Siena	.12	.06	.01

42 / 1991 Courtside Draft Pix

☐ 9 Myron Brown Slippery Rock	.10	.05	.01
☐ 10 Randy Brown New Mexico State	.15	.07	.01
☐ 11 Darrin Chancellor Southern Mississippi	.08	.04	.01
☐ 12 Pete Chilcutt North Carolina	.20	.10	.02
☐ 13 Chris Corchiani North Carolina St.	.15	.07	.01
☐ 14 John Crotty Virginia	.10	.05	.01
☐ 15 Dale Davis Clemson	.35	.17	.03
☐ 16 Marty Dow San Diego State	.08	.04	.01
☐ 17 Richard Dumas Oklahoma State	.08	.04	.01
☐ 18 LeRon Ellis Syracuse	.12	.06	.01
☐ 19 Tony Farmer Nebraska	.08	.04	.01
☐ 20 Roy Fisher California	.08	.04	.01
☐ 21 Rick Fox North Carolina	1.00	.50	.10
☐ 22 Chad Gallagher Creighton	.08	.04	.01
☐ 23 Chris Gatling Old Dominion	.40	.20	.04
☐ 24 Sean Green Iona	.15	.07	.01
☐ 25 Reggie Hanson Kentucky	.08	.04	.01
☐ 26 Donald Hodge Temple	.35	.17	.03
☐ 27 Steve Hood James Madison	.10	.05	.01
☐ 28 Keith Hughes Rutgers	.08	.04	.01
☐ 29 Mike Iuzzolino St.Francis	.35	.17	.03
☐ 30 Keith Jennings East Tenn. State	.15	.07	.01
☐ 31 Larry Johnson UNLV	5.00	2.50	.50
☐ 32 Treg Lee Ohio State	.08	.04	.01
☐ 33 Cedric Lewis Maryland	.08	.04	.01
☐ 34 Kevin Lynch Minnesota	.15	.07	.01
☐ 35 Mark Macon Temple	.35	.17	.03
☐ 36 Jason Matthews Pittsburgh	.08	.04	.01
☐ 37 Eric Murdock Providence	.30	.15	.03

1991 Courtside Draft Pix / 43

☐ 38 Jimmy Oliver Purdue	.20	.10	.02
☐ 39 Doug Overton LaSalle	.08	.04	.01
☐ 40 Elliot Perry Memphis State	.15	.07	.01
☐ 41 Brian Shorter Pittsburgh	.08	.04	.01
☐ 42 Alvaro Teheran Houston	.05	.02	.00
☐ 43 Joey Wright Texas	.08	.04	.01
☐ 44 Joe Wylie Miami (FL)	.08	.04	.01
☐ 45 Larry Johnson Collegiate Player of the Year	1.50	.75	.15
☐ NNO Larry Johnson SP (Sendaway)	5.00	2.50	.50

1991 Courtside Holograms

These three holograms were issued in a plastic sleeve within a paper envelope. According to information printed on the envelope, 99,000 sets were produced. Each hologram features the player photo against a parquet basketball floor background, with a subtitle at the bottom of the card face. Framed by turquoise borders above and on the right, the backs present stats (biographical), college record (year by year statistics), and profile. The cards are unnumbered and checklisted below in alphabetical order.

	MINT	EXC	G-VG
COMPLETE SET (3)	5.00	2.50	.50
COMMON PLAYER (1-3)	.60	.30	.06

44 / 1991 Courtside Holograms

☐ 1 Greg Anthony	.80	.40	.08
1990 National Champions			
☐ 2 Larry Johnson	4.50	2.25	.45
1990 Player of the Year			
☐ 3 Mark Macon	.60	.30	.06
First Round Draft Pick			

1961-62 Fleer

The 1961 Fleer set was Fleer's only major basketball issue until the 1986-87 season. The cards in the set measure the standard, 2 1/2" by 3 1/2". Cards numbered 45 to 66 are action shots (designated IA) of players elsewhere in the set. No known scarcities exist, although the set is quite popular since it contains the first basketball cards of many of the game's all-time greats including Elgin Baylor, Wilt Chamberlain, Oscar Robertson, and Jerry West. Many of the cards are frequently found with centering problems.

	NRMT	VG-E	GOOD
COMPLETE SET (66)	4500.00	2100.00	500.00
COMMON PLAYER (1-44)	15.00	7.50	1.50
COMMON PLAYER IA (45-66)	11.00	5.50	1.10
☐ 1 Al Attles	70.00	15.00	3.00
Philadelphia Warriors			
☐ 2 Paul Arizin	27.00	13.50	2.70
Philadelphia Warriors			
☐ 3 Elgin Baylor	300.00	150.00	30.00
Los Angeles Lakers			
☐ 4 Walt Bellamy	36.00	18.00	3.60
Chicago Packers			

1961-62 Fleer / 45

☐ 5	Arlen Bockhorn Cincinnati Royals	15.00	7.50	1.50
☐ 6	Bob Boozer Cincinnati Royals	18.00	9.00	1.80
☐ 7	Carl Braun Boston Celtics	18.00	9.00	1.80
☐ 8	Wilt Chamberlain Philadelphia Warriors	1500.00	600.00	175.00
☐ 9	Larry Costello Syracuse Nationals	20.00	10.00	2.00
☐ 10	Bob Cousy Boston Celtics	135.00	60.00	12.00
☐ 11	Walter Dukes Detroit Pistons	15.00	7.50	1.50
☐ 12	Wayne Embry Cincinnati Royals	35.00	17.50	3.50
☐ 13	Dave Gambee Syracuse Nationals	15.00	7.50	1.50
☐ 14	Tom Gola Philadelphia Warriors	27.00	13.50	2.70
☐ 15	Sihugo Green St. Louis Hawks	20.00	10.00	2.00
☐ 16	Hal Greer Syracuse Nationals	45.00	22.50	4.50
☐ 17	Richie Guerin New York Knicks	28.00	14.00	2.80
☐ 18	Cliff Hagan St. Louis Hawks	27.00	13.50	2.70
☐ 19	Tom Heinsohn Boston Celtics	50.00	25.00	5.00
☐ 20	Bailey Howell Detroit Pistons	25.00	12.50	2.50
☐ 21	Rod Hundley Los Angeles Lakers	27.00	13.50	2.70
☐ 22	K.C. Jones Boston Celtics	50.00	25.00	5.00
☐ 23	Sam Jones Boston Celtics	50.00	25.00	5.00
☐ 24	Phil Jordan New York Knicks	15.00	7.50	1.50
☐ 25	John Kerr Syracuse Nationals	25.00	12.50	2.50
☐ 26	Rudy LaRusso Los Angeles Lakers	25.00	12.50	2.50
☐ 27	George Lee Detroit Pistons	15.00	7.50	1.50
☐ 28	Bob Leonard Chicago Packers	15.00	7.50	1.50
☐ 29	Clyde Lovellette St. Louis Hawks	25.00	12.50	2.50
☐ 30	John McCarthy St. Louis Hawks	15.00	7.50	1.50
☐ 31	Tom Meschery Philadelphia Warriors	21.00	10.50	2.10
☐ 32	Willie Naulls New York Knicks	18.00	9.00	1.80
☐ 33	Don Ohl Detroit Pistons	20.00	10.00	2.00

46 / 1961-62 Fleer

☐ 34	Bob Pettit 65.00	32.50	6.50
	St. Louis Hawks		
☐ 35	Frank Ramsey 27.00	13.50	2.70
	Boston Celtics		
☐ 36	Oscar Robertson 450.00	225.00	45.00
	Cincinnati Royals		
☐ 37	Guy Rodgers 21.00	10.50	2.10
	Philadelphia Warriors		
☐ 38	Bill Russell 500.00	250.00	50.00
	Boston Celtics		
☐ 39	Dolph Schayes 30.00	15.00	3.00
	Syracuse Nationals		
☐ 40	Frank Selvy 15.00	7.50	1.50
	Los Angeles Lakers		
☐ 41	Gene Shue 20.00	10.00	2.00
	Detroit Pistons		
☐ 42	Jack Twyman 25.00	12.50	2.50
	Cincinnati Royals		
☐ 43	Jerry West 675.00	325.00	65.00
	Los Angeles Lakers		
☐ 44	Len Wilkens UER 65.00	32.50	6.50
	St. Louis Hawks		
	(Misspelled Wilkins		
	on card front)		
☐ 45	Paul Arizin IA 15.00	7.50	1.50
	Philadelphia Warriors		
☐ 46	Elgin Baylor IA 85.00	42.50	8.50
	Los Angeles Lakers		
☐ 47	Wilt Chamberlain IA 300.00	150.00	30.00
	Philadelphia Warriors		
☐ 48	Larry Costello IA 12.00	6.00	1.20
	Syracuse Nationals		
☐ 49	Bob Cousy IA 50.00	25.00	5.00
	Boston Celtics		
☐ 50	Walter Dukes IA 11.00	5.50	1.10
	Detroit Pistons		
☐ 51	Tom Gola IA 15.00	7.50	1.50
	Philadelphia Warriors		
☐ 52	Richie Guerin IA 15.00	7.50	1.50
	New York Knicks		
☐ 53	Cliff Hagan IA 16.00	8.00	1.60
	St. Louis Hawks		
☐ 54	Tom Heinsohn IA 25.00	12.50	2.50
	Boston Celtics		
☐ 55	Bailey Howell IA 12.00	6.00	1.20
	Detroit Pistons		
☐ 56	John Kerr IA 14.00	7.00	1.40
	Syracuse Nationals		
☐ 57	Rudy LaRusso IA 14.00	7.00	1.40
	Los Angeles Lakers		
☐ 58	Clyde Lovellette IA 14.00	7.00	1.40
	St. Louis Hawks		
☐ 59	Bob Pettit IA 30.00	15.00	3.00
	St. Louis Hawks		
☐ 60	Frank Ramsey IA 14.00	7.00	1.40
	Boston Celtics		
☐ 61	Oscar Robertson IA 125.00	60.00	12.50
	Cincinnati Royals		

1986-87 Fleer / 47

☐ 62	Bill Russell IA	200.00	100.00	20.00
	Boston Celtics			
☐ 63	Dolph Schayes IA	17.00	8.50	1.70
	Syracuse Nationals			
☐ 64	Gene Shue IA	12.00	6.00	1.20
	Detroit Pistons			
☐ 65	Jack Twyman IA	14.00	7.00	1.40
	Cincinnati Royals			
☐ 66	Jerry West IA	210.00	75.00	15.00
	Los Angeles Lakers			

1986-87 Fleer

This 132-card set features prominent players in the NBA. Cards measure the standard 2 1/2" by 3 1/2". The photo on the front is inside a red, white, and blue frame. A Fleer "Premier" logo is pictured in the upper corner of the obverse. The card backs are printed in red and blue on white card stock. The card numbers correspond to the alphabetical order of the player's names. Each retail wax pack contained 12 player cards, a piece of gum, and an insert sticker card. Several cards have special "Traded" notations on them if the player was traded after his picture was selected. Since only the Star Company had been issuing basketball cards nationally since 1983, most of the players in this Fleer set already had cards which are considered XRC's, extended rookie cards. However, since this Fleer set was the first nationally available set in packs since the 1981-82 Topps issue, most of the players in the set could be considered rookie cards. Therefore, the key rookie cards in this set, who had already had cards in previous Star sets are Charles Barkley, Clyde Drexler, Patrick Ewing, Michael Jordan, Hakeem Olajuwon, Isiah Thomas, and Dominique Wilkins. The key rookie cards in this set, who had not previously appeared on cards, are Karl Malone and Chris Mullin. It's important to note that some of the more expensive cards in this set (especially Michael Jordan) have been counterfeited in the past few years. Checking key detailed printing areas such as the "Fleer Premier" logo on the front and the players' association logo on the back under eight or ten power magnification usually detects the legitimate from the counterfeits.

48 / 1986-87 Fleer

	MINT	EXC	G-VG
COMPLETE SET (132)	900.00	450.00	90.00
COMMON PLAYER (1-132)	1.25	.60	.12
☐ 1 Kareem Abdul-Jabbar Los Angeles Lakers	12.00	6.00	1.20
☐ 2 Alvan Adams Phoenix Suns	1.25	.60	.12
☐ 3 Mark Aguirre Dallas Mavericks	4.00	2.00	.40
☐ 4 Danny Ainge Boston Celtics	6.00	3.00	.60
☐ 5 John Bagley Cleveland Cavaliers	2.50	1.25	.25
☐ 6 Thurl Bailey Utah Jazz	1.50	.75	.15
☐ 7 Charles Barkley Philadelphia 76ers	65.00	32.50	6.50
☐ 8 Benoit Benjamin Los Angeles Clippers	4.00	2.00	.40
☐ 9 Larry Bird Boston Celtics	20.00	10.00	2.00
☐ 10 Otis Birdsong New Jersey Nets	1.25	.60	.12
☐ 11 Rolando Blackman Dallas Mavericks	6.50	3.25	.65
☐ 12 Manute Bol Washington Bullets	3.00	1.50	.30
☐ 13 Sam Bowie Portland Trail Blazers	3.00	1.50	.30
☐ 14 Joe Barry Carroll Golden State Warriors	1.25	.60	.12
☐ 15 Tom Chambers Seattle Supersonics	12.50	6.25	1.25
☐ 16 Maurice Cheeks Philadelphia 76ers	1.50	.75	.15
☐ 17 Michael Cooper Los Angeles Lakers	1.50	.75	.15
☐ 18 Wayne Cooper Denver Nuggets	1.25	.60	.12
☐ 19 Pat Cummings New York Knicks	1.25	.60	.12
☐ 20 Terry Cummings Milwaukee Bucks	7.00	3.50	.70
☐ 21 Adrian Dantley Utah Jazz	1.50	.75	.15
☐ 22 Brad Davis Dallas Mavericks	1.50	.75	.15
☐ 23 Walter Davis Phoenix Suns	1.50	.75	.15
☐ 24 Darryl Dawkins New Jersey Nets	1.50	.75	.15
☐ 25 Larry Drew Sacramento Kings	1.50	.75	.15
☐ 26 Clyde Drexler Portland Trail Blazers	80.00	40.00	8.00
☐ 27 Joe Dumars Detroit Pistons	25.00	12.50	2.50

1986-87 Fleer / 49

☐ 28	Mark Eaton 2.00	1.00	.20
	Utah Jazz		
☐ 29	James Edwards 1.50	.75	.15
	Phoenix Suns		
☐ 30	Alex English 2.25	1.10	.22
	Denver Nuggets		
☐ 31	Julius Erving 12.00	6.00	1.20
	Philadelphia 76ers		
☐ 32	Patrick Ewing 70.00	35.00	7.00
	New York Knicks		
☐ 33	Vern Fleming 1.50	.75	.15
	Indiana Pacers		
☐ 34	Sleepy Floyd 1.50	.75	.15
	Golden State Warriors		
☐ 35	World B. Free 1.50	.75	.15
	Cleveland Cavaliers		
☐ 36	George Gervin 2.50	1.25	.25
	Chicago Bulls		
☐ 37	Artis Gilmore 1.75	.85	.17
	San Antonio Spurs		
☐ 38	Mike Gminski 1.25	.60	.12
	New Jersey Nets		
☐ 39	Rickey Green 1.50	.75	.15
	Utah Jazz		
☐ 40	Sidney Green 1.25	.60	.12
	Chicago Bulls		
☐ 41	David Greenwood 1.25	.60	.12
	San Antonio Spurs		
☐ 42	Darrell Griffith 1.50	.75	.15
	Utah Jazz		
☐ 43	Bill Hanzlik 1.25	.60	.12
	Denver Nuggets		
☐ 44	Derek Harper 4.00	2.00	.40
	Dallas Mavericks		
☐ 45	Gerald Henderson 1.25	.60	.12
	Seattle Supersonics		
☐ 46	Roy Hinson 1.50	.75	.15
	Philadelphia 76ers		
☐ 47	Craig Hodges 2.50	1.25	.25
	Milwaukee Bucks		
☐ 48	Phil Hubbard 1.25	.60	.12
	Cleveland Cavaliers		
☐ 49	Jay Humphries 2.50	1.25	.25
	Phoenix Suns		
☐ 50	Dennis Johnson 1.75	.85	.17
	Boston Celtics		
☐ 51	Eddie Johnson 3.50	1.75	.35
	Sacramento Kings		
☐ 52	Frank Johnson 1.25	.60	.12
	Washington Bullets		
☐ 53	Magic Johnson 36.00	18.00	3.60
	Los Angeles Lakers		
☐ 54	Marques Johnson 1.50	.75	.15
	Los Angeles Clippers (Decimal point missing, rookie year scoring avg.)		
☐ 55	Steve Johnson UER 1.25	.60	.12
	San Antonio Spurs		

50 / 1986-87 Fleer

☐ 56	Vinnie Johnson (photo actually David Greenwood) 1.50	.75	.15
	Detroit Pistons		
☐ 57	Michael Jordan 550.00	275.00	55.00
	Chicago Bulls		
☐ 58	Clark Kellogg 1.50	.75	.15
	Indiana Pacers		
☐ 59	Albert King 1.25	.60	.12
	New Jersey Nets		
☐ 60	Bernard King 2.00	1.00	.20
	New York Knicks		
☐ 61	Bill Laimbeer 2.00	1.00	.20
	Detroit Pistons		
☐ 62	Allen Leavell 1.25	.60	.12
	Houston Rockets		
☐ 63	Lafayette Lever 1.75	.85	.17
	Denver Nuggets		
☐ 64	Alton Lister 1.50	.75	.15
	Seattle Supersonics		
☐ 65	Lewis Lloyd 1.25	.60	.12
	Houston Rockets		
☐ 66	Maurice Lucas 1.50	.75	.15
	Los Angeles Lakers		
☐ 67	Jeff Malone 10.00	5.00	1.00
	Washington Bullets		
☐ 68	Karl Malone 65.00	32.50	6.50
	Utah Jazz		
☐ 69	Moses Malone 4.00	2.00	.40
	Washington Bullets		
☐ 70	Cedric Maxwell 1.50	.75	.15
	Los Angeles Clippers		
☐ 71	Rodney McCray 1.75	.85	.17
	Houston Rockets		
☐ 72	Xavier McDaniel 13.00	6.50	1.30
	Seattle Supersonics		
☐ 73	Kevin McHale 3.00	1.50	.30
	Boston Celtics		
☐ 74	Mike Mitchell 1.25	.60	.12
	San Antonio Spurs		
☐ 75	Sidney Moncrief 1.75	.85	.17
	Milwaukee Bucks		
☐ 76	Johnny Moore 1.25	.60	.12
	San Antonio Spurs		
☐ 77	Chris Mullin 55.00	27.50	5.50
	Golden State Warriors		
☐ 78	Larry Nance 11.00	5.50	1.10
	Phoenix Suns		
☐ 79	Calvin Natt 1.25	.60	.12
	Denver Nuggets		
☐ 80	Norm Nixon 1.25	.60	.12
	Los Angeles Clippers		
☐ 81	Charles Oakley 3.00	1.50	.30
	Chicago Bulls		
☐ 82	Hakeem Olajuwon 45.00	22.50	4.50
	Houston Rockets		
☐ 83	Louis Orr 1.25	.60	.12
	New York Knicks		

1986-87 Fleer / 51

☐ 84	Robert Parish UER Boston Celtics	4.00	2.00	.40
☐ 85	Jim Paxson Portland Trail Blazers	1.25	.60	.12
☐ 86	Sam Perkins Dallas Mavericks	8.00	4.00	.80
☐ 87	Ricky Pierce Milwaukee Bucks	8.00	4.00	.80
☐ 88	Paul Pressey Milwaukee Bucks	1.50	.75	.15
☐ 89	Kurt Rambis Los Angeles Lakers	1.50	.75	.15
☐ 90	Robert Reid Houston Rockets	1.25	.60	.12
☐ 91	Doc Rivers Atlanta Hawks	2.75	1.35	.27
☐ 92	Alvin Robertson San Antonio Spurs	4.00	2.00	.40
☐ 93	Cliff Robinson Philadelphia 76ers	1.25	.60	.12
☐ 94	Tree Rollins Atlanta Hawks	1.25	.60	.12
☐ 95	Dan Roundfield Washington Bullets	1.25	.60	.12
☐ 96	Jeff Ruland Philadelphia 76ers	1.50	.75	.15
☐ 97	Ralph Sampson Houston Rockets	1.75	.85	.17
☐ 98	Danny Schayes Denver Nuggets	1.50	.75	.15
☐ 99	Byron Scott Los Angeles Lakers	5.00	2.50	.50
☐ 100	Purvis Short Golden State Warriors	1.25	.60	.12
☐ 101	Jerry Sichting Boston Celtics	1.25	.60	.12
☐ 102	Jack Sikma Milwaukee Bucks	1.50	.75	.15
☐ 103	Derek Smith Los Angeles Clippers	1.50	.75	.15
☐ 104	Larry Smith Golden State Warriors	1.25	.60	.12
☐ 105	Rory Sparrow New York Knicks	1.25	.60	.12
☐ 106	Steve Stipanovich Indiana Pacers	1.50	.75	.15
☐ 107	Terry Teagle Golden State Warriors	2.00	1.00	.20
☐ 108	Reggie Theus Sacramento Kings	1.50	.75	.15
☐ 109	Isiah Thomas Detroit Pistons	30.00	15.00	3.00
☐ 110	LaSalle Thompson Sacramento Kings	1.50	.75	.15
☐ 111	Mychal Thompson Portland Trail Blazers	1.50	.75	.15
☐ 112	Sedale Threatt Philadelphia 76ers	4.50	2.25	.45

52 / 1986-87 Fleer

☐ 113 Wayman Tisdale 5.00		2.50	.50
Indiana Pacers			
☐ 114 Andrew Toney 1.50		.75	.15
Philadelphia 76ers			
☐ 115 Kelly Tripucka 1.50		.75	.15
Detroit Pistons			
☐ 116 Mel Turpin 1.50		.75	.15
Cleveland Cavaliers			
☐ 117 Kiki Vandeweghe 1.50		.75	.15
Portland Trail Blazers			
☐ 118 Jay Vincent 1.25		.60	.12
Dallas Mavericks			
☐ 119 Bill Walton 3.25		1.60	.32
Boston Celtics			
(Missing decimal points			
on four lines of			
FG Percentage)			
☐ 120 Spud Webb 6.50		3.25	.65
Atlanta Hawks			
☐ 121 Dominique Wilkins 30.00		15.00	3.00
Atlanta Hawks			
☐ 122 Gerald Wilkins 5.00		2.50	.50
New York Knicks			
☐ 123 Buck Williams 11.00		5.50	1.10
New Jersey Nets			
☐ 124 Gus Williams 1.50		.75	.15
Washington Bullets			
☐ 125 Herb Williams 1.50		.75	.15
Indiana Pacers			
☐ 126 Kevin Willis 8.00		4.00	.80
Atlanta Hawks			
☐ 127 Randy Wittman 1.25		.60	.12
Atlanta Hawks			
☐ 128 Al Wood 1.25		.60	.12
Seattle Supersonics			
☐ 129 Mike Woodson 1.25		.60	.12
Sacramento Kings			
☐ 130 Orlando Woolridge 3.50		1.75	.35
Chicago Bulls			
☐ 131 James Worthy 25.00		12.50	2.50
Los Angeles Lakers			
☐ 132 Checklist 1-132 .... 1.50		.75	.15

1986-87 Fleer Sticker Inserts

This set of 11 stickers was distributed in the wax packs (one per pack) with the Fleer regular 132-card issue. The stickers are 2 1/2" by 3 1/2". The backs of the sticker cards are printed in blue and red on white card stock.

	MINT	EXC	G-VG
COMPLETE SET (11)	75.00	37.50	7.50
COMMON PLAYER (1-11)	1.00	.50	.10

☐ 1	Kareem Abdul-Jabbar	5.00	2.50	.50
	Los Angeles Lakers			
☐ 2	Larry Bird	9.00	4.50	.90
	Boston Celtics			
☐ 3	Adrian Dantley	1.00	.50	.10
	Utah Jazz			
☐ 4	Alex English	1.00	.50	.10
	Denver Nuggets			
☐ 5	Julius Erving	5.00	2.50	.50
	Philadelphia 76ers			
☐ 6	Patrick Ewing	12.00	6.00	1.20
	New York Knicks			
☐ 7	Magic Johnson	13.50	6.50	1.35
	Los Angeles Lakers			
☐ 8	Michael Jordan	50.00	25.00	5.00
	Chicago Bulls			
☐ 9	Hakeem Olajuwon	6.50	3.25	.65
	Houston Rockets			
☐ 10	Isiah Thomas	5.00	2.50	.50
	Detroit Pistons			
☐ 11	Dominique Wilkins	5.00	2.50	.50
	Atlanta Hawks			

1987-88 Fleer

The 1987-88 Fleer basketball set contains 132 standard size (2 1/2" by 3 1/2") cards featuring 131 of the NBA's better-known players, plus a checklist. The fronts are white with gray horizontal stripes. The backs are red, white, and blue and show each player's complete NBA statistics. The cards are numbered essentially in alphabetical order. This set was issued in wax packs, each

54 / 1987-88 Fleer

containing 12 cards. The key "pure" rookie cards in this set are Brad Daugherty, A.C. Green, Ron Harper, Chuck Person, Terry Porter, Detlef Schrempf, and Hot Rod Williams. Other key rookie cards in this set, who had already had cards in previous Star sets, are Jerome Kersey, John Paxson, and Otis Thorpe.

	MINT	EXC	G-VG
COMPLETE SET (132)	265.00	115.00	22.00
COMMON PLAYER (1-132)	.50	.25	.05
☐ 1 Kareem Abdul-Jabbar	8.00	4.00	.80
Los Angeles Lakers			
☐ 2 Alvan Adams	.50	.25	.05
Phoenix Suns			
☐ 3 Mark Aguirre	1.00	.50	.10
Dallas Mavericks			
☐ 4 Danny Ainge	1.50	.75	.15
Boston Celtics			
☐ 5 John Bagley	.75	.35	.07
Cleveland Cavaliers			
☐ 6 Thurl Bailey UER	.50	.25	.05
Utah Jazz			
(reverse negative)			
☐ 7 Greg Ballard	.50	.25	.05
Golden State Warriors			
☐ 8 Gene Banks	.50	.25	.05
Chicago Bulls			
☐ 9 Charles Barkley	17.00	8.50	1.70
Philadelphia 76ers			
☐ 10 Benoit Benjamin	1.00	.50	.10
Los Angeles Clippers			
☐ 11 Larry Bird	13.00	6.50	1.30
Boston Celtics			
☐ 12 Rolando Blackman	1.50	.75	.15
Dallas Mavericks			
☐ 13 Manute Bol	.75	.35	.07
Washington Bullets			

1987-88 Fleer / 55

☐ 14	Tony Brown	.50	.25	.05
	New Jersey Nets			
☐ 15	Michael Cage	1.50	.75	.15
	Los Angeles Clippers			
☐ 16	Joe Barry Carroll	.50	.25	.05
	Golden State Warriors			
☐ 17	Bill Cartwright	.75	.35	.07
	New York Knicks			
☐ 18	Terry Catledge	1.50	.75	.15
	Washington Bullets			
☐ 19	Tom Chambers	3.50	1.75	.35
	Seattle Supersonics			
☐ 20	Maurice Cheeks	.75	.35	.07
	Philadelphia 76ers			
☐ 21	Michael Cooper	.75	.35	.07
	Los Angeles Lakers			
☐ 22	Dave Corzine	.50	.25	.05
	Chicago Bulls			
☐ 23	Terry Cummings	1.75	.85	.17
	Milwaukee Bucks			
☐ 24	Adrian Dantley	.75	.35	.07
	Detroit Pistons			
☐ 25	Brad Daugherty	24.00	12.00	2.40
	Cleveland Cavaliers			
☐ 26	Walter Davis	.75	.35	.07
	Phoenix Suns			
☐ 27	Johnny Dawkins	3.00	1.50	.30
	San Antonio Spurs			
☐ 28	James Donaldson	.75	.35	.07
	Dallas Mavericks			
☐ 29	Larry Drew	.50	.25	.05
	Los Angeles Clippers			
☐ 30	Clyde Drexler	20.00	10.00	2.00
	Portland Trail Blazers			
☐ 31	Joe Dumars	7.00	3.50	.70
	Detroit Pistons			
☐ 32	Mark Eaton	.75	.35	.07
	Utah Jazz			
☐ 33	Dale Ellis	3.00	1.50	.30
	Seattle Supersonics			
☐ 34	Alex English	1.00	.50	.10
	Denver Nuggets			
☐ 35	Julius Erving	8.00	4.00	.80
	Philadelphia 76ers			
☐ 36	Mike Evans	.50	.25	.05
	Denver Nuggets			
☐ 37	Patrick Ewing	18.00	9.00	1.80
	New York Knicks			
☐ 38	Vern Fleming	.50	.25	.05
	Indiana Pacers			
☐ 39	Sleepy Floyd	.50	.25	.05
	Golden State Warriors			
☐ 40	Artis Gilmore	1.00	.50	.10
	San Antonio Spurs			
☐ 41	Mike Gminski UER	.50	.25	.05
	New Jersey Nets			
	(reversed negative)			

56 / 1987-88 Fleer

☐ 42	A.C. Green Los Angeles Lakers	4.50	2.25	.45
☐ 43	Rickey Green Utah Jazz	.50	.25	.05
☐ 44	Sidney Green Detroit Pistons	.50	.25	.05
☐ 45	David Greenwood San Antonio Spurs	.50	.25	.05
☐ 46	Darrell Griffith Utah Jazz	.50	.25	.05
☐ 47	Bill Hanzlik Denver Nuggets	.50	.25	.05
☐ 48	Derek Harper Dallas Mavericks	1.00	.50	.10
☐ 49	Ron Harper Cleveland Cavaliers	6.00	3.00	.60
☐ 50	Gerald Henderson New York Knicks	.50	.25	.05
☐ 51	Roy Hinson Philadelphia 76ers	.50	.25	.05
☐ 52	Craig Hodges Milwaukee Bucks	.75	.35	.07
☐ 53	Phil Hubbard Cleveland Cavaliers	.50	.25	.05
☐ 54	Dennis Johnson Boston Celtics	.75	.35	.07
☐ 55	Eddie Johnson Sacramento Kings	1.00	.50	.10
☐ 56	Magic Johnson Los Angeles Lakers	22.00	11.00	2.20
☐ 57	Steve Johnson Portland Trail Blazers	.50	.25	.05
☐ 58	Vinnie Johnson Detroit Pistons	.75	.35	.07
☐ 59	Michael Jordan Chicago Bulls	125.00	60.00	12.50
☐ 60	Jerome Kersey Portland Trail Blazers	12.50	6.25	1.25
☐ 61	Bill Laimbeer Detroit Pistons	1.00	.50	.10
☐ 62	Lafayette Lever UER Denver Nuggets (Photo actually Otis Smith)	.75	.35	.07
☐ 63	Cliff Levingston Atlanta Hawks	1.50	.75	.15
☐ 64	Alton Lister Seattle Supersonics	.50	.25	.05
☐ 65	John Long Indiana Pacers	.50	.25	.05
☐ 66	John Lucas Milwaukee Bucks	.50	.25	.05
☐ 67	Jeff Malone Washington Bullets	2.50	1.25	.25
☐ 68	Karl Malone Utah Jazz	17.00	8.50	1.70
☐ 69	Moses Malone Washington Bullets	3.00	1.50	.30

1987-88 Fleer / 57

☐ 70	Cedric Maxwell .... .75 Houston Rockets	.35	.07
☐ 71	Tim McCormick .... .75 Philadelphia 76ers	.35	.07
☐ 72	Rodney McCray .... .75 Houston Rockets	.35	.07
☐ 73	Xavier McDaniel .... 3.50 Seattle Supersonics	1.75	.35
☐ 74	Kevin McHale .... 2.00 Boston Celtics	1.00	.20
☐ 75	Nate McMillan .... 1.25 Seattle Supersonics	.60	.12
☐ 76	Sidney Moncrief .... .75 Milwaukee Bucks	.35	.07
☐ 77	Chris Mullin .... 15.00 Golden State Warriors	7.50	1.50
☐ 78	Larry Nance .... 2.50 Phoenix Suns	1.25	.25
☐ 79	Charles Oakley .... .75 Chicago Bulls	.35	.07
☐ 80	Hakeem Olajuwon .... 12.50 Houston Rockets	6.25	1.25
☐ 81	Robert Parish UER .... 3.00 Boston Celtics (Misspelled Parrish on both sides)	1.50	.30
☐ 82	Jim Paxson .... .50 Portland Trail Blazers	.25	.05
☐ 83	John Paxson .... 7.00 Chicago Bulls	3.50	.70
☐ 84	Sam Perkins .... 2.00 Dallas Mavericks	1.00	.20
☐ 85	Chuck Person .... 6.50 Indiana Pacers	3.25	.65
☐ 86	Jim Peterson .... .75 Houston Rockets	.35	.07
☐ 87	Ricky Pierce .... 1.75 Milwaukee Bucks	.85	.17
☐ 88	Ed Pinckney .... 1.75 Phoenix Suns	.85	.17
☐ 89	Terry Porter .... 17.00 Portland Trail Blazers (College Wisconsin, should be Wisconsin - Stevens Point)	8.50	1.70
☐ 90	Paul Pressey .... .50 Milwaukee Bucks	.25	.05
☐ 91	Robert Reid .... .50 Houston Rockets	.25	.05
☐ 92	Doc Rivers .... .75 Atlanta Hawks	.35	.07
☐ 93	Alvin Robertson .... 1.00 San Antonio Spurs	.50	.10
☐ 94	Tree Rollins .... .50 Atlanta Hawks	.25	.05
☐ 95	Ralph Sampson .... .75 Houston Rockets	.35	.07

58 / 1987-88 Fleer

☐ 96 Mike Sanders .75		.35	.07
Phoenix Suns			
☐ 97 Detlef Schrempf 8.00		4.00	.80
Dallas Mavericks			
☐ 98 Byron Scott 1.25		.60	.12
Los Angeles Lakers			
☐ 99 Jerry Sichting .50		.25	.05
Boston Celtics			
☐ 100 Jack Sikma .75		.35	.07
Milwaukee Bucks			
☐ 101 Larry Smith .50		.25	.05
Golden State Warriors			
☐ 102 Rory Sparrow .50		.25	.05
New York Knicks			
☐ 103 Steve Stipanovich .50		.25	.05
Indiana Pacers			
☐ 104 Jon Sundvold .75		.35	.07
San Antonio Spurs			
☐ 105 Reggie Theus .75		.35	.07
Sacramento Kings			
☐ 106 Isiah Thomas 9.00		4.50	.90
Detroit Pistons			
☐ 107 LaSalle Thompson .50		.25	.05
Sacramento Kings			
☐ 108 Mychal Thompson .75		.35	.07
Los Angeles Lakers			
☐ 109 Otis Thorpe 7.00		3.50	.70
Sacramento Kings			
☐ 110 Sedale Threatt 1.00		.50	.10
Chicago Bulls			
☐ 111 Waymon Tisdale 1.25		.60	.12
Indiana Pacers			
☐ 112 Kelly Tripucka .75		.35	.07
Utah Jazz			
☐ 113 Trent Tucker .75		.35	.07
New York Knicks			
☐ 114 Terry Tyler .50		.25	.05
Sacramento Kings			
☐ 115 Darnell Valentine .50		.25	.05
Los Angeles Clippers			
☐ 116 Kiki Vandeweghe .75		.35	.07
Portland Trail Blazers			
☐ 117 Darrell Walker .75		.35	.07
Denver Nuggets			
☐ 118 Dominique Wilkins 9.00		4.50	.90
Atlanta Hawks			
☐ 119 Gerald Wilkins 1.00		.50	.10
New York Knicks			
☐ 120 Buck Williams 3.00		1.50	.30
New Jersey Nets			
☐ 121 Herb Williams .75		.35	.07
Indiana Pacers			
☐ 122 John Williams .75		.35	.07
Washington Bullets			
☐ 123 John Williams 5.00		2.50	.50
Cleveland Cavaliers			
☐ 124 Kevin Willis 2.00		1.00	.20
Atlanta Hawks			

1987-88 Fleer Sticker Inserts / 59

☐ 125 David Wingate	.75	.35	.07
Philadelphia 76ers			
☐ 126 Randy Wittman	.50	.25	.05
Atlanta Hawks			
☐ 127 Leon Wood	.50	.25	.05
New Jersey Nets			
☐ 128 Mike Woodson	.50	.25	.05
Los Angeles Clippers			
☐ 129 Orlando Woolridge	1.00	.50	.10
New Jersey Nets			
☐ 130 James Worthy	7.00	3.50	.70
Los Angeles Lakers			
☐ 131 Danny Young	.75	.35	.07
Seattle Supersonics			
☐ 132 Checklist Card	.75	.35	.07

1987-88 Fleer Sticker Inserts

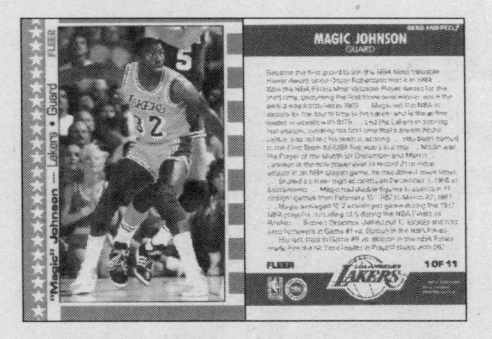

The 1987-88 Fleer Stickers set is an 11-card standard size (2 1/2" by 3 1/2") set issued as an insert with the regular 132-card set. The fronts are red, white, blue, and yellow. The backs are white and blue, and contain career highlights. One sticker was included in each wax pack. Virtually all cards from this set have wax-stained backs as a result of the packaging.

	MINT	EXC	G-VG
COMPLETE SET (11)	35.00	17.50	3.50
COMMON PLAYER (1-11)	.50	.25	.05
☐ 1 Magic Johnson	9.00	4.50	.90
Los Angeles Lakers			
☐ 2 Michael Jordan	25.00	12.50	2.50
Chicago Bulls			
(In text, votes mis-			

60 / 1987-88 Fleer Sticker Inserts

spelled as voites)
☐ 3 Hakeem Olajuwon UER 3.75	1.85	.37
Houston Rockets		
(Misspelled Olajuwan		
on card back)		
☐ 4 Larry Bird 5.00	2.50	.50
Boston Celtics		
☐ 5 Kevin McHale .... .75	.35	.07
Boston Celtics		
☐ 6 Charles Barkley 5.50	2.75	.55
Philadelphia 76ers		
☐ 7 Dominique Wilkins 3.00	1.50	.30
Atlanta Hawks		
☐ 8 Kareem Abdul-Jabbar 3.00	1.50	.30
Los Angeles Lakers		
☐ 9 Mark Aguirre .... .50	.25	.05
Dallas Mavericks		
☐ 10 Chuck Person 1.00	.50	.10
Indiana Pacers		
☐ 11 Alex English .... .50	.25	.05
Denver Nuggets		

1988-89 Fleer

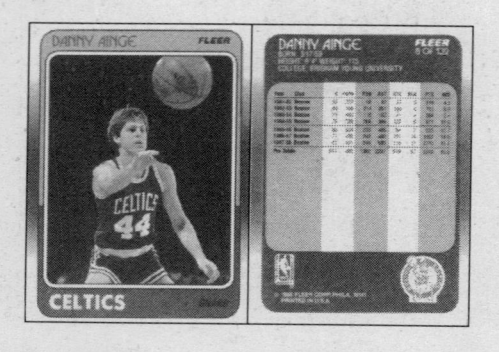

The 1988-89 Fleer basketball set contains 132 standard size (2 1/2" by 3 1/2") cards. There are 119 regular cards, plus 12 All-Star cards and a checklist. The outer borders are white and gray, while the inner borders correspond to the team colors. The backs are greenish, and show full NBA statistics with limited biographical information. The set is ordered alphabetically in team subsets (with a few exceptions due to late trades). The teams themselves are also presented in alphabetical order, Atlanta Hawks (1-6, 98, and 118), Boston Celtics (8-12), Charlotte Hornets (13-14), Chicago Bulls (15-17 and 19-21), Cleveland Cavaliers (22-26), Dallas Mavericks (27-

1988-89 Fleer / 61

32), Denver Nuggets (33-38), Detroit Pistons (39-45), Golden State Warriors (46-49), Houston Rockets (50-54 and 63), Indiana Pacers (55-60), Los Angeles Clippers (61), Los Angeles Lakers (64-70), Miami Heat (71-72), Milwaukee Bucks (73-76), New Jersey Nets (77-79 and 102), New York Knicks (18 and 80-84), Philadelphia 76ers (85-88), Phoenix Suns (89-91 and 106), Portland Trail Blazers (92-96), Sacramento Kings (7, 97, and 99-100), San Antonio Spurs (101 and 103-105), Seattle Supersonics (62 and 107-110), Utah Jazz (111-115), Washington Bullets (116-117 and 119), and All-Stars (120-131). This set was issued in wax packs of 12 cards. The key rookie cards in this set are Michael Adams, Kevin Duckworth, Horace Grant, Reggie Miller, Derrick McKey, Scottie Pippen, Mark Price, Dennis Rodman, and Kenny Smith. There is also a rookie card of John Stockton who had previously only appeared in Star Company sets.

	MINT	EXC	G-VG
COMPLETE SET (132)	150.00	75.00	15.00
COMMON PLAYER (1-132)	.20	.10	.02
☐ 1 Antoine Carr	1.00	.30	.06
☐ 2 Cliff Levingston	.30	.15	.03
☐ 3 Doc Rivers	.30	.15	.03
☐ 4 Spud Webb	.75	.35	.07
☐ 5 Dominique Wilkins	3.50	1.75	.35
☐ 6 Kevin Willis	1.00	.50	.10
☐ 7 Randy Wittman	.20	.10	.02
☐ 8 Danny Ainge	.75	.35	.07
☐ 9 Larry Bird	6.00	3.00	.60
☐ 10 Dennis Johnson	.30	.15	.03
☐ 11 Kevin McHale	1.00	.50	.10
☐ 12 Robert Parish	1.25	.60	.12
☐ 13 Tyrone Bogues	1.00	.50	.10
☐ 14 Dell Curry	1.50	.75	.15
☐ 15 Dave Corzine	.20	.10	.02
☐ 16 Horace Grant	12.00	6.00	1.20
☐ 17 Michael Jordan	36.00	18.00	3.60
☐ 18 Charles Oakley	.30	.15	.03
☐ 19 John Paxson	1.00	.50	.10
☐ 20 Scottie Pippen UER (Misspelled Pippin on card back)	55.00	27.50	5.50
☐ 21 Brad Sellers	.30	.15	.03
☐ 22 Brad Daugherty	6.00	3.00	.60
☐ 23 Ron Harper	1.00	.50	.10
☐ 24 Larry Nance	1.25	.60	.12
☐ 25 Mark Price	9.00	4.50	.90
☐ 26 Hot Rod Williams	.75	.35	.07
☐ 27 Mark Aguirre	.50	.25	.05
☐ 28 Rolando Blackman	.75	.35	.07
☐ 29 James Donaldson	.20	.10	.02
☐ 30 Derek Harper	.50	.25	.05
☐ 31 Sam Perkins	1.00	.50	.10
☐ 32 Roy Tarpley	.60	.30	.06
☐ 33 Michael Adams	3.50	1.75	.35
☐ 34 Alex English	.60	.30	.06
☐ 35 Lafayette Lever	.30	.15	.03
☐ 36 Blair Rasmussen	.60	.30	.06
☐ 37 Danny Schayes	.30	.15	.03
☐ 38 Jay Vincent	.20	.10	.02
☐ 39 Adrian Dantley	.40	.20	.04
☐ 40 Joe Dumars	3.00	1.50	.30

62 / 1988-89 Fleer

☐ 41	Vinnie Johnson	.30	.15	.03
☐ 42	Bill Laimbeer	.40	.20	.04
☐ 43	Dennis Rodman	9.00	4.50	.90
☐ 44	John Salley	2.00	1.00	.20
☐ 45	Isiah Thomas	3.25	1.60	.32
☐ 46	Winston Garland	.50	.25	.05
☐ 47	Rod Higgins	.30	.15	.03
☐ 48	Chris Mullin	5.50	2.75	.55
☐ 49	Ralph Sampson	.30	.15	.03
☐ 50	Joe Barry Carroll	.20	.10	.02
☐ 51	Sleepy Floyd	.30	.15	.03
☐ 52	Rodney McCray	.30	.15	.03
☐ 53	Hakeem Olajuwon	4.00	2.00	.40
☐ 54	Purvis Short	.20	.10	.02
☐ 55	Vern Fleming	.20	.10	.02
☐ 56	John Long	.20	.10	.02
☐ 57	Reggie Miller	9.00	4.50	.90
☐ 58	Chuck Person	1.00	.50	.10
☐ 59	Steve Stipanovich	.30	.15	.03
☐ 60	Waymon Tisdale	.60	.30	.06
☐ 61	Benoit Benjamin	.50	.25	.05
☐ 62	Michael Cage	.30	.15	.03
☐ 63	Mike Woodson	.20	.10	.02
☐ 64	Kareem Abdul-Jabbar	4.00	2.00	.40
☐ 65	Michael Cooper	.40	.20	.04
☐ 66	A.C. Green	.75	.35	.07
☐ 67	Magic Johnson	10.00	5.00	1.00
☐ 68	Byron Scott	.60	.30	.06
☐ 69	Mychal Thompson	.30	.15	.03
☐ 70	James Worthy	3.00	1.50	.30
☐ 71	Duane Washington	.30	.15	.03
☐ 72	Kevin Williams	.20	.10	.02
☐ 73	Randy Breuer	.30	.15	.03
☐ 74	Terry Cummings	.75	.35	.07
☐ 75	Paul Pressey	.20	.10	.02
☐ 76	Jack Sikma	.30	.15	.03
☐ 77	John Bagley	.30	.15	.03
☐ 78	Roy Hinson	.20	.10	.02
☐ 79	Buck Williams	1.25	.60	.12
☐ 80	Patrick Ewing	6.50	3.25	.65
☐ 81	Sidney Green	.20	.10	.02
☐ 82	Mark Jackson	2.25	1.10	.22
☐ 83	Kenny Walker	.30	.15	.03
☐ 84	Gerald Wilkins	.50	.25	.05
☐ 85	Charles Barkley	5.50	2.75	.55
☐ 86	Maurice Cheeks	.40	.20	.04
☐ 87	Mike Gminski	.20	.10	.02
☐ 88	Cliff Robinson	.20	.10	.02
☐ 89	Armon Gilliam	1.75	.85	.17
☐ 90	Eddie Johnson	.40	.20	.04
☐ 91	Mark West	.50	.25	.05
☐ 92	Clyde Drexler	7.00	3.50	.70
☐ 93	Kevin Duckworth	2.50	1.25	.25
☐ 94	Steve Johnson	.20	.10	.02
☐ 95	Jerome Kersey	3.00	1.50	.30
☐ 96	Terry Porter	4.50	2.25	.45

(College Wisconsin,

1988-89 Fleer / 63

  should be Wisconsin -
  Stevens Point)
☐ 97   Joe Kleine .... .35   .17   .03
☐ 98   Reggie Theus .... .30   .15   .03
☐ 99   Otis Thorpe .... 1.00   .50   .10
☐ 100 Kenny Smith .... 2.00   1.00   .20
  (College NC State,
  should be North
  Carolina)
☐ 101 Greg Anderson .... .90   .45   .09
☐ 102 Walter Berry .... .35   .17   .03
☐ 103 Frank Brickowski .... .35   .17   .03
☐ 104 Johnny Dawkins .... .35   .17   .03
☐ 105 Alvin Robertson .... .50   .25   .05
☐ 106 Tom Chambers .... 1.00   .50   .10
  (Born 6/2/59,
  should be 6/21/59)
☐ 107 Dale Ellis .... .40   .20   .04
☐ 108 Xavier McDaniel .... 1.00   .50   .10
☐ 109 Derrick McKey .... 2.00   1.00   .20
☐ 110 Nate McMillan UER .... .30   .15   .03
  (Photo actually
  Kevin Williams)
☐ 111 Thurl Bailey .... .20   .10   .02
☐ 112 Mark Eaton .... .30   .15   .03
☐ 113 Bobby Hansen .... .30   .15   .03
☐ 114 Karl Malone .... 5.50   2.75   .55
☐ 115 John Stockton 22.00   11.00   2.20
☐ 116 Bernard King .... .60   .30   .06
☐ 117 Jeff Malone .... 1.00   .50   .10
☐ 118 Moses Malone .... 1.00   .50   .10
☐ 119 John Williams .... .30   .15   .03
☐ 120 Michael Jordan AS 12.00   6.00   1.20
  Chicago Bulls
☐ 121 Mark Jackson AS .... .50   .25   .05
  New York Knicks
☐ 122 Byron Scott AS .... .30   .15   .03
  Los Angeles Lakers
☐ 123 Magic Johnson AS .... 4.50   2.25   .45
  Los Angeles Lakers
☐ 124 Larry Bird AS .... 2.75   1.35   .27
  Boston Celtics
☐ 125 Dominique Wilkins AS .... 1.50   .75   .15
  Atlanta Hawks
☐ 126 Hakeem Olajuwon AS .... 1.75   .85   .17
  Houston Rockets
☐ 127 John Stockton AS .... 5.50   2.75   .55
  Utah Jazz
☐ 128 Alvin Robertson AS .... .30   .15   .03
  San Antonio Spurs
☐ 129 Charles Barkley AS .... 2.50   1.25   .25
  Philadelphia 76ers
  (Back says Buck Williams
  is member of Jets,
  should be Nets)
☐ 130 Patrick Ewing AS .... 2.50   1.25   .25
  New York Knicks

64 / 1988-89 Fleer

☐ 131 Mark Eaton AS	.30	.15	.03
Utah Jazz			
☐ 132 Checklist Card	.30	.15	.03

1988-89 Fleer Sticker Inserts

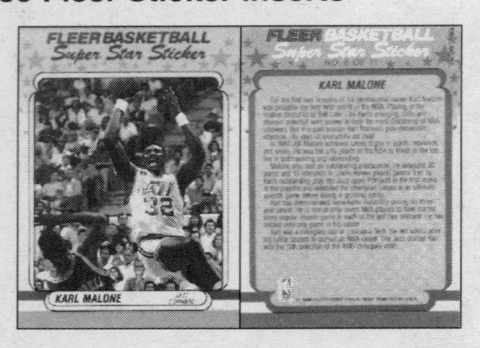

The 1988-89 Fleer Sticker set is an 11-card standard size (2 1/2" by 3 1/2") set issued as an insert with the regular 132-card set. The fronts are baby blue, red, and white. The backs are blue and pink and contain career highlights. The stickers were packed randomly in the wax packs. The set is ordered alphabetically. Virtually all cards from this set have wax-stained backs as a result of the packaging.

	MINT	EXC	G-VG
COMPLETE SET (11)	12.50	6.25	1.25
COMMON PLAYER (1-11)	.30	.15	.03
☐ 1 Mark Aguirre	.30	.15	.03
Dallas Mavericks			
☐ 2 Larry Bird	2.00	1.00	.20
Boston Celtics			
☐ 3 Clyde Drexler	2.00	1.00	.20
Portland Trail Blazers			
☐ 4 Alex English	.30	.15	.03
Denver Nuggets			
☐ 5 Patrick Ewing	1.75	.85	.17
New York Knicks			
☐ 6 Magic Johnson	3.00	1.50	.30
Los Angeles Lakers			
☐ 7 Michael Jordan	8.00	4.00	.80
Chicago Bulls			
☐ 8 Karl Malone	1.50	.75	.15
Utah Jazz			

1989-90 Fleer / 65

☐ 9 Kevin McHale .... .40	.20	.04
Boston Celtics		
☐ 10 Isiah Thomas 1.00	.50	.10
Detroit Pistons		
☐ 11 Dominique Wilkins 1.00	.50	.10
Atlanta Hawks		

1989-90 Fleer

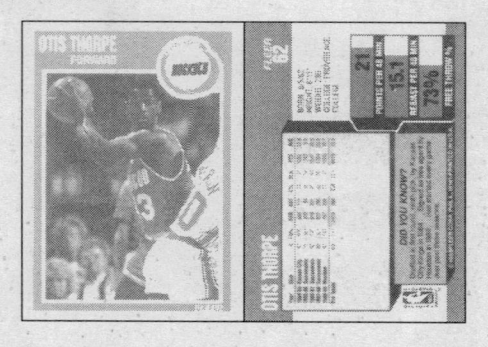

The 1989-90 Fleer basketball set consists of 168 cards measuring the standard size (2 1/2" by 3 1/2"). The fronts feature color action player photos, with various color borders between white inner and outer borders. The player's name and position appear in the upper left corner, with the team logo superimposed over the upper right corner of the picture. The horizontally oriented backs have black lettering on red, pink, and white background and present career statistics, biographical information, and a performance index. The set is ordered alphabetically in team subsets (with a few exceptions due to late trades). The teams themselves are also presented in alphabetical order, Atlanta Hawks (1-7), Boston Celtics (8-14), Charlotte Hornets (15-18), Chicago Bulls (19-23), Cleveland Cavaliers (25-31), Dallas Mavericks (32-37), Denver Nuggets (38-43), Detroit Pistons (44-51), Golden State Warriors (52-57), Houston Rockets (58-63), Indiana Pacers (64-68), Los Angeles Clippers (69-74), Los Angeles Lakers (75-80), Miami Heat (81-84), Milwaukee Bucks (85-91), Minnesota Timberwolves (92-94), New Jersey Nets (95-99), New York Knicks (100-107), Orlando Magic (108-111), Philadelphia 76ers (112-118), Phoenix Suns (119-125), Portland Trail Blazers (126-132), Sacramento Kings (133-139), San Antonio Spurs (140-144), Seattle Supersonics (24 and 145-150), Utah Jazz (151-156), Washington Bullets (157-162), and All-Star Game Combos (163-167). Rookie Cards included in this set are Willie Anderson, Rex Chapman, Hersey Hawkins, Jeff Hornacek, Kevin Johnson, Reggie Lewis, Dan Majerle, Danny Manning, Vernon Maxwell, Ken Norman, Mitch Richmond, Rony Seikaly, Brian Shaw, Scott Skiles, Charles Smith, and Rod Strickland.

	MINT	EXC	G-VG
COMPLETE SET (168)	35.00	17.50	3.50
COMMON PLAYER (1-168)	.06	.03	.00

66 / 1989-90 Fleer

☐ 1 John Battle	.30	.15	.03
☐ 2 Jon Koncak	.10	.05	.01
☐ 3 Cliff Levingston	.06	.03	.00
☐ 4 Moses Malone	.40	.20	.04
☐ 5 Glenn Rivers	.10	.05	.01
☐ 6 Spud Webb UER	.25	.12	.02
(Points per 48 minutes incorrect at 2.6)			
☐ 7 Dominique Wilkins	.90	.45	.09
☐ 8 Larry Bird	2.25	1.10	.22
☐ 9 Dennis Johnson	.12	.06	.01
☐ 10 Reggie Lewis	5.50	2.75	.55
☐ 11 Kevin McHale	.40	.20	.04
☐ 12 Robert Parish	.50	.25	.05
☐ 13 Ed Pinckney	.10	.05	.01
☐ 14 Brian Shaw	.75	.35	.07
☐ 15 Rex Chapman	.50	.25	.05
☐ 16 Kurt Rambis	.10	.05	.01
☐ 17 Robert Reid	.06	.03	.00
☐ 18 Kelly Tripucka	.10	.05	.01
☐ 19 Bill Cartwright UER	.10	.05	.01
(First season 1978-80, should be 1979-80)			
☐ 20 Horace Grant	1.50	.75	.15
☐ 21 Michael Jordan	8.00	4.00	.80
☐ 22 John Paxson	.35	.17	.03
☐ 23 Scottie Pippen	8.00	4.00	.80
☐ 24 Brad Sellers	.06	.03	.00
☐ 25 Brad Daugherty	1.75	.85	.17
☐ 26 Craig Ehlo	1.25	.60	.12
☐ 27 Ron Harper	.25	.12	.02
☐ 28 Larry Nance	.35	.17	.03
☐ 29 Mark Price	1.25	.60	.12
☐ 30 Mike Sanders	.10	.05	.01
☐ 31A John Williams ERR Cleveland Cavaliers	1.00	.50	.10
☐ 31B John Williams COR Cleveland Cavaliers	.25	.12	.02
☐ 32 Rolando Blackman UER	.25	.12	.02
(Career blocks and points listed as 1961 and 2127, should be 196 and 12,127)			
☐ 33 Adrian Dantley	.20	.10	.02
☐ 34 James Donaldson	.06	.03	.00
☐ 35 Derek Harper	.15	.07	.01
☐ 36 Sam Perkins	.30	.15	.03
☐ 37 Herb Williams	.10	.05	.01
☐ 38 Michael Adams	.50	.25	.05
☐ 39 Walter Davis	.12	.06	.01
☐ 40 Alex English	.20	.10	.02
☐ 41 Lafayette Lever	.10	.05	.01
☐ 42 Blair Rasmussen	.06	.03	.00
☐ 43 Dan Schayes	.10	.05	.01
☐ 44 Mark Aguirre	.12	.06	.01
☐ 45 Joe Dumars	.60	.30	.06
☐ 46 James Edwards	.10	.05	.01
☐ 47 Vinnie Johnson	.12	.06	.01

1989-90 Fleer / 67

☐ 48	Bill Laimbeer	.15	.07	.01
☐ 49	Dennis Rodman	1.25	.60	.12
☐ 50	Isiah Thomas	.90	.45	.09
☐ 51	John Salley	.15	.07	.01
☐ 52	Manute Bol	.12	.06	.01
☐ 53	Winston Garland	.06	.03	.00
☐ 54	Rod Higgins	.06	.03	.00
☐ 55	Chris Mullin	1.50	.75	.15
☐ 56	Mitch Richmond	3.00	1.50	.30
☐ 57	Terry Teagle	.10	.05	.01
☐ 58	Derrick Chievous UER (Stats correctly say 81 games in '88-89, text says 82)	.12	.06	.01
☐ 59	Sleepy Floyd	.10	.05	.01
☐ 60	Tim McCormick	.06	.03	.00
☐ 61	Hakeem Olajuwon	1.25	.60	.12
☐ 62	Otis Thorpe	.35	.17	.03
☐ 63	Mike Woodson	.06	.03	.00
☐ 64	Vern Fleming	.10	.05	.01
☐ 65	Reggie Miller	1.25	.60	.12
☐ 66	Chuck Person	.35	.17	.03
☐ 67	Detlef Schrempf	1.00	.50	.10
☐ 68	Rik Smits	.50	.25	.05
☐ 69	Benoit Benjamin	.15	.07	.01
☐ 70	Gary Grant	.40	.20	.04
☐ 71	Danny Manning	3.50	1.75	.35
☐ 72	Ken Norman	.75	.35	.07
☐ 73	Charles Smith	1.50	.75	.15
☐ 74	Reggie Williams	.75	.35	.07
☐ 75	Michael Cooper	.12	.06	.01
☐ 76	A.C. Green	.25	.12	.02
☐ 77	Magic Johnson	4.50	2.25	.45
☐ 78	Byron Scott	.20	.10	.02
☐ 79	Mychal Thompson	.10	.05	.01
☐ 80	James Worthy	.60	.30	.06
☐ 81	Kevin Edwards	.30	.15	.03
☐ 82	Grant Long	1.00	.50	.10
☐ 83	Rony Seikaly	2.00	1.00	.20
☐ 84	Rory Sparrow	.06	.03	.00
☐ 85	Greg Anderson UER (Stats show 1988-89 as 19888-89)	.10	.05	.01
☐ 86	Jay Humphries	.10	.05	.01
☐ 87	Larry Krystkowiak	.20	.10	.02
☐ 88	Ricky Pierce	.30	.15	.03
☐ 89	Paul Pressey	.10	.05	.01
☐ 90	Alvin Robertson	.10	.05	.01
☐ 91	Jack Sikma	.10	.05	.01
☐ 92	Steve Johnson	.06	.03	.00
☐ 93	Rick Mahorn	.10	.05	.01
☐ 94	David Rivers	.10	.05	.01
☐ 95	Joe Barry Carroll	.06	.03	.00
☐ 96	Lester Conner UER (Garden State in stats, should be Golden State)	.10	.05	.01
☐ 97	Roy Hinson	.06	.03	.00

68 / 1989-90 Fleer

☐ 98 Mike McGee	.10	.05	.01
☐ 99 Chris Morris	.50	.25	.05
☐ 100 Patrick Ewing	1.75	.85	.17
☐ 101 Mark Jackson	.30	.15	.03
☐ 102 Johnny Newman	.50	.25	.05
☐ 103 Charles Oakley	.12	.06	.01
☐ 104 Rod Strickland	1.00	.50	.10
☐ 105 Trent Tucker	.06	.03	.00
☐ 106 Kiki Vandeweghe	.10	.05	.01
☐ 107A Gerald Wilkins (U. of Tennessee)	.12	.06	.01
☐ 107B Gerald Wilkins (U. of Tenn.)	.12	.06	.01
☐ 108 Terry Catledge	.12	.06	.01
☐ 109 Dave Corzine	.06	.03	.00
☐ 110 Scott Skiles	.75	.35	.07
☐ 111 Reggie Theus	.12	.06	.01
☐ 112 Ron Anderson	.30	.15	.03
☐ 113 Charles Barkley	1.50	.75	.15
☐ 114 Scott Brooks	.20	.10	.02
☐ 115 Maurice Cheeks	.15	.07	.01
☐ 116 Mike Gminski	.10	.05	.01
☐ 117 Hersey Hawkins UER (Born 9/29/65, should be 9/9/65)	3.50	1.75	.35
☐ 118 Chris Welp	.10	.05	.01
☐ 119 Tom Chambers	.35	.17	.03
☐ 120 Armon Gilliam	.20	.10	.02
☐ 121 Jeff Hornacek	2.00	1.00	.20
☐ 122 Eddie Johnson	.12	.06	.01
☐ 123 Kevin Johnson	9.00	4.50	.90
☐ 124 Dan Majerle	2.00	1.00	.20
☐ 125 Mark West	.06	.03	.00
☐ 126 Richard Anderson	.10	.05	.01
☐ 127 Mark Bryant	.30	.15	.03
☐ 128 Clyde Drexler	2.00	1.00	.20
☐ 129 Kevin Duckworth	.25	.12	.02
☐ 130 Jerome Kersey	.90	.45	.09
☐ 131 Terry Porter	1.25	.60	.12
☐ 132 Buck Williams	.40	.20	.04
☐ 133 Danny Ainge	.25	.12	.02
☐ 134 Ricky Berry	.10	.05	.01
☐ 135 Rodney McCray	.10	.05	.01
☐ 136 Jim Petersen	.06	.03	.00
☐ 137 Harold Pressley	.10	.05	.01
☐ 138 Kenny Smith	.20	.10	.02
☐ 139 Wayman Tisdale	.20	.10	.02
☐ 140 Willie Anderson	.75	.35	.07
☐ 141 Frank Brickowski	.10	.05	.01
☐ 142 Terry Cummings	.25	.12	.02
☐ 143 Johnny Dawkins	.12	.06	.01
☐ 144 Vern Maxwell	.75	.35	.07
☐ 145 Michael Cage	.06	.03	.00
☐ 146 Dale Ellis	.12	.06	.01
☐ 147 Alton Lister	.06	.03	.00
☐ 148 Xavier McDaniel	.40	.20	.04
☐ 149 Derrick McKey	.25	.12	.02

1989-90 Fleer All-Stars / 69

☐ 150 Nate McMillan	.06	.03	.00
☐ 151 Thurl Bailey	.10	.05	.01
☐ 152 Mark Eaton	.10	.05	.01
☐ 153 Darrell Griffith	.10	.05	.01
☐ 154 Eric Leckner	.10	.05	.01
☐ 155 Karl Malone	1.50	.75	.15
☐ 156 John Stockton	3.00	1.50	.30
☐ 157 Mark Alarie	.10	.05	.01
☐ 158 Ledell Eackles	.60	.30	.06
☐ 159 Bernard King	.20	.10	.02
☐ 160 Jeff Malone	.35	.17	.03
☐ 161 Darrell Walker	.06	.03	.00
☐ 162A John Williams ERR Washington Bullets	.75	.35	.07
☐ 162B John Williams COR Washington Bullets	.10	.05	.01
☐ 163 All Star Game Karl Malone John Stockton	.40	.20	.04
☐ 164 All Star Game Hakeem Olajuwon Clyde Drexler	.40	.20	.04
☐ 165 All Star Game Dominique Wilkins Moses Malone	.30	.15	.03
☐ 166 All Star Game UER Brad Daugherty Mark Price (Bio says Nance had 204 blocks, should be 206)	.40	.20	.04
☐ 167 All Star Game Patrick Ewing Mark Jackson	.40	.20	.04
☐ 168 Checklist Card	.10	.01	.00

1989-90 Fleer All-Stars

This set of 11 insert stickers features NBA All-Stars and measures the standard size (2 1/2" by 3 1/2"). The front has a color action player photo in the shape of a cup silhouette. An aqua stripe with dark blue stars traverses the card top, and the same pattern reappears about halfway down the card face. The words "Fleer '89 All-Stars" appear at the top of the picture, with the player's name and position immediately below the picture. The back has a star pattern similar to the front. A career summary is printed in blue on a white background. The stickers are numbered on the back and checklisted below accordingly. One was inserted in each wax pack.

	MINT	EXC	G-VG
COMPLETE SET (11)	5.00	2.50	.50
COMMON STICKER (1-11)	.10	.05	.01
☐ 1 Karl Malone Utah Jazz	.75	.35	.07

70 / 1989-90 Fleer All-Stars

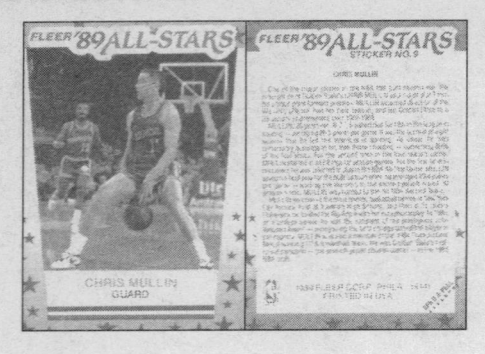

☐ 2	Hakeem Olajuwon	.50	.25	.05
	Houston Rockets			
☐ 3	Michael Jordan	2.50	1.25	.25
	Chicago Bulls			
☐ 4	Charles Barkley	.75	.35	.07
	Philadelphia 76ers			
☐ 5	Magic Johnson	1.50	.75	.15
	Los Angeles Lakers			
☐ 6	Isiah Thomas	.40	.20	.04
	Detroit Pistons			
☐ 7	Patrick Ewing	.75	.35	.07
	New York Knicks			
☐ 8	Dale Ellis	.10	.05	.01
	Seattle Supersonics			
☐ 9	Chris Mullin	.75	.35	.07
	Golden State Warriors			
☐ 10	Larry Bird	1.00	.50	.10
	Boston Celtics			
☐ 11	Tom Chambers	.15	.07	.01
	Phoenix Suns			

1990-91 Fleer

The 1990-91 Fleer set contains 198 cards measuring the standard size (2 1/2" by 3 1/2"). The fronts feature a color action player photo, with a white inner border and a two-color (red on top and bottom, blue on sides) outer border on a white card face. The team logo is superimposed at the upper left corner of the picture, with the player's name and position appearing below the picture. The backs are printed in black, gray, and yellow, and present biographical and statistical

1990-91 Fleer / 71

information. The cards are numbered on the back. The set is ordered alphabetically in team subsets (with a few exceptions due to late trades). The teams themselves are also presented in alphabetical order, Atlanta Hawks (1-7), Boston Celtics (8-15), Charlotte Hornets (16-21), Chicago Bulls (22-30 and 120), Cleveland Cavaliers (31-37), Dallas Mavericks (38-45 and 50), Denver Nuggets (46-53), Detroit Pistons (54-61), Golden State Warriors (62-68), Houston Rockets (69-75), Indiana Pacers (76-83), Los Angeles Clippers (84-89), Los Angeles Lakers (90-97), Miami Heat (98-103), Milwaukee Bucks (104-110), Minnesota Timberwolves (111-116 and 140), New Jersey Nets (117-123 and 136), New York Knicks (124-131), Orlando Magic (132-135 and 137), Philadelphia 76ers (138-139 and 141-145), Phoenix Suns (146-153), Portland Trail Blazers (154-161), Sacramento Kings (162-167 and 186-187), San Antonio Spurs (168-174), Seattle Supersonics (175-181), Utah Jazz (182-189 and 195), and Washington Bullets (164, 190-194, and 196). The description, All-American, is properly capitalized on the back of cards 134 and 144, but is not capitalized on cards 20, 29, 51, 53, 59, 70, 119, 130, 178, and 192. The key rookies in this set are Nick Anderson, B.J. Armstrong, Vlade Divac, Sherman Douglas, Sean Elliott, Pervis Ellison, Danny Ferry, Tim Hardaway, Shawn Kemp, Sarunas Marciulionis, Glen Rice, Pooh Richardson, and Cliff Robinson.

	MINT	EXC	G-VG
COMPLETE SET (198)	10.00	5.00	1.00
COMMON PLAYER (1-198)	.03	.01	.00
☐ 1 John Battle UER (Drafted in '84, should be '85)	.06	.03	.00
☐ 2 Cliff Levingston	.03	.01	.00
☐ 3 Moses Malone	.10	.05	.01
☐ 4 Kenny Smith	.06	.03	.00
☐ 5 Spud Webb	.06	.03	.00
☐ 6 Dominique Wilkins	.15	.07	.01
☐ 7 Kevin Willis	.10	.05	.01
☐ 8 Larry Bird	.35	.17	.03
☐ 9 Dennis Johnson	.08	.04	.01
☐ 10 Joe Kleine	.03	.01	.00
☐ 11 Reggie Lewis	.25	.12	.02

72 / 1990-91 Fleer

☐ 12 Kevin McHale	.10	.05	.01
☐ 13 Robert Parish	.12	.06	.01
☐ 14 Jim Paxson	.03	.01	.00
☐ 15 Ed Pinckney	.03	.01	.00
☐ 16 Tyrone Bogues	.03	.01	.00
☐ 17 Rex Chapman	.06	.03	.00
☐ 18 Dell Curry	.03	.01	.00
☐ 19 Armon Gilliam	.03	.01	.00
☐ 20 J.R. Reid	.15	.07	.01
☐ 21 Kelly Tripucka	.03	.01	.00
☐ 22 B.J. Armstrong	.40	.20	.04
☐ 23A Bill Cartwright ERR (No decimal points in FGP and FTP)	.50	.25	.05
☐ 23B Bill Cartwright COR	.06	.03	.00
☐ 24 Horace Grant	.20	.10	.02
☐ 25 Craig Hodges	.03	.01	.00
☐ 26 Michael Jordan UER (Led NBA in scoring 4 years, not 3)	1.50	.75	.15
☐ 27 Stacey King UER (Comma missing between progressed and Stacy)	.25	.12	.02
☐ 28 John Paxson	.06	.03	.00
☐ 29 Will Perdue	.10	.05	.01
☐ 30 Scottie Pippen UER (Born AR, not AK)	.60	.30	.06
☐ 31 Brad Daugherty	.20	.10	.02
☐ 32 Craig Ehlo	.06	.03	.00
☐ 33 Danny Ferry	.20	.10	.02
☐ 34 Steve Kerr	.03	.01	.00
☐ 35 Larry Nance	.10	.05	.01
☐ 36 Mark Price UER (Drafted by Cleveland, should be Dallas)	.20	.10	.02
☐ 37 Hot Rod Williams	.08	.04	.01
☐ 38 Rolando Blackman	.06	.03	.00
☐ 39A Adrian Dantley ERR (No decimal points in FGP and FTP)	.50	.25	.05
☐ 39B Adrian Dantley COR	.08	.04	.01
☐ 40 Brad Davis	.03	.01	.00
☐ 41 James Donaldson UER (Text says in committed, should be is committed)	.03	.01	.00
☐ 42 Derek Harper	.06	.03	.00
☐ 43 Sam Perkins UER (First line of text should be intact)	.10	.05	.01
☐ 44 Bill Wennington	.03	.01	.00
☐ 45 Herb Williams	.03	.01	.00
☐ 46 Michael Adams	.08	.04	.01
☐ 47 Walter Davis	.06	.03	.00
☐ 48 Alex English UER (Stats missing from '76-77 through '79-80)	.08	.04	.01
☐ 49 Bill Hanzlik	.03	.01	.00

1990-91 Fleer / 73

☐ 50	Lafayette Lever UER	.06	.03	.00
	(Born AR, not AK)			
☐ 51	Todd Lichti	.10	.05	.01
☐ 52	Blair Rasmussen	.03	.01	.00
☐ 53	Dan Schayes	.03	.01	.00
☐ 54	Mark Aguirre	.06	.03	.00
☐ 55	Joe Dumars	.12	.06	.01
☐ 56	James Edwards	.03	.01	.00
☐ 57	Vinnie Johnson	.06	.03	.00
☐ 58	Bill Laimbeer	.08	.04	.01
☐ 59	Dennis Rodman	.20	.10	.02
☐ 60	John Salley	.06	.03	.00
☐ 61	Isiah Thomas	.15	.07	.01
☐ 62	Manute Bol	.03	.01	.00
☐ 63	Tim Hardaway	1.50	.75	.15
☐ 64	Rod Higgins	.03	.01	.00
☐ 65	Sarunas Marciulionis	.40	.20	.04
☐ 66	Chris Mullin	.25	.12	.02
☐ 67	Mitch Richmond	.15	.07	.01
☐ 68	Terry Teagle	.03	.01	.00
☐ 69	Anthony Bowie UER	.15	.07	.01
	(Seasons, not seasons)			
☐ 70	Eric Floyd	.06	.03	.00
☐ 71	Buck Johnson	.03	.01	.00
☐ 72	Vernon Maxwell	.06	.03	.00
☐ 73	Hakeem Olajuwon	.25	.12	.02
☐ 74	Otis Thorpe	.06	.03	.00
☐ 75	Mitchell Wiggins	.03	.01	.00
☐ 76	Vern Fleming	.03	.01	.00
☐ 77	George McCloud	.10	.05	.01
☐ 78	Reggie Miller	.20	.10	.02
☐ 79	Chuck Person	.08	.04	.01
☐ 80	Mike Sanders	.06	.03	.00
☐ 81	Detlef Schrempf	.10	.05	.01
☐ 82	Rik Smits	.08	.04	.01
☐ 83	LaSalle Thompson	.03	.01	.00
☐ 84	Benoit Benjamin	.06	.03	.00
☐ 85	Winston Garland	.03	.01	.00
☐ 86	Ron Harper	.06	.03	.00
☐ 87	Danny Manning	.15	.07	.01
☐ 88	Ken Norman	.08	.04	.01
☐ 89	Charles Smith	.10	.05	.01
☐ 90	Michael Cooper	.06	.03	.00
☐ 91	Vlade Divac	.30	.15	.03
☐ 92	A.C. Green	.06	.03	.00
☐ 93	Magic Johnson	.75	.35	.07
☐ 94	Byron Scott	.06	.03	.00
☐ 95	Mychal Thompson UER	.03	.01	.00
	(Missing '78-79 stats from Portland)			
☐ 96	Orlando Woolridge	.03	.01	.00
☐ 97	James Worthy	.15	.07	.01
☐ 98	Sherman Douglas	.20	.10	.02
☐ 99	Kevin Edwards	.03	.01	.00
☐ 100	Grant Long	.06	.03	.00
☐ 101	Glen Rice	.90	.45	.09
☐ 102	Rony Seikaly UER	.15	.07	.01
	(Ron on front)			

74 / 1990-91 Fleer

☐ 103 Billy Thompson	.06	.03	.00
☐ 104 Jeff Grayer	.15	.07	.01
☐ 105 Jay Humphries	.03	.01	.00
☐ 106 Ricky Pierce	.06	.03	.00
☐ 107 Paul Pressey	.03	.01	.00
☐ 108 Fred Roberts	.06	.03	.00
☐ 109 Alvin Robertson	.06	.03	.00
☐ 110 Jack Sikma	.06	.03	.00
☐ 111 Randy Breuer	.03	.01	.00
☐ 112 Tony Campbell	.10	.05	.01
☐ 113 Tyrone Corbin	.06	.03	.00
☐ 114 Sam Mitchell UER	.15	.07	.01
(Mercer University, not Mercer College)			
☐ 115 Tod Murphy UER	.06	.03	.00
(Born Long Beach, not Lakewood)			
☐ 116 Pooh Richardson	.40	.20	.04
☐ 117 Mookie Blaylock	.20	.10	.02
☐ 118 Sam Bowie	.06	.03	.00
☐ 119 Lester Conner	.03	.01	.00
☐ 120 Dennis Hopson	.06	.03	.00
☐ 121 Chris Morris	.06	.03	.00
☐ 122 Charles Shackleford	.06	.03	.00
☐ 123 Purvis Short	.03	.01	.00
☐ 124 Maurice Cheeks	.06	.03	.00
☐ 125 Patrick Ewing	.30	.15	.03
☐ 126 Mark Jackson	.06	.03	.00
☐ 127A Johnny Newman ERR	.50	.25	.05
(Jr. misprinted as J. on card back)			
☐ 127B Johnny Newman COR	.06	.03	.00
☐ 128 Charles Oakley	.06	.03	.00
☐ 129 Trent Tucker	.03	.01	.00
☐ 130 Kenny Walker	.03	.01	.00
☐ 131 Gerald Wilkins	.06	.03	.00
☐ 132 Nick Anderson	.40	.20	.04
☐ 133 Terry Catledge	.03	.01	.00
☐ 134 Sidney Green	.03	.01	.00
☐ 135 Otis Smith	.06	.03	.00
☐ 136 Reggie Theus	.06	.03	.00
☐ 137 Sam Vincent	.03	.01	.00
☐ 138 Ron Anderson	.06	.03	.00
☐ 139 Charles Barkley UER	.25	.12	.02
(FG Percentage .545.)			
☐ 140 Scott Brooks UER	.03	.01	.00
('89-89 Philadelphia in wrong typeface)			
☐ 141 Johnny Dawkins	.03	.01	.00
☐ 142 Mike Gminski	.03	.01	.00
☐ 143 Hersey Hawkins	.15	.07	.01
☐ 144 Rick Mahorn	.06	.03	.00
☐ 145 Derek Smith	.03	.01	.00
☐ 146 Tom Chambers	.10	.05	.01
☐ 147 Jeff Hornacek	.15	.07	.01
☐ 148 Eddie Johnson	.06	.03	.00
☐ 149 Kevin Johnson	.25	.12	.02

1990-91 Fleer / 75

☐ 150A Dan Majerle ERR (Award in 1988; three-time selection)	.50	.25	.05
☐ 150B Dan Majerle COR (Award in 1989; three-time selection)	.15	.07	.01
☐ 151 Tim Perry	.20	.10	.02
☐ 152 Kurt Rambis	.06	.03	.00
☐ 153 Mark West	.03	.01	.00
☐ 154 Clyde Drexler	.30	.15	.03
☐ 155 Kevin Duckworth	.03	.01	.00
☐ 156 Byron Irvin	.08	.04	.01
☐ 157 Jerome Kersey	.10	.05	.01
☐ 158 Terry Porter	.15	.07	.01
☐ 159 Cliff Robinson	.40	.20	.04
☐ 160 Buck Williams	.10	.05	.01
☐ 161 Danny Young	.03	.01	.00
☐ 162 Danny Ainge	.06	.03	.00
☐ 163 Antoine Carr	.03	.01	.00
☐ 164 Pervis Ellison	.60	.30	.06
☐ 165 Rodney McCray	.03	.01	.00
☐ 166 Harold Pressley	.03	.01	.00
☐ 167 Wayman Tisdale	.08	.04	.01
☐ 168 Willie Anderson	.08	.04	.01
☐ 169 Frank Brickowski	.03	.01	.00
☐ 170 Terry Cummings	.08	.04	.01
☐ 171 Sean Elliott	.40	.20	.04
☐ 172 David Robinson	1.50	.75	.15
☐ 173 Rod Strickland	.08	.04	.01
☐ 174 David Wingate	.03	.01	.00
☐ 175 Dana Barros	.20	.10	.02
☐ 176 Michael Cage UER (Born AR, not AK)	.03	.01	.00
☐ 177 Dale Ellis	.06	.03	.00
☐ 178 Shawn Kemp	1.50	.75	.15
☐ 179 Xavier McDaniel	.10	.05	.01
☐ 180 Derrick McKey	.06	.03	.00
☐ 181 Nate McMillan	.03	.01	.00
☐ 182 Thurl Bailey	.03	.01	.00
☐ 183 Mike Brown	.06	.03	.00
☐ 184 Mark Eaton	.03	.01	.00
☐ 185 Blue Edwards	.20	.10	.02
☐ 186 Bob Hansen	.03	.01	.00
☐ 187 Eric Leckner	.03	.01	.00
☐ 188 Karl Malone	.25	.12	.02
☐ 189 John Stockton	.25	.12	.02
☐ 190 Mark Alarie	.03	.01	.00
☐ 191 Ledell Eackles	.06	.03	.00
☐ 192A Harvey Grant (First name on card front in black)	1.00	.50	.10
☐ 192B Harvey Grant (First name on card front in white)	.15	.07	.01
☐ 193 Tom Hammonds	.15	.07	.01
☐ 194 Bernard King	.06	.03	.00
☐ 195 Jeff Malone	.10	.05	.01

76 / 1990-91 Fleer

☐ 196 Darrell Walker	.03	.01	.00
☐ 197 Checklist Card	.06	.01	.00
☐ 198 Checklist Card	.06	.01	.00

1990-91 Fleer All-Stars

These All-Star inserts measure the standard size (2 1/2" by 3 1/2"). The fronts feature a color action photo, framed by a basketball hoop and net on an aqua background. An orange stripe at the top represents the bottom of the backboard and has the words "Fleer '90 All-Stars." The player's name and position are given at the bottom between stars. The backs are printed in blue and pink with white borders and have career summaries. The cards are numbered on the back. These inserts were not included in every wax pack and hence they are a little more difficult to find than the Fleer All-Star inserts of the previous years.

	MINT	EXC	G-VG
COMPLETE SET (12)	6.00	3.00	.60
COMMON PLAYER (1-12)	.30	.15	.03
☐ 1 Charles Barkley Philadelphia 76ers	.60	.30	.06
☐ 2 Larry Bird Boston Celtics	.90	.45	.09
☐ 3 Hakeem Olajuwon Houston Rockets	.50	.25	.05
☐ 4 Magic Johnson Los Angeles Lakers	1.50	.75	.15
☐ 5 Michael Jordan Chicago Bulls	2.50	1.25	.25
☐ 6 Isiah Thomas Detroit Pistons	.40	.20	.04

1990-91 Fleer Rookie Sensations / 77

☐ 7 Karl Malone Utah Jazz	.60	.30	.06
☐ 8 Tom Chambers Phoenix Suns	.30	.15	.03
☐ 9 John Stockton Utah Jazz	.60	.30	.06
☐ 10 David Robinson San Antonio Spurs	2.00	1.00	.20
☐ 11 Clyde Drexler Portland Trail Blazers	.75	.35	.07
☐ 12 Patrick Ewing New York Knicks	.75	.35	.07

1990-91 Fleer Rookie Sensations

These rookie sensation cards measure the standard size (2 1/2" by 3 1/2"). The fronts feature color action player photos, with white and red borders on an aqua background. A basketball overlays the lower left corner of the picture, with the words "Rookie Sensation" in yellow lettering, and the player's name appearing in white lettering in the bottom red border. The backs are printed in black and red on gray background (with white borders), and present summaries of their college careers and rookie seasons. The cards are numbered on the back. These inserts were distributed intermittently in cello packs and thus are considered a tough insert set to complete.

	MINT	EXC	G-VG
COMPLETE SET (10)	80.00	40.00	8.00
COMMON PLAYER (1-10)	2.50	1.25	.25

☐ 1 David Robinson UER
   San Antonio Spurs
   (Text has 1988-90 season,
   should be 1989-90)
	35.00	17.50	3.50

78 / 1990-91 Fleer Rookie Sensations

☐ 2 Sean Elliott UER	6.00	3.00	.60
San Antonio Spurs			
(Misspelled Elliot			
on card front)			
☐ 3 Glen Rice	16.00	8.00	1.60
Miami Heat			
☐ 4 J.R. Reid	2.50	1.25	.25
Charlotte Hornets			
☐ 5 Stacey King	4.00	2.00	.40
Chicago Bulls			
☐ 6 Pooh Richardson	6.00	3.00	.60
Minnesota Timberwolves			
☐ 7 Nick Anderson	6.00	3.00	.60
Orlando Magic			
☐ 8 Tim Hardaway	35.00	17.50	3.50
Golden State Warriors			
☐ 9 Vlade Divac	4.00	2.00	.40
Los Angeles Lakers			
☐ 10 Sherman Douglas	3.50	1.75	.35
Miami Heat			

1990-91 Fleer Update

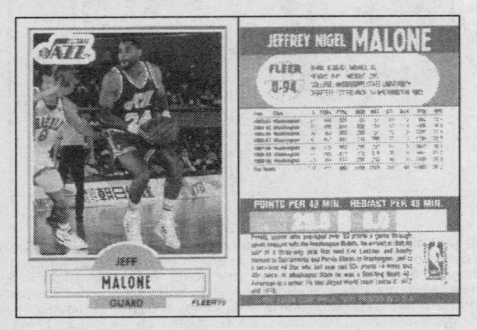

The cards are the same size (2 1/2" by 3 1/2") and design as the regular issue. The set numbering is arranged alphabetically by team as follows: Atlanta Hawks (1-5), Boston Celtics (6-10), Charlotte Hornets (11-13), Chicago Bulls (14-15), Cleveland Cavaliers (16-18), Dallas Mavericks (19-23), Cleveland Cavaliers (24-27), Detroit Pistons (28-30), Golden State Warriors (31-34), Houston Rockets (35-36), Indiana Pacers (37-39), Los Angeles Clippers (40-42), Los Angeles Lakers (43-46), Miami Heat (47-50), Milwaukee Bucks (51-55), Minnesota Timberwolves (56-58), New Jersey Nets (59-62), New York Knicks (63-66), Orlando Magic (67), Philadelphia 76ers (68-73), Phoenix Suns (74-77), Portland Trail Blazers (78-81), Sacramento Kings (82-87), San

1990-91 Fleer Update / 79

Antonio Spurs (88-91), Seattle Supersonics (92-93), Utah Jazz (94-96), and Washington Bullets (97-99). The key rookies in this set are Dee Brown (his only major 1990-91 card), Derrick Coleman, Kendall Gill, Gary Payton, Drazen Petrovic, Dennis Scott, and Lionel Simmons.

	MINT	EXC	G-VG
COMPLETE SET (100)	14.00	7.00	1.40
COMMON PLAYER (1-100)	.04	.02	.00
☐ U1 Jon Koncak	.07	.03	.01
☐ U2 Tim McCormick	.04	.02	.00
☐ U3 Glenn Rivers	.07	.03	.01
☐ U4 Rumeal Robinson	.35	.17	.03
☐ U5 Trevor Wilson	.07	.03	.01
☐ U6 Dee Brown	1.50	.75	.15
☐ U7 Dave Popson	.07	.03	.01
☐ U8 Kevin Gamble	.07	.03	.01
☐ U9 Brian Shaw	.12	.06	.01
☐ U10 Michael Smith	.07	.03	.01
☐ U11 Kendall Gill	5.00	2.50	.50
☐ U12 Johnny Newman	.07	.03	.01
☐ U13 Steve Scheffler	.07	.03	.01
☐ U14 Dennis Hopson	.07	.03	.01
☐ U15 Cliff Levingston	.04	.02	.00
☐ U16 Chucky Brown	.10	.05	.01
☐ U17 John Morton	.07	.03	.01
☐ U18 Gerald Paddio	.07	.03	.01
☐ U19 Alex English	.07	.03	.01
☐ U20 Fat Lever	.07	.03	.01
☐ U21 Rodney McCray	.04	.02	.00
☐ U22 Roy Tarpley	.07	.03	.01
☐ U23 Randy White	.10	.05	.01
☐ U24 Anthony Cook	.07	.03	.01
☐ U25 Chris Jackson	.40	.20	.04
☐ U26 Marcus Liberty	.60	.30	.06
☐ U27 Orlando Woolridge	.04	.02	.00
☐ U28 William Bedford	.10	.05	.01
☐ U29 Lance Blanks	.10	.05	.01
☐ U30 Scott Hastings	.04	.02	.00
☐ U31 Tyrone Hill	.40	.20	.04
☐ U32 Les Jepsen	.10	.05	.01
☐ U33 Steve Johnson	.04	.02	.00
☐ U34 Kevin Pritchard	.07	.03	.01
☐ U35 Dave Jamerson	.10	.05	.01
☐ U36 Kenny Smith	.07	.03	.01
☐ U37 Greg Dreiling	.07	.03	.01
☐ U38 Kenny Williams	.07	.03	.01
☐ U39 Micheal Williams UER	.20	.10	.02
☐ U40 Gary Grant	.30	.15	.03
☐ U41 Bo Kimble	.04	.02	.00
☐ U42 Loy Vaught	.10	.05	.01
☐ U43 Elden Campbell	.40	.20	.04
☐ U44 Sam Perkins	.50	.25	.05
☐ U45 Tony Smith	.10	.05	.01
☐ U46 Terry Teagle	.15	.07	.01
☐ U47 Willie Burton	.04	.02	.00
☐ U48 Bimbo Coles	.40	.20	.04
☐ U49 Terry Davis	.40	.20	.04
	.25	.12	.02

80 / 1990-91 Fleer Update

☐ U50 Alec Kessler	.10	.05	.01
☐ U51 Greg Anderson	.04	.02	.00
☐ U52 Frank Brickowski	.04	.02	.00
☐ U53 Steve Henson	.07	.03	.01
☐ U54 Brad Lohaus	.07	.03	.01
☐ U55 Dan Schayes	.04	.02	.00
☐ U56 Gerald Glass	.40	.20	.04
☐ U57 Felton Spencer	.25	.12	.02
☐ U58 Doug West	.40	.20	.04
☐ U59 Jud Buechler	.15	.07	.01
☐ U60 Derrick Coleman	3.00	1.50	.30
☐ U61 Tate George	.07	.03	.01
☐ U62 Reggie Theus	.07	.03	.01
☐ U63 Greg Grant	.07	.03	.01
☐ U64 Jerrod Mustaf	.25	.12	.02
☐ U65 Eddie Lee Wilkins	.07	.03	.01
☐ U66 Michael Ansley	.07	.03	.01
☐ U67 Jerry Reynolds	.07	.03	.01
☐ U68 Dennis Scott	.90	.45	.09
☐ U69 Manute Bol	.04	.02	.00
☐ U70 Armon Gilliam	.04	.02	.00
☐ U71 Brian Oliver	.10	.05	.01
☐ U72 Kenny Payne	.10	.05	.01
☐ U73 Jayson Williams	.15	.07	.01
☐ U74 Kenny Battle	.12	.06	.01
☐ U75 Cedric Ceballos	.75	.35	.07
☐ U76 Negele Knight	.40	.20	.04
☐ U77 Xavier McDaniel	.10	.05	.01
☐ U78 Alaa Abdelnaby	.30	.15	.03
☐ U79 Danny Ainge	.10	.05	.01
☐ U80 Mark Bryant	.04	.02	.00
☐ U81 Drazen Petrovic	1.25	.60	.12
☐ U82 Anthony Bonner	.30	.15	.03
☐ U83 Duane Causwell	.30	.15	.03
☐ U84 Bobby Hansen	.04	.02	.00
☐ U85 Eric Leckner	.07	.03	.01
☐ U86 Travis Mays	.25	.12	.02
☐ U87 Lionel Simmons	1.50	.75	.15
☐ U88 Sidney Green	.04	.02	.00
☐ U89 Tony Massenburg	.07	.03	.01
☐ U90 Paul Pressey	.04	.02	.00
☐ U91 Dwayne Schintzius	.07	.03	.01
☐ U92 Gary Payton	.90	.45	.09
☐ U93 Olden Polynice	.04	.02	.00
☐ U94 Jeff Malone	.10	.05	.01
☐ U95 Walter Palmer	.07	.03	.01
☐ U96 Delaney Rudd	.10	.05	.01
☐ U97 Pervis Ellison	1.25	.60	.12
☐ U98 A.J. English	.35	.17	.03
☐ U99 Greg Foster	.07	.03	.01
☐ U100 Checklist Card	.07	.01	.00

1991-92 Fleer

The 1991-92 Fleer basketball card set contains 240 cards measuring the standard size (2 1/2" by 3 1/2"). The fronts features color action player photos, bordered by a red stripe on the bottom, and gray and red stripes on the top. A 3/4" blue stripe checkered with black NBA logos runs the length of the card and serves as the left border of the picture. The team logo, player's name, and position are printed in white lettering in this stripe. The picture is bordered on the right side by a thin gray stripe and a thicker blue one. The backs present career summaries and are printed with black lettering on various pastel colors, superimposed over a wooden basketball floor background. The cards are numbered and checklisted below alphabetically within and according to teams as follows: Atlanta Hawks (1-7), Boston Celtics (8-16), Charlotte Hornets (17-24), Chicago Bulls (25-33), Cleveland Cavaliers (34-41), Dallas Mavericks (42-48), Denver Nuggets (49-56), Detroit Pistons (57-64), Golden State Warriors (65-72), Houston Rockets (73-80), Indiana Pacers (81-88), L.A. Clippers (86-96), L.A. Lakers (97-104), Miami Heat (105-112), Milwaukee Bucks (113-120), Minnesota Timberwolves (121-127), New Jersey Nets (128-134), New York Knicks (135-142), Orlando Magic (143-149), Philadelphia 76ers (150-157), Phoenix Suns (158-165), Portland Trail Blazers (166-173), Sacramento Kings (174-181), San Antonio Spurs (182-188), Seattle Supersonics (189-196), Utah Jazz (197-203), and Washington Bullets (204-209). Other subsets within the set are All-Stars (210-219), League Leaders (220-226), Slam Dunk (227-232), and All Star Game Highlights (233-238). There are no key Rookie Cards in this first series.

	MINT	EXC	G-VG
COMPLETE SET (240)	6.00	3.00	.60
COMMON PLAYER (1-240)	.03	.01	.00
☐ 1 John Battle	.06	.03	.00
☐ 2 Jon Koncak	.03	.01	.00
☐ 3 Rumeal Robinson	.06	.03	.00
☐ 4 Spud Webb	.06	.03	.00
☐ 5 Bob Weiss CO	.03	.01	.00
☐ 6 Dominique Wilkins	.12	.06	.01
☐ 7 Kevin Willis	.08	.04	.01
☐ 8 Larry Bird	.25	.12	.02

82 / 1991-92 Fleer

☐ 9	Dee Brown	.20	.10	.02
☐ 10	Chris Ford CO	.03	.01	.00
☐ 11	Kevin Gamble	.06	.03	.00
☐ 12	Reggie Lewis	.12	.06	.01
☐ 13	Kevin McHale	.08	.04	.01
☐ 14	Robert Parish	.10	.05	.01
☐ 15	Ed Pinckney	.03	.01	.00
☐ 16	Brian Shaw	.06	.03	.00
☐ 17	Tyrone Bogues	.03	.01	.00
☐ 18	Rex Chapman	.06	.03	.00
☐ 19	Dell Curry	.03	.01	.00
☐ 20	Kendall Gill	.50	.25	.05
☐ 21	Eric Leckner	.03	.01	.00
☐ 22	Gene Littles CO	.03	.01	.00
☐ 23	Johnny Newman	.03	.01	.00
☐ 24	J.R. Reid	.06	.03	.00
☐ 25	B.J. Armstrong	.10	.05	.01
☐ 26	Bill Cartwright	.06	.03	.00
☐ 27	Horace Grant	.10	.05	.01
☐ 28	Phil Jackson CO	.03	.01	.00
☐ 29	Michael Jordan	1.00	.50	.10
☐ 30	Cliff Levingston	.03	.01	.00
☐ 31	John Paxson	.06	.03	.00
☐ 32	Will Perdue	.06	.03	.00
☐ 33	Scottie Pippen	.30	.15	.03
☐ 34	Brad Daugherty	.12	.06	.01
☐ 35	Craig Ehlo	.06	.03	.00
☐ 36	Danny Ferry	.06	.03	.00
☐ 37	Larry Nance	.08	.04	.01
☐ 38	Mark Price	.12	.06	.01
☐ 39	Darnell Valentine	.03	.01	.00
☐ 40	Hot Rod Williams	.06	.03	.00
☐ 41	Lenny Wilkens CO	.06	.03	.00
☐ 42	Richie Adubato CO	.03	.01	.00
☐ 43	Rolando Blackman	.06	.03	.00
☐ 44	James Donaldson	.03	.01	.00
☐ 45	Derek Harper	.06	.03	.00
☐ 46	Rodney McCray	.03	.01	.00
☐ 47	Randy White	.06	.03	.00
☐ 48	Herb Williams	.08	.04	.01
☐ 49	Chris Jackson	.03	.01	.00
☐ 50	Marcus Liberty	.15	.07	.01
☐ 51	Todd Lichti	.03	.01	.00
☐ 52	Blair Rasmussen	.03	.01	.00
☐ 53	Paul Westhead CO	.03	.01	.00
☐ 54	Reggie Williams	.06	.03	.00
☐ 55	Joe Wolf	.03	.01	.00
☐ 56	Orlando Woolridge	.03	.01	.00
☐ 57	Mark Aguirre	.06	.03	.00
☐ 58	Chuck Daly CO	.06	.03	.00
☐ 59	Joe Dumars	.10	.05	.01
☐ 60	James Edwards	.03	.01	.00
☐ 61	Vinnie Johnson	.03	.01	.00
☐ 62	Bill Laimbeer	.06	.03	.00
☐ 63	Dennis Rodman	.10	.05	.01
☐ 64	Isiah Thomas	.12	.06	.01
☐ 65	Tim Hardaway	.50	.25	.05

1991-92 Fleer / 83

☐	66	Rod Higgins	.03	.01	.00
☐	67	Tyrone Hill	.08	.04	.01
☐	68	Sarunas Marciulionis	.12	.06	.01
☐	69	Chris Mullin	.15	.07	.01
☐	70	Don Nelson CO	.03	.01	.00
☐	71	Mitch Richmond	.10	.05	.01
☐	72	Tom Tolbert	.03	.01	.00
☐	73	Don Chaney CO	.03	.01	.00
☐	74	Eric (Sleepy) Floyd	.03	.01	.00
☐	75	Buck Johnson	.03	.01	.00
☐	76	Vernon Maxwell	.06	.03	.00
☐	77	Hakeem Olajuwon	.12	.06	.01
☐	78	Kenny Smith	.03	.01	.00
☐	79	Larry Smith	.03	.01	.00
☐	80	Otis Thorpe	.06	.03	.00
☐	81	Vern Fleming	.03	.01	.00
☐	82	Bob Hill CO	.06	.03	.00
☐	83	Reggie Miller	.10	.05	.01
☐	84	Chuck Person	.06	.03	.00
☐	85	Detlef Schrempf	.06	.03	.00
☐	86	Rik Smits	.06	.03	.00
☐	87	LaSalle Thompson	.03	.01	.00
☐	88	Micheal Williams	.06	.03	.00
☐	89	Gary Grant	.03	.01	.00
☐	90	Ron Harper	.06	.03	.00
☐	91	Bo Kimble	.06	.03	.00
☐	92	Danny Manning	.10	.05	.01
☐	93	Ken Norman	.06	.03	.00
☐	94	Olden Polynice	.03	.01	.00
☐	95	Mike Schuler CO	.03	.01	.00
☐	96	Charles Smith	.08	.04	.01
☐	97	Vlade Divac	.08	.04	.01
☐	98	Mike Dunleavy CO	.03	.01	.00
☐	99	A.C. Green	.06	.03	.00
☐	100	Magic Johnson	.60	.30	.06
☐	101	Sam Perkins	.08	.04	.01
☐	102	Byron Scott	.06	.03	.00
☐	103	Terry Teagle	.03	.01	.00
☐	104	James Worthy	.10	.05	.01
☐	105	Willie Burton	.06	.03	.00
☐	106	Bimbo Coles	.10	.05	.01
☐	107	Sherman Douglas	.06	.03	.00
☐	108	Kevin Edwards	.03	.01	.00
☐	109	Grant Long	.03	.01	.00
☐	110	Kevin Loughery CO	.03	.01	.00
☐	111	Glen Rice	.25	.12	.02
☐	112	Rony Seikaly	.08	.04	.01
☐	113	Frank Brickowski	.03	.01	.00
☐	114	Dale Ellis	.06	.03	.00
☐	115	Del Harris CO	.03	.01	.00
☐	116	Jay Humphries	.03	.01	.00
☐	117	Fred Roberts	.03	.01	.00
☐	118	Alvin Robertson	.06	.03	.00
☐	119	Dan Schayes	.03	.01	.00
☐	120	Jack Sikma	.06	.03	.00
☐	121	Tony Campbell	.06	.03	.00
☐	122	Tyrone Corbin	.06	.03	.00

84 / 1991-92 Fleer

☐ 123 Sam Mitchell	.03	.01	.00
☐ 124 Tod Murphy	.03	.01	.00
☐ 125 Pooh Richardson	.10	.05	.01
☐ 126 Jim Rodgers CO	.03	.01	.00
☐ 127 Felton Spencer	.06	.03	.00
☐ 128 Mookie Blaylock	.06	.03	.00
☐ 129 Sam Bowie	.06	.03	.00
☐ 130 Derrick Coleman	.30	.15	.03
☐ 131 Chris Dudley	.03	.01	.00
☐ 132 Bill Fitch CO	.03	.01	.00
☐ 133 Chris Morris	.06	.03	.00
☐ 134 Drazen Petrovic	.15	.07	.01
☐ 135 Maurice Cheeks	.06	.03	.00
☐ 136 Patrick Ewing	.20	.10	.02
☐ 137 Mark Jackson	.06	.03	.00
☐ 138 Charles Oakley	.06	.03	.00
☐ 139 Pat Riley CO	.06	.03	.00
☐ 140 Trent Tucker	.03	.01	.00
☐ 141 Kiki Vandeweghe	.06	.03	.00
☐ 142 Gerald Wilkins	.06	.03	.00
☐ 143 Nick Anderson	.10	.05	.01
☐ 144 Terry Catledge	.03	.01	.00
☐ 145 Matt Guokas CO	.03	.01	.00
☐ 146 Jerry Reynolds	.03	.01	.00
☐ 147 Dennis Scott	.10	.05	.01
☐ 148 Scott Skiles	.06	.03	.00
☐ 149 Otis Smith	.03	.01	.00
☐ 150 Ron Anderson	.03	.01	.00
☐ 151 Charles Barkley	.15	.07	.01
☐ 152 Johnny Dawkins	.03	.01	.00
☐ 153 Armon Gilliam	.03	.01	.00
☐ 154 Hersey Hawkins	.08	.04	.01
☐ 155 Jim Lynam CO	.03	.01	.00
☐ 156 Rick Mahorn	.06	.03	.00
☐ 157 Brian Oliver	.06	.03	.00
☐ 158 Tom Chambers	.08	.04	.01
☐ 159 Cotton Fitzsimmons CO	.03	.01	.00
☐ 160 Jeff Hornacek	.10	.05	.01
☐ 161 Kevin Johnson	.15	.07	.01
☐ 162 Negele Knight	.06	.03	.00
☐ 163 Dan Majerle	.10	.05	.01
☐ 164 Xavier McDaniel	.08	.04	.01
☐ 165 Mark West	.03	.01	.00
☐ 166 Rick Adelman CO	.03	.01	.00
☐ 167 Danny Ainge	.06	.03	.00
☐ 168 Clyde Drexler	.20	.10	.02
☐ 169 Kevin Duckworth	.03	.01	.00
☐ 170 Jerome Kersey	.08	.04	.01
☐ 171 Terry Porter	.10	.05	.01
☐ 172 Cliff Robinson	.10	.05	.01
☐ 173 Buck Williams	.08	.04	.01
☐ 174 Antoine Carr	.03	.01	.00
☐ 175 Duane Causwell	.06	.03	.00
☐ 176 Jim Les	.08	.04	.01
☐ 177 Travis Mays	.06	.03	.00
☐ 178 Dick Motta CO	.03	.01	.00
☐ 179 Lionel Simmons	.15	.07	.01

1991-92 Fleer / 85

☐ 180 Rory Sparrow	.03	.01	.00
☐ 181 Wayman Tisdale	.06	.03	.00
☐ 182 Willie Anderson	.06	.03	.00
☐ 183 Larry Brown CO	.03	.01	.00
☐ 184 Terry Cummings	.08	.04	.01
☐ 185 Sean Elliott	.10	.05	.01
☐ 186 Paul Pressey	.03	.01	.00
☐ 187 David Robinson	.60	.30	.06
☐ 188 Rod Strickland	.06	.03	.00
☐ 189 Benoit Benjamin	.03	.01	.00
☐ 190 Eddie Johnson	.06	.03	.00
☐ 191 K.C. Jones CO	.03	.01	.00
☐ 192 Shawn Kemp	.50	.25	.05
☐ 193 Derrick McKey	.06	.03	.00
☐ 194 Gary Payton	.10	.05	.01
☐ 195 Ricky Pierce	.06	.03	.00
☐ 196 Sedale Threatt	.06	.03	.00
☐ 197 Thurl Bailey	.03	.01	.00
☐ 198 Mark Eaton	.03	.01	.00
☐ 199 Blue Edwards	.03	.01	.00
☐ 200 Jeff Malone	.08	.04	.01
☐ 201 Karl Malone	.15	.07	.01
☐ 202 Jerry Sloan CO	.03	.01	.00
☐ 203 John Stockton	.15	.07	.01
☐ 204 Ledell Eackles	.03	.01	.00
☐ 205 Pervis Ellison	.15	.07	.01
☐ 206 A.J. English	.10	.05	.01
☐ 207 Harvey Grant	.06	.03	.00
☐ 208 Bernard King	.08	.04	.01
☐ 209 Wes Unseld CO	.06	.03	.00
☐ 210 Kevin Johnson AS	.10	.05	.01
☐ 211 Michael Jordan AS	.40	.20	.04
☐ 212 Dominique Wilkins AS	.08	.04	.01
☐ 213 Charles Barkley AS	.10	.05	.01
☐ 214 Hakeem Olajuwon AS	.08	.04	.01
☐ 215 Patrick Ewing AS	.10	.05	.01
☐ 216 Tim Hardaway AS	.20	.10	.02
☐ 217 John Stockton AS	.10	.05	.01
☐ 218 Chris Mullin AS	.10	.05	.01
☐ 219 Karl Malone AS	.10	.05	.01
☐ 220 Michael Jordan LL	.40	.20	.04
☐ 221 John Stockton LL	.10	.05	.01
☐ 222 Alvin Robertson LL	.06	.03	.00
☐ 223 Hakeem Olajuwon LL	.08	.04	.01
☐ 224 Buck Williams LL	.06	.03	.00
☐ 225 David Robinson LL	.25	.12	.02
☐ 226 Reggie Miller LL	.08	.04	.01
☐ 227 Blue Edwards SD	.08	.04	.01
☐ 228 Dee Brown SD	.15	.07	.01
☐ 229 Rex Chapman SD	.06	.03	.00
☐ 230 Kenny Smith SD	.03	.01	.00
☐ 231 Shawn Kemp SD	.20	.10	.02
☐ 232 Kendall Gill SD	.25	.12	.02
☐ 233 '91 All Star Game	.06	.03	.00
Enemies - A Love Story (East Bench Scene)			
☐ 234 '91 All Star Game	.06	.03	.00

86 / 1991-92 Fleer

A Game of Contrasts (Drexler over McHale)			
☐ 235 '91 All Star Game Showtime (Alvin Robertson)	.03	.01	.00
☐ 236 '91 All Star Game Unstoppable Force vs. Unbeatable Man (Ewing rejects K.Malone)	.06	.03	.00
☐ 237 '91 All Star Game Just Me and the Boys (Rebounding Scene)	.06	.03	.00
☐ 238 '91 All Star Game Unforgettable (Jordan reverse lay-in)	.10	.05	.01
☐ 239 Checklist 1-120	.06	.01	.00
☐ 240 Checklist 121-240	.06	.01	.00

1991-92 Fleer Pro Visions

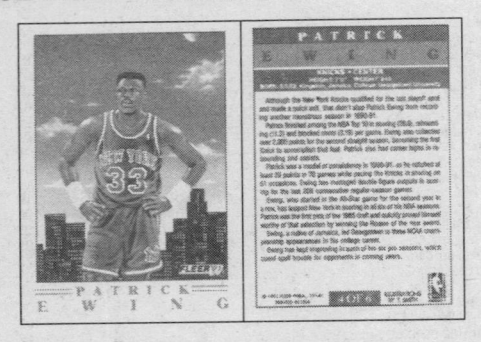

This six-card set measures the standard size (2 1/2" by 3 1/2") and showcases outstanding NBA players. The set was distributed as a random insert in 1991-92 Fleer wax packs. The fronts feature a color player portrait by sports artist Terry Smith. The portrait is bordered on all sides by white, with the player's name in red lettering below the picture. The backs present biographical information and career summary in black lettering on a color background (with white borders). The cards are numbered on the back.

	MINT	EXC	G-VG
COMPLETE SET (6)	1.50	.75	.15
COMMON PLAYER (1-6)	.25	.12	.02

1991-92 Fleer Rookie Sensations / 87

☐ 1 David Robinson	.60	.30	.06
San Antonio Spurs			
☐ 2 Michael Jordan	.75	.35	.07
Chicago Bulls			
☐ 3 Charles Barkley	.25	.12	.02
Philadelphia 76ers			
☐ 4 Patrick Ewing	.25	.12	.02
New York Knicks			
☐ 5 Karl Malone	.25	.12	.02
Utah Jazz			
☐ 6 Magic Johnson	.60	.30	.06
Los Angeles Lakers			

1991-92 Fleer Rookie Sensations

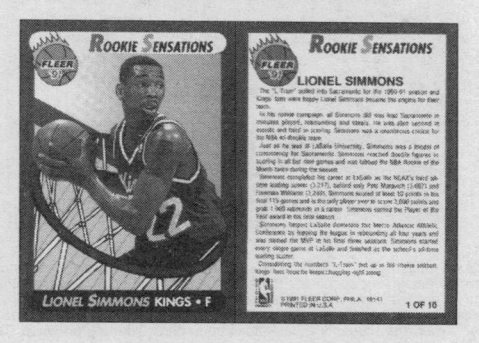

This ten-card set showcases outstanding rookies from the 1990-91 season and measures the standard size (2 1/2" by 3 1/2"). The set was distributed as a random insert in 1991-92 Fleer cello packs. The fronts feature a color player photo inside a basketball rim and net. The picture is bordered in magenta on all sides. The words "Rookie Sensations" appear above the picture, and player information is given below the picture. An orange basketball with the words "Fleer '91" appears in the upper left corner on both sides of the card. The back has a magenta border and includes highlights of the player's rookie season. The cards are numbered on the back.

	MINT	EXC	G-VG
COMPLETE SET (10)	20.00	10.00	2.00
COMMON PLAYER (1-10)	.75	.35	.07
☐ 1 Lionel Simmons	3.00	1.50	.30
☐ 2 Dennis Scott	2.00	1.00	.20
☐ 3 Derrick Coleman	4.50	2.25	.45
☐ 4 Kendall Gill	8.00	4.00	.80

88 / 1991-92 Fleer Rookie Sensations

☐ 5 Travis Mays	.75	.35	.07
☐ 6 Felton Spencer	.75	.35	.07
☐ 7 Willie Burton	.75	.35	.07
☐ 8 Chris Jackson	1.00	.50	.10
☐ 9 Gary Payton	2.00	1.00	.20
☐ 10 Dee Brown	3.00	1.50	.30

1991-92 Fleer Schoolyard Stars

This six-card set measures the standard size (2 1/2" by 3 1/2"). The set was distributed only in 1991-92 Fleer rak packs (one per pack). The front features color action player photos. The photos are bordered on the left and bottom by a black stripe and a broken pink stripe. Yellow stripes traverse the card top and bottom, and the background is a gray cement-colored design. The back has a similar layout and presents a basketball tip in black lettering on white. The cards are numbered on the back.

	MINT	EXC	G-VG
COMPLETE SET (6)	2.50	1.25	.25
COMMON PLAYER (1-6)	.30	.15	.03
☐ 1 Chris Mullin Golden State Warriors	1.00	.50	.10
☐ 2 Isiah Thomas Detroit Pistons	.75	.35	.07
☐ 3 Kevin McHale Boston Celtics	.40	.20	.04
☐ 4 Kevin Johnson Phoenix Suns	1.00	.50	.10
☐ 5 Karl Malone Utah Jazz	1.00	.50	.10
☐ 6 Alvin Robertson Milwaukee Bucks	.30	.15	.03

1991-92 Fleer Update

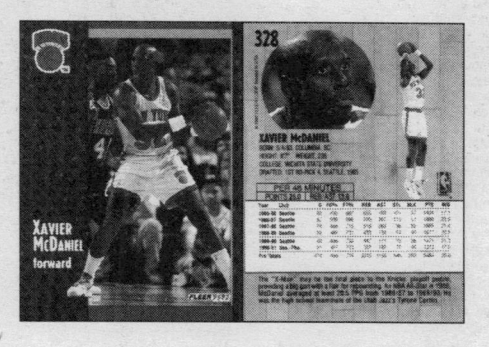

The 1991-92 Fleer Update basketball set contains 160 standard-size (2 1/2" by 3 1/2") cards and features hot rookies and traded veterans. The set was only distributed in wax packs. Special Dikembe Mutombo and Dominique Wilkins cards were randomly and intermittently inserted in the packs, and each player signed over 2,000 of his cards. The fronts feature the same design as the first series, with color player photos and a 3/4" blue checkered stripe serving as a left border. The backs have a close-up photo, biography, and statistics on a wooden basketball floor background. The cards are numbered on the back and checklisted below alphabetically according to teams as follows: Atlanta Hawks (241-246), Boston Celtics (247-251), Charlotte Hornets (252-255), Chicago Bulls (256-259), Cleveland Cavaliers (260-265), Dallas Mavericks (266-271), Denver Nuggets (272-277), Detroit Pistons (278-283), Golden State Warriors (284-288), Houston Rockets (289-292), Indiana Pacers (293-295), Los Angeles Clippers (296-299), Los Angeles Lakers (300-304), Miami Heat (305-309), Milwaukee Bucks (310-315), Minnesota Timberwolves (316-321), New Jersey Nets (322-325), New York Knicks (326-330), Orlando Magic (331-334), Philadelphia 76ers (335-338), Phoenix Suns (339-343), Portland Trail Blazers (344-346), Sacramento Kings (347-352), San Antonio Spurs (353-356), Seattle Supersonics (357-361), Utah Jazz (362-366), and Washington Bullets (367-371). Team Leaders (372-398) and checklist cards (399-400) round out the set. The key rookie cards in this extended set are Stacey Augmon, Larry Johnson, Dikembe Mutumbo, Billy Owens, and Steve Smith.

	MINT	EXC	G-VG
COMPLETE SET (160)	8.00	4.00	.80
COMMON PLAYER (241-400)	.03	.01	.00
☐ 241 Stacey Augmon	.75	.35	.07
☐ 242 Maurice Cheeks	.06	.03	.00
☐ 243 Paul Graham	.20	.10	.02
☐ 244 Rodney Monroe	.15	.07	.01
☐ 245 Blair Rasmussen	.03	.01	.00
☐ 246 Alexander Volkov	.08	.04	.01
☐ 247 John Bagley	.06	.03	.00
☐ 248 Rick Fox	.75	.35	.07
☐ 249 Rickey Green	.03	.01	.00

90 / 1991-92 Fleer Update

☐ 250	Joe Kleine	.03	.01	.00
☐ 251	Stojko Vrankovic	.10	.05	.01
☐ 252	Allan Bristow CO	.03	.01	.00
☐ 253	Kenny Gattison	.10	.05	.01
☐ 254	Mike Gminski	.03	.01	.00
☐ 255	Larry Johnson	4.00	2.00	.40
☐ 256	Bobby Hansen	.03	.01	.00
☐ 257	Craig Hodges	.03	.01	.00
☐ 258	Stacey King	.06	.03	.00
☐ 259	Scott Williams	.25	.12	.02
☐ 260	John Battle	.03	.01	.00
☐ 261	Winston Bennett	.03	.01	.00
☐ 262	Terrell Brandon	.35	.17	.03
☐ 263	Henry James	.08	.04	.01
☐ 264	Steve Kerr	.03	.01	.00
☐ 265	Jimmy Oliver	.10	.05	.01
☐ 266	Brad Davis	.03	.01	.00
☐ 267	Terry Davis	.06	.03	.00
☐ 268	Donald Hodge	.25	.12	.02
☐ 269	Mike Iuzzolino	.20	.10	.02
☐ 270	Fat Lever	.06	.03	.00
☐ 271	Doug Smith	.35	.17	.03
☐ 272	Greg Anderson	.03	.01	.00
☐ 273	Kevin Brooks	.08	.04	.01
☐ 274	Walter Davis	.06	.03	.00
☐ 275	Winston Garland	.03	.01	.00
☐ 276	Mark Macon	.30	.15	.03
☐ 277A	Dikembe Mutombo (Fleer '91 on front)	2.00	1.00	.20
☐ 277A	Dikembe Mutombo (Fleer '91-92 on front)	2.00	1.00	.20
☐ 278	William Bedford	.03	.01	.00
☐ 279	Lance Blanks	.06	.03	.00
☐ 280	John Salley	.06	.03	.00
☐ 281	Charles Thomas	.08	.04	.01
☐ 282	Darrell Walker	.03	.01	.00
☐ 283	Orlando Woolridge	.06	.03	.00
☐ 284	Victor Alexander	.15	.07	.01
☐ 285	Vincent Askew	.10	.05	.01
☐ 286	Mario Elie	.15	.07	.01
☐ 287	Alton Lister	.03	.01	.00
☐ 288	Billy Owens	2.00	1.00	.20
☐ 289	Matt Bullard	.12	.06	.01
☐ 290	Carl Herrera	.12	.06	.01
☐ 291	Tree Rollins	.03	.01	.00
☐ 292	John Turner	.08	.04	.01
☐ 293	Dale Davis UER (Photo on back actually Sean Green)	.20	.10	.02
☐ 294	Sean Green	.08	.04	.01
☐ 295	Kenny Williams	.06	.03	.00
☐ 296	James Edwards	.03	.01	.00
☐ 297	LeRon Ellis	.08	.04	.01
☐ 298	Doc Rivers	.06	.03	.00
☐ 299	Loy Vaught	.08	.04	.01
☐ 300	Elden Campbell	.10	.05	.01
☐ 301	Jack Haley	.03	.01	.00

1991-92 Fleer Update / 91

☐	302	Keith Owens	.08	.04	.01
☐	303	Tony Smith	.06	.03	.00
☐	304	Sedale Threatt	.06	.03	.00
☐	305	Keith Askins	.08	.04	.01
☐	306	Alec Kessler	.06	.03	.00
☐	307	John Morton	.03	.01	.00
☐	308	Alan Ogg	.08	.04	.01
☐	309	Steve Smith	.90	.45	.09
☐	310	Lester Conner	.03	.01	.00
☐	311	Jeff Grayer	.03	.01	.00
☐	312	Frank Hamblen CO	.06	.03	.00
☐	313	Steve Henson	.03	.01	.00
☐	314	Larry Krystkowiak	.03	.01	.00
☐	315	Moses Malone	.10	.05	.01
☐	316	Thurl Bailey	.03	.01	.00
☐	317	Randy Breuer	.03	.01	.00
☐	318	Scott Brooks	.03	.01	.00
☐	319	Gerald Glass	.10	.05	.01
☐	320	Luc Longley	.15	.07	.01
☐	321	Doug West	.08	.04	.01
☐	322	Kenny Anderson	.75	.35	.07
☐	323	Tate George	.06	.03	.00
☐	324	Terry Mills	.12	.06	.01
☐	325	Greg Anthony	.30	.15	.03
☐	326	Anthony Mason	.25	.12	.02
☐	327	Tim McCormick	.03	.01	.00
☐	328	Xavier McDaniel	.08	.04	.01
☐	329	Brian Quinnett	.03	.01	.00
☐	330	John Starks	.50	.25	.05
☐	331	Stanley Roberts	.60	.30	.06
☐	332	Jeff Turner	.03	.01	.00
☐	333	Sam Vincent	.03	.01	.00
☐	334	Brian Williams	.30	.15	.03
☐	335	Manute Bol	.03	.01	.00
☐	336	Kenny Payne	.03	.01	.00
☐	337	Charles Shackleford	.03	.01	.00
☐	338	Jayson Williams	.06	.03	.00
☐	339	Cedric Ceballos	.12	.06	.01
☐	340	Andrew Lang	.10	.05	.01
☐	341	Jerrod Mustaf	.08	.04	.01
☐	342	Tim Perry	.06	.03	.00
☐	343	Kurt Rambis	.06	.03	.00
☐	344	Alaa Abdelnaby	.08	.04	.01
☐	345	Robert Pack	.50	.25	.05
☐	346	Danny Young	.03	.01	.00
☐	347	Anthony Bonner	.06	.03	.00
☐	348	Pete Chilcutt	.10	.05	.01
☐	349	Rex Hughes	.06	.03	.00
☐	350	Mitch Richmond	.10	.05	.01
☐	351	Dwayne Schintzius	.06	.03	.00
☐	352	Spud Webb	.06	.03	.00
☐	353	Antoine Carr	.03	.01	.00
☐	354	Sidney Green	.03	.01	.00
☐	355	Vinnie Johnson	.03	.01	.00
☐	356	Greg Sutton	.08	.04	.01
☐	357	Dana Barros	.03	.01	.00
☐	358	Michael Cage	.03	.01	.00

92 / 1991-92 Fleer Update

☐ 359 Marty Conlon	.08	.04	.01
☐ 360 Rich King	.10	.05	.01
☐ 361 Nate McMillan	.03	.01	.00
☐ 362 David Benoit	.30	.15	.03
☐ 363 Mike Brown	.03	.01	.00
☐ 364 Tyrone Corbin	.06	.03	.00
☐ 365 Eric Murdock	.15	.07	.01
☐ 366 Delaney Rudd	.03	.01	.00
☐ 367 Michael Adams	.08	.04	.01
☐ 368 Tom Hammonds	.06	.03	.00
☐ 369 Larry Stewart	.25	.12	.02
☐ 370 Andre Turner	.08	.04	.01
☐ 371 David Wingate	.03	.01	.00
☐ 372 Dominique Wilkins TL	.08	.04	.01
Atlanta Hawks			
☐ 373 Larry Bird TL	.15	.07	.01
Boston Celtics			
☐ 374 Rex Chapman TL	.06	.03	.00
Charlotte Hornets			
☐ 375 Michael Jordan TL	.40	.20	.04
Chicago Bulls			
☐ 376 Brad Daugherty TL	.08	.04	.01
Cleveland Cavaliers			
☐ 377 Derek Harper TL	.06	.03	.00
Dallas Mavericks			
☐ 378 Dikembe Mutombo TL	.30	.15	.03
Denver Nuggets			
☐ 379 Joe Dumars TL	.08	.04	.01
Detroit Pistons			
☐ 380 Chris Mullin TL	.10	.05	.01
Golden State Warriors			
☐ 381 Hakeem Olajuwon TL	.08	.04	.01
Houston Rockets			
☐ 382 Chuck Person TL	.06	.03	.00
Indiana Pacers			
☐ 383 Charles Smith TL	.06	.03	.00
Los Angeles Clippers			
☐ 384 James Worthy TL	.08	.04	.01
Los Angeles Lakers			
☐ 385 Glen Rice TL	.15	.07	.01
Miami Heat			
☐ 386 Alvin Robertson TL	.03	.01	.00
Milwaukee Bucks			
☐ 387 Tony Campbell TL	.03	.01	.00
Minnesota Timberwolves			
☐ 388 Derrick Coleman TL	.20	.10	.02
New Jersey Nets			
☐ 389 Patrick Ewing TL	.10	.05	.01
New York Knicks			
☐ 390 Scott Skiles TL	.03	.01	.00
Orlando Magic			
☐ 391 Charles Barkley TL	.10	.05	.01
Philadelphia 76ers			
☐ 392 Kevin Johnson TL	.10	.05	.01
Phoenix Suns			
☐ 393 Clyde Drexler TL	.12	.06	.01
Portland Trail Blazers			

1991 Front Row 50 / 93

☐ 394	Lionel Simmons TL Sacramento Kings	.10	.05	.01
☐ 395	David Robinson TL San Antonio Spurs	.25	.12	.02
☐ 396	Ricky Pierce TL Seattle Supersonics	.03	.01	.00
☐ 397	John Stockton TL Utah Jazz	.10	.05	.01
☐ 398	Michael Adams TL Washington Bullets	.03	.01	.00
☐ 399	Checklist	.06	.01	.00
☐ 400	Checklist	.06	.01	.00

1991 Front Row 50

The 1991 Front Row Basketball Draft Pick set contains 50 cards measuring the standard-size (2 1/2" by 3 1/2"). For the American version, Front Row produced approximately 150,000 factory sets and 600 wax cases, for a total press run of about 167,000 sets. The factory sets come with an official certificate of authenticity that bears a unique serial number. Two bilingual versions were also printed. The Japanese/English version features the same players as in the American version, but with different production quantities (62,000 factory sets and 600 wax cases). The Italian/English version features many different players and has 100 cards, with production quantities of 30,000 factory sets and 3,000 wax cases. Finally the bonus card in the American version could be redeemed for two Italian Promotional cards and an additional card number 50 to replace the returned bonus card. The front design features glossy color action player photos with white borders. The player's name appears in a green stripe beneath the picture. The backs have different smaller color photos (upper right corner) as well as biography, college statistics, and achievements superimposed on a gray background with an orange basketball. The set also includes a second (career highlights) card of some players (39-43), and a subset devoted to Larry Johnson (44-49). The cards are numbered on the back.

94 / 1991 Front Row 50

	MINT	EXC	G-VG
COMPLETE SET (50)	10.00	5.00	1.00
COMMON PLAYER (1-50)	.05	.02	.00

- ☐ 1 Larry Johnson .... 5.00 — 2.50 — .50
  UNLV
- ☐ 2 Kenny Anderson .... 1.50 — .75 — .15
  Georgia Tech
- ☐ 3 Rick Fox .... 1.00 — .50 — .10
  North Carolina
- ☐ 4 Pete Chilcutt .... .20 — .10 — .02
  North Carolina
- ☐ 5 George Ackles .... .08 — .04 — .01
  UNLV
- ☐ 6 Mark Macon .... .35 — .17 — .03
  Temple
- ☐ 7 Greg Anthony .... .40 — .20 — .04
  UNLV
- ☐ 8 Mike Iuzzolino .... .35 — .17 — .03
  St. Francis
- ☐ 9 Anthony Avent .... .20 — .10 — .02
  Seton Hall
- ☐ 10 Terrell Brandon .... .40 — .20 — .04
  Oregon
- ☐ 11 Kevin Brooks .... .15 — .07 — .01
  SW Louisiana
- ☐ 12 Myron Brown .... .10 — .05 — .01
  Slippery Rock
- ☐ 13 Chris Corchiani .... .15 — .07 — .01
  North Carolina State
- ☐ 14 Chris Gatling .... .40 — .20 — .04
  Old Dominion
- ☐ 15 Marcus Kennedy .... .08 — .04 — .01
  Eastern Michigan
- ☐ 16 Eric Murdock .... .30 — .15 — .03
  Providence
- ☐ 17 Tony Farmer .... .08 — .04 — .01
  Nebraska
- ☐ 18 Keith Hughes .... .08 — .04 — .01
  Rutgers
- ☐ 19 Kevin Lynch .... .15 — .07 — .01
  Minnesota
- ☐ 20 Chad Gallagher .... .08 — .04 — .01
  Creighton
- ☐ 21 Darrin Chancellor .... .08 — .04 — .01
  Southern Mississippi
- ☐ 22 Jimmy Oliver .... .20 — .10 — .02
  Purdue
- ☐ 23 Von McDade .... .08 — .04 — .01
  Wisconsin-Milwaukee
- ☐ 24 Donald Hodge .... .35 — .17 — .03
  Temple
- ☐ 25 Randy Brown .... .15 — .07 — .01
  New Mexico State
- ☐ 26 Doug Overton .... .08 — .04 — .01
  LaSalle
- ☐ 27 LeRon Ellis .... .12 — .06 — .01
  Syracuse

1991 Front Row Update / 95

☐ 28	Sean Green Iona	.15	.07	.01
☐ 29	Elliot Perry Memphis State	.15	.07	.01
☐ 30	Richard Dumas Oklahoma State	.08	.04	.01
☐ 31	Dale Davis Clemson	.35	.17	.03
☐ 32	Lamont Strothers Christopher Newport	.15	.07	.01
☐ 33	Steve Hood James Madison	.10	.05	.01
☐ 34	Joey Wright Texas	.08	.04	.01
☐ 35	Patrick Eddie Mississippi	.12	.06	.01
☐ 36	Joe Wylie Miami	.08	.04	.01
☐ 37	Bobby Phills Southern	.10	.05	.01
☐ 38	Alvaro Teheran Houston	.05	.02	.00
☐ 39	Dale Davis Career Highlights	.10	.05	.01
☐ 40	Rick Fox Career Highlights	.30	.15	.03
☐ 41	Terrell Brandon Career Highlights	.12	.06	.01
☐ 42	Greg Anthony Career Highlights	.12	.06	.01
☐ 43	Mark Macon Career Highlights	.10	.05	.01
☐ 44	Larry Johnson Career Highlights	.50	.25	.05
☐ 45	Larry Johnson First in the Nation	.50	.25	.05
☐ 46	Larry Johnson Power	.50	.25	.05
☐ 47	Larry Johnson A Class Act	.50	.25	.05
☐ 48	Larry Johnson Flashback	.50	.25	.05
☐ 49	Larry Johnson Up Close and Personal	.50	.25	.05
☐ 50A	Bonus Card	.75	.35	.07
☐ 50B	Marty Conlon	.25	.12	.02

1991 Front Row Update

The 1991 Front Row Update basketball set completes the 1991 Front Row Draft Picks set. Each set was accompanied by an certificate of authenticity that bears a unique serial number, with the production run reported to be 50,000 sets. The cards measure the standard size (2 1/2" by

96 / 1991 Front Row Update

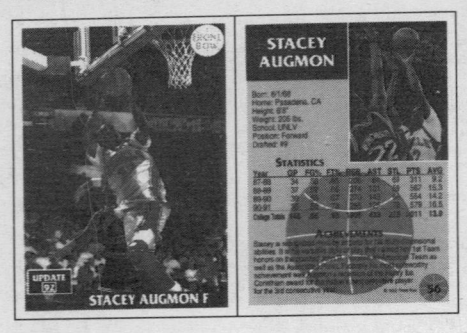

3 1/2"). The fronts feature glossy color action player photos enclosed by white borders. A basketball backboard and rim with the words "Update 92" appears in the lower left corner, with the player's name and position in a dark green stripe beneath the picture. On a gray background with an orange basketball, the backs carry biography, color close-up photo, statistics, and achievements. The cards are numbered on the back.

	MINT	EXC	G-VG
COMPLETE SET (50)	9.00	4.50	.90
COMMON PLAYER (51-100)	.05	.02	.00
☐ 51 Billy Owens	2.50	1.25	.25
Syracuse			
☐ 52 Dikembe Mutombo	1.75	.85	.17
Georgetown			
☐ 53 Steve Smith	1.50	.75	.15
Michigan State			
☐ 54 Luc Longley	.25	.12	.02
New Mexico			
☐ 55 Doug Smith	.40	.20	.04
Missouri			
☐ 56 Stacey Augmon	1.00	.50	.10
UNLV			
☐ 57 Brian Williams	.50	.25	.05
Arizona			
☐ 58 Stanley Roberts	.90	.45	.09
LSU			
☐ 59 Rodney Monroe	.25	.12	.02
North Carolina State			
☐ 60 Isaac Austin	.10	.05	.01
Arizona State			
☐ 61 Rich King	.10	.05	.01
Nebraska			
☐ 62 Victor Alexander	.20	.10	.02
Iowa State			
☐ 63 LaBradford Smith	.20	.10	.02
Louisville			

1991 Front Row Update / 97

☐ 64	Greg Sutton Oklahoma City	.12	.06	.01
☐ 65	John Turner Phillips	.10	.05	.01
☐ 66	Joao Viana Nassuna	.10	.05	.01
☐ 67	Charles Thomas Eastern Michigan	.08	.04	.01
☐ 68	Carl Thomas Eastern Michigan	.08	.04	.01
☐ 69	Tharon Mayes Florida State	.08	.04	.01
☐ 70	David Benoit Alabama	.35	.17	.03
☐ 71	Corey Crowder Kentucky Wesleyan	.08	.04	.01
☐ 72	Larry Stewart Coppin State	.35	.17	.03
☐ 73	Steve Bardo Illinois	.08	.04	.01
☐ 74	Paris McCurdy Ball State	.05	.02	.00
☐ 75	Robert Pack USC	.50	.25	.05
☐ 76	Doug Lee Purdue	.08	.04	.01
☐ 77	Tom Copa Marquette	.05	.02	.00
☐ 78	Keith Owens UCLA	.10	.05	.01
☐ 79	Mike Goodson Pittsburgh	.05	.02	.00
☐ 80	John Crotty Virginia	.10	.05	.01
☐ 81	Sean Muto St. John's	.05	.02	.00
☐ 82	Chancellor Nichols James Madison	.05	.02	.00
☐ 83	Stevie Thompson Syracuse	.08	.04	.01
☐ 84	Demetrius Calip Michigan	.08	.04	.01
☐ 85	Clifford Martin Idaho	.05	.02	.00
☐ 86	Andy Kennedy Alabama (Birmingham)	.03	.04	.01
☐ 87	Oliver Taylor Seton Hall	.05	.02	.00
☐ 88	Gary Waites Alabama	.05	.02	.00
☐ 89	Matt Roe Maryland	.08	.04	.01
☐ 90	Cedric Lewis Maryland	.08	.04	.01
☐ 91	Emanuel Davis Deleware State	.05	.02	.00
☐ 92	Jackie Jones Oklahoma	.08	.04	.01

98 / 1991 Front Row Update

- ☐ 93 Clifford Scales .... .05 .02 .00
  Nebraska
- ☐ 94 Cameron Burns .... .05 .02 .00
  Mississippi State
- ☐ 95 Clinton Venable .... .08 .04 .01
  Bowling Green
- ☐ 96 Ken Redfield .... .08 .04 .01
  Michigan State
- ☐ 97 Melvin Newbern .... .08 .04 .01
  Minnesota
- ☐ 98 Chris Harris .... .05 .02 .00
  Illinois (Chicago)
- ☐ 99 Bonus Card .... .75 .35 .07
- ☐ 100 Checklist .... .05 .02 .00

1991 Front Row Italian/English 100

The 1991 Front Row Italian/English Basketball Draft Pick set contains 100 cards measuring standard size (2 1/2" by 3 1/2"). Each factory set comes with an official certificate of authenticity that bears a unique serial number. This set is distinguished from the American version by length (100 instead of 50 cards), different production quantities (30,000 factory sets and 3,000 wax cases), and a red stripe on the card front. The front design features glossy color action player photos with white borders. The player's name appears in a red stripe beneath the picture. The backs have different smaller color photos (upper right corner) as well as biography, college statistics, and achievements superimposed on a gray background with an orange basketball. The set also includes a second (career highlights) card of some players (39-43), a subset devoted to Larry Johnson (44-49), and two "Retrospect" cards (96-97). The cards are numbered on the back.

	MINT	EXC	G-VG
COMPLETE SET (100)	12.00	6.00	1.20
COMMON PLAYER (1-50)	.05	.02	.00

1991 Front Row Italian/English 100 / 99

COMMON PLAYER (51-100)	.05	.02	.00
☐ 1 Larry Johnson UNLV	5.00	2.50	.50
☐ 2 Kenny Anderson Georgia Tech	1.50	.75	.15
☐ 3 Rick Fox North Carolina	1.00	.50	.10
☐ 4 Pete Chilcutt North Carolina	.20	.10	.02
☐ 5 George Ackles UNLV	.08	.04	.01
☐ 6 Mark Macon Temple	.35	.17	.03
☐ 7 Greg Anthony UNLV	.40	.20	.04
☐ 8 Mike Iuzzolino St. Francis	.35	.17	.03
☐ 9 Anthony Avent Seton Hall	.20	.10	.02
☐ 10 Terrell Brandon Oregon	.40	.20	.04
☐ 11 Kevin Brooks SW Louisiana	.15	.07	.01
☐ 12 Myron Brown Slippery Rock	.10	.05	.01
☐ 13 Chris Corchiani North Carolina State	.15	.07	.01
☐ 14 Chris Gatling Old Dominion	.40	.20	.04
☐ 15 Marcus Kennedy Eastern Michigan	.08	.04	.01
☐ 16 Eric Murdock Providence	.30	.15	.03
☐ 17 Tony Farmer Nebraska	.08	.04	.01
☐ 18 Keith Hughes Rutgers	.08	.04	.01
☐ 19 Kevin Lynch Minnesota	.15	.07	.01
☐ 20 Chad Gallagher Creighton	.08	.04	.01
☐ 21 Darrin Chancellor Southern Mississippi	.08	.04	.01
☐ 22 Jimmy Oliver Purdue	.20	.10	.02
☐ 23 Von McDade Wisconsin-Milwaukee	.08	.04	.01
☐ 24 Donald Hodge Temple	.35	.17	.03
☐ 25 Randy Brown New Mexico State	.15	.07	.01
☐ 26 Doug Overton LaSalle	.08	.04	.01
☐ 27 LeRon Ellis Syracuse	.12	.06	.01
☐ 28 Sean Green Iona	.15	.07	.01

100 / 1991 Front Row Italian/English 100

☐ 29	Elliot Perry Memphis State	.15	.07	.01
☐ 30	Richard Dumas Oklahoma State	.08	.04	.01
☐ 31	Dale Davis Clemson	.35	.17	.03
☐ 32	Lamont Strothers Christopher Newport	.15	.07	.01
☐ 33	Steve Hood James Madison	.10	.05	.01
☐ 34	Joey Wright Texas	.08	.04	.01
☐ 35	Patrick Eddie Mississippi	.12	.06	.01
☐ 36	Joe Wylie Miami	.08	.04	.01
☐ 37	Bobby Phills Southern	.10	.05	.01
☐ 38	Alvaro Teheran Houston	.05	.02	.00
☐ 39	Dale Davis Career Highlights	.10	.05	.01
☐ 40	Rick Fox Career Highlights	.30	.15	.03
☐ 41	Terrell Brandon Career Highlights	.12	.06	.01
☐ 42	Greg Anthony Career Highlights	.12	.06	.01
☐ 43	Mark Macon Career Highlights	.10	.05	.01
☐ 44	Larry Johnson Career Highlights	.50	.25	.05
☐ 45	Larry Johnson First in the Nation	.50	.25	.05
☐ 46	Larry Johnson Power	.50	.25	.05
☐ 47	Larry Johnson A Class Act	.50	.25	.05
☐ 48	Larry Johnson Flashback	.50	.25	.05
☐ 49	Larry Johnson Up Close and Personal	.50	.25	.05
☐ 50A	Bonus Card	.75	.35	.07
☐ 50B	Marty Conlon	.25	.12	.02
☐ 51	Mike Goodson Pittsburgh	.05	.02	.00
☐ 52	Drexel Deveaux Tampa	.05	.02	.00
☐ 53	Sean Muto St. John's	.05	.02	.00
☐ 54	Keith Owens UCLA	.15	.07	.01
☐ 55	Joao Viana Nassuna	.05	.02	.00
☐ 56	Chancellor Nichols James Madison	.05	.02	.00
☐ 57	Charles Thomas Eastern Michigan	.12	.06	.01

1991 Front Row Italian/English 100 / 101

☐ 58 Carl Thomas Eastern Michigan	.08	.04	.01
☐ 59 Anthony Blakley Panhandle State	.05	.02	.00
☐ 60 Demetrius Calip Michigan	.12	.06	.01
☐ 61 Dale Turnquist Bethel College	.05	.02	.00
☐ 62 Carlos Funchess Northeast Louisiana	.05	.02	.00
☐ 63 Tharon Mayes Florida State	.12	.06	.01
☐ 64 Andy Kennedy Alabama - Birmingham	.08	.04	.01
☐ 65 Oliver Taylor Seton Hall	.05	.02	.00
☐ 66 David Benoit Alabama	.50	.25	.05
☐ 67 Gary Waites Alabama	.05	.02	.00
☐ 68 Corey Crowder Kentucky Wesleyan	.10	.05	.01
☐ 69 Sydney Grider Southwestern Louisiana	.05	.02	.00
☐ 70 Derek Strong Xavier	.08	.04	.01
☐ 71 Larry Stewart Coppin State	.50	.25	.05
☐ 72 Matt Roe Maryland	.08	.04	.01
☐ 73 Cedric Lewis Maryland	.08	.04	.01
☐ 74 Anthony Houston St. Mary's	.05	.02	.00
☐ 75 Steve Bardo Illinois	.08	.04	.01
☐ 76 Marc Brown Siena	.12	.06	.01
☐ 77 Michael Cutright McNeese State	.05	.02	.00
☐ 78 Emanuel Davis Deleware State	.05	.02	.00
☐ 79 Paris McCurdy Ball State	.05	.02	.00
☐ 80 Jackie Jones Oklahoma State	.08	.04	.01
☐ 81 Mark Peterson Rutgers	.05	.02	.00
☐ 82 Clifford Scales Nebraska	.05	.02	.00
☐ 83 Robert Pack USC	.75	.35	.07
☐ 84 Doug Lee Purdue	.12	.06	.01
☐ 85 Cameron Burns Mississippi State	.05	.02	.00
☐ 86 Tom Copa Marquette	.05	.02	.00

102 / 1991 Front Row Italian/English 100

☐ 87	Clinton Venable Bowling Green State	.08	.04	.01
☐ 88	Ken Redfield Michigan State	.08	.04	.01
☐ 89	Melvin Newbern Minnesota	.08	.04	.01
☐ 90	Darren Henrie David Lipscomb	.05	.02	.00
☐ 91	Chris Harris Illinois (Chicago)	.05	.02	.00
☐ 92	John Crotty Virginia	.10	.05	.01
☐ 93	Paul Graham Ohio	.40	.20	.04
☐ 94	Stevie Thompson Syracuse	.10	.05	.01
☐ 95	Clifford Martin Idaho	.05	.02	.00
☐ 96	Brian Shaw UC Santa Barbara	.12	.06	.01
☐ 97	Danny Ferry Duke	.12	.06	.01
☐ 98	Doug Loescher	.05	.02	.00
☐ 99	Checklist	.05	.02	.00
☐ 100	Bonus Card	.75	.35	.07

1991 Front Row Italian Promos

The American version of the 1991 Front Row Draft Pick set (50) included a bonus card that could be redeemed for two Italian promo cards through a mail-in offer. This promo set consists of ten cards measuring the standard size (2 1/2" by 3 1/2"). The color player photos on the front are bordered in white, and the player's name appears in a red stripe beneath the picture. On a gray background with an orange Front Row basketball logo, the backs read "Italian Promo Card" and "20,000 Ten Card Sets Produced" although the back of the Bonus Card says "50,000 Sets Produced". The cards are unnumbered and checklisted below in alphabetical order.

	MINT	EXC	G-VG
COMPLETE SET (10)	3.00	1.50	.30
COMMON PLAYER (1-10)	.15	.07	.01
☐ 1 Steve Bardo Illinois	.15	.07	.01
☐ 2 Corey Crowder Kentucky Wesleyan	.20	.10	.02
☐ 3 Danny Ferry Duke	.30	.15	.03
☐ 4 Doug Lee Purdue	.25	.12	.02
☐ 5 Tharon Mayes Florida State	.25	.12	.02
☐ 6 Robert Pack USC	1.00	.50	.10

☐ 7 Brian Shaw	.35	.17	.03
Cal (Santa Barbara)			
☐ 8 Larry Stewart	.75	.35	.07
Coppen State			
☐ 9 Carl Thomas	.15	.07	.01
Eastern Michigan			
☐ 10 Charles Thomas	.25	.12	.02
Eastern Michigan			

1991-92 Front Row Premier

The 1991-92 Front Row Premier set contains 120 standard-size (2 1/2" by 3 1/2") cards. No factory sets were made, and the production run was limited to 2,500 waxbox cases, with 360 cards per box. The set included five bonus cards (86, 88, 90, 91, 93) that were redeemable through a mail-in offer for unnamed player cards. Moreover, limited edition cards as well as gold, silver, and autographed cards were randomly inserted in the wax packs. The glossy color player photos on the fronts are enclosed by borders with different shades of white and blue. The player's name appears in a silver stripe beneath the picture. The backs have biography, statistics, and achievements superimposed on an orange basketball icon. The cards are numbered on the back.

	MINT	EXC	G-VG
COMPLETE SET (120)	14.00	7.00	1.40
COMMON PLAYER (1-120)	.05	.02	.00
☐ 1 Rich King	.10	.05	.01
Nebraska			
☐ 2 Kenny Anderson	1.00	.50	.10
Georgia Tech			

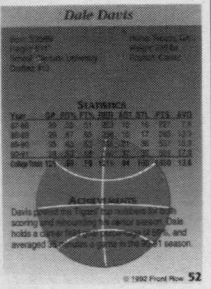

104 / 1991-92 Front Row Premier

☐ 3 Billy Owens ACC	.60	.30	.06
Syracuse			
☐ 4 Ken Redfield	.08	.04	.01
Michigan State			
☐ 5 Robert Pack	.50	.25	.05
USC			
☐ 6 Clinton Venable	.08	.04	.01
Bowling Green			
☐ 7 Tom Copa	.05	.02	.00
Marquette			
☐ 8 Rick Fox HL	.15	.07	.01
North Carolina			
☐ 9 Cameron Burns	.05	.02	.00
Mississippi State			
☐ 10 Doug Lee	.08	.04	.01
Purdue			
☐ 11 LaBradford Smith	.20	.10	.02
Louisville			
☐ 12 Clifford Scales	.05	.02	.00
Nebraska			
☐ 13 Mark Peterson	.05	.02	.00
Rutgers			
☐ 14 Jackie Jones	.05	.02	.00
Oklahoma			
☐ 15 Paris McCurdy	.05	.02	.00
Ball State			
☐ 16 Dikembe Mutombo ACC	.50	.25	.05
Georgetown			
☐ 17 Emanuel Davis	.05	.02	.00
Delaware State			
☐ 18 Michael Cutright	.05	.02	.00
McNeese State			
☐ 19 Marc Brown	.08	.04	.01
Siena			
☐ 20 Steve Bardo	.08	.04	.01
Illinois			

1991-92 Front Row Premier / 105

- [ ] 21 John Turner .... .10 .05 .01
  Phillips
- [ ] 22 Anthony Houston .... .05 .02 .00
  St. Mary's
- [ ] 23 Cedric Lewis .... .08 .04 .01
  Maryland
- [ ] 24 Matt Roe .... .08 .04 .01
  Maryland
- [ ] 25 Larry Stewart .... .35 .17 .03
  Coppin State
- [ ] 26 Derek Strong .... .08 .04 .01
  Xavier
- [ ] 27 Sydney Grider .... .05 .02 .00
  Southwestern Louisiana
- [ ] 28 Corey Crowder .... .08 .04 .01
  Kentucky Wesleyan
- [ ] 29 Gary Waites .... .05 .02 .00
  Alabama
- [ ] 30 David Benoit .... .35 .17 .03
  Alabama
- [ ] 31 Larry Johnson ACC .... .75 .35 .07
  UNLV
- [ ] 32 Oliver Taylor UER .... .05 .02 .00
  Seton Hall
  (Chris Corchiani's name
  on back)
- [ ] 33 Andy Kennedy .... .08 .04 .01
  Alabama-Birmingham
- [ ] 34 Tharon Mayes .... .08 .04 .01
  Florida State
- [ ] 35 Carlos Funchess .... .05 .02 .00
  Northeast Louisiana
- [ ] 36 Dale Turnquist .... .05 .02 .00
  Bethel
- [ ] 37 Luc Longley .... .25 .12 .02
  New Mexico
- [ ] 38 Demetrius Calip .... .08 .04 .01
  Michigan
- [ ] 39 Anthony Blakley .... .05 .02 .00
  Panhandle State
- [ ] 40 Carl Thomas .... .08 .04 .01
  Eastern Michigan
- [ ] 41 Charles Thomas .... .08 .04 .01
  Eastern Michigan
- [ ] 42 Chancellor Nichols .... .05 .02 .00
  James Madison
- [ ] 43 Joao Viana .... .10 .05 .01
  Nassuna
- [ ] 44 Keith Owens .... .10 .05 .01
  UCLA
- [ ] 45 Sean Muto .... .05 .02 .00
  St. Johns
- [ ] 46 Drexel Deveaux .... .05 .02 .00
  Tampa
- [ ] 47 Stacey Augmon ACC .... .25 .12 .02
  UNLV
- [ ] 48 Mike Goodson .... .05 .02 .00
  Pittsburgh

106 / 1991-92 Front Row Premier

☐ 49	Marty Conlon .... .08	.04	.01
	Providence		
☐ 50	Mark Macon .... .25	.12	.02
	Temple		
☐ 51	Greg Anthony .... .30	.15	.03
	UNLV		
☐ 52	Dale Davis .... .25	.12	.02
	Clemson		
☐ 53	Isaac Austin .... .10	.05	.01
	Arizona State		
☐ 54	Alvaro Teheran .... .05	.02	.00
	Houston		
☐ 55	Bobby Phills .... .08	.04	.01
	Southern		
☐ 56	Joe Wylie .... .08	.04	.01
	Miami		
☐ 57	Patrick Eddie .... .08	.04	.01
	Mississippi		
☐ 58	Joey Wright .... .08	.04	.01
	Texas		
☐ 59	Steve Hood .... .08	.04	.01
	James Maidson		
☐ 60	Lamont Strothers .... .10	.05	.01
	Christopher Newport		
☐ 61	Victor Alexander .... .20	.10	.02
	Iowa State		
☐ 62	Richard Dumas .... .08	.04	.01
	Oklahoma State		
☐ 63	Elliot Perry .... .10	.05	.01
	Memphis State		
☐ 64	Sean Green .... .10	.05	.01
	Iona		
☐ 65	Rick Fox .... .90	.45	.09
	North Carolina		
☐ 66	LeRon Ellis .... .10	.05	.01
	Syracuse		
☐ 67	Doug Overton .... .08	.04	.01
	LaSalle		
☐ 68	Randy Brown .... .10	.05	.01
	New Mexico State		
☐ 69	Donald Hodge .... .25	.12	.02
	Temple		
☐ 70	Von McDade .... .08	.04	.01
	Wisconsin-Milwaukee		
☐ 71	Greg Sutton .... .12	.06	.01
	Oral Roberts		
☐ 72	Jimmy Oliver .... .15	.07	.01
	Purdue		
☐ 73	Terrell Brandon HL .... .10	.05	.01
	Oregon		
☐ 74	Darrin Chancellor .... .05	.02	.00
	Southern Mississippi		
☐ 75	Chad Gallagher .... .05	.02	.00
	Creighton		
☐ 76	Kevin Lynch .... .10	.05	.01
	Minnesota		
☐ 77	Keith Hughes .... .08	.04	.01
	Rutgers		

1991-92 Front Row Premier / 107

☐ 78 Tony Farmer Nebraska	.05	.02	.00
☐ 79 Eric Murdock Providence	.20	.10	.02
☐ 80 Marcus Kennedy Eastern Michigan	.08	.04	.01
☐ 81 Larry Johnson UNLV	4.00	2.00	.40
☐ 82 Stacey Augmon UNLV	1.00	.50	.10
☐ 83 Dikembe Mutombo Georgetown	1.75	.85	.17
☐ 84 Steve Smith Michigan State	1.50	.75	.15
☐ 85 Billy Owens Syracuse	2.50	1.25	.25
☐ 86 Bonus Card 1 Stanley Roberts LSU	.30	.15	.03
☐ 87 Brian Shaw UC Santa Barbara	.10	.05	.01
☐ 88 Bonus Card 2 Rodney Monroe North Carolina State	.20	.10	.02
☐ 89 LaBradford Smith HL Louisville	.08	.04	.01
☐ 90 Bonus Card 3 Mark Randall Kansas	.15	.07	.01
☐ 91 Bonus Card 4 Brian Williams Arizona	.25	.12	.02
☐ 92 Danny Ferry (Flashback) Duke	.08	.04	.01
☐ 93 Bonus Card 5 Shawn Vandiver Colorado	.15	.07	.01
☐ 94 Doug Smith HL Missouri	.10	.05	.01
☐ 95 Luc Longley HL New Mexico	.10	.05	.01
☐ 96 Billy Owens HL Syracuse	.60	.30	.06
☐ 97 Steve Smith HL Michigan State	.35	.17	.03
☐ 98 Dikembe Mutombo HL Georgetown	.50	.25	.05
☐ 99 Stacey Augmon HL UNLV	.25	.12	.02
☐ 100 Larry Johnson HL UNLV	.75	.35	.07
☐ 101 Chris Gatling Old Dominion	.30	.15	.03
☐ 102 Chris Corchiani North Carolina State	.10	.05	.01
☐ 103 Myron Brown Slippery Rock	.08	.04	.01

108 / 1991-92 Front Row Premier

☐ 104 Kevin Brooks	.10	.05	.01
Southwestern Louisiana			
☐ 105 Anthony Avent	.12	.06	.01
Seton Hall			
☐ 106 Steve Smith ACC	.35	.17	.03
Michigan State			
☐ 107 Mike Iuzzolino	.25	.12	.02
Saint Francis			
☐ 108 George Ackles	.08	.04	.01
UNLV			
☐ 109 Melvin Newbern	.08	.04	.01
Minnesota			
☐ 110 Robert Pack HL	.20	.10	.02
USC			
☐ 111 Darren Henrie	.05	.02	.00
David Lipscomb			
☐ 112 Chris Harris	.05	.02	.00
Illinois-Chicago			
☐ 113 John Crotty	.08	.04	.01
Virginia			
☐ 114 Terrell Brandon	.30	.15	.03
Oregon			
☐ 115 Paul Graham	.25	.12	.02
Ohio			
☐ 116 Stevie Thompson	.08	.04	.01
Syracuse			
☐ 117 Clifford Martin	.05	.02	.00
Idaho			
☐ 118 Doug Smith	.40	.20	.04
Missouri			
☐ 119 Pete Chilcutt	.12	.06	.01
North Carolina			
☐ 120 Checklist Card	.05	.02	.00

1989-90 Hoops I

The 1989-90 Hoops sets contains 300 cards measuring the standard size (2 1/2" by 3 1/2"). The fronts feature color action player photos, bordered by a basketball lane in one of the team's colors. On a white card face the player's name appears in black lettering above the picture. The backs have head shots of the players, biographical information, and statistics, all printed on a pale yellow background with white borders. The cards are numbered on the backs. The key rookie in this set is David Robinson's card number 138, which only appeared in this first series of Hoops. Other Rookie Cards included in this series are Willie Anderson, Rex Chapman, Harvey Grant, Hersey Hawkins, Jeff Hornacek, Kevin Johnson, Reggie Lewis, Dan Majerle, Danny Manning, Vernon Maxwell, Ken Norman, Mitch Richmond, Rony Seikaly, Brian Shaw, Scott Skiles, Charles Smith, Rod Strickland, and Micheal Williams. Beware of David Robinson counterfeit cards which are distinguishable primarily by comparison to a real card or under magnification.

	MINT	EXC	G-VG
COMPLETE SET (300)	45.00	22.50	4.50
COMMON PLAYER (1-300)	.03	.01	.00

1989-90 Hoops I / 109

COMMON PLAYER SP (1-300)	.20	.10	.02
☐ 1 Joe Dumars	.25	.12	.02
Detroit Pistons			
☐ 2 Wayne Rollins	.03	.01	.00
Cleveland Cavaliers			
☐ 3 Kenny Walker	.03	.01	.00
New York Knicks			
☐ 4 Mychal Thompson	.03	.01	.00
Los Angeles Lakers			
☐ 5 Alvin Robertson SP	.20	.10	.02
San Antonio Spurs			
☐ 6 Vinny Del Negro	.10	.05	.01
Sacramento Kings			
☐ 7 Greg Anderson SP	.20	.10	.02
San Antonio Spurs			
☐ 8 Rod Strickland	.40	.20	.04
New York Knicks			
☐ 9 Ed Pinckney	.06	.03	.00
Boston Celtics			
☐ 10 Dale Ellis	.06	.03	.00
Seattle Supersonics			
☐ 11 Chuck Daly CO	.20	.10	.02
Detroit Pistons			
☐ 12 Eric Leckner	.08	.04	.01
Utah Jazz			
☐ 13 Charles Davis	.03	.01	.00
Chicago Bulls			
☐ 14 Cotton Fitzsimmons CO	.03	.01	.00
Phoenix Suns			
(No NBA logo on back			
in bottom right)			
☐ 15 Byron Scott	.08	.04	.01
Los Angeles Lakers			
☐ 16 Derrick Chievous	.08	.04	.01
Houston Rockets			

110 / 1989-90 Hoops I

☐ 17	Reggie Lewis 1.75	.85	.17
	Boston Celtics		
☐ 18	Jim Paxson .... .03	.01	.00
	Boston Celtics		
☐ 19	Tony Campbell .... .35	.17	.03
	Los Angeles Lakers		
☐ 20	Rolando Blackman .... .10	.05	.01
	Dallas Mavericks		
☐ 21	Michael Jordan AS .... .75	.35	.07
	Chicago Bulls		
☐ 22	Cliff Levingston .... .06	.03	.00
	Atlanta Hawks		
☐ 23	Roy Tarpley .... .06	.03	.00
	Dallas Mavericks		
☐ 24	Harold Pressley UER .... .08	.04	.01
	Sacramento Kings		
	(Cinderella misspelled		
	as cindarella)		
☐ 25	Larry Nance .... .15	.07	.01
	Cleveland Cavaliers		
☐ 26	Chris Morris .... .20	.10	.02
	New Jersey Nets		
☐ 27	Bob Hansen UER .... .03	.01	.00
	Utah Jazz		
	(Drafted in '84,		
	should say '83)		
☐ 28	Mark Price AS .... .10	.05	.01
	Cleveland Cavaliers		
☐ 29	Reggie Miller .... .40	.20	.04
	Indiana Pacers		
☐ 30	Karl Malone .... .40	.20	.04
	Utah Jazz		
☐ 31	Sidney Lowe SP .... .20	.10	.02
	Charlotte Hornets		
☐ 32	Ron Anderson .... .03	.01	.00
	Philadelphia 76ers		
☐ 33	Mike Gminski .... .03	.01	.00
	Philadelphia 76ers		
☐ 34	Scott Brooks .... .10	.05	.01
	Philadelphia 76ers		
☐ 35	Kevin Johnson 2.50	1.25	.25
	Phoenix Suns		
☐ 36	Mark Bryant .... .12	.06	.01
	Portland Trail Blazers		
☐ 37	Rik Smits .... .20	.10	.02
	Indiana Pacers		
☐ 38	Tim Perry .... .35	.17	.03
	Phoenix Suns		
☐ 39	Ralph Sampson .... .06	.03	.00
	Golden State Warriors		
☐ 40	Danny Manning UER 1.00	.50	.10
	Los Angeles Clippers		
	(Missing 1988		
	in draft info)		
☐ 41	Kevin Edwards .... .15	.07	.01
	Miami Heat		
☐ 42	Paul Mokeski .... .03	.01	.00
	Milwaukee Bucks		

1989-90 Hoops I / 111

☐ 43	Dale Ellis AS	.06	.03	.00
	Seattle Supersonics			
☐ 44	Walter Berry	.03	.01	.00
	Houston Rockets			
☐ 45	Chuck Person	.12	.06	.01
	Indiana Pacers			
☐ 46	Rick Mahorn SP	.20	.10	.02
	Detroit Pistons			
☐ 47	Joe Kleine	.03	.01	.00
	Boston Celtics			
☐ 48	Brad Daugherty AS	.20	.10	.02
	Cleveland Cavaliers			
☐ 49	Mike Woodson	.03	.01	.00
	Houston Rockets			
☐ 50	Brad Daugherty	.50	.25	.05
	Cleveland Cavaliers			
☐ 51	Shelton Jones SP	.25	.12	.02
	Philadelphia 76ers			
☐ 52	Michael Adams	.20	.10	.02
	Denver Nuggets			
☐ 53	Wes Unseld CO	.10	.05	.01
	Washington Bullets			
☐ 54	Rex Chapman	.20	.10	.02
	Charlotte Hornets			
☐ 55	Kelly Tripucka	.03	.01	.00
	Charlotte Hornets			
☐ 56	Rickey Green	.03	.01	.00
	Milwaukee Bucks			
☐ 57	Frank Johnson SP	.20	.10	.02
	Houston Rockets			
☐ 58	Johnny Newman	.20	.10	.02
	New York Knicks			
☐ 59	Billy Thompson	.10	.05	.01
	Miami Heat			
☐ 60	Stu Jackson CO	.06	.03	.00
	New York Knicks			
☐ 61	Walter Davis	.06	.03	.00
	Denver Nuggets			
☐ 62	Brian Shaw SP UER	.50	.25	.05
	Boston Celtics (Gary Grant led rookies in assists, not Shaw)			
☐ 63	Gerald Wilkins	.06	.03	.00
	New York Knicks			
☐ 64	Armon Gilliam	.10	.05	.01
	Phoenix Suns			
☐ 65	Maurice Cheeks SP	.25	.12	.02
	Philadelphia 76ers			
☐ 66	Jack Sikma	.06	.03	.00
	Milwaukee Bucks			
☐ 67	Harvey Grant	.90	.45	.09
	Washington Bullets			
☐ 68	Jim Lynam CO	.03	.01	.00
	Philadelphia 76ers			
☐ 69	Clyde Drexler AS	.25	.12	.02
	Portland Trail Blazers			
☐ 70	Xavier McDaniel	.15	.07	.01
	Seattle Supersonics			

112 / 1989-90 Hoops I

☐ 71	Danny Young	.03	.01	.00
	Portland Trail Blazers			
☐ 72	Fennis Dembo	.08	.04	.01
	Detroit Pistons			
☐ 73	Mark Acres SP	.20	.10	.02
	Boston Celtics			
☐ 74	Brad Lohaus SP	.25	.12	.02
	Sacramento Kings			
☐ 75	Manute Bol	.06	.03	.00
	Golden State Warriors			
☐ 76	Purvis Short	.03	.01	.00
	Houston Rockets			
☐ 77	Allen Leavell	.03	.01	.00
	Houston Rockets			
☐ 78	Johnny Dawkins SP	.20	.10	.02
	San Antonio Spurs			
☐ 79	Paul Pressey	.03	.01	.00
	Milwaukee Bucks			
☐ 80	Patrick Ewing	.50	.25	.05
	New York Knicks			
☐ 81	Bill Wennington	.10	.05	.01
	Dallas Mavericks			
☐ 82	Danny Schayes	.06	.03	.00
	Denver Nuggets			
☐ 83	Derek Smith	.03	.01	.00
	Philadelphia 76ers			
☐ 84	Moses Malone AS	.08	.04	.01
	Atlanta Hawks			
☐ 85	Jeff Malone	.15	.07	.01
	Washington Bullets			
☐ 86	Otis Smith SP	.25	.12	.02
	Golden State Warriors			
☐ 87	Trent Tucker	.03	.01	.00
	New York Knicks			
☐ 88	Robert Reid	.03	.01	.00
	Charlotte Hornets			
☐ 89	John Paxson	.15	.07	.01
	Chicago Bulls			
☐ 90	Chris Mullin	.40	.20	.04
	Golden State Warriors			
☐ 91	Tom Garrick	.08	.04	.01
	Los Angeles Clippers			
☐ 92	Willis Reed CO SP UER	.30	.15	.03
	New Jersey Nets (Gambling, should be Grambling)			
☐ 93	Dave Corzine SP	.20	.10	.02
	Chicago Bulls			
☐ 94	Mark Alarie	.08	.04	.01
	Washington Bullets			
☐ 95	Mark Aguirre	.08	.04	.01
	Detroit Pistons			
☐ 96	Charles Barkley AS	.20	.10	.02
	Philadelphia 76ers			
☐ 97	Sidney Green SP	.20	.10	.02
	New York Knicks			
☐ 98	Kevin Willis	.20	.10	.02
	Atlanta Hawks			

1989-90 Hoops I / 113

☐ 99 Dave Hoppen Charlotte Hornets	.08	.04	.01
☐ 100 Terry Cummings SP Milwaukee Bucks	.30	.15	.03
☐ 101 Dwayne Washington SP Miami Heat	.20	.10	.02
☐ 102 Larry Brown CO San Antonio Spurs	.03	.01	.00
☐ 103 Kevin Duckworth Portland Trail Blazers	.08	.04	.01
☐ 104 Uwe Blab SP Dallas Mavericks	.30	.15	.03
☐ 105 Terry Porter Portland Trail Blazers	.35	.17	.03
☐ 106 Craig Ehlo Cleveland Cavaliers	.50	.25	.05
☐ 107 Don Casey CO Los Angeles Clippers	.03	.01	.00
☐ 108 Pat Riley CO Los Angeles Lakers	.06	.03	.00
☐ 109 John Salley Detroit Pistons	.08	.04	.01
☐ 110 Charles Barkley Philadelphia 76ers	.40	.20	.04
☐ 111 Sam Bowie SP Portland Trail Blazers	.25	.12	.02
☐ 112 Earl Cureton Charlotte Hornets	.08	.04	.01
☐ 113 Craig Hodges UER Chicago Bulls (3-pointing shooting)	.06	.03	.00
☐ 114 Benoit Benjamin Los Angeles Clippers	.06	.03	.00
☐ 115A Spud Webb ERR SP Atlanta Hawks (Signed 9/27/89)	.35	.17	.03
☐ 115B Spud Webb COR Atlanta Hawks (Second series; signed 9/26/85)	.15	.07	.01
☐ 116 Karl Malone AS Utah Jazz	.20	.10	.02
☐ 117 Sleepy Floyd Houston Rockets	.06	.03	.00
☐ 118 John Williams Cleveland Cavaliers	.10	.05	.01
☐ 119 Michael Holton Charlotte Hornets	.03	.01	.00
☐ 120 Alex English Denver Nuggets	.10	.05	.01
☐ 121 Dennis Johnson Boston Celtics	.08	.04	.01
☐ 122 Wayne Cooper SP Denver Nuggets	.20	.10	.02
☐ 123A Don Chaney CO Houston Rockets (Line next to NBA coaching record)	.30	.15	.03

114 / 1989-90 Hoops I

☐ 123B Don Chaney CO	.06	.03	.00
Houston Rockets (No line)			
☐ 124 A.C. Green	.08	.04	.01
Los Angeles Lakers			
☐ 125 Adrian Dantley	.12	.06	.01
Dallas Mavericks			
☐ 126 Del Harris CO	.03	.01	.00
Milwaukee Bucks			
☐ 127 Dick Harter CO	.03	.01	.00
Charlotte Hornets			
☐ 128 Reggie Williams	.30	.15	.03
Los Angeles Clippers			
☐ 129 Bill Hanzlik	.03	.01	.00
Denver Nuggets			
☐ 130 Dominique Wilkins	.30	.15	.03
Atlanta Hawks			
☐ 131 Herb Williams	.06	.03	.00
Dallas Mavericks			
☐ 132 Steve Johnson SP	.20	.10	.02
Portland Trail Blazers			
☐ 133 Alex English AS	.06	.03	.00
Denver Nuggets			
☐ 134 Darrell Walker	.03	.01	.00
Washington Bullets			
☐ 135 Bill Laimbeer	.08	.04	.01
Detroit Pistons			
☐ 136 Fred Roberts	.10	.05	.01
Milwaukee Bucks			
☐ 137 Hersey Hawkins	1.00	.50	.10
Philadelphia 76ers			
☐ 138 David Robinson SP	33.00	15.00	3.00
San Antonio Spurs			
☐ 139 Brad Sellers SP	.20	.10	.02
Chicago Bulls			
☐ 140 John Stockton	.75	.35	.07
Utah Jazz			
☐ 141 Grant Long	.35	.17	.03
Miami Heat			
☐ 142 Marc Iavaroni SP	.20	.10	.02
Utah Jazz			
☐ 143 Steve Alford SP	.25	.12	.02
Golden State Warriors			
☐ 144 Jeff Lamp SP	.20	.10	.02
Los Angeles Lakers			
☐ 145 Buck Williams SP UER	.35	.17	.03
New Jersey Nets (Won ROY in '81, should say '82)			
☐ 146 Mark Jackson AS	.06	.03	.00
New York Knicks			
☐ 147 Jim Petersen	.03	.01	.00
Sacramento Kings			
☐ 148 Steve Stipanovich SP	.20	.10	.02
Indiana Pacers			
☐ 149 Sam Vincent SP	.30	.15	.03
Chicago Bulls			

1989-90 Hoops I / 115

☐ 150 Larry Bird	.60	.30	.06
Boston Celtics			
☐ 151 Jon Koncak	.08	.04	.01
Atlanta Hawks			
☐ 152 Olden Polynice	.25	.12	.02
Seattle Supersonics			
☐ 153 Randy Breuer	.03	.01	.00
Milwaukee Bucks			
☐ 154 John Battle	.15	.07	.01
Atlanta Hawks			
☐ 155 Mark Eaton	.06	.03	.00
Utah Jazz			
☐ 156 Kevin McHale AS UER	.08	.04	.01
Boston Celtics			
(No TM on Celtics			
logo on back)			
☐ 157 Jerry Sichting SP	.20	.10	.02
Portland Trail Blazers			
☐ 158 Pat Cummings SP	.20	.10	.02
Miami Heat			
☐ 159 Patrick Ewing AS	.20	.10	.02
New York Knicks			
☐ 160 Mark Price	.40	.20	.04
Cleveland Cavaliers			
☐ 161 Jerry Reynolds CO	.03	.01	.00
Sacramento Kings			
☐ 162 Ken Norman	.30	.15	.03
Los Angeles Clippers			
☐ 163 John Bagley SP UER	.25	.12	.02
New Jersey Nets			
(Picked in '83,			
should say '82)			
☐ 164 Christian Welp SP	.25	.12	.02
Philadelphia 76ers			
☐ 165 Reggie Theus SP	.25	.12	.02
Atlanta Hawks			
☐ 166 Magic Johnson AS	.75	.35	.07
Los Angeles Lakers			
☐ 167 John Long UER	.03	.01	.00
Detroit Pistons			
(Picked in '79,			
should say '78)			
☐ 168 Larry Smith SP	.20	.10	.02
Golden State Warriors			
☐ 169 Charles Shackleford	.10	.05	.01
New Jersey Nets			
☐ 170 Tom Chambers	.12	.06	.01
Phoenix Suns			
☐ 171A John MacLeod CO SP	.30	.15	.03
Dallas Mavericks			
ERR (NBA logo in			
wrong place)			
☐ 171B John MacLeod CO	.06	.03	.00
Dallas Mavericks			
COR (Second series)			
☐ 172 Ron Rothstein CO	.03	.01	.00
Miami Heat			

116 / 1989-90 Hoops I

☐ 173 Joe Wolf	.08	.04	.01
Los Angeles Clippers			
☐ 174 Mark Eaton AS	.03	.01	.00
Utah Jazz			
☐ 175 Jon Sundvold	.03	.01	.00
Miami Heat			
☐ 176 Scott Hastings SP	.20	.10	.02
Miami Heat			
☐ 177 Isiah Thomas AS	.12	.06	.01
Detroit Pistons			
☐ 178 Hakeem Olajuwon AS	.15	.07	.01
Houston Rockets			
☐ 179 Mike Fratello CO	.03	.01	.00
Atlanta Hawks			
☐ 180 Hakeem Olajuwon	.35	.17	.03
Houston Rockets			
☐ 181 Randolph Keys	.08	.04	.01
Cleveland Cavaliers			
☐ 182 Richard Anderson UER	.03	.01	.00
Portland Trail Blazers			
(Trail Blazers on front			
should be all caps)			
☐ 183 Dan Majerle	.75	.35	.07
Phoenix Suns			
☐ 184 Derek Harper	.08	.04	.01
Dallas Mavericks			
☐ 185 Robert Parish	.20	.10	.02
Boston Celtics			
☐ 186 Ricky Berry SP	.20	.10	.02
Sacramento Kings			
☐ 187 Michael Cooper	.08	.04	.01
Los Angeles Lakers			
☐ 188 Vinnie Johnson	.06	.03	.00
Detroit Pistons			
☐ 189 James Donaldson	.03	.01	.00
Dallas Mavericks			
☐ 190 Clyde Drexler UER	.50	.25	.05
Portland Trail Blazers			
(4th pick, should			
be 14th)			
☐ 191 Jay Vincent SP	.20	.10	.02
San Antonio Spurs			
☐ 192 Nate McMillan	.03	.01	.00
Seattle Supersonics			
☐ 193 Kevin Duckworth AS	.06	.03	.00
Portland Trail Blazers			
☐ 194 Ledell Eackles	.25	.12	.02
Washington Bullets			
☐ 195 Eddie Johnson	.06	.03	.00
Phoenix Suns			
☐ 196 Terry Teagle	.06	.03	.00
Golden State Warriors			
☐ 197 Tom Chambers AS	.08	.04	.01
Phoenix Suns			
☐ 198 Joe Barry Carroll	.03	.01	.00
New Jersey Nets			
☐ 199 Dennis Hopson	.12	.06	.01
New Jersey Nets			

1989-90 Hoops I / 117

☐ 200 Michael Jordan	2.50	1.25	.25
Chicago Bulls			
☐ 201 Jerome Lane	.10	.05	.01
Denver Nuggets			
☐ 202 Greg Kite	.06	.03	.00
Charlotte Hornets			
☐ 203 David Rivers SP	.25	.12	.02
Los Angeles Lakers			
☐ 204 Sylvester Gray	.08	.04	.01
Miami Heat			
☐ 205 Ron Harper	.12	.06	.01
Cleveland Cavaliers			
☐ 206 Frank Brickowski	.03	.01	.00
San Antonio Spurs			
☐ 207 Rory Sparrow	.03	.01	.00
Miami Heat			
☐ 208 Gerald Henderson	.03	.01	.00
Philadelphia 76ers			
☐ 209 Rod Higgins UER	.03	.01	.00
Golden State Warriors			
('85-86 stats should			
also include San			
Antonio and Seattle)			
☐ 210 James Worthy	.25	.12	.02
Los Angeles Lakers			
☐ 211 Dennis Rodman	.40	.20	.04
Detroit Pistons			
☐ 212 Ricky Pierce	.15	.07	.01
Milwaukee Bucks			
☐ 213 Charles Oakley	.08	.04	.01
New York Knicks			
☐ 214 Steve Colter	.03	.01	.00
Washington Bullets			
☐ 215 Danny Ainge	.10	.05	.01
Sacramento Kings			
☐ 216 Lenny Wilkens CO UER	.08	.04	.01
Cleveland Cavaliers			
(No NBA logo on back			
in bottom right)			
☐ 217 Larry Nance AS	.08	.04	.01
Cleveland Cavaliers			
☐ 218 Muggsy Bogues	.06	.03	.00
Charlotte Hornets			
☐ 219 James Worthy AS	.12	.06	.01
Los Angeles Lakers			
☐ 220 Lafayette Lever	.06	.03	.00
Denver Nuggets			
☐ 221 Quintin Dailey SP	.20	.10	.02
Los Angeles Clippers			
☐ 222 Lester Conner	.03	.01	.00
New Jersey Nets			
☐ 223 Jose Ortiz	.10	.05	.01
Utah Jazz			
☐ 224 Micheal Williams SP	1.00	.50	.10
Detroit Pistons			
☐ 225 Wayman Tisdale	.10	.05	.01
Sacramento Kings			

118 / 1989-90 Hoops I

☐ 226 Mike Sanders SP Cleveland Cavaliers	.20	.10	.02
☐ 227 Jim Farmer SP Utah Jazz	.25	.12	.02
☐ 228 Mark West Phoenix Suns	.03	.01	.00
☐ 229 Jeff Hornacek Phoenix Suns	.75	.35	.07
☐ 230 Chris Mullin AS Golden State Warriors	.20	.10	.02
☐ 231 Vern Fleming Indiana Pacers	.06	.03	.00
☐ 232 Kenny Smith Sacramento Kings	.10	.05	.01
☐ 233 Derrick McKey Seattle Supersonics	.15	.07	.01
☐ 234 Dominique Wilkins AS Atlanta Hawks	.15	.07	.01
☐ 235 Willie Anderson San Antonio Spurs	.30	.15	.03
☐ 236 Keith Lee SP New Jersey Nets	.25	.12	.02
☐ 237 Buck Johnson Houston Rockets	.15	.07	.01
☐ 238 Randy Wittman Indiana Pacers	.03	.01	.00
☐ 239 Terry Catledge SP Washington Bullets	.20	.10	.02
☐ 240 Bernard King Washington Bullets	.10	.05	.01
☐ 241 Darrell Griffith Utah Jazz	.03	.01	.00
☐ 242 Horace Grant Chicago Bulls	.50	.25	.05
☐ 243 Rony Seikaly Miami Heat	.75	.35	.07
☐ 244 Scottie Pippen Chicago Bulls	2.50	1.25	.25
☐ 245 Michael Cage UER Seattle Supersonics (Picked in '85, should say '84)	.03	.01	.00
☐ 246 Kurt Rambis Charlotte Hornets	.06	.03	.00
☐ 247 Morlon Wiley SP Dallas Mavericks	.25	.12	.02
☐ 248 Ronnie Grandison Boston Celtics	.08	.04	.01
☐ 249 Scott Skiles SP Indiana Pacers	.75	.35	.07
☐ 250 Isiah Thomas Detroit Pistons	.30	.15	.03
☐ 251 Thurl Bailey Utah Jazz	.03	.01	.00
☐ 252 Doc Rivers Atlanta Hawks	.06	.03	.00
☐ 253 Stuart Gray SP Indiana Pacers	.20	.10	.02

1989-90 Hoops I / 119

☐ 254 John Williams	.06	.03	.00
Washington Bullets			
☐ 255 Bill Cartwright	.06	.03	.00
Chicago Bulls			
☐ 256 Terry Cummings AS	.06	.03	.00
Milwaukee Bucks			
☐ 257 Rodney McCray	.06	.03	.00
Sacramento Kings			
☐ 258 Larry Krystkowiak	.10	.05	.01
Milwaukee Bucks			
☐ 259 Will Perdue	.40	.20	.04
Chicago Bulls			
☐ 260 Mitch Richmond	1.25	.60	.12
Golden State Warriors			
☐ 261 Blair Rasmussen	.03	.01	.00
Denver Nuggets			
☐ 262 Charles Smith	.60	.30	.06
Los Angeles Clippers			
☐ 263 Tyrone Corbin SP	.40	.20	.04
Phoenix Suns			
☐ 264 Kelvin Upshaw	.08	.04	.01
Boston Celtics			
☐ 265 Otis Thorpe	.20	.10	.02
Houston Rockets			
☐ 266 Phil Jackson CO	.06	.03	.00
Chicago Bulls			
☐ 267 Jerry Sloan CO	.03	.01	.00
Utah Jazz			
☐ 268 John Shasky	.08	.04	.01
Miami Heat			
☐ 269A Bernie Bickerstaff CO SP	.30	.15	.03
Seattle Supersonics			
ERR (Born 2/11/44)			
☐ 269B Bernie Bickerstaff CO	.08	.04	.01
Seattle Supersonics			
COR (Second series;			
Born 11/2/43)			
☐ 270 Magic Johnson	1.50	.75	.15
Los Angeles Lakers			
☐ 271 Vernon Maxwell	.30	.15	.03
San Antonio Spurs			
☐ 272 Tim McCormick	.03	.01	.00
Houston Rockets			
☐ 273 Don Nelson CO	.03	.01	.00
Golden State Warriors			
☐ 274 Gary Grant	.15	.07	.01
Los Angeles Clippers			
☐ 275 Sidney Moncrief SP	.30	.15	.03
Milwaukee Bucks			
☐ 276 Roy Hinson	.03	.01	.00
New Jersey Nets			
☐ 277 Jimmy Rodgers CO	.03	.01	.00
Boston Celtics			
☐ 278 Antoine Carr	.06	.03	.00
Atlanta Hawks			
☐ 279A Orlando Woolridge SP	.30	.15	.03
Los Angeles Lakers			
ERR (No Trademark)			

120 / 1989-90 Hoops I

☐ 279B Orlando Woolridge	.08	.04	.01
Los Angeles Lakers COR (Second series)			
☐ 280 Kevin McHale	.15	.07	.01
Boston Celtics			
☐ 281 LaSalle Thompson	.03	.01	.00
Indiana Pacers			
☐ 282 Detlef Schrempf	.30	.15	.03
Indiana Pacers			
☐ 283 Doug Moe CO	.03	.01	.00
Denver Nuggets			
☐ 284A James Edwards	.30	.15	.03
Detroit Pistons (Small black line next to card number)			
☐ 284B James Edwards	.06	.03	.00
Detroit Pistons (No small black line)			
☐ 285 Jerome Kersey	.30	.15	.03
Portland Trail Blazers			
☐ 286 Sam Perkins	.15	.07	.01
Dallas Mavericks			
☐ 287 Sedale Threatt	.08	.04	.01
Seattle Supersonics			
☐ 288 Tim Kempton SP	.25	.12	.02
Charlotte Hornets			
☐ 289 Mark McNamara	.03	.01	.00
Los Angeles Lakers			
☐ 290 Moses Malone	.15	.07	.01
Atlanta Hawks			
☐ 291 Rick Adelman CO UER	.06	.03	.00
Portland Trail Blazers (Chemekata misspelled as Chemkota)			
☐ 292 Dick Versace CO	.03	.01	.00
Indiana Pacers			
☐ 293 Alton Lister SP	.20	.10	.02
Seattle Supersonics			
☐ 294 Winston Garland	.03	.01	.00
Golden State Warriors			
☐ 295 Kiki Vandeweghe	.06	.03	.00
New York Knicks			
☐ 296 Brad Davis	.03	.01	.00
Dallas Mavericks			
☐ 297 John Stockton AS	.20	.10	.02
Utah Jazz			
☐ 298 Jay Humphries	.06	.03	.00
Milwaukee Bucks			
☐ 299 Dell Curry	.06	.03	.00
Charlotte Hornets			
☐ 300 Mark Jackson	.12	.06	.01
New York Knicks			

1989-90 Hoops II

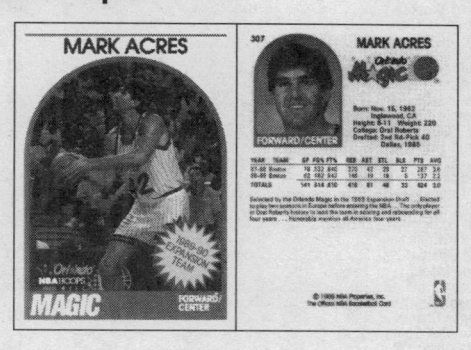

The design of the cards in the 53-card Hoops II set is identical to that of the first series. This set features the expansion teams (Minnesota and Orlando), traded players, a special NBA Championship card of the Detroit Pistons, and a David Robinson In Action card. The cards are standard size (2 1/2" by 3 1/2") and numbered on the back in continuation of the first series. Cards numbered 301, 305, 307, 308, 318, 322, 328, 339, and 343 all have basketball misspelled as baasketball on the bottom of the card back. The key rookie in this set is Kevin Gamble. Since the original card number 353 Detroit Pistons World Champs was so difficult for collectors to find in packs, Hoops produced another edition of the card that was available direct from the company for free with additional copies available for only 35 cents per card.

	MINT	EXC	G-VG
COMPLETE SET (52)	6.00	3.00	.60
COMMON PLAYER (301-352)	.05	.02	.00
☐ 301 Morlon Wiley	.08	.04	.01
Orlando Magic			
☐ 302 Reggie Theus	.08	.04	.01
Orlando Magic			
☐ 303 Otis Smith	.08	.04	.01
Orlando Magic			
☐ 304 Tod Murphy	.10	.05	.01
Minnesota Timberwolves			
☐ 305 Sidney Green	.05	.02	.00
Orlando Magic			
☐ 306 Shelton Jones	.08	.04	.01
Milwaukee Bucks			
☐ 307 Mark Acres	.05	.02	.00
Orlando Magic			
☐ 308 Terry Catledge	.08	.04	.01
Orlando Magic			
☐ 309 Larry Smith	.05	.02	.00
Houston Rockets			

122 / 1989-90 Hoops II

☐ 310 David Robinson IA	5.00	2.50	.50
San Antonio Spurs			
☐ 311 Johnny Dawkins	.08	.04	.01
Philadelphia 76ers			
☐ 312 Terry Cummings	.15	.07	.01
San Antonio Spurs			
☐ 313 Sidney Lowe	.05	.02	.00
Minnesota Timberwolves			
☐ 314 Bill Musselman CO	.05	.02	.00
Minnesota Timberwolves			
☐ 315 Buck Williams UER	.15	.07	.01
Portland Trail Blazers			
(Won ROY in '81,			
should say '82)			
☐ 316 Mel Turpin	.05	.02	.00
Washington Bullets			
☐ 317 Scott Hastings	.05	.02	.00
Detroit Pistons			
☐ 318 Scott Skiles	.20	.10	.02
Orlando Magic			
☐ 319 Tyrone Corbin	.12	.06	.01
Minnesota Timberwolves			
☐ 320 Maurice Cheeks	.08	.04	.01
San Antonio Spurs			
☐ 321 Matt Goukas CO	.05	.02	.00
Orlando Magic			
☐ 322 Jeff Turner	.08	.04	.01
Orlando Magic			
☐ 323 David Wingate	.05	.02	.00
San Antonio Spurs			
☐ 324 Steve Johnson	.05	.02	.00
Minnesota Timberwolves			
☐ 325 Alton Lister	.05	.02	.00
Golden State Warriors			
☐ 326 Ken Bannister	.08	.04	.01
Los Angeles Clippers			
☐ 327 Bill Fitch CO UER	.05	.02	.00
New Jersey Nets			
(Copyright missing			
on bottom of back)			
☐ 328 Sam Vincent	.08	.04	.01
Orlando Magic			
☐ 329 Larry Drew	.05	.02	.00
Los Angeles Lakers			
☐ 330 Rick Mahorn	.08	.04	.01
Minnesota Timberwolves			
☐ 331 Christian Welp	.05	.02	.00
San Antonio Spurs			
☐ 332 Brad Lohaus	.08	.04	.01
Minnesota Timberwolves			
☐ 333 Frank Johnson	.05	.02	.00
Orlando Magic			
☐ 334 Jim Farmer	.08	.04	.01
Minnesota Timberwolves			
☐ 335 Wayne Cooper	.05	.02	.00
Portland Trail Blazers			
☐ 336 Mike Brown	.12	.06	.01
Utah Jazz			

1990-91 Hoops I / 123

☐ 337 Sam Bowie	.10	.05	.01
New Jersey Nets			
☐ 338 Kevin Gamble	.50	.25	.05
Boston Celtics			
☐ 339 Jerry Ice Reynolds	.15	.07	.01
Orlando Magic			
☐ 340 Mike Sanders	.08	.04	.01
Indiana Pacers			
☐ 341 Bill Jones UER	.08	.04	.01
New Jersey Nets			
(Center on front, should be F)			
☐ 342 Greg Anderson	.08	.04	.01
Milwaukee Bucks			
☐ 343 Dave Corzine	.05	.02	.00
Orlando Magic			
☐ 344 Micheal Williams UER	.35	.17	.03
Phoenix Suns			
☐ 345 Jay Vincent	.05	.02	.00
Philadelphia 76ers			
☐ 346 David Rivers	.08	.04	.01
Minnesota Timberwolves			
☐ 347 Caldwell Jones UER	.08	.04	.01
San Antonio Spurs			
(He was not starting center on '83 Sixers)			
☐ 348 Brad Sellers	.05	.02	.00
Seattle Supersonics			
☐ 349 Scott Roth	.08	.04	.01
Minnesota Timberwolves			
☐ 350 Alvin Robertson	.08	.04	.01
Milwaukee Bucks			
☐ 351 Steve Kerr	.20	.10	.02
Cleveland Cavaliers			
☐ 352 Stuart Gray	.05	.02	.00
Charlotte Hornets			
☐ 353A World Champions SP	7.50	3.75	.75
Detroit Pistons			
☐ 353B World Champions UER	.40	.20	.04
Detroit Pistons			
(George Blaha misspelled Blanha)			

1990-91 Hoops I

The 1990-91 Hoops basketball set contains 336 cards measuring the standard size (2 1/2" by 3 1/2"). On the front the color action player photo appears in the shape of a basketball lane, bordered by gold on the All-Star cards (1-26) and by silver on the regular issues (27-331, 336). The player's name and the stripe below the picture are printed in one of the team's colors. The team logo at the lower right corner rounds out the card face. The back of the regular issue has a color head shot and biographical information as well as college and pro statistics, framed by a basketball lane. The cards are numbered on the back and arranged alphabetically according

124 / 1990-91 Hoops I

to teams as follows: Atlanta Hawks (27-37), Boston Celtics (38-48), Charlotte Hornets (49-59), Chicago Bulls (60-69), Cleveland Cavaliers (70-80), Dallas Mavericks (81-90), Denver Nuggets (91-100), Detroit Pistons (101-111), Golden State Warriors (112-122), Houston Rockets (123-131), Indiana Pacers (132-141), Los Angeles Clippers (142-152), Los Angeles Lakers (153-163), Miami Heat (164-172), Milwaukee Bucks (173-183), Minnesota Timberwolves (184-192), New Jersey Nets (193-201), New York Knicks (202-212), Orlando Magic (213-223), Philadelphia 76ers (224-232), Phoenix Suns (233-242), Portland Trail Blazers (243-252), Sacramento Kings (253-262), San Antonio Spurs (263-273), Seattle Supersonics (274-284), Utah Jazz (285-294), and Washington Bullets (295-304). The coaches cards number 305-331. Some of the All-Star cards (card numbers 2, 6, and 8) can be found with or without a printing mistake, i.e., no T in the trademark logo on the card back. A few of the cards (card numbers 14, 66, 144, and 279) refer to the player as "all America" rather than "All America". The following cards can be found with or without a black line under the card number, height, and birthplace: 20, 23, 24, 29, and 87. Rookie Cards included in this set are Nick Anderson, B.J. Armstrong, Vlade Divac, Sherman Douglas, Sean Elliott, Pervis Ellison, Danny Ferry, Tim Hardaway, Shawn Kemp, Sarunas Marciulionis, Drazen Petrovic, Glen Rice, Pooh Richardson, and Cliff Robinson.

	MINT	EXC	G-VG
COMPLETE SET (336)	8.00	4.00	.80
COMMON PLAYER (1-336)	.03	.01	.00
COMMON AS PLAYER (1-26)	.06	.03	.00
COMMON PLAYER SP	.06	.03	.00
☐ 1 Charles Barkley AS SP	.25	.12	.02
Philadelphia 76ers			
☐ 2 Larry Bird AS SP	.30	.15	.03
Boston Celtics			
☐ 3 Joe Dumars AS SP	.12	.06	.01
Detroit Pistons			
☐ 4 Patrick Ewing AS SP	.30	.15	.03
New York Knicks			
(A-S blocks listed as			
1, should be 5) UER			
☐ 5 Michael Jordan AS SP	1.25	.60	.12
Chicago Bulls			
(Won Slam Dunk in			

1990-91 Hoops I / 125

'87 and '88,
not '86 and '88) UER
- [ ] 6 Kevin McHale AS SP .... .10 .05 .01
  Boston Celtics
- [ ] 7 Reggie Miller AS SP .... .12 .06 .01
  Indiana Pacers
- [ ] 8 Robert Parish AS SP .... .12 .06 .01
  Boston Celtics
- [ ] 9 Scottie Pippen AS SP .... .40 .20 .04
  Chicago Bulls
- [ ] 10 Dennis Rodman AS SP .... .12 .06 .01
  Detroit Pistons
- [ ] 11 Isiah Thomas AS SP .... .15 .07 .01
  Detroit Pistons
- [ ] 12 Dominique Wilkins .... .15 .07 .01
  AS SP
  Atlanta Hawks
- [ ] 13A All-Star Checklist SP .... .40 .20 .04
  ERR (No card number)
- [ ] 13B All-Star Checklist SP .... .10 .05 .01
  COR (Card number on back)
- [ ] 14 Rolando Blackman AS SP .... .08 .04 .01
  Dallas Mavericks
- [ ] 15 Tom Chambers AS SP .... .08 .04 .01
  Phoenix Suns
- [ ] 16 Clyde Drexler AS SP .... .30 .15 .03
  Portland Trail Blazers
- [ ] 17 A.C. Green AS SP .... .06 .03 .00
  Los Angeles Lakers
- [ ] 18 Magic Johnson AS SP .... .75 .35 .07
  Los Angeles Lakers
- [ ] 19 Kevin Johnson AS SP .... .25 .12 .02
  Phoenix Suns
- [ ] 20 Lafayette Lever AS SP .... .06 .03 .00
  Denver Nuggets
- [ ] 21 Karl Malone AS SP .... .25 .12 .02
  Utah Jazz
- [ ] 22 Chris Mullin AS SP .... .25 .12 .02
  Golden State Warriors
- [ ] 23 Hakeem Olajuwon AS SP .... .20 .10 .02
  Houston Rockets
- [ ] 24 David Robinson AS SP .... 1.00 .50 .10
  San Antonio Spurs
- [ ] 25 John Stockton AS SP .... .25 .12 .02
  Utah Jazz
- [ ] 26 James Worthy AS SP .... .12 .06 .01
  Los Angeles Lakers
- [ ] 27 John Battle .... .03 .01 .00
  Atlanta Hawks
- [ ] 28 Jon Koncak .... .03 .01 .00
  Atlanta Hawks
- [ ] 29 Cliff Levingston SP .... .06 .03 .00
  Atlanta Hawks
- [ ] 30 John Long SP .... .06 .03 .00
  Atlanta Hawks
- [ ] 31 Moses Malone .... .12 .06 .01
  Atlanta Hawks

126 / 1990-91 Hoops I

☐ 32 Doc Rivers	.06	.03	.00
Atlanta Hawks			
☐ 33 Kenny Smith SP	.06	.03	.00
Atlanta Hawks			
☐ 34 Alexander Volkov	.12	.06	.01
Atlanta Hawks			
☐ 35 Spud Webb	.06	.03	.00
Atlanta Hawks			
☐ 36 Dominique Wilkins	.15	.07	.01
Atlanta Hawks			
☐ 37 Kevin Willis	.10	.05	.01
Atlanta Hawks			
☐ 38 John Bagley	.06	.03	.00
Boston Celtics			
☐ 39 Larry Bird	.35	.17	.03
Boston Celtics			
☐ 40 Kevin Gamble	.10	.05	.01
Boston Celtics			
☐ 41 Dennis Johnson SP	.10	.05	.01
Boston Celtics			
☐ 42 Joe Kleine	.03	.01	.00
Boston Celtics			
☐ 43 Reggie Lewis	.25	.12	.02
Boston Celtics			
☐ 44 Kevin McHale	.10	.05	.01
Boston Celtics			
☐ 45 Robert Parish	.12	.06	.01
Boston Celtics			
☐ 46 Jim Paxson SP	.06	.03	.00
Boston Celtics			
☐ 47 Ed Pinckney	.03	.01	.00
Boston Celtics			
☐ 48 Brian Shaw	.08	.04	.01
Boston Celtics			
☐ 49 Richard Anderson SP	.06	.03	.00
Charlotte Hornets			
☐ 50 Muggsy Bogues	.03	.01	.00
Charlotte Hornets			
☐ 51 Rex Chapman	.06	.03	.00
Charlotte Hornets			
☐ 52 Dell Curry	.03	.01	.00
Charlotte Hornets			
☐ 53 Kenny Gattison	.20	.10	.02
Charlotte Hornets			
☐ 54 Armon Gilliam	.03	.01	.00
Charlotte Hornets			
☐ 55 Dave Hoppen	.03	.01	.00
Charlotte Hornets			
☐ 56 Randolph Keys	.03	.01	.00
Charlotte Hornets			
☐ 57 J.R. Reid	.15	.07	.01
Charlotte Hornets			
☐ 58 Robert Reid SP	.06	.03	.00
Charlotte Hornets			
☐ 59 Kelly Tripucka	.03	.01	.00
Charlotte Hornets			
☐ 60 B.J. Armstrong	.40	.20	.04
Chicago Bulls			

1990-91 Hoops I / 127

☐ 61	Bill Cartwright Chicago Bulls	.06	.03	.00
☐ 62	Charles Davis SP Chicago Bulls	.06	.03	.00
☐ 63	Horace Grant Chicago Bulls	.20	.10	.02
☐ 64	Craig Hodges Chicago Bulls	.03	.01	.00
☐ 65	Michael Jordan Chicago Bulls	1.50	.75	.15
☐ 66	Stacey King Chicago Bulls	.25	.12	.02
☐ 67	John Paxson Chicago Bulls	.08	.04	.01
☐ 68	Will Perdue Chicago Bulls	.06	.03	.00
☐ 69	Scottie Pippen Chicago Bulls	.60	.30	.06
☐ 70	Winston Bennett Cleveland Cavaliers	.08	.04	.01
☐ 71	Chucky Brown Cleveland Cavaliers	.08	.04	.01
☐ 72	Derrick Chievous Cleveland Cavaliers	.03	.01	.00
☐ 73	Brad Daugherty Cleveland Cavaliers	.20	.10	.02
☐ 74	Craig Ehlo Cleveland Cavaliers	.06	.03	.00
☐ 75	Steve Kerr Cleveland Cavaliers	.03	.01	.00
☐ 76	Paul Mokeski SP Cleveland Cavaliers	.06	.03	.00
☐ 77	John Morton Cleveland Cavaliers	.08	.04	.01
☐ 78	Larry Nance Cleveland Cavaliers	.10	.05	.01
☐ 79	Mark Price Cleveland Cavaliers	.20	.10	.02
☐ 80	Hot Rod Williams Cleveland Cavaliers	.08	.04	.01
☐ 81	Steve Alford Dallas Mavericks	.06	.03	.00
☐ 82	Rolando Blackman Dallas Mavericks	.08	.04	.01
☐ 83	Adrian Dantley SP Dallas Mavericks	.10	.05	.01
☐ 84	Brad Davis Dallas Mavericks	.03	.01	.00
☐ 85	James Donaldson Dallas Mavericks	.03	.01	.00
☐ 86	Derek Harper Dallas Mavericks	.06	.03	.00
☐ 87	Sam Perkins SP Dallas Mavericks	.12	.06	.01
☐ 88	Roy Tarpley Dallas Mavericks	.06	.03	.00
☐ 89	Bill Wennington SP Dallas Mavericks	.06	.03	.00

128 / 1990-91 Hoops I

☐ 90 Herb Williams .... .03	.01	.00
Dallas Mavericks		
☐ 91 Michael Adams .... .08	.04	.01
Denver Nuggets		
☐ 92 Joe Barry Carroll SP .... .08	.04	.01
Denver Nuggets		
☐ 93 Walter Davis UER .... .06	.03	.00
Denver Nuggets		
(Born NC, not PA)		
☐ 94 Alex English SP .... .10	.05	.01
Denver Nuggets		
☐ 95 Bill Hanzlik .... .03	.01	.00
Denver Nuggets		
☐ 96 Jerome Lane .... .03	.01	.00
Denver Nuggets		
☐ 97 Lafayette Lever SP .... .08	.04	.01
Denver Nuggets		
☐ 98 Todd Lichti .... .10	.05	.01
Denver Nuggets		
☐ 99 Blair Rasmussen .... .03	.01	.00
Denver Nuggets		
☐ 100 Danny Schayes SP .... .06	.03	.00
Denver Nuggets		
☐ 101 Mark Aguirre .... .06	.03	.00
Detroit Pistons		
☐ 102 William Bedford .... .08	.04	.01
Detroit Pistons		
☐ 103 Joe Dumars .... .12	.06	.01
Detroit Pistons		
☐ 104 James Edwards .... .03	.01	.00
Detroit Pistons		
☐ 105 Scott Hastings .... .03	.01	.00
Detroit Pistons		
☐ 106 Gerald Henderson SP .... .06	.03	.00
Detroit Pistons		
☐ 107 Vinnie Johnson .... .06	.03	.00
Detroit Pistons		
☐ 108 Bill Laimbeer .... .08	.04	.01
Detroit Pistons		
☐ 109 Dennis Rodman .... .20	.10	.02
Detroit Pistons		
☐ 110 John Salley .... .06	.03	.00
Detroit Pistons		
☐ 111 Isiah Thomas UER .... .15	.07	.01
Detroit Pistons		
(No position listed		
on the card)		
☐ 112 Manute Bol SP .... .08	.04	.01
Golden State Warriors		
☐ 113 Tim Hardaway 1.50	.75	.15
Golden State Warriors		
☐ 114 Rod Higgins .... .03	.01	.00
Golden State Warriors		
☐ 115 Sarunas Marciulionis .... .40	.20	.04
Golden State Warriors		
☐ 116 Chris Mullin UER .... .25	.12	.02
Golden State Warriors		
(Born Brooklyn, NY,		

1990-91 Hoops I / 129

not New York, NY)

☐ 117 Jim Petersen Golden State Warriors	.03	.01	.00
☐ 118 Mitch Richmond Golden State Warriors	.15	.07	.01
☐ 119 Mike Smrek Golden State Warriors	.10	.05	.01
☐ 120 Terry Teagle SP Golden State Warriors	.06	.03	.00
☐ 121 Tom Tolbert Golden State Warriors	.08	.04	.01
☐ 122 Christian Welp SP Golden State Warriors	.06	.03	.00
☐ 123 Byron Dinkins SP Houston Rockets	.10	.05	.01
☐ 124 Eric(Sleepy) Floyd Houston Rockets	.06	.03	.00
☐ 125 Buck Johnson Houston Rockets	.06	.03	.00
☐ 126 Vernon Maxwell Houston Rockets	.06	.03	.00
☐ 127 Hakeem Olajuwon Houston Rockets	.25	.12	.02
☐ 128 Larry Smith Houston Rockets	.03	.01	.00
☐ 129 Otis Thorpe Houston Rockets	.06	.03	.00
☐ 130 Mitchell Wiggins SP Houston Rockets	.06	.03	.00
☐ 131 Mike Woodson Houston Rockets	.03	.01	.00
☐ 132 Greg Dreiling Indiana Pacers	.08	.04	.01
☐ 133 Vern Fleming Indiana Pacers	.03	.01	.00
☐ 134 Rickey Green SP Indiana Pacers	.06	.03	.00
☐ 135 Reggie Miller Indiana Pacers	.20	.10	.02
☐ 136 Chuck Person Indiana Pacers	.08	.04	.01
☐ 137 Mike Sanders Indiana Pacers	.06	.03	.00
☐ 138 Detlef Schrempf Indiana Pacers	.10	.05	.01
☐ 139 Rik Smits Indiana Pacers	.08	.04	.01
☐ 140 LaSalle Thompson Indiana Pacers	.03	.01	.00
☐ 141 Randy Wittman Indiana Pacers	.03	.01	.00
☐ 142 Benoit Benjamin Los Angeles Clippers	.06	.03	.00
☐ 143 Winston Garland Los Angeles Clippers	.03	.01	.00
☐ 144 Tom Garrick Los Angeles Clippers	.03	.01	.00
☐ 145 Gary Grant	.03	.01	.00

130 / 1990-91 Hoops I

☐ 146 Ron Harper Los Angeles Clippers	.06	.03	.00
☐ 147 Danny Manning Los Angeles Clippers	.15	.07	.01
☐ 148 Jeff Martin Los Angeles Clippers	.08	.04	.01
☐ 149 Ken Norman Los Angeles Clippers	.08	.04	.01
☐ 150 David Rivers SP Los Angeles Clippers	.06	.03	.00
☐ 151 Charles Smith Los Angeles Clippers	.12	.06	.01
☐ 152 Joe Wolf SP Los Angeles Clippers	.06	.03	.00
☐ 153 Michael Cooper SP Los Angeles Lakers	.10	.05	.01
☐ 154 Vlade Divac UER Los Angeles Lakers (Height 6'11", should be 7'1")	.30	.15	.03
☐ 155 Larry Drew Los Angeles Lakers	.03	.01	.00
☐ 156 A.C. Green Los Angeles Lakers	.06	.03	.00
☐ 157 Magic Johnson Los Angeles Lakers	.75	.35	.07
☐ 158 Mark McNamara SP Los Angeles Lakers	.06	.03	.00
☐ 159 Byron Scott Los Angeles Lakers	.06	.03	.00
☐ 160 Mychal Thompson Los Angeles Lakers	.03	.01	.00
☐ 161 Jay Vincent SP Los Angeles Lakers	.06	.03	.00
☐ 162 Orlando Woolridge SP Los Angeles Lakers	.08	.04	.01
☐ 163 James Worthy Los Angeles Lakers	.12	.06	.01
☐ 164 Sherman Douglas Miami Heat	.20	.10	.02
☐ 165 Kevin Edwards Miami Heat	.03	.01	.00
☐ 166 Tellis Frank SP Miami Heat	.10	.05	.01
☐ 167 Grant Long Miami Heat	.06	.03	.00
☐ 168 Glen Rice Miami Heat	.90	.45	.09
☐ 169A Rony Seikaly Miami Heat (Athens)	.15	.07	.01
☐ 169B Rony Seikaly Miami Heat (Beirut)	.15	.07	.01
☐ 170 Rory Sparrow SP Miami Heat	.06	.03	.00

1990-91 Hoops I / 131

☐ 171A Jon Sundvold Miami Heat (First series)	.06	.03	.00
☐ 171B Billy Thompson Miami Heat (Second series)	.06	.03	.00
☐ 172A Billy Thompson Miami Heat (First series)	.06	.03	.00
☐ 172B Jon Sundvold Miami Heat (Second series)	.06	.03	.00
☐ 173 Greg Anderson Milwaukee Bucks	.03	.01	.00
☐ 174 Jeff Grayer Milwaukee Bucks	.15	.07	.01
☐ 175 Jay Humphries Milwaukee Bucks	.03	.01	.00
☐ 176 Frank Kornet Milwaukee Bucks	.08	.04	.01
☐ 177 Larry Krystkowiak Milwaukee Bucks	.03	.01	.00
☐ 178 Brad Lohaus Milwaukee Bucks	.06	.03	.00
☐ 179 Ricky Pierce Milwaukee Bucks	.06	.03	.00
☐ 180 Paul Pressey SP Milwaukee Bucks	.06	.03	.00
☐ 181 Fred Roberts Milwaukee Bucks	.06	.03	.00
☐ 182 Alvin Robertson Milwaukee Bucks	.06	.03	.00
☐ 183 Jack Sikma Milwaukee Bucks	.06	.03	.00
☐ 184 Randy Breuer Minnesota Timberwolves	.03	.01	.00
☐ 185 Tony Campbell Minnesota Timberwolves	.06	.03	.00
☐ 186 Tyrone Corbin Minnesota Timberwolves	.06	.03	.00
☐ 187 Sidney Lowe SP Minnesota Timberwolves	.06	.03	.00
☐ 188 Sam Mitchell Minnesota Timberwolves	.15	.07	.01
☐ 189 Tod Murphy Minnesota Timberwolves	.06	.03	.00
☐ 190 Pooh Richardson Minnesota Timberwolves	.35	.17	.03
☐ 191 Scott Roth SP Minnesota Timberwolves	.06	.03	.00
☐ 192 Brad Sellers SP Minnesota Timberwolves	.06	.03	.00
☐ 193 Mookie Blaylock New Jersey Nets	.25	.12	.02
☐ 194 Sam Bowie New Jersey Nets	.06	.03	.00
☐ 195 Lester Conner New Jersey Nets	.03	.01	.00

132 / 1990-91 Hoops I

☐ 196 Derrick Gervin	.08	.04	.01
New Jersey Nets			
☐ 197 Jack Haley	.08	.04	.01
New Jersey Nets			
☐ 198 Roy Hinson	.03	.01	.00
New Jersey Nets			
☐ 199 Dennis Hopson SP	.06	.03	.00
New Jersey Nets			
☐ 200 Chris Morris	.06	.03	.00
New Jersey Nets			
☐ 201 Purvis Short SP	.06	.03	.00
New Jersey Nets			
☐ 202 Maurice Cheeks	.08	.04	.01
New York Knicks			
☐ 203 Patrick Ewing	.30	.15	.03
New York Knicks			
☐ 204 Stuart Gray	.03	.01	.00
New York Knicks			
☐ 205 Mark Jackson	.06	.03	.00
New York Knicks			
☐ 206 Johnny Newman SP	.08	.04	.01
New York Knicks			
☐ 207 Charles Oakley	.06	.03	.00
New York Knicks			
☐ 208 Trent Tucker	.03	.01	.00
New York Knicks			
☐ 209 Kiki Vandeweghe	.06	.03	.00
New York Knicks			
☐ 210 Kenny Walker	.03	.01	.00
New York Knicks			
☐ 211 Eddie Lee Wilkins	.03	.01	.00
New York Knicks			
☐ 212 Gerald Wilkins	.06	.03	.00
New York Knicks			
☐ 213 Mark Acres	.03	.01	.00
Orlando Magic			
☐ 214 Nick Anderson	.50	.25	.05
Orlando Magic			
☐ 215 Michael Ansley UER	.08	.04	.01
Orlando Magic			
(Ranked first, not third)			
☐ 216 Terry Catledge	.06	.03	.00
Orlando Magic			
☐ 217 Dave Corzine SP	.06	.03	.00
Orlando Magic			
☐ 218 Sidney Green SP	.06	.03	.00
Orlando Magic			
☐ 219 Jerry Reynolds	.03	.01	.00
Orlando Magic			
☐ 220 Scott Skiles	.08	.04	.01
Orlando Magic			
☐ 221 Otis Smith	.03	.01	.00
Orlando Magic			
☐ 222 Reggie Theus SP	.08	.04	.01
Orlando Magic			
☐ 223A Sam Vincent	.50	.25	.05
Orlando Magic			
(First series, shows			

1990-91 Hoops I / 133

 12 Michael Jordan)
- [ ] 223B Sam Vincent .... .06   .03   .00
  Orlando Magic
  (Second series, shows
  Sam dribbling)
- [ ] 224 Ron Anderson .... .03   .01   .00
  Philadelphia 76ers
- [ ] 225 Charles Barkley .... .25   .12   .02
  Philadelphia 76ers
- [ ] 226 Scott Brooks SP UER .... .06   .03   .00
  Philadelphia 76ers
  (Born French Camp,
  not Lathron, Cal.)
- [ ] 227 Johnny Dawkins .... .03   .01   .00
  Philadelphia 76ers
- [ ] 228 Mike Gminski .... .03   .01   .00
  Philadelphia 76ers
- [ ] 229 Hersey Hawkins .... .15   .07   .01
  Philadelphia 76ers
- [ ] 230 Rick Mahorn .... .06   .03   .00
  Philadelphia 76ers
- [ ] 231 Derek Smith SP .... .06   .03   .00
  Philadelphia 76ers
- [ ] 232 Bob Thornton .... .08   .04   .01
  Philadelphia 76ers
- [ ] 233 Kenny Battle .... .10   .05   .01
  Phoenix Suns
- [ ] 234A Tom Chambers .... .10   .05   .01
  Phoenix Suns
  (First series;
  Forward on front)
- [ ] 234B Tom Chambers .... .10   .05   .01
  Phoenix Suns
  (Second series;
  Guard on front)
- [ ] 235 Greg Grant SP .... .10   .05   .01
  Phoenix Suns
- [ ] 236 Jeff Hornacek .... .15   .07   .01
  Phoenix Suns
- [ ] 237 Eddie Johnson .... .06   .03   .00
  Phoenix Suns
- [ ] 238A Kevin Johnson .... .30   .15   .03
  Phoenix Suns
  (First series;
  Guard on front)
- [ ] 238B Kevin Johnson .... .30   .15   .03
  Phoenix Suns
  (Second series;
  Forward on front)
- [ ] 239 Dan Majerle .... .15   .07   .01
  Phoenix Suns
- [ ] 240 Tim Perry .... .08   .04   .01
  Phoenix Suns
- [ ] 241 Kurt Rambis .... .06   .03   .00
  Phoenix Suns
- [ ] 242 Mark West .... .03   .01   .00
  Phoenix Suns
- [ ] 243 Mark Bryant .... .03   .01   .00

134 / 1990-91 Hoops I

Portland Trail Blazers			
☐ 244 Wayne Cooper .... .03	.01	.00
Portland Trail Blazers			
☐ 245 Clyde Drexler .... .30	.15	.03
Portland Trail Blazers			
☐ 246 Kevin Duckworth .... .03	.01	.00
Portland Trail Blazers			
☐ 247 Jerome Kersey .... .12	.06	.01
Portland Trail Blazers			
☐ 248 Drazen Petrovic .... .50	.25	.05
Portland Trail Blazers			
☐ 249A Terry Porter ERR .... .50	.25	.05
Portland Trail Blazers			
(No NBA symbol on back)			
☐ 249B Terry Porter COR .... .15	.07	.01
Portland Trail Blazers			
☐ 250 Cliff Robinson .... .40	.20	.04
Portland Trail Blazers			
☐ 251 Buck Williams .... .10	.05	.01
Portland Trail Blazers			
☐ 252 Danny Young .... .03	.01	.00
Portland Trail Blazers			
☐ 253 Danny Ainge SP .... .08	.04	.01
Sacramento Kings			
☐ 254 Randy Allen SP .... .10	.05	.01
Sacramento Kings			
☐ 255 Antoine Carr .... .06	.03	.00
Sacramento Kings			
☐ 256 Vinny Del Negro SP .... .08	.04	.01
Sacramento Kings			
☐ 257 Pervis Ellison SP .... .75	.35	.07
Sacramento Kings			
☐ 258 Greg Kite SP .... .06	.03	.00
Sacramento Kings			
☐ 259 Rodney McCray SP .... .08	.04	.01
Sacramento Kings			
☐ 260 Harold Pressley SP .... .08	.04	.01
Sacramento Kings			
☐ 261 Ralph Sampson .... .06	.03	.00
Sacramento Kings			
☐ 262 Wayman Tisdale .... .08	.04	.01
Sacramento Kings			
☐ 263 Willie Anderson .... .08	.04	.01
San Antonio Spurs			
☐ 264 Uwe Blab SP .... .06	.03	.00
San Antonio Spurs			
☐ 265 Frank Brickowski SP .... .06	.03	.00
San Antonio Spurs			
☐ 266 Terry Cummings .... .08	.04	.01
San Antonio Spurs			
☐ 267 Sean Elliott .... .40	.20	.04
San Antonio Spurs			
☐ 268 Caldwell Jones SP .... .06	.03	.00
San Antonio Spurs			
☐ 269 Johnny Moore SP .... .06	.03	.00
San Antonio Spurs			
☐ 270 David Robinson 1.25	.60	.12
San Antonio Spurs			

1990-91 Hoops I / 135

☐ 271 Rod Strickland	.08	.04	.01
San Antonio Spurs			
☐ 272 Reggie Williams	.06	.03	.00
San Antonio Spurs			
☐ 273 David Wingate SP	.06	.03	.00
San Antonio Spurs			
☐ 274 Dana Barros UER	.20	.10	.02
Seattle Supersonics			
(Born April, not March)			
☐ 275 Michael Cage UER	.03	.01	.00
Seattle Supersonics			
(Drafted '84, not '85)			
☐ 276 Quintin Dailey	.03	.01	.00
Seattle Supersonics			
☐ 277 Dale Ellis	.06	.03	.00
Seattle Supersonics			
☐ 278 Steve Johnson SP	.06	.03	.00
Seattle Supersonics			
☐ 279 Shawn Kemp	1.50	.75	.15
Seattle Supersonics			
☐ 280 Xavier McDaniel	.10	.05	.01
Seattle Supersonics			
☐ 281 Derrick McKey	.06	.03	.00
Seattle Supersonics			
☐ 282 Nate McMillan	.03	.01	.00
Seattle Supersonics			
☐ 283 Olden Polynice	.03	.01	.00
Seattle Supersonics			
☐ 284 Sedale Threatt	.06	.03	.00
Seattle Supersonics			
☐ 285 Thurl Bailey	.06	.03	.00
Utah Jazz			
☐ 286 Mike Brown	.03	.01	.00
Utah Jazz			
☐ 287 Mark Eaton UER	.06	.03	.00
Utah Jazz			
(72nd pick, not 82nd)			
☐ 288 Blue Edwards	.20	.10	.02
Utah Jazz			
☐ 289 Darrell Griffith	.03	.01	.00
Utah Jazz			
☐ 290 Robert Hansen SP	.06	.03	.00
Utah Jazz			
☐ 291 Eric Leckner SP	.08	.04	.01
Utah Jazz			
☐ 292 Karl Malone	.25	.12	.02
Utah Jazz			
☐ 293 Delaney Rudd	.08	.04	.01
Utah Jazz			
☐ 294 John Stockton	.25	.12	.02
Utah Jazz			
☐ 295 Mark Alarie	.03	.01	.00
Washington Bullets			
☐ 296 Ledell Eackles SP	.10	.05	.01
Washington Bullets			
☐ 297 Harvey Grant	.06	.03	.00
Washington Bullets			
☐ 298A Tom Hammonds	.15	.07	.01

136 / 1990-91 Hoops I

Washington Bullets (No rookie logo on front)			
☐ 298B Tom Hammonds	.15	.07	.01
Washington Bullets (Rookie logo on front)			
☐ 299 Charles Jones	.03	.01	.00
Washington Bullets			
☐ 300 Bernard King	.08	.04	.01
Washington Bullets			
☐ 301 Jeff Malone SP	.12	.06	.01
Washington Bullets			
☐ 302 Mel Turpin SP	.08	.04	.01
Washington Bullets			
☐ 303 Darrell Walker	.03	.01	.00
Washington Bullets			
☐ 304 John Williams	.03	.01	.00
Washington Bullets			
☐ 305 Bob Weiss CO	.03	.01	.00
Atlanta Hawks			
☐ 306 Chris Ford CO	.03	.01	.00
Boston Celtics			
☐ 307 Gene Littles CO	.03	.01	.00
Charlotte Hornets			
☐ 308 Phil Jackson CO	.03	.01	.00
Chicago Bulls			
☐ 309 Lenny Wilkens CO	.08	.04	.01
Cleveland Cavaliers			
☐ 310 Richie Adubato CO	.03	.01	.00
Dallas Mavericks			
☐ 311 Doug Moe CO SP	.10	.05	.01
Denver Nuggets			
☐ 312 Chuck Daly CO	.06	.03	.00
Detroit Pistons			
☐ 313 Don Nelson CO	.03	.01	.00
Golden State Warriors			
☐ 314 Don Chaney CO	.03	.01	.00
Houston Rockets			
☐ 315 Dick Versace CO	.03	.01	.00
Indiana Pacers			
☐ 316 Mike Schuler CO	.03	.01	.00
Los Angeles Clippers			
☐ 317 Pat Riley CO SP	.10	.05	.01
Los Angeles Lakers			
☐ 318 Ron Rothstein CO	.03	.01	.00
Miami Heat			
☐ 319 Del Harris CO	.03	.01	.00
Milwaukee Bucks			
☐ 320 Bill Musselman CO	.03	.01	.00
Minnesota Timberwolves			
☐ 321 Bill Fitch CO	.03	.01	.00
New Jersey Nets			
☐ 322 Stu Jackson CO	.03	.01	.00
New York Knicks			
☐ 323 Matt Guokas CO	.03	.01	.00
Orlando Magic			
☐ 324 Jim Lynam CO	.03	.01	.00
Philadelphia 76ers			
☐ 325 Cotton Fitzsimmons CO	.03	.01	.00

		Phoenix Suns			
☐	326	Rick Adelman CO	.06	.03	.00
		Portland Trail Blazers			
☐	327	Dick Motta CO	.03	.01	.00
		Sacramento Kings			
☐	328	Larry Brown CO	.03	.01	.00
		San Antonio Spurs			
☐	329	K.C. Jones CO	.08	.04	.01
		Seattle Supersonics			
☐	330	Jerry Sloan CO	.03	.01	.00
		Utah Jazz			
☐	331	Wes Unseld CO	.06	.03	.00
		Washington Bullets			
☐	332	Checklist 1 SP	.08	.04	.01
☐	333	Checklist 2 SP	.08	.04	.01
☐	334	Checklist 3 SP	.08	.04	.01
☐	335	Checklist 4 SP	.08	.04	.01
☐	336	Danny Ferry SP	.25	.12	.02
		Cleveland Cavaliers			
☐	NNO	David Robinson and	2.25	1.10	.22
		All-Rookie Team			
		(No stats on back)			
☐	NNO	David Robinson and	15.00	7.50	1.50
		All-Rookie Team			
		(Stats on back)			

1990-91 Hoops II

The design of the cards in the 104-card Hoops II set is identical to that of the first series. This set features NBA finals (337-342), coaches (343-354), team checklists (355-381), inside stuff (382-385), stay in school (386-387), don't foul out (388-389), lottery selections (390-400), and updates (401-438). The cards are standard size (2 1/2" by 3 1/2") and are numbered on the back in

138 / 1990-91 Hoops II

continuation of the first series. The key rookies in the set are the eleven lottery picks (390-400) led by Derrick Coleman, Kendall Gill, and Lionel Simmons.

	MINT	EXC	G-VG
COMPLETE SET (104)	6.00	3.00	.60
COMMON PLAYER (337-440)	.03	.01	.00
☐ 337 NBA Final Game 1	.06	.03	.00
☐ 338 NBA Final Game 2	.06	.03	.00
☐ 339 NBA Final Game 3	.06	.03	.00
☐ 340 NBA Final Game 4	.06	.03	.00
☐ 341A NBA Final Game 5 ERR	.10	.05	.01
(No headline on back)			
☐ 341B NBA Final Game 5 COR	.10	.05	.01
☐ 342 Championship Card UER	.10	.05	.01
(Player named as Sidney Green is really David Greenwood)			
☐ 343 K.C. Jones CO	.06	.03	.00
Seattle Supersonics			
☐ 344 Wes Unseld CO	.06	.03	.00
Washington Bullets			
☐ 345 Don Nelson CO	.03	.01	.00
Golden State Warriors			
☐ 346 Bob Weiss CO	.03	.01	.00
Atlanta Hawks			
☐ 347 Chris Ford CO	.03	.01	.00
Boston Celtics			
☐ 348 Phil Jackson CO	.06	.03	.00
Chicago Bulls			
☐ 349 Lenny Wilkens CO	.06	.03	.00
Cleveland Cavaliers			
☐ 350 Don Chaney CO	.03	.01	.00
Houston Rockets			
☐ 351 Mike Dunleavy CO	.03	.01	.00
Los Angeles Lakers			
☐ 352 Matt Guokas CO	.03	.01	.00
Orlando Magic			
☐ 353 Rick Adelman CO	.06	.03	.00
Portland Trail Blazers			
☐ 354 Jerry Sloan CO	.03	.01	.00
Utah Jazz			
☐ 355 Dominique Wilkins TC	.08	.04	.01
Atlanta Hawks			
☐ 356 Larry Bird TC	.15	.07	.01
Boston Celtics			
☐ 357 Rex Chapman TC	.06	.03	.00
Charlotte Hornets			
☐ 358 Michael Jordan TC	.50	.25	.05
Chicago Bulls			
☐ 359 Mark Price TC	.08	.04	.01
Cleveland Cavaliers			
☐ 360 Rolando Blackman TC	.06	.03	.00
Dallas Mavericks			
☐ 361 Michael Adams TC	.06	.03	.00
Denver Nuggets			
☐ 362 Joe Dumars TC UER	.08	.04	.01
Detroit Pistons			

1990-91 Hoops II / 139

(Gerald Henderson's name
and number not listed)
- ☐ 363 Chris Mullin TC .... .12 .06 .01
  Golden State Warriors
- ☐ 364 Hakeem Olajuwon TC .... .12 .06 .01
  Houston Rockets
- ☐ 365 Reggie Miller TC .... .08 .04 .01
  Indiana Pacers
- ☐ 366 Danny Manning TC .... .08 .04 .01
  Los Angeles Clippers
- ☐ 367 Magic Johnson TC UER .... .35 .17 .03
  Los Angeles Lakers
  (Dunleavy listed as 439,
  should be 351)
- ☐ 368 Rony Seikaly TC .... .08 .04 .01
  Miami Heat
- ☐ 369 Alvin Robertson TC .... .06 .03 .00
  Milwaukee Bucks
- ☐ 370 Pooh Richardson TC .... .10 .05 .01
  Minnesota Timberwolves
- ☐ 371 Chris Morris TC .... .06 .03 .00
  New Jersey Nets
- ☐ 372 Patrick Ewing TC .... .15 .07 .01
  New York Knicks
- ☐ 373 Nick Anderson TC .... .12 .06 .01
  Orlando Magic
- ☐ 374 Charles Barkley TC .... .12 .06 .01
  Philadelphia 76ers
- ☐ 375 Kevin Johnson TC .... .12 .06 .01
  Phoenix Suns
- ☐ 376 Clyde Drexler TC .... .15 .07 .01
  Portland Trail Blazers
- ☐ 377 Wayman Tisdale TC .... .06 .03 .00
  Sacramento Kings
- ☐ 378A David Robinson TC .... .50 .25 .05
  San Antonio Spurs
  (basketball fully
  visible)
- ☐ 378A David Robinson TC .... .50 .25 .05
  San Antonio Spurs
  (basketball partially
  visible)
- ☐ 379 Xavier McDaniel TC .... .06 .03 .00
  Seattle Supersonics
- ☐ 380 Karl Malone TC .... .12 .06 .01
  Utah Jazz
- ☐ 381 Bernard King TC .... .06 .03 .00
  Washington Bullets
  Inside Stuff
- ☐ 382 Michael Jordan .... .75 .35 .07
  Playground
- ☐ 383 Lights, Camera, ... .12 .06 .01
  NBA Action
  (Karl Malone
  on horseback)
- ☐ 384 European Imports .... .10 .05 .01
  (Vlade Divac and
  Sarunas Marciulionis)

140 / 1990-91 Hoops II

☐ 385 Super Streaks	1.00	.50	.10
Stay In School			
(Magic Johnson and			
Michael Jordan)			
☐ 386 Johnny Newman	.06	.03	.00
Charlotte Hornets			
(Stay in School)			
☐ 387 Dell Curry	.06	.03	.00
Charlotte Hornets			
(Stay in School)			
☐ 388 Patrick Ewing	.15	.07	.01
New York Knicks			
(Don't Foul Out)			
☐ 389 Isiah Thomas	.08	.04	.01
Detroit Pistons			
(Don't Foul Out)			
☐ 390 Derrick Coleman LS	1.50	.75	.15
New Jersey Nets			
☐ 391 Gary Payton LS	.50	.25	.05
Seattle Supersonics			
☐ 392 Chris Jackson LS	.25	.12	.02
Denver Nuggets			
☐ 393 Dennis Scott LS	.50	.25	.05
Los Angeles Lakers			
☐ 394 Kendall Gill LS	2.00	1.00	.20
Charlotte Hornets			
☐ 395 Felton Spencer LS	.15	.07	.01
Minnesota Timberwolves			
☐ 396 Lionel Simmons LS	.75	.35	.07
Sacramento Kings			
☐ 397 Bo Kimble LS	.10	.05	.01
Los Angeles Clippers			
☐ 398 Willie Burton LS	.20	.10	.02
Miami Heat			
☐ 399 Rumeal Robinson LS	.20	.10	.02
Atlanta Hawks			
☐ 400 Tyrone Hill LS	.20	.10	.02
Golden State Warriors			
☐ 401 Tim McCormick	.03	.01	.00
Atlanta Hawks			
☐ 402 Sidney Moncrief	.06	.03	.00
Atlanta Hawks			
☐ 403 Johnny Newman	.06	.03	.00
Charlotte Hornets			
☐ 404 Dennis Hopson	.06	.03	.00
Chicago Bulls			
☐ 405 Cliff Levingston	.03	.01	.00
Chicago Bulls			
☐ 406 Danny Ferry	.08	.04	.01
Cleveland Cavaliers			
☐ 407 Alex English	.08	.04	.01
Dallas Mavericks			
☐ 408 Lafayette Lever	.06	.03	.00
Dallas Mavericks			
☐ 409 Rodney McCray	.03	.01	.00
Dallas Mavericks			
☐ 410 Mike Dunleavy CO	.03	.01	.00
Los Angeles Lakers			

1990-91 Hoops II / 141

☐ 411 Orlando Woolridge Denver Nuggets	.06	.03	.00
☐ 412 Joe Wolf Denver Nuggets	.03	.01	.00
☐ 413 Tree Rollins Detroit Pistons	.03	.01	.00
☐ 414 Kenny Smith Houston Rockets	.06	.03	.00
☐ 415 Sam Perkins Los Angeles Lakers	.10	.05	.01
☐ 416 Terry Teagle Los Angeles Lakers	.03	.01	.00
☐ 417 Frank Brickowski Milwaukee Bucks	.03	.01	.00
☐ 418 Danny Schayes Milwaukee Bucks	.03	.01	.00
☐ 419 Scott Brooks Minnesota Timberwolves	.03	.01	.00
☐ 420 Reggie Theus New Jersey Nets	.06	.03	.00
☐ 421 Greg Grant New York Knicks	.03	.01	.00
☐ 422 Paul Westhead CO Denver Nuggets	.03	.01	.00
☐ 423 Greg Kite Orlando Magic	.03	.01	.00
☐ 424 Manute Bol Philadelphia 76ers	.03	.01	.00
☐ 425 Rickey Green Philadelphia 76ers	.03	.01	.00
☐ 426 Ed Nealy Phoenix Suns	.03	.01	.00
☐ 427 Danny Ainge Portland Trail Blazers	.06	.03	.00
☐ 428 Bobby Hansen Sacramento Kings	.03	.01	.00
☐ 429 Eric Leckner Charlotte Hornets	.06	.03	.00
☐ 430 Rory Sparrow Sacramento Kings	.03	.01	.00
☐ 431 Bill Wennington Sacramento Kings	.03	.01	.00
☐ 432 Paul Pressey San Antonio Spurs	.03	.01	.00
☐ 433 David Greenwood San Antonio Spurs	.03	.01	.00
☐ 434 Mark McNamara Orlando Magic	.03	.01	.00
☐ 435 Sidney Green Orlando Magic	.03	.01	.00
☐ 436 Dave Corzine Orlando Magic	.03	.01	.00
☐ 437 Jeff Malone Utah Jazz	.10	.05	.01
☐ 438 Pervis Ellison Washington Bullets	.35	.17	.03
☐ 439 Checklist 5	.06	.01	.00
☐ 440 Checklist 6	.06	.01	.00

142 / 1991-92 Hoops I

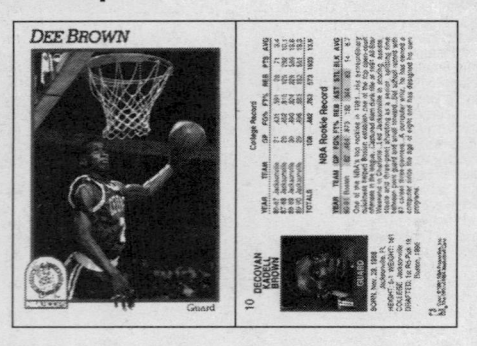

1991-92 Hoops I

The 1991-92 Hoops I basketball set contains 330 cards measuring the standard size (2 1/2" by 3 1/2"). The fronts feature color action player photos, with different color borders on a white card face. The player's name is printed in black lettering in the upper left corner, and the team logo is superimposed over the lower left corner of the picture. In a horizontal format the backs have color head shots and biographical information on the left side, while the right side presents college and pro statistics. The cards are numbered on the back and checklisted below alphabetically within and according to teams as follows: Atlanta Hawks (1-8), Boston Celtics (9-17), Charlotte Hornets (18-25), Chicago Bulls (26-34), Cleveland Cavaliers (35-42), Dallas Mavericks (43-50), Denver Nuggets (51-58), Detroit Pistons (59-66), Golden State Warriors (67-74), Houston Rockets (75-82), Indiana Pacers (83-90), Los Angeles Clippers (91-98), Los Angeles Lakers (99-106), Miami Heat (107-114), Milwaukee Bucks (115-122), Minnesota Timberwolves (123-130), New Jersey Nets (131-138), New York Knicks (139-146), Orlando Magic (147-154), Philadelphia 76ers (155-162), Phoenix Suns (163-170), Portland Trail Blazers (171-179), Sacramento Kings (180-187), San Antonio Spurs (188-196), Seattle Supersonics (197-204), Utah Jazz (205-212), and Washington Bullets (213-220). Other subsets included in this set are coaches (221-247), All-Stars East (248-260), All-Stars West (261-273), teams (274-300), Centennial Card honoring James Naismith (301), Inside Stuff (302-305), League Leaders (306-313), Milestones (314-318), NBA yearbook (319-324), Stay in School (325-326), Don't Drive and Drink (327), and Checklists (328-330). There are no key rookie cards in this series. A special short-printed Naismith card, numbered CC1, was inserted into wax packs. It features a colorized photo of Dr. Naismith standing between two peach baskets like those used in the first basketball game. The back narrates the invention of the game of basketball. An unnumbered Centennial Card featuring the Centennial Logo was also available via a mail-in offer.

	MINT	EXC	G-VG
COMPLETE SET (330)	8.00	4.00	.80
COMMON PLAYER (1-330)	.03	.01	.00
☐ 1 John Battle	.06	.03	.00
☐ 2 Moses Malone UER	.10	.05	.01
(119 rebounds 1982-83, should be 1194)			

1991-92 Hoops I / 143

☐ 3	Sidney Moncrief	.06	.03	.00
☐ 4	Doc Rivers	.06	.03	.00
☐ 5	Rumeal Robinson UER	.06	.03	.00
	(Back says 11th pick in 1990, should be 10th)			
☐ 6	Spud Webb	.06	.03	.00
☐ 7	Dominique Wilkins	.12	.06	.01
☐ 8	Kevin Willis	.08	.04	.01
☐ 9	Larry Bird	.25	.12	.02
☐ 10	Dee Brown	.25	.12	.02
☐ 11	Kevin Gamble	.06	.03	.00
☐ 12	Joe Kleine	.03	.01	.00
☐ 13	Reggie Lewis	.12	.06	.01
☐ 14	Kevin McHale	.08	.04	.01
☐ 15	Robert Parish	.10	.05	.01
☐ 16	Ed Pinckney	.03	.01	.00
☐ 17	Brian Shaw	.06	.03	.00
☐ 18	Muggsy Bogues	.03	.01	.00
☐ 19	Rex Chapman	.06	.03	.00
☐ 20	Dell Curry	.03	.01	.00
☐ 21	Kendall Gill	.50	.25	.05
☐ 22	Mike Gminski	.03	.01	.00
☐ 23	Johnny Newman	.03	.01	.00
☐ 24	J.R. Reid	.06	.03	.00
☐ 25	Kelly Tripucka	.03	.01	.00
☐ 26	B.J. Armstrong	.10	.05	.01
	(B.J. on front, Benjamin Roy on back)			
☐ 27	Bill Cartwright	.06	.03	.00
☐ 28	Horace Grant	.10	.05	.01
☐ 29	Craig Hodges	.03	.01	.00
☐ 30	Michael Jordan	1.00	.50	.10
☐ 31	Stacey King	.06	.03	.00
☐ 32	Cliff Levingston	.03	.01	.00
☐ 33	John Paxson	.06	.03	.00
☐ 34	Scottie Pippen	.30	.15	.03
☐ 35	Chucky Brown	.03	.01	.00
☐ 36	Brad Daugherty	.12	.06	.01
☐ 37	Craig Ehlo	.06	.03	.00
☐ 38	Danny Ferry	.06	.03	.00
☐ 39	Larry Nance	.08	.04	.01
☐ 40	Mark Price	.12	.06	.01
☐ 41	Darnell Valentine	.03	.01	.00
☐ 42	Hot Rod Williams	.06	.03	.00
☐ 43	Rolando Blackman	.06	.03	.00
☐ 44	Brad Davis	.03	.01	.00
☐ 45	James Donaldson	.03	.01	.00
☐ 46	Derek Harper	.06	.03	.00
☐ 47	Fat Lever	.06	.03	.00
☐ 48	Rodney McCray	.03	.01	.00
☐ 49	Roy Tarpley	.06	.03	.00
☐ 50	Herb Williams	.03	.01	.00
☐ 51	Michael Adams	.06	.03	.00
☐ 52	Chris Jackson UER	.08	.04	.01
	(Born in Mississippi, not Michigan)			
☐ 53	Jerome Lane	.03	.01	.00

144 / 1991-92 Hoops I

☐ 54	Todd Lichti	.03	.01	.00
☐ 55	Blair Rasmussen	.03	.01	.00
☐ 56	Reggie Williams	.06	.03	.00
☐ 57	Joe Wolf	.03	.01	.00
☐ 58	Orlando Woolridge	.06	.03	.00
☐ 59	Mark Aguirre	.06	.03	.00
☐ 60	Joe Dumars	.10	.05	.01
☐ 61	James Edwards	.03	.01	.00
☐ 62	Vinnie Johnson	.03	.01	.00
☐ 63	Bill Laimbeer	.06	.03	.00
☐ 64	Dennis Rodman	.10	.05	.01
☐ 65	John Salley	.06	.03	.00
☐ 66	Isiah Thomas	.12	.06	.01
☐ 67	Tim Hardaway	.50	.25	.05
☐ 68	Rod Higgins	.03	.01	.00
☐ 69	Tyrone Hill	.08	.04	.01
☐ 70	Alton Lister	.03	.01	.00
☐ 71	Sarunas Marciulionis	.12	.06	.01
☐ 72	Chris Mullin	.15	.07	.01
☐ 73	Mitch Richmond	.10	.05	.01
☐ 74	Tom Tolbert	.03	.01	.00
☐ 75	Eric(Sleepy) Floyd	.06	.03	.00
☐ 76	Buck Johnson	.03	.01	.00
☐ 77	Vernon Maxwell	.06	.03	.00
☐ 78	Hakeem Olajuwon	.12	.06	.01
☐ 79	Kenny Smith	.03	.01	.00
☐ 80	Larry Smith	.03	.01	.00
☐ 81	Otis Thorpe	.06	.03	.00
☐ 82	David Wood	.08	.04	.01
☐ 83	Vern Fleming	.03	.01	.00
☐ 84	Reggie Miller	.10	.05	.01
☐ 85	Chuck Person	.06	.03	.00
☐ 86	Mike Sanders	.06	.03	.00
☐ 87	Detlef Schrempf	.06	.03	.00
☐ 88	Rik Smits	.06	.03	.00
☐ 89	LaSalle Thompson	.03	.01	.00
☐ 90	Micheal Williams	.06	.03	.00
☐ 91	Winston Garland	.03	.01	.00
☐ 92	Gary Grant	.03	.01	.00
☐ 93	Ron Harper	.06	.03	.00
☐ 94	Danny Manning	.10	.05	.01
☐ 95	Jeff Martin	.03	.01	.00
☐ 96	Ken Norman	.06	.03	.00
☐ 97	Olden Polynice	.03	.01	.00
☐ 98	Charles Smith	.08	.04	.01
☐ 99	Vlade Divac	.10	.05	.01
☐ 100	A.C. Green	.06	.03	.00
☐ 101	Magic Johnson	.60	.30	.06
☐ 102	Sam Perkins	.08	.04	.01
☐ 103	Byron Scott	.06	.03	.00
☐ 104	Terry Teagle	.03	.01	.00
☐ 105	Mychal Thompson	.03	.01	.00
☐ 106	James Worthy	.10	.05	.01
☐ 107	Willie Burton	.06	.03	.00
☐ 108	Bimbo Coles	.10	.05	.01
☐ 109	Terry Davis	.06	.03	.00
☐ 110	Sherman Douglas	.06	.03	.00

1991-92 Hoops I / 145

☐ 111	Kevin Edwards	.03	.01	.00
☐ 112	Alec Kessler	.06	.03	.00
☐ 113	Glen Rice	.25	.12	.02
☐ 114	Rony Seikaly	.08	.04	.01
☐ 115	Frank Brickowski	.03	.01	.00
☐ 116	Dale Ellis	.06	.03	.00
☐ 117	Jay Humphries	.03	.01	.00
☐ 118	Brad Lohaus	.03	.01	.00
☐ 119	Fred Roberts	.03	.01	.00
☐ 120	Alvin Robertson	.06	.03	.00
☐ 121	Danny Schayes	.03	.01	.00
☐ 122	Jack Sikma	.06	.03	.00
☐ 123	Randy Breuer	.03	.01	.00
☐ 124	Tony Campbell	.03	.01	.00
☐ 125	Tyrone Corbin	.03	.01	.00
☐ 126	Gerald Glass	.12	.06	.01
☐ 127	Sam Mitchell	.03	.01	.00
☐ 128	Tod Murphy	.03	.01	.00
☐ 129	Pooh Richardson	.10	.05	.01
☐ 130	Felton Spencer	.06	.03	.00
☐ 131	Mookie Blaylock	.06	.03	.00
☐ 132	Sam Bowie	.06	.03	.00
☐ 133	Jud Buechler	.03	.01	.00
☐ 134	Derrick Coleman	.30	.15	.03
☐ 135	Chris Dudley	.03	.01	.00
☐ 136	Chris Morris	.06	.03	.00
☐ 137	Drazen Petrovic	.15	.07	.01
☐ 138	Reggie Theus	.06	.03	.00
☐ 139	Maurice Cheeks	.06	.03	.00
☐ 140	Patrick Ewing	.20	.10	.02
☐ 141	Mark Jackson	.06	.03	.00
☐ 142	Charles Oakley	.06	.03	.00
☐ 143	Trent Tucker	.03	.01	.00
☐ 144	Kiki Vandeweghe	.06	.03	.00
☐ 145	Kenny Walker	.03	.01	.00
☐ 146	Gerald Wilkins	.06	.03	.00
☐ 147	Nick Anderson	.12	.06	.01
☐ 148	Michael Ansley	.03	.01	.00
☐ 149	Terry Catledge	.03	.01	.00
☐ 150	Jerry Reynolds	.03	.01	.00
☐ 151	Dennis Scott	.10	.05	.01
☐ 152	Scott Skiles	.06	.03	.00
☐ 153	Otis Smith	.03	.01	.00
☐ 154	Sam Vincent	.03	.01	.00
☐ 155	Ron Anderson	.03	.01	.00
☐ 156	Charles Barkley	.15	.07	.01
☐ 157	Manute Bol	.03	.01	.00
☐ 158	Johnny Dawkins	.06	.03	.00
☐ 159	Armon Gilliam	.03	.01	.00
☐ 160	Rickey Green	.03	.01	.00
☐ 161	Hersey Hawkins	.08	.04	.01
☐ 162	Rick Mahorn	.06	.03	.00
☐ 163	Tom Chambers	.08	.04	.01
☐ 164	Jeff Hornacek	.10	.05	.01
☐ 165	Kevin Johnson	.15	.07	.01
☐ 166	Andrew Lang	.10	.05	.01
☐ 167	Dan Majerle	.10	.05	.01

146 / 1991-92 Hoops I

☐ 168 Xavier McDaniel	.08	.04	.01
☐ 169 Kurt Rambis	.06	.03	.00
☐ 170 Mark West	.03	.01	.00
☐ 171 Danny Ainge	.06	.03	.00
☐ 172 Mark Bryant	.03	.01	.00
☐ 173 Walter Davis	.06	.03	.00
☐ 174 Clyde Drexler	.20	.10	.02
☐ 175 Kevin Duckworth	.03	.01	.00
☐ 176 Jerome Kersey	.08	.04	.01
☐ 177 Terry Porter	.10	.05	.01
☐ 178 Cliff Robinson	.10	.05	.01
☐ 179 Buck Williams	.08	.04	.01
☐ 180 Anthony Bonner	.08	.04	.01
☐ 181 Antoine Carr	.03	.01	.00
☐ 182 Duane Causwell	.06	.03	.00
☐ 183 Bobby Hansen	.03	.01	.00
☐ 184 Travis Mays	.06	.03	.00
☐ 185 Lionel Simmons	.20	.10	.02
☐ 186 Rory Sparrow	.03	.01	.00
☐ 187 Wayman Tisdale	.06	.03	.00
☐ 188 Willie Anderson	.06	.03	.00
☐ 189 Terry Cummings	.08	.04	.01
☐ 190 Sean Elliott	.12	.06	.01
☐ 191 Sidney Green	.03	.01	.00
☐ 192 David Greenwood	.03	.01	.00
☐ 193 Paul Pressey	.03	.01	.00
☐ 194 David Robinson	.60	.30	.06
☐ 195 Dwayne Schintzius	.06	.03	.00
☐ 196 Rod Strickland	.06	.03	.00
☐ 197 Benoit Benjamin	.03	.01	.00
☐ 198 Michael Cage	.03	.01	.00
☐ 199 Eddie Johnson	.06	.03	.00
☐ 200 Shawn Kemp	.50	.25	.05
☐ 201 Derrick McKey	.06	.03	.00
☐ 202 Gary Payton	.10	.05	.01
☐ 203 Ricky Pierce	.06	.03	.00
☐ 204 Sedale Threatt	.06	.03	.00
☐ 205 Thurl Bailey	.03	.01	.00
☐ 206 Mike Brown	.03	.01	.00
☐ 207 Mark Eaton	.03	.01	.00
☐ 208 Blue Edwards UER (Forward/guard on front, guard on back)	.03	.01	.00
☐ 209 Darrell Griffith	.03	.01	.00
☐ 210 Jeff Malone	.08	.04	.01
☐ 211 Karl Malone	.15	.07	.01
☐ 212 John Stockton	.15	.07	.01
☐ 213 Ledell Eackles	.03	.01	.00
☐ 214 Pervis Ellison	.15	.07	.01
☐ 215 A.J. English	.10	.05	.01
☐ 216 Harvey Grant (Shown boxing out twin brother Horace)	.08	.04	.01
☐ 217 Charles Jones	.03	.01	.00
☐ 218 Bernard King	.06	.03	.00
☐ 219 Darrell Walker	.03	.01	.00
☐ 220 John Williams	.03	.01	.00

1991-92 Hoops I / 147

☐ 221	Bob Weiss CO	.03	.01	.00
☐ 222	Chris Ford CO	.03	.01	.00
☐ 223	Gene Littles CO	.03	.01	.00
☐ 224	Phil Jackson CO	.06	.03	.00
☐ 225	Lenny Wilkens CO	.06	.03	.00
☐ 226	Richie Adubato CO	.03	.01	.00
☐ 227	Paul Westhead CO	.03	.01	.00
☐ 228	Chuck Daly CO	.06	.03	.00
☐ 229	Don Nelson CO	.03	.01	.00
☐ 230	Don Chaney CO	.03	.01	.00
☐ 231	Bob Hill CO UER (Coached under Ted Owens, not Ted Owen)	.06	.03	.00
☐ 232	Mike Schuler CO	.03	.01	.00
☐ 233	Mike Dunleavy CO	.03	.01	.00
☐ 234	Kevin Loughery CO	.03	.01	.00
☐ 235	Del Harris CO	.03	.01	.00
☐ 236	Jimmy Rodgers CO	.03	.01	.00
☐ 237	Bill Fitch CO	.03	.01	.00
☐ 238	Pat Riley CO	.06	.03	.00
☐ 239	Matt Guokas CO	.03	.01	.00
☐ 240	Jim Lynam CO	.03	.01	.00
☐ 241	Cotton Fitzsimmons CO	.03	.01	.00
☐ 242	Rick Adelman CO	.06	.03	.00
☐ 243	Dick Motta CO	.03	.01	.00
☐ 244	Larry Brown CO	.06	.03	.00
☐ 245	K.C. Jones CO	.06	.03	.00
☐ 246	Jerry Sloan CO	.03	.01	.00
☐ 247	Wes Unseld CO	.06	.03	.00
☐ 248	Charles Barkley AS	.10	.05	.01
☐ 249	Brad Daugherty AS	.08	.04	.01
☐ 250	Joe Dumars AS	.08	.04	.01
☐ 251	Patrick Ewing AS	.10	.05	.01
☐ 252	Hersey Hawkins AS	.06	.03	.00
☐ 253	Michael Jordan AS	.40	.20	.04
☐ 254	Bernard King AS	.06	.03	.00
☐ 255	Kevin McHale AS	.08	.04	.01
☐ 256	Robert Parish AS	.08	.04	.01
☐ 257	Ricky Pierce AS	.06	.03	.00
☐ 258	Alvin Robertson AS	.03	.01	.00
☐ 259	Dominique Wilkins AS	.08	.04	.01
☐ 260	Chris Ford CO AS	.03	.01	.00
☐ 261	Tom Chambers AS	.06	.03	.00
☐ 262	Clyde Drexler AS	.12	.06	.01
☐ 263	Kevin Duckworth AS	.03	.01	.00
☐ 264	Tim Hardaway AS	.20	.10	.02
☐ 265	Kevin Johnson AS	.10	.05	.01
☐ 266	Magic Johnson AS	.30	.15	.03
☐ 267	Karl Malone AS	.10	.05	.01
☐ 268	Chris Mullen AS	.10	.05	.01
☐ 269	Terry Porter AS	.06	.03	.00
☐ 270	David Robinson AS	.20	.10	.02
☐ 271	John Stockton AS	.10	.05	.01
☐ 272	James Worthy AS	.08	.04	.01
☐ 273	Rick Adelman CO AS	.03	.01	.00
☐ 274	Atlanta Hawks Team Card UER	.06	.03	.00

148 / 1991-92 Hoops I

(Actually began as Tri-Cities Blackhawks)			
☐ 275 Boston Celtics .... .06		.03	.00
Team Card UER			
(No NBA Hoops logo on card front)			
☐ 276 Charlotte Hornets .... .06		.03	.00
Team Card			
☐ 277 Chicago Bulls .... .06		.03	.00
Team Card			
☐ 278 Cleveland Cavaliers .... .06		.03	.00
Team Card			
☐ 279 Dallas Mavericks .... .06		.03	.00
Team Card			
☐ 280 Denver Nuggets .... .06		.03	.00
Team Card			
☐ 281 Detroit Pistons .... .06		.03	.00
Team Card UER			
(Pistons not NBA Finalists until 1988; Ft. Wayne Pistons in Finals in 1955 and 1956)			
☐ 282 Golden State Warriors .... .06		.03	.00
Team Card			
☐ 283 Houston Rockets .... .06		.03	.00
Team Card			
☐ 284 Indiana Pacers .... .06		.03	.00
Team Card			
☐ 285 Los Angeles Clippers .... .06		.03	.00
Team Card			
☐ 286 Los Angeles Lakers .... .06		.03	.00
Team Card			
☐ 287 Miami Heat .... .06		.03	.00
Team Card			
☐ 288 Milwaukee Bucks .... .06		.03	.00
Team Card			
☐ 289 Minnesota Timberwolves .... .06		.03	.00
Team Card			
☐ 290 New Jersey Nets .... .06		.03	.00
Team Card			
☐ 291 New York Knicks .... .06		.03	.00
Team Card UER			
(Golden State not mentioned as an active charter member of NBA)			
☐ 292 Orlando Magic .... .06		.03	.00
Team Card			
☐ 293 Philadelphia 76ers .... .06		.03	.00
Team Card			
☐ 294 Phoenix Suns .... .06		.03	.00
Team Card			
☐ 295 Portland Trail Blazers .... .06		.03	.00
Team Card			
☐ 296 Sacramento Kings .... .06		.03	.00
Team Card			
☐ 297 San Antonio Spurs .... .06		.03	.00
Team Card			

1991-92 Hoops I / 149

☐ 298 Seattle Supersonics Team Card	.06	.03	.00
☐ 299 Utah Jazz Team Card	.06	.03	.00
☐ 300 Washington Bullets Team Card	.06	.03	.00
☐ 301 Centennial Card James Naismith	.10	.05	.01
☐ 302 Kevin Johnson IS	.10	.05	.01
☐ 303 Reggie Miller IS	.08	.04	.01
☐ 304 Hakeem Olajuwon IS	.08	.04	.01
☐ 305 Robert Parish IS	.08	.04	.01
☐ 306 Scoring Leaders Michael Jordan Karl Malone	.35	.17	.03
☐ 307 3-Point FG Percent League Leaders Jim Les Trent Tucker	.06	.03	.00
☐ 308 Free Throw Percent League Leaders Reggie Miller Jeff Malone	.06	.03	.00
☐ 309 Blocks League Leaders Hakeem Olajuwon David Robinson	.20	.10	.02
☐ 310 Steals League Leaders Alvin Robertson John Stockton	.06	.03	.00
☐ 311 Rebounds LL UER David Robinson Dennis Rodman (Robinson credited as playing for Houston)	.15	.07	.01
☐ 312 Assists League Leaders John Stockton Magic Johnson	.20	.10	.02
☐ 313 Field Goal Percent League Leaders Buck Williams Robert Parish	.06	.03	.00
☐ 314 Larry Bird UER Milestone (Should be card 315 to fit Milestone sequence)	.15	.07	.01
☐ 315 A.English/M.Malone Milestone UER (Should be card 314 and be a League Leader card)	.08	.04	.01
☐ 316 Magic Johnson Milestone	.30	.15	.03
☐ 317 Michael Jordan Milestone	.40	.20	.04
☐ 318 Moses Malone Milestone	.08	.04	.01
☐ 319 Larry Bird NBA Yearbook	.15	.07	.01

150 / 1991-92 Hoops I

☐ 320 Maurice Cheeks NBA Yearbook Look Back	.06	.03	.00
☐ 321 Magic Johnson NBA Yearbook Look Back	.30	.15	.03
☐ 322 Bernard King NBA Yearbook Look Back	.06	.03	.00
☐ 323 Moses Malone NBA Yearbook Look Back	.08	.04	.01
☐ 324 Robert Parish NBA Yearbook Look Back	.08	.04	.01
☐ 325 All-Star Jam Jammin' With Will Smith (Stay in School)	.06	.03	.00
☐ 326 All-Star Jam Jammin' With The Boys and Will Smith (Stay in School)	.06	.03	.00
☐ 327 David Robinson Leave Alcohol Out	.25	.12	.02
☐ 328 Checklist 1	.06	.01	.00
☐ 329 Checklist 2 UER (Card front is from 330)	.06	.01	.00
☐ 330 Checklist 3 UER (Card front is from 329; card 327 listed oper- ation, should be celebration)	.06	.01	.00
☐ CC1 Dr.James Naismith SP	5.00	2.50	.50
☐ NNO Centennial Card (Sendaway)	.50	.25	.05

1991-92 Hoops Slam Dunk Champions

The six-card subset features the winners of the All-Star weekend slam dunk competition from 1986 to 1991. The cards measure the standard size (2 1/2" by 3 1/2") and were only available in first series 47-card rack packs. The front has a color photo of the player dunking the ball, with royal blue borders on a white card face. The player's name appears in orange lettering in a purple stripe above the picture, and the year the player won is given in a "Slam Dunk Champion" emblem overlaying the lower left corner of the picture. The design of the back is similar to the front, only with an extended caption on a yellow-green background. A drawing of a basketball entering a rim appears at the upper left corner. The cards are numbered on the back by Roman numerals.

	MINT	EXC	G-VG
COMPLETE SET (6)	4.00	2.00	.40
COMMON PLAYER (1-6)	.30	.15	.03

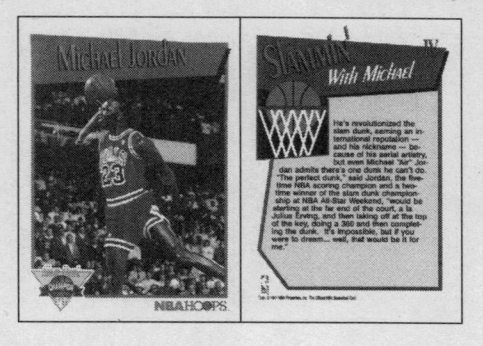

☐ 1 Larry Nance (Numbered I)	.40	.20	.04
☐ 2 Dominique Wilkins (Numbered II)	1.00	.50	.10
☐ 3 Spud Webb (Numbered III)	.30	.15	.03
☐ 4 Michael Jordan (Numbered IV)	3.00	1.50	.30
☐ 5 Kenny Walker (Numbered V)	.30	.15	.03
☐ 6 Dee Brown (Numbered VI)	1.00	.50	.10

1991-92 Hoops II

The 1991-92 Hoops II basketball set contains 260 cards measuring the standard size (2 1/2" by 3 1/2"). Series II packs also featured a randomly packed Gold Foil USA Basketball logo card. On a white card face, the fronts feature color player photos inside different color frames. The player's name appears above the picture, while the team logo appears at the lower left corner. In a horizontal format, the backs have a color head shot, biography, and complete statistics (college and pro). The cards are numbered on the back and checklisted below alphabetically according to and within teams as follows: Atlanta Hawks (331-337), Boston Celtics (338-341), Charlotte Hornets (342-344), Chicago Bulls (345-346), Cleveland Cavaliers (347-351), Dallas Mavericks (352-353), Denver Nuggets (354-359), Detroit Pistons (360-367), Houston Rockets (368-371), Indiana Pacers (372-375), Los Angeles Clippers (376-381), Los Angeles Lakers (382-385), Miami Heat (386-389), Milwaukee Bucks (390-394), Minnesota Timberwolves (395-397), New Jersey Nets (398-401), New York Knicks (402-406), Orlando Magic (407-410), Philadelphia 76ers (411-416), Phoenix Suns (417-422), Portland Trail Blazers (423-425), Sacramento Kings (426-431), San Antonio Spurs (432-437), Seattle Supersonics (438-441), Utah Jazz (442), and

152 / 1991-92 Hoops II

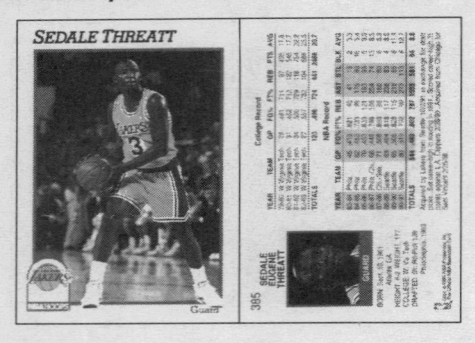

Washington Bullets (443-448). The set includes the following special cards and subsets: Supreme Court (449-502), Art Cards (503-529), Active Leaders (530-537), NBA Hoops Tribune (538-543), Stay in School (544-545), Draft Picks (546-556), USA Basketball 1976 (557), USA Basketball 1984 (558-564), USA Basketball 1988 (565-574), and USA Basketball 1992 (575-588). The key rookie cards in this series are Stacey Augmon, Larry Johnson, Dikembe Mutumbo, Billy Owens, and Steve Smith. A special individually numbered (out of 10,000) "Head of the Class" (showing the top six draft picks from 1991) card was made available to the first 10,000 fans requesting one along with three wrappers from each series of 1991-92 Hoops cards.

	MINT	EXC	G-VG
COMPLETE SET (260)	16.00	8.00	1.60
COMMON PLAYER (331-590)	.03	.01	.00
☐ 331 Maurice Cheeks	.06	.03	.00
☐ 332 Duane Ferrell	.03	.01	.00
☐ 333 Jon Koncak	.03	.01	.00
☐ 334 Gary Leonard	.08	.04	.01
☐ 335 Travis Mays	.06	.03	.00
☐ 336 Blair Rasmussen	.03	.01	.00
☐ 337 Alexander Volkov	.06	.03	.00
☐ 338 John Bagley	.06	.03	.00
☐ 339 Rickey Green UER	.03	.01	.00
(Ricky on front)			
☐ 340 Derek Smith	.03	.01	.00
☐ 341 Stojko Vrankovic	.10	.05	.01
☐ 342 Anthony Frederick	.15	.07	.01
☐ 343 Kenny Gattison	.06	.03	.00
☐ 344 Eric Leckner	.03	.01	.00
☐ 345 Will Perdue	.03	.01	.00
☐ 346 Scott Williams	.25	.12	.02
☐ 347 John Battle	.03	.01	.00
☐ 348 Winston Bennett	.03	.01	.00
☐ 349 Henry James	.08	.04	.01
☐ 350 Steve Kerr	.03	.01	.00
☐ 351 John Morton	.03	.01	.00

☐	352	Terry Davis	.06	.03	.00
☐	353	Randy White	.03	.01	.00
☐	354	Greg Anderson	.03	.01	.00
☐	355	Anthony Cook	.06	.03	.00
☐	356	Walter Davis	.06	.03	.00
☐	357	Winston Garland	.03	.01	.00
☐	358	Scott Hastings	.03	.01	.00
☐	359	Marcus Liberty	.15	.07	.01
☐	360	William Bedford	.03	.01	.00
☐	361	Lance Blanks	.06	.03	.00
☐	362	Brad Sellers	.03	.01	.00
☐	363	Darrell Walker	.03	.01	.00
☐	364	Orlando Woolridge	.06	.03	.00
☐	365	Vincent Askew	.10	.05	.01
☐	366	Mario Elie	.15	.07	.01
☐	367	Jim Petersen	.03	.01	.00
☐	368	Matt Bullard	.12	.06	.01
☐	369	Gerald Henderson	.03	.01	.00
☐	370	Dave Jamerson	.06	.03	.00
☐	371	Tree Rollins	.03	.01	.00
☐	372	Greg Dreiling	.03	.01	.00
☐	373	George McCloud	.06	.03	.00
☐	374	Kenny Williams	.03	.01	.00
☐	375	Randy Wittman	.03	.01	.00
☐	376	Tony Brown	.03	.01	.00
☐	377	Lanard Copeland	.03	.01	.00
☐	378	James Edwards	.03	.01	.00
☐	379	Bo Kimble	.06	.03	.00
☐	380	Doc Rivers	.06	.03	.00
☐	381	Loy Vaught	.10	.05	.01
☐	382	Elden Campbell	.10	.05	.01
☐	383	Jack Haley	.03	.01	.00
☐	384	Tony Smith	.06	.03	.00
☐	385	Sedale Threatt	.06	.03	.00
☐	386	Keith Askins	.08	.04	.01
☐	387	Grant Long	.03	.01	.00
☐	388	Alan Ogg	.08	.04	.01
☐	389	Jon Sundvold	.03	.01	.00
☐	390	Lester Conner	.03	.01	.00
☐	391	Jeff Grayer	.03	.01	.00
☐	392	Steve Henson	.03	.01	.00
☐	393	Larry Krystkowiak	.03	.01	.00
☐	394	Moses Malone	.10	.05	.01
☐	395	Scott Brooks	.03	.01	.00
☐	396	Tellis Frank	.03	.01	.00
☐	397	Doug West	.06	.03	.00
☐	398	Rafael Addison	.10	.05	.01
☐	399	Dave Feitl	.08	.04	.01
☐	400	Tate George	.06	.03	.00
☐	401	Terry Mills	.12	.06	.01
☐	402	Tim McCormick	.03	.01	.00
☐	403	Xavier McDaniel	.08	.04	.01
☐	404	Anthony Mason	.25	.12	.02
☐	405	Brian Quinnett	.03	.01	.00
☐	406	John Starks	.50	.25	.05
☐	407	Mark Acres	.03	.01	.00
☐	408	Greg Kite	.03	.01	.00

154 / 1991-92 Hoops II

☐ 409	Jeff Turner	.03	.01	.00
☐ 410	Morlon Wiley	.03	.01	.00
☐ 411	Dave Hoppen	.03	.01	.00
☐ 412	Brian Oliver	.06	.03	.00
☐ 413	Kenny Payne	.03	.01	.00
☐ 414	Charles Shackleford	.03	.01	.00
☐ 415	Mitchell Wiggins	.03	.01	.00
☐ 416	Jayson Williams	.06	.03	.00
☐ 417	Cedric Ceballos	.12	.06	.01
☐ 418	Negele Knight	.08	.04	.01
☐ 419	Andrew Lang	.06	.03	.00
☐ 420	Jerrod Mustaf	.08	.04	.01
☐ 421	Ed Nealy	.03	.01	.00
☐ 422	Tim Perry	.06	.03	.00
☐ 423	Alaa Abdelnaby	.08	.04	.01
☐ 424	Wayne Cooper	.03	.01	.00
☐ 425	Danny Young	.03	.01	.00
☐ 426	Dennis Hopson	.06	.03	.00
☐ 427	Les Jepsen	.03	.01	.00
☐ 428	Jim Les	.08	.04	.01
☐ 429	Mitch Richmond	.10	.05	.01
☐ 430	Dwayne Schintzius	.06	.03	.00
☐ 431	Spud Webb	.06	.03	.00
☐ 432	Jud Buechler	.06	.03	.00
☐ 433	Antoine Carr	.03	.01	.00
☐ 434	Tom Garrick	.03	.01	.00
☐ 435	Sean Higgins	.10	.05	.01
☐ 436	Avery Johnson	.03	.01	.00
☐ 437	Tony Massenburg	.03	.01	.00
☐ 438	Dana Barros	.06	.03	.00
☐ 439	Quintin Dailey	.03	.01	.00
☐ 440	Bart Kofoed	.08	.04	.01
☐ 441	Nate McMillan	.03	.01	.00
☐ 442	Delaney Rudd	.03	.01	.00
☐ 443	Michael Adams	.08	.04	.01
☐ 444	Mark Alarie	.03	.01	.00
☐ 445	Greg Foster	.03	.01	.00
☐ 446	Tom Hammonds	.06	.03	.00
☐ 447	Andre Turner	.08	.04	.01
☐ 448	David Wingate	.03	.01	.00
☐ 449	Dominique Wilkins SC	.08	.04	.01
☐ 450	Kevin Willis SC	.06	.03	.00
☐ 451	Larry Bird SC	.15	.07	.01
☐ 452	Robert Parish SC	.08	.04	.01
☐ 453	Rex Chapman SC	.06	.03	.00
☐ 454	Kendall Gill SC	.25	.12	.02
☐ 455	Michael Jordan SC	.40	.20	.04
☐ 456	Scottie Pippen SC	.15	.07	.01
☐ 457	Brad Daugherty SC	.08	.04	.01
☐ 458	Larry Nance SC	.06	.03	.00
☐ 459	Rolando Blackman SC	.06	.03	.00
☐ 460	Derek Harper SC	.06	.03	.00
☐ 461	Chris Jackson SC	.06	.03	.00
☐ 462	Todd Lichti SC	.03	.01	.00
☐ 463	Joe Dumars SC	.08	.04	.01
☐ 464	Isiah Thomas SC	.08	.04	.01
☐ 465	Tim Hardaway SC	.20	.10	.02

1991-92 Hoops II / 155

☐ 466	Chris Mullin SC	.10	.05	.01
☐ 467	Hakeem Olajuwon SC	.08	.04	.01
☐ 468	Otis Thorpe SC	.03	.01	.00
☐ 469	Reggie Miller SC	.08	.04	.01
☐ 470	Detlef Schrempf SC	.06	.03	.00
☐ 471	Ron Harper SC	.06	.03	.00
☐ 472	Charles Smith SC	.06	.03	.00
☐ 473	Magic Johnson SC	.30	.15	.03
☐ 474	James Worthy SC	.08	.04	.01
☐ 475	Sherman Douglas SC	.06	.03	.00
☐ 476	Rony Seikaly SC	.08	.04	.01
☐ 477	Jay Humphries SC	.03	.01	.00
☐ 478	Alvin Robertson SC	.03	.01	.00
☐ 479	Tyrone Corbin SC	.03	.01	.00
☐ 480	Pooh Richardson SC	.08	.04	.01
☐ 481	Sam Bowie SC	.03	.01	.00
☐ 482	Derrick Coleman SC	.15	.07	.01
☐ 483	Patrick Ewing SC	.10	.05	.01
☐ 484	Charles Oakley SC	.03	.01	.00
☐ 485	Dennis Scott SC	.08	.04	.01
☐ 486	Scott Skiles SC	.03	.01	.00
☐ 487	Charles Barkley SC	.10	.05	.01
☐ 488	Hersey Hawkins SC	.06	.03	.00
☐ 489	Tom Chambers SC	.06	.03	.00
☐ 490	Kevin Johnson SC	.10	.05	.01
☐ 491	Clyde Drexler SC	.12	.06	.01
☐ 492	Terry Porter SC	.08	.04	.01
☐ 493	Lionel Simmons SC	.10	.05	.01
☐ 494	Wayman Tisdale SC	.06	.03	.00
☐ 495	Terry Cummings SC	.06	.03	.00
☐ 496	David Robinson SC	.20	.10	.02
☐ 497	Shawn Kemp SC	.20	.10	.02
☐ 498	Ricky Pierce SC	.06	.03	.00
☐ 499	Karl Malone SC	.10	.05	.01
☐ 500	John Stockton SC	.10	.05	.01
☐ 501	Harvey Grant SC	.06	.03	.00
☐ 502	Bernard King SC	.06	.03	.00
☐ 503	Travis Mays Art	.06	.03	.00
☐ 504	Kevin McHale Art	.08	.04	.01
☐ 505	Muggsy Bogues Art	.03	.01	.00
☐ 506	Scottie Pippen Art	.15	.07	.01
☐ 507	Brad Daugherty Art	.08	.04	.01
☐ 508	Derek Harper Art	.06	.03	.00
☐ 509	Chris Jackson Art	.06	.03	.00
☐ 510	Isiah Thomas Art	.08	.04	.01
☐ 511	Tim Hardaway Art	.20	.10	.02
☐ 512	Otis Thorpe Art	.03	.01	.00
☐ 513	Chuck Person Art	.06	.03	.00
☐ 514	Ron Harper Art	.06	.03	.00
☐ 515	James Worthy Art	.08	.04	.01
☐ 516	Sherman Douglas Art	.06	.03	.00
☐ 517	Dale Ellis Art	.06	.03	.00
☐ 518	Tony Campbell Art	.03	.01	.00
☐ 519	Derrick Coleman Art	.15	.07	.01
☐ 520	Gerald Wilkins Art	.03	.01	.00
☐ 521	Scott Skiles Art	.03	.01	.00
☐ 522	Manute Bol Art	.03	.01	.00

156 / 1991-92 Hoops II

- ☐ 523 Tom Chambers Art .... .06 .03 .00
- ☐ 524 Terry Porter Art .... .08 .04 .01
- ☐ 525 Lionel Simmons Art .... .10 .05 .01
- ☐ 526 Sean Elliott Art .... .10 .05 .01
- ☐ 527 Shawn Kemp Art .... .20 .10 .02
- ☐ 528 John Stockton Art .... .10 .05 .01
- ☐ 529 Harvey Grant Art .... .06 .03 .00
- ☐ 530 Michael Adams .... .06 .03 .00
  All-Time Active Leader
  Three-Point Field Goals
- ☐ 531 Charles Barkley .... .10 .05 .01
  All-Time Active Leader
  Field Goal Percentage
- ☐ 532 Larry Bird .... .15 .07 .01
  All-Time Active Leader
  Free Throw Percentage
- ☐ 533 Maurice Cheeks .... .06 .03 .00
  All-Time Active Leader
  Steals
- ☐ 534 Mark Eaton .... .03 .01 .00
  All-Time Active Leader
  Blocks
- ☐ 535 Magic Johnson .... .30 .15 .03
  All-Time Active Leader
  Assists
- ☐ 536 Michael Jordan .... .40 .20 .04
  All-Time Active Leader
  Scoring Average
- ☐ 537 Moses Malone .... .08 .04 .01
  All-Time Active Leader
  Rebounds
- ☐ 538 NBA Finals Game 1 .... .06 .03 .00
  Perkins' Three Pointer
  (Sam Perkins)
- ☐ 539 NBA Finals Game 2 .... .08 .04 .01
  Bulls Rout Lakers
  (Pippen against Worthy)
- ☐ 540 NBA Finals Game 3 .... .06 .03 .00
  Bulls Win OT Thriller
  (Vlade Divac lay-in)
- ☐ 541 NBA Finals Game 4 .... .06 .03 .00
  Bulls One Game Away
  (John Paxson jumper)
- ☐ 542 NBA Finals Game 5 .... .10 .05 .01
  Jordan, Bulls Win
  First Title
  (Jordan reverses
  over Vlade Divac)
- ☐ 543 Championship Card .... .10 .05 .01
  Chicago Bulls Champs
  (Michael Jordan
  kissing trophy)
- ☐ 544 Otis Smith .... .03 .01 .00
  Stay in School
- ☐ 545 Jeff Turner .... .03 .01 .00
  Stay in School
- ☐ 546 Larry Johnson .... 4.00 2.00 .40

1991-92 Hoops II / 157

☐	547	Kenny Anderson	.75	.35	.07
☐	548	Billy Owens	2.00	1.00	.20
☐	549	Dikembe Mutombo	2.00	1.00	.20
☐	550	Steve Smith	.90	.45	.09
☐	551	Doug Smith	.35	.17	.03
☐	552	Luc Longley	.15	.07	.01
☐	553	Mark Macon	.30	.15	.03
☐	554	Stacey Augmon	.75	.35	.07
☐	555	Brian Williams	.30	.15	.03
☐	556	Terrell Brandon	.35	.17	.03
☐	557	Walter Davis Team USA 1976	.06	.03	.00
☐	558	Vern Fleming Team USA 1984	.06	.03	.00
☐	559	Joe Kleine Team USA 1984	.06	.03	.00
☐	560	Jon Koncak Team USA 1984	.06	.03	.00
☐	561	Sam Perkins Team USA 1984	.10	.05	.01
☐	562	Alvin Robertson Team USA 1984	.06	.03	.00
☐	563	Wayman Tisdale Team USA 1984	.06	.03	.00
☐	564	Jeff Turner Team USA 1984	.06	.03	.00
☐	565	Willie Anderson Team USA 1988	.06	.03	.00
☐	566	Stacey Augmon Team USA 1988	.40	.20	.04
☐	567	Bimbo Coles Team USA 1988	.10	.05	.01
☐	568	Jeff Grayer Team USA 1988	.06	.03	.00
☐	569	Hersey Hawkins Team USA 1988	.12	.06	.01
☐	570	Dan Majerle Team USA 1988	.10	.05	.01
☐	571	Danny Manning Team USA 1988	.10	.05	.01
☐	572	J.R. Reid Team USA 1988	.06	.03	.00
☐	573	Mitch Richmond Team USA 1988	.10	.05	.01
☐	574	Charles Smith Team USA 1988	.10	.05	.01
☐	575	Charles Barkley Team USA 1992	.50	.25	.05
☐	576	Larry Bird Team USA 1992	.75	.35	.07
☐	577	Patrick Ewing Team USA 1992	.60	.30	.06
☐	578	Magic Johnson Team USA 1992	1.50	.75	.15
☐	579	Michael Jordan Team USA 1992	2.00	1.00	.20
☐	580	Karl Malone	.50	.25	.05

158 / 1991-92 Hoops II

Team USA 1992			
☐ 581 Chris Mullin	.50	.25	.05
Team USA 1992			
☐ 582 Scottie Pippen	.90	.45	.09
Team USA 1992			
☐ 583 David Robinson	1.50	.75	.15
Team USA 1992			
☐ 584 John Stockton	.50	.25	.05
Team USA 1992			
☐ 585 Chuck Daly CO	.15	.07	.01
Team USA 1992			
☐ 586 Lenny Wilkens CO	.12	.06	.01
Team USA 1992			
☐ 587 P.J. Carlesimo CO	.15	.07	.01
Team USA 1992			
☐ 588 Mike Krzyzewski CO	.30	.15	.03
Team USA 1992			
☐ 589 Checklist Card 1	.06	.01	.00
☐ 590 Checklist Card 2	.06	.01	.00
☐ NNO Team USA SP	10.00	5.00	1.00
Title Card			
☐ xx Head of the Class SP	25.00	12.50	2.50
Kenny Anderson			
Larry Johnson			
Dikembe Mutombo			
Billy Owens			
Doug Smith			
Steve Smith			

1991-92 Hoops All-Star MVP's

This six-card standard-size (2 1/2" by 3 1/2") set commemorates the most valuable player of the NBA All-Star games from 1986 to 1991. One card was inserted in each series II rack pack. On a white card face, the front features non-action color photos framed by either a blue (7, 9, 12) or red (8, 10, 11) border. The top thicker border is jagged and displays the player's name, while the year the award was received appears in a colored box in the lower left corner. The backs have the same design and feature a color action photo from the All-Star game. The cards are numbered on the back by Roman numerals.

	MINT	EXC	G-VG
COMPLETE SET (6)	7.00	3.50	.70
COMMON PLAYER (7-12)	.30	.15	.03
☐ 7 Isiah Thomas	1.00	.50	.10
(Numbered VII)			
☐ 8 Tom Chambers	.30	.15	.03
(Numbered VIII)			
☐ 9 Michael Jordan	3.00	1.50	.30
(Numbered IX)			
☐ 10 Karl Malone	1.50	.75	.15
(Numbered X)			

1990-91 Sky Box / 159

☐ 11 Magic Johnson .... 2.00   1.00   .20
   (Numbered XI)
☐ 12 Charles Barkley .... 1.50   .75   .15
   (Numbered XII)

1990-91 SkyBox

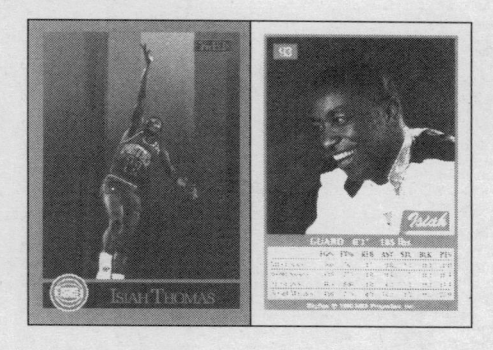

The 1990-91 SkyBox set contains 300 cards featuring NBA players. The cards measure the standard size (2 1/2" by 3 1/2"). The front features an action shot of the player on a computer-

160 / 1990-91 Sky Box

generated background consisting of various color stripes and geometric shapes. The player's name appears in a black stripe below the photo, with the team logo superimposed at the left lower corner. The photo is bordered in gold. The back presents head shots of the player, with gold borders on white background. Player statistics are given in a box below the photo. The cards are numbered on the back and checklisted below alphabetically according to team names as follows: Atlanta Hawks (1-12), Boston Celtics (13-24), Charlotte Hornets (25-36), Chicago Bulls (37-47), Cleveland Cavaliers (48-58), Dallas Mavericks (59-70), Denver Nuggets (71-81), Detroit Pistons (82-93), Golden State Warriors (94-104), Houston Rockets (105-113), Indiana Pacers (114-123), Los Angeles Clippers (124-133), Los Angeles Lakers (134-143), Miami Heat (144-154), Milwaukee Bucks (155-166), Minnesota Timberwolves (167-175), New Jersey Nets (176-185), New York Knicks (186-197), Orlando Magic (198-209), Philadelphia 76ers (210-219), Phoenix Suns (220-230), Portland Trail Blazers (231-241), Sacramento Kings (242-251), San Antonio Spurs (252-262), Seattle Supersonics (263-273), Utah Jazz (274-284), and Washington Bullets (285-294). Rookie Cards included in this set are Nick Anderson, B.J. Armstrong, Vlade Divac, Sherman Douglas, Sean Elliott, Pervis Ellison, Danny Ferry, Tim Hardaway, Shawn Kemp, Sarunas Marciulionis, Drazen Petrovic, Glen Rice, Pooh Richardson, and Cliff Robinson. Cards that were deleted by SkyBox for the second series are marked in the checklist below by SP.

	MINT	EXC	G-VG
COMPLETE SET (300)	15.00	7.50	1.50
COMMON PLAYER (1-300)	.04	.02	.00
COMMON PLAYER SP	.07	.03	.01
☐ 1 John Battle Atlanta Hawks	.07	.03	.01
☐ 2 Duane Ferrell SP Atlanta Hawks	.20	.10	.02
☐ 3 Jon Koncak Atlanta Hawks	.04	.02	.00
☐ 4 Cliff Levingston SP Atlanta Hawks	.07	.03	.01
☐ 5 John Long SP Atlanta Hawks	.07	.03	.01
☐ 6 Moses Malone Atlanta Hawks	.15	.07	.01
☐ 7 Glenn Rivers Atlanta Hawks	.07	.03	.01
☐ 8 Kenny Smith SP Atlanta Hawks	.07	.03	.01
☐ 9 Alexander Volkov Atlanta Hawks	.15	.07	.01
☐ 10 Spud Webb Atlanta Hawks	.10	.05	.01
☐ 11 Dominique Wilkins Atlanta Hawks	.20	.10	.02
☐ 12 Kevin Willis Atlanta Hawks	.12	.06	.01
☐ 13 John Bagley Boston Celtics	.07	.03	.01
☐ 14 Larry Bird Boston Celtics	.50	.25	.05
☐ 15 Kevin Gamble Boston Celtics	.12	.06	.01
☐ 16 Dennis Johnson SP Boston Celtics	.12	.06	.01
☐ 17 Joe Kleine Boston Celtics	.04	.02	.00
☐ 18 Reggie Lewis Boston Celtics	.35	.17	.03

1990-91 Sky Box / 161

☐ 19	Boston Celtics Kevin McHale	.15	.07	.01
☐ 20	Boston Celtics Robert Parish	.15	.07	.01
☐ 21	Boston Celtics Jim Paxson SP	.07	.03	.01
☐ 22	Boston Celtics Ed Pinckney	.04	.02	.00
☐ 23	Boston Celtics Brian Shaw	.10	.05	.01
☐ 24	Boston Celtics Michael Smith	.07	.03	.01
☐ 25	Boston Celtics Richard Anderson SP	.07	.03	.01
☐ 26	Charlotte Hornets Tyrone Bogues	.04	.02	.00
☐ 27	Charlotte Hornets Rex Chapman	.10	.05	.01
☐ 28	Charlotte Hornets Dell Curry	.07	.03	.01
☐ 29	Charlotte Hornets Armon Gilliam	.04	.02	.00
☐ 30	Charlotte Hornets Michael Holton SP	.07	.03	.01
☐ 31	Charlotte Hornets Dave Hoppen	.04	.02	.00
☐ 32	Charlotte Hornets J.R. Reid	.20	.10	.02
☐ 33	Charlotte Hornets Robert Reid SP	.07	.03	.01
☐ 34	Charlotte Hornets Brian Rowsom SP	.20	.10	.02
☐ 35	Charlotte Hornets Kelly Tripucka	.04	.02	.00
☐ 36	Charlotte Hornets Micheal Williams SP UER	.35	.17	.03
☐ 37	Charlotte Hornets B.J. Armstrong	.60	.30	.06
☐ 38	Chicago Bulls Bill Cartwright	.07	.03	.01
☐ 39	Chicago Bulls Horace Grant	.30	.15	.03
☐ 40	Chicago Bulls Craig Hodges	.04	.02	.00
☐ 41	Chicago Bulls Michael Jordan	2.50	1.25	.25
☐ 42	Chicago Bulls Stacey King	.35	.17	.03
☐ 43	Chicago Bulls Ed Nealy SP	.07	.03	.01
☐ 44	Chicago Bulls John Paxson	.10	.05	.01
☐ 45	Chicago Bulls Will Perdue	.10	.05	.01
☐ 46	Chicago Bulls Scottie Pippen	1.00	.50	.10
☐ 47	Chicago Bulls Jeff Sanders SP	.10	.05	.01

162 / 1990-91 Sky Box

	Chicago Bulls			
☐ 48	Winston Bennett	.07	.03	.01
	Cleveland Cavaliers			
☐ 49	Chucky Brown	.10	.05	.01
	Cleveland Cavaliers			
☐ 50	Brad Daugherty	.30	.15	.03
	Cleveland Cavaliers			
☐ 51	Craig Ehlo	.12	.06	.01
	Cleveland Cavaliers			
☐ 52	Steve Kerr	.04	.02	.00
	Cleveland Cavaliers			
☐ 53	Paul Mokeski SP	.07	.03	.01
	Cleveland Cavaliers			
☐ 54	John Morton	.07	.03	.01
	Cleveland Cavaliers			
☐ 55	Larry Nance	.12	.06	.01
	Cleveland Cavaliers			
☐ 56	Mark Price	.30	.15	.03
	Cleveland Cavaliers			
☐ 57	Tree Rollins SP	.07	.03	.01
	Cleveland Cavaliers			
☐ 58	Hot Rod Williams	.10	.05	.01
	Cleveland Cavaliers			
☐ 59	Steve Alford	.07	.03	.01
	Dallas Mavericks			
☐ 60	Rolando Blackman	.10	.05	.01
	Dallas Mavericks			
☐ 61	Adrian Dantley SP	.12	.06	.01
	Dallas Mavericks			
☐ 62	Brad Davis	.04	.02	.00
	Dallas Mavericks			
☐ 63	James Donaldson	.04	.02	.00
	Dallas Mavericks			
☐ 64	Derek Harper	.07	.03	.01
	Dallas Mavericks			
☐ 65	Anthony Jones SP	.10	.05	.01
	Dallas Mavericks			
☐ 66	Sam Perkins SP	.15	.07	.01
	Dallas Mavericks			
☐ 67	Roy Tarpley	.07	.03	.01
	Dallas Mavericks			
☐ 68	Bill Wennington SP	.07	.03	.01
	Dallas Mavericks			
☐ 69	Randy White	.10	.05	.01
	Dallas Mavericks			
☐ 70	Herb Williams	.04	.02	.00
	Dallas Mavericks			
☐ 71	Michael Adams	.10	.05	.01
	Denver Nuggets			
☐ 72	Joe Barry Carroll SP	.07	.03	.01
	Denver Nuggets			
☐ 73	Walter Davis	.07	.03	.01
	Denver Nuggets			
☐ 74	Alex English SP	.12	.06	.01
	Denver Nuggets			
☐ 75	Bill Hanzlik	.04	.02	.00
	Denver Nuggets			
☐ 76	Tim Kempton SP	.07	.03	.01

1990-91 Sky Box / 163

☐ 77	Denver Nuggets Jerome Lane	.04	.02	.00
☐ 78	Denver Nuggets Lafayette Lever SP	.10	.05	.01
☐ 79	Denver Nuggets Todd Lichti	.12	.06	.01
☐ 80	Denver Nuggets Blair Rasmussen	.04	.02	.00
☐ 81	Denver Nuggets Dan Schayes SP	.07	.03	.01
☐ 82	Denver Nuggets Mark Aguirre	.10	.05	.01
☐ 83	Detroit Pistons William Bedford	.07	.03	.01
☐ 84	Detroit Pistons Joe Dumars	.20	.10	.02
☐ 85	Detroit Pistons James Edwards	.04	.02	.00
☐ 86	Detroit Pistons David Greenwood SP	.07	.03	.01
☐ 87	Detroit Pistons Scott Hastings	.04	.02	.00
☐ 88	Detroit Pistons Gerald Henderson SP	.07	.03	.01
☐ 89	Detroit Pistons Vinnie Johnson	.07	.03	.01
☐ 90	Detroit Pistons Bill Laimbeer	.10	.05	.01
☐ 91A	Detroit Pistons Dennis Rodman (SkyBox logo in upper right corner)	.30	.15	.03
☐ 91B	Detroit Pistons Dennis Rodman (SkyBox logo in upper left corner)	.30	.15	.03
☐ 92	Detroit Pistons John Salley	.10	.05	.01
☐ 93	Detroit Pistons Isiah Thomas	.20	.10	.02
☐ 94	Detroit Pistons Manute Bol SP	.10	.05	.01
☐ 95	Golden State Warriors Tim Hardaway	2.50	1.25	.25
☐ 96	Golden State Warriors Rod Higgins	.04	.02	.00
☐ 97	Golden State Warriors Sarunas Marciulionis	.60	.30	.06
☐ 98	Golden State Warriors Chris Mullin	.35	.17	.03
☐ 99	Golden State Warriors Jim Petersen	.04	.02	.00
☐ 100	Golden State Warriors Mitch Richmond	.20	.10	.02
☐ 101	Golden State Warriors Mike Smrek	.12	.06	.01
☐ 102	Golden State Warriors Terry Teagle SP	.07	.03	.01

164 / 1990-91 Sky Box

Golden State Warriors			
☐ 103 Tom Tolbert	.10	.05	.01
Golden State Warriors			
☐ 104 Kelvin Upshaw SP	.10	.05	.01
Golden State Warriors			
☐ 105 Anthony Bowie SP	.25	.12	.02
Houston Rockets			
☐ 106 Adrian Caldwell	.10	.05	.01
Houston Rockets			
☐ 107 Eric(Sleepy) Floyd	.07	.03	.01
Houston Rockets			
☐ 108 Buck Johnson	.04	.02	.00
Houston Rockets			
☐ 109 Vernon Maxwell	.07	.03	.01
Houston Rockets			
☐ 110 Hakeem Olajuwon	.30	.15	.03
Houston Rockets			
☐ 111 Larry Smith	.04	.02	.00
Houston Rockets			
☐ 112A Otis Thorpe ERR	.75	.35	.07
Houston Rockets (Front photo actually Mitchell Wiggins)			
☐ 112B Otis Thorpe COR	.12	.06	.01
Houston Rockets			
☐ 113A M. Wiggins SP ERR	.75	.35	.07
Houston Rockets (Front photo actually Otis Thorpe)			
☐ 113B M. Wiggins SP COR	.10	.05	.01
Houston Rockets			
☐ 114 Vern Fleming	.04	.02	.00
Indiana Pacers			
☐ 115 Rickey Green SP	.07	.03	.01
Indiana Pacers			
☐ 116 George McCloud	.12	.06	.01
Indiana Pacers			
☐ 117 Reggie Miller	.30	.15	.03
Indiana Pacers			
☐ 118A Dyron Nix SP ERR	2.50	1.25	.25
Indiana Pacers (Back photo actually Wayman Tisdale)			
☐ 118B Dyron Nix SP COR	.10	.05	.01
Indiana Pacers			
☐ 119 Chuck Person	.10	.05	.01
Indiana Pacers			
☐ 120 Mike Sanders	.07	.03	.01
Indiana Pacers			
☐ 121 Detlef Schrempf	.15	.07	.01
Indiana Pacers			
☐ 122 Rik Smits	.10	.05	.01
Indiana Pacers			
☐ 123 LaSalle Thompson	.04	.02	.00
Indiana Pacers			
☐ 124 Benoit Benjamin	.07	.03	.01
Los Angeles Clippers			
☐ 125 Winston Garland	.04	.02	.00

1990-91 Sky Box / 165

Los Angeles Clippers			
☐ 126 Tom Garrick	.07	.03	.01
Los Angeles Clippers			
☐ 127 Gary Grant	.04	.02	.00
Los Angeles Clippers			
☐ 128 Ron Harper	.10	.05	.01
Los Angeles Clippers			
☐ 129 Danny Manning	.25	.12	.02
Los Angeles Clippers			
☐ 130 Jeff Martin	.10	.05	.01
Los Angeles Clippers			
☐ 131 Ken Norman	.10	.05	.01
Los Angeles Clippers			
☐ 132 Charles Smith	.15	.07	.01
Los Angeles Clippers			
☐ 133 Joe Wolf SP	.07	.03	.01
Los Angeles Clippers			
☐ 134 Michael Cooper SP	.12	.06	.01
Los Angeles Lakers			
☐ 135 Vlade Divac	.40	.20	.04
Los Angeles Lakers			
☐ 136 Larry Drew	.04	.02	.00
Los Angeles Lakers			
☐ 137 A.C. Green	.07	.03	.01
Los Angeles Lakers			
☐ 138 Magic Johnson	1.00	.50	.10
Los Angeles Lakers			
☐ 139 Mark McNamara SP	.07	.03	.01
Los Angeles Lakers			
☐ 140 Byron Scott	.07	.03	.01
Los Angeles Lakers			
☐ 141 Mychal Thompson	.04	.02	.00
Los Angeles Lakers			
☐ 142 Orlando Woolridge SP	.10	.05	.01
Los Angeles Lakers			
☐ 143 James Worthy	.20	.10	.02
Los Angeles Lakers			
☐ 144 Terry Davis	.20	.10	.02
Miami Heat			
☐ 145 Sherman Douglas	.30	.15	.03
Miami Heat			
☐ 146 Kevin Edwards	.07	.03	.01
Miami Heat			
☐ 147 Tellis Frank SP	.10	.05	.01
Miami Heat			
☐ 148 Scott Haffner SP	.10	.05	.01
Miami Heat			
☐ 149 Grant Long	.10	.05	.01
Miami Heat			
☐ 150 Glen Rice	1.50	.75	.15
Miami Heat			
☐ 151 Rony Seikaly	.20	.10	.02
Miami Heat			
☐ 152 Rory Sparrow SP	.07	.03	.01
Miami Heat			
☐ 153 Jon Sundvold	.04	.02	.00
Miami Heat			
☐ 154 Billy Thompson	.04	.02	.00

166 / 1990-91 Sky Box

Miami Heat			
☐ 155 Greg Anderson	.04	.02	.00
Milwaukee Bucks			
☐ 156 Ben Coleman SP	.10	.05	.01
Milwaukee Bucks			
☐ 157 Jeff Grayer	.20	.10	.02
Milwaukee Bucks			
☐ 158 Jay Humphries	.04	.02	.00
Milwaukee Bucks			
☐ 159 Frank Kornet	.07	.03	.01
Milwaukee Bucks			
☐ 160 Larry Krystkowiak	.04	.02	.00
Milwaukee Bucks			
☐ 161 Brad Lohaus	.07	.03	.01
Milwaukee Bucks			
☐ 162 Ricky Pierce	.07	.03	.01
Milwaukee Bucks			
☐ 163 Paul Pressey SP	.07	.03	.01
Milwaukee Bucks			
☐ 164 Fred Roberts	.07	.03	.01
Milwaukee Bucks			
☐ 165 Alvin Robertson	.07	.03	.01
Milwaukee Bucks			
☐ 166 Jack Sikma	.07	.03	.01
Milwaukee Bucks			
☐ 167 Randy Breuer	.04	.02	.00
Minnesota Timberwolves			
☐ 168 Tony Campbell	.07	.03	.01
Minnesota Timberwolves			
☐ 169 Tyrone Corbin	.07	.03	.01
Minnesota Timberwolves			
☐ 170 Sidney Lowe SP	.07	.03	.01
Minnesota Timberwolves			
☐ 171 Sam Mitchell	.20	.10	.02
Minnesota Timberwolves			
☐ 172 Tod Murphy	.07	.03	.01
Minnesota Timberwolves			
☐ 173 Pooh Richardson	.60	.30	.06
Minnesota Timberwolves			
☐ 174 Donald Royal SP	.10	.05	.01
Minnesota Timberwolves			
☐ 175 Brad Sellers SP	.07	.03	.01
Minnesota Timberwolves			
☐ 176 Mookie Blaylock	.25	.12	.02
New Jersey Nets			
☐ 177 Sam Bowie	.07	.03	.01
New Jersey Nets			
☐ 178 Lester Conner	.04	.02	.00
New Jersey Nets			
☐ 179 Derrick Gervin	.10	.05	.01
New Jersey Nets			
☐ 180 Jack Haley	.10	.05	.01
New Jersey Nets			
☐ 181 Roy Hinson	.04	.02	.00
New Jersey Nets			
☐ 182 Dennis Hopson SP	.10	.05	.01
New Jersey Nets			
☐ 183 Chris Morris	.07	.03	.01

1990-91 Sky Box / 167

☐ 184 Pete Myers SP — New Jersey Nets	.10	.05	.01
☐ 185 Purvis Short SP — New Jersey Nets	.07	.03	.01
☐ 186 Maurice Cheeks — New Jersey Nets	.10	.05	.01
☐ 187 Patrick Ewing — New York Knicks	.35	.17	.03
☐ 188 Stuart Gray — New York Knicks	.04	.02	.00
☐ 189 Mark Jackson — New York Knicks	.07	.03	.01
☐ 190 Johnny Newman SP — New York Knicks	.10	.05	.01
☐ 191 Charles Oakley — New York Knicks	.07	.03	.01
☐ 192 Brian Quinnett — New York Knicks	.10	.05	.01
☐ 193 Trent Tucker — New York Knicks	.04	.02	.00
☐ 194 Kiki Vandeweghe — New York Knicks	.07	.03	.01
☐ 195 Kenny Walker — New York Knicks	.04	.02	.00
☐ 196 Eddie Lee Wilkins — New York Knicks	.04	.02	.00
☐ 197 Gerald Wilkins — New York Knicks	.07	.03	.01
☐ 198 Mark Acres — Orlando Magic	.04	.02	.00
☐ 199 Nick Anderson — Orlando Magic	.60	.30	.06
☐ 200 Michael Ansley — Orlando Magic	.07	.03	.01
☐ 201 Terry Catledge — Orlando Magic	.07	.03	.01
☐ 202 Dave Corzine SP — Orlando Magic	.07	.03	.01
☐ 203 Sidney Green SP — Orlando Magic	.07	.03	.01
☐ 204 Jerry Reynolds — Orlando Magic	.07	.03	.01
☐ 205 Scott Skiles — Orlando Magic	.10	.05	.01
☐ 206 Otis Smith — Orlando Magic	.07	.03	.01
☐ 207 Reggie Theus SP — Orlando Magic	.10	.05	.01
☐ 208 Jeff Turner — Orlando Magic	.04	.02	.00
☐ 209 Sam Vincent — Orlando Magic	.07	.03	.01
☐ 210 Ron Anderson — Philadelphia 76ers	.04	.02	.00
☐ 211 Charles Barkley — Philadelphia 76ers	.35	.17	.03
☐ 212 Scott Brooks SP	.07	.03	.01

168 / 1990-91 Sky Box

Philadelphia 76ers			
☐ 213 Lanard Copeland SP	.07	.03	.01
Philadelphia 76ers			
☐ 214 Johnny Dawkins	.04	.02	.00
Philadelphia 76ers			
☐ 215 Mike Gminski	.04	.02	.00
Philadelphia 76ers			
☐ 216 Hersey Hawkins	.20	.10	.02
Philadelphia 76ers			
☐ 217 Rick Mahorn	.07	.03	.01
Philadelphia 76ers			
☐ 218 Derek Smith SP	.07	.03	.01
Philadelphia 76ers			
☐ 219 Bob Thornton	.07	.03	.01
Philadelphia 76ers			
☐ 220 Tom Chambers	.12	.06	.01
Phoenix Suns			
☐ 221 Greg Grant SP	.12	.06	.01
Phoenix Suns			
☐ 222 Jeff Hornacek	.20	.10	.02
Phoenix Suns			
☐ 223 Eddie Johnson	.07	.03	.01
Phoenix Suns			
☐ 224A Kevin Johnson	.40	.20	.04
Phoenix Suns (SkyBox logo in lower right corner)			
☐ 224B Kevin Johnson	.40	.20	.04
Phoenix Suns (SkyBox logo in upper right corner)			
☐ 225 Andrew Lang	.30	.15	.03
Phoenix Suns			
☐ 226 Dan Majerle	.20	.10	.02
Phoenix Suns			
☐ 227 Mike McGee SP	.07	.03	.01
Phoenix Suns			
☐ 228 Tim Perry	.07	.03	.01
Phoenix Suns			
☐ 229 Kurt Rambis	.07	.03	.01
Phoenix Suns			
☐ 230 Mark West	.04	.02	.00
Phoenix Suns			
☐ 231 Mark Bryant	.07	.03	.01
Portland Trail Blazers			
☐ 232 Wayne Cooper	.04	.02	.00
Portland Trail Blazers			
☐ 233 Clyde Drexler	.40	.20	.04
Portland Trail Blazers			
☐ 234 Kevin Duckworth	.04	.02	.00
Portland Trail Blazers			
☐ 235 Byron Irvin SP	.12	.06	.01
Portland Trail Blazers			
☐ 236 Jerome Kersey	.15	.07	.01
Portland Trail Blazers			
☐ 237 Drazen Petrovic	.75	.35	.07
Portland Trail Blazers			
☐ 238 Terry Porter	.20	.10	.02

1990-91 Sky Box / 169

	Portland Trail Blazers		
☐ 239 Cliff Robinson	.60	.30	.06
	Portland Trail Blazers		
☐ 240 Buck Williams	.12	.06	.01
	Portland Trail Blazers		
☐ 241 Danny Young	.04	.02	.00
	Portland Trail Blazers		
☐ 242 Danny Ainge SP	.10	.05	.01
	Sacramento Kings		
☐ 243 Randy Allen SP	.10	.05	.01
	Sacramento Kings		
☐ 244A Antoine Carr SP	.12	.06	.01
	Sacramento Kings (Wearing Atlanta jersey on back)		
☐ 244B Antoine Carr	.07	.03	.01
	Sacramento Kings (Wearing Sacramento jersey on back)		
☐ 245 Vinny Del Negro SP	.10	.05	.01
	Sacramento Kings		
☐ 246 Pervis Ellison	1.25	.60	.12
	Sacramento Kings		
☐ 247 Greg Kite SP	.07	.03	.01
	Sacramento Kings		
☐ 248 Rodney McCray SP	.07	.03	.01
	Sacramento Kings		
☐ 249 Harold Pressley SP	.07	.03	.01
	Sacramento Kings		
☐ 250 Ralph Sampson	.07	.03	.01
	Sacramento Kings		
☐ 251 Wayman Tisdale	.10	.05	.01
	Sacramento Kings		
☐ 252 Willie Anderson	.10	.05	.01
	San Antonio Spurs		
☐ 253 Uwe Blab SP	.07	.03	.01
	San Antonio Spurs		
☐ 254 Frank Brickowski SP	.07	.03	.01
	San Antonio Spurs		
☐ 255 Terry Cummings	.10	.05	.01
	San Antonio Spurs		
☐ 256 Sean Elliott	.60	.30	.06
	San Antonio Spurs		
☐ 257 Caldwell Jones SP	.07	.03	.01
	San Antonio Spurs		
☐ 258 Johnny Moore SP	.07	.03	.01
	San Antonio Spurs		
☐ 259 Zarko Paspalj SP	.12	.06	.01
	San Antonio Spurs		
☐ 260 David Robinson	2.00	1.00	.20
	San Antonio Spurs		
☐ 261 Rod Strickland	.10	.05	.01
	San Antonio Spurs		
☐ 262 David Wingate SP	.07	.03	.01
	San Antonio Spurs		
☐ 263 Dana Barros	.30	.15	.03
	Seattle Supersonics		
☐ 264 Michael Cage	.04	.02	.00

170 / 1990-91 Sky Box

☐ 265 Quintin Dailey — Seattle Supersonics	.04	.02	.00
☐ 266 Dale Ellis — Seattle Supersonics	.07	.03	.01
☐ 267 Steve Johnson SP — Seattle Supersonics	.07	.03	.01
☐ 268 Shawn Kemp — Seattle Supersonics	2.50	1.25	.25
☐ 269 Xavier McDaniel — Seattle Supersonics	.12	.06	.01
☐ 270 Derrick McKey — Seattle Supersonics	.07	.03	.01
☐ 271A Nate McMillan SP ERR — Seattle Supersonics (Back photo actually Olden Polynice; first series)	.12	.06	.01
☐ 271B Nate McMillan COR — Seattle Supersonics (second series)	.07	.03	.01
☐ 272 Olden Polynice — Seattle Supersonics	.07	.03	.01
☐ 273 Sedale Threatt — Seattle Supersonics	.07	.03	.01
☐ 274 Thurl Bailey — Utah Jazz	.07	.03	.01
☐ 275 Mike Brown — Utah Jazz	.07	.03	.01
☐ 276 Mark Eaton — Utah Jazz	.04	.02	.00
☐ 277 Blue Edwards — Utah Jazz	.30	.15	.03
☐ 278 Darrell Griffith — Utah Jazz	.07	.03	.01
☐ 279 Bobby Hansen SP — Utah Jazz	.07	.03	.01
☐ 280 Eric Johnson — Utah Jazz	.07	.03	.01
☐ 281 Eric Leckner SP — Utah Jazz	.07	.03	.01
☐ 282 Karl Malone — Utah Jazz	.30	.15	.03
☐ 283 Delaney Rudd — Utah Jazz	.10	.05	.01
☐ 284 John Stockton — Utah Jazz	.30	.15	.03
☐ 285 Mark Alarie — Washington Bullets	.04	.02	.00
☐ 286 Steve Colter SP — Washington Bullets	.07	.03	.01
☐ 287 Ledell Eackles SP — Washington Bullets	.10	.05	.01
☐ 288 Harvey Grant — Washington Bullets	.20	.10	.02
☐ 289 Tom Hammonds — Washington Bullets	.25	.12	.02
☐ 290 Charles Jones — Washington Bullets	.04	.02	.00

1990-91 Sky Box II / 171

	Washington Bullets			
☐ 291	Bernard King	.10	.05	.01
	Washington Bullets			
☐ 292	Jeff Malone SP	.15	.07	.01
	Washington Bullets			
☐ 293	Darrell Walker	.04	.02	.00
	Washington Bullets			
☐ 294	John Williams	.04	.02	.00
	Washington Bullets			
☐ 295	Checklist 1 SP	.07	.01	.00
☐ 296	Checklist 2 SP	.07	.01	.00
☐ 297	Checklist 3 SP	.07	.01	.00
☐ 298	Checklist 4 SP	.07	.01	.00
☐ 299	Checklist 5 SP	.07	.01	.00
☐ 300	Danny Ferry SP	.30	.15	.03
	Cleveland Cavaliers			

1990-91 SkyBox II

This 123-card set measures the standard size (2 1/2" by 3 1/2") and has the same design as the regular issue 1990-91 SkyBox. The backs of the coaches' cards each feature a quote. The cards are numbered on the back in continuation of the first series and checklisted below as follows: coaches (301-327), team checklists (328-354), lottery picks (355-365), updates (366-420), and card checklists (421-423). The key rookies in the second series are the eleven lottery picks (355-365) led by Derrick Coleman, Kendall Gill, Gary Payton, Dennis Scott, and Lionel Simmons.

	MINT	EXC	G-VG
COMPLETE SET (123)	9.00	4.50	.90
COMMON PLAYER (301-423)	.04	.02	.00
☐ 301 Bob Weiss CO	.04	.02	.00
Atlanta Hawks			

172 / 1990-91 Sky Box II

☐ 302 Chris Ford CO	.04	.02	.00
Boston Celtics			
☐ 303 Gene Littles CO	.04	.02	.00
Charlotte Hornets			
☐ 304 Phil Jackson CO	.07	.03	.01
Chicago Bulls			
☐ 305 Lenny Wilkens CO	.07	.03	.01
Cleveland Cavaliers			
☐ 306 Richie Adubato CO	.04	.02	.00
Dallas Mavericks			
☐ 307 Paul Westhead CO	.04	.02	.00
Denver Nuggets			
☐ 308 Chuck Daly CO	.07	.03	.01
Detroit Pistons			
☐ 309 Don Nelson CO	.04	.02	.00
Golden State Warriors			
☐ 310 Don Chaney CO	.04	.02	.00
Houston Rockets			
☐ 311 Dick Versace CO	.04	.02	.00
Indiana Pacers			
☐ 312 Mike Schuler CO	.04	.02	.00
Los Angeles Clippers			
☐ 313 Mike Dunleavy CO	.04	.02	.00
Los Angeles Lakers			
☐ 314 Ron Rothstein CO	.04	.02	.00
Miami Heat			
☐ 315 Del Harris CO	.04	.02	.00
Milwaukee Bucks			
☐ 316 Bill Musselman CO	.04	.02	.00
Minnesota Timberwolves			
☐ 317 Bill Fitch CO	.04	.02	.00
Houston Rockets			
☐ 318 Stu Jackson CO	.04	.02	.00
New York Knicks			
☐ 319 Matt Guokas CO	.04	.02	.00
Orlando Magic			
☐ 320 Jim Lynam CO	.04	.02	.00
Philadelphia 76ers			
☐ 321 Cotton Fitzsimmons CO	.04	.02	.00
Phoenix Suns			
☐ 322 Rick Adelman CO	.07	.03	.01
Portland Trail Blazers			
☐ 323 Dick Motta CO	.04	.02	.00
Sacramento Kings			
☐ 324 Larry Brown CO	.04	.02	.00
San Antonio Spurs			
☐ 325 K.C. Jones CO	.04	.02	.00
Seattle Supersonics			
☐ 326 Jerry Sloan CO	.04	.02	.00
Utah Jazz			
☐ 327 Wes Unseld CO	.07	.03	.01
Washington Bullets			
☐ 328 Atlanta Hawks TC	.04	.02	.00
☐ 329 Boston Celtics TC	.04	.02	.00
☐ 330 Charlotte Hornets TC	.04	.02	.00
☐ 331 Chicago Bulls TC	.04	.02	.00
☐ 332 Cleveland Cavaliers TC	.04	.02	.00

1990-91 Sky Box II / 173

☐ 333 Dallas Mavericks TC	.04	.02	.00
☐ 334 Denver Nuggets TC	.04	.02	.00
☐ 335 Detroit Pistons TC	.04	.02	.00
☐ 336 Golden State Warriors TC	.04	.02	.00
☐ 337 Houston Rockets TC	.04	.02	.00
☐ 338 Indiana Pacers TC	.04	.02	.00
☐ 339 Los Angeles Clippers TC	.04	.02	.00
☐ 340 Los Angeles Lakers TC	.04	.02	.00
☐ 341 Miami Heat TC	.04	.02	.00
☐ 342 Milwaukee Bucks TC	.04	.02	.00
☐ 343 Minnesota Timberwolves TC	.04	.02	.00
☐ 344 New Jersey Nets TC	.04	.02	.00
☐ 345 New York Knicks TC	.04	.02	.00
☐ 346 Orlando Magic TC	.04	.02	.00
☐ 347 Philadelphia 76ers TC	.04	.02	.00
☐ 348 Phoenix Suns TC	.04	.02	.00
☐ 349 Portland Trail Blazers TC	.04	.02	.00
☐ 350 Sacramento Kings TC	.04	.02	.00
☐ 351 San Antonio Spurs TC	.04	.02	.00
☐ 352 Seattle SuperSonics TC	.04	.02	.00
☐ 353 Utah Jazz TC	.04	.02	.00
☐ 354 Washington Bullets TC	.04	.02	.00
☐ 355 Rumeal Robinson LP Atlanta Hawks	.30	.15	.03
☐ 356 Kendall Gill LP Charlotte Hornets	3.00	1.50	.30
☐ 357 Chris Jackson LP Denver Nuggets	.35	.17	.03
☐ 358 Tyrone Hill LP Golden State Warriors	.30	.15	.03
☐ 359 Bo Kimble LP Los Angeles Clippers	.10	.05	.01
☐ 360 Willie Burton LP Miami Heat	.30	.15	.03
☐ 361 Felton Spencer LP Minnesota Timberwolves	.20	.10	.02
☐ 362 Derrick Coleman LP New Jersey Nets	2.00	1.00	.20
☐ 363 Dennis Scott LP Orlando Magic	.75	.35	.07
☐ 364 Lionel Simmons LP Sacramento Kings	1.00	.50	.10
☐ 365 Gary Payton LP Seattle Supersonics	.75	.35	.07
☐ 366 Tim McCormick Atlanta Hawks	.04	.02	.00
☐ 367 Sidney Moncrief Atlanta Hawks	.07	.03	.01
☐ 368 Kenny Gattison Charlotte Hornets	.20	.10	.02
☐ 369 Randolph Keys Charlotte Hornets	.04	.02	.00
☐ 370 Johnny Newman Charlotte Hornets	.07	.03	.01
☐ 371 Dennis Hopson Chicago Bulls	.07	.03	.01
☐ 372 Cliff Levingston	.04	.02	.00

174 / 1990-91 Sky Box II

Chicago Bulls			
☐ 373 Derrick Chievous	.04	.02	.00
Cleveland Cavaliers			
☐ 374 Danny Ferry	.10	.05	.01
Cleveland Cavaliers			
☐ 375 Alex English	.07	.03	.01
Dallas Mavericks			
☐ 376 Lafayette Lever	.07	.03	.01
Dallas Mavericks			
☐ 377 Rodney McCray	.04	.02	.00
Dallas Mavericks			
☐ 378 T.R. Dunn	.04	.02	.00
Denver Nuggets			
☐ 379 Corey Gaines	.07	.03	.01
Denver Nuggets			
☐ 380 Avery Johnson	.10	.05	.01
San Antonio Spurs			
☐ 381 Joe Wolf	.04	.02	.00
Denver Nuggets			
☐ 382 Orlando Woolridge	.07	.03	.01
Denver Nuggets			
☐ 383 Wayne Rollins	.04	.02	.00
Detroit Pistons			
☐ 384 Steve Johnson	.04	.02	.00
Seattle Supersonics			
☐ 385 Kenny Smith	.07	.03	.01
Houston Rockets			
☐ 386 Mike Woodson	.04	.02	.00
Cleveland Cavaliers			
☐ 387 Greg Dreiling	.07	.03	.01
Indiana Pacers			
☐ 388 Micheal Williams	.20	.10	.02
Indiana Pacers			
☐ 389 Randy Wittman	.04	.02	.00
Indiana Pacers			
☐ 390 Ken Bannister	.04	.02	.00
Los Angeles Clippers			
☐ 391 Sam Perkins	.10	.05	.01
Los Angeles Lakers			
☐ 392 Terry Teagle	.04	.02	.00
Los Angeles Lakers			
☐ 393 Milt Wagner	.07	.03	.01
Miami Heat			
☐ 394 Frank Brickowski	.04	.02	.00
Milwaukee Bucks			
☐ 395 Dan Schayes	.04	.02	.00
Milwaukee Bucks			
☐ 396 Scott Brooks	.04	.02	.00
Minnesota Timberwolves			
☐ 397 Doug West	.30	.15	.03
Minnesota Timberwolves			
☐ 398 Chris Dudley	.12	.06	.01
New Jersey Nets			
☐ 399 Reggie Theus	.07	.03	.01
New Jersey Nets			
☐ 400 Greg Grant	.04	.02	.00
New York Knicks			

1990-91 Sky Box II / 175

☐ 401 Greg Kite Orlando Magic	.04	.02	.00
☐ 402 Mark McNamara Orlando Magic	.04	.02	.00
☐ 403 Manute Bol Philadelphia 76ers	.04	.02	.00
☐ 404 Rickey Green Philadelphia 76ers	.04	.02	.00
☐ 405 Kenny Battle Denver Nuggets	.12	.06	.01
☐ 406 Ed Nealy Phoenix Suns	.04	.02	.00
☐ 407 Danny Ainge Portland Trail Blazers	.10	.05	.01
☐ 408 Steve Colter Sacramento Kings	.04	.02	.00
☐ 409 Bobby Hansen Sacramento Kings	.04	.02	.00
☐ 410 Eric Leckner Charlotte Hornets	.07	.03	.01
☐ 411 Rory Sparrow Sacramento Kings	.04	.02	.00
☐ 412 Bill Wennington Sacramento Kings	.04	.02	.00
☐ 413 Sidney Green San Antonio Spurs	.04	.02	.00
☐ 414 David Greenwood San Antonio Spurs	.04	.02	.00
☐ 415 Paul Pressey San Antonio Spurs	.04	.02	.00
☐ 416 Reggie Williams San Antonio Spurs	.07	.03	.01
☐ 417 Dave Corzine Orlando Magic	.04	.02	.00
☐ 418 Jeff Malone Utah Jazz	.12	.06	.01
☐ 419 Pervis Ellison Washington Bullets	.40	.20	.04
☐ 420 Byron Irvin Washington Bullets	.10	.05	.01
☐ 421 Checklist 1	.07	.01	.00
☐ 422 Checklist 2	.07	.01	.00
☐ 423 Checklist 3	.07	.01	.00
☐ NNO SkyBox Salutes the NBA SP	4.50	2.00	.40

176 / 1991-92 Sky Box I

1991-92 SkyBox I

The 1991-92 SkyBox Series I basketball set contains 350 cards measuring the standard size (2 1/2" by 3 1/2"). The fronts feature color action player photos overlaying multi-colored computer-generated geometric shapes and stripes. The pictures are borderless and the card face is white. The player's name appears in different color lettering at the bottom of each card, with the team logo in the lower right corner. In a trapezoid shape, the backs have non-action color player photos. At the bottom biographical and statistical information appear inside a color-striped diagonal. The cards are numbered and checklisted below alphabetically within and according to teams as follows: Atlanta Hawks (1-11), Boston Celtics (12-22), Charlotte Hornets (23-33), Chicago Bulls (34-44), Cleveland Cavaliers (45-55), Dallas Mavericks (56-66), Denver Nuggets (67-77), Detroit Pistons (78-88), Golden State Warriors (89-99), Houston Rockets (100-110), Indiana Pacers (111-121), Los Angeles Clippers (122-132), Los Angeles Lakers (133-143), Miami Heat (144-154), Milwaukee Bucks (155-165), Minnesota Timberwolves (166-176), New Jersey Nets (177-187), New York Knicks (188-198), Orlando Magic (199-209), Philadelphia 76ers (210-220), Phoenix Suns (221-231), Portland Trail Blazers (232-242), Sacramento Kings (243-253), San Antonio Spurs (254-264), Seattle Supersonics (265-275), Utah Jazz (276-286), and Washington Bullets (287-297). Other subsets included in this set are Stats (298-307), Best Single Game Performance (308-312), NBA All-Star Weekend Highlights (313-317), NBA All-Rookie Team (318-322), GQ's "NBA All-Star Style Team" (323-327), Centennial Highlights (328-332), Great Moments from the NBA Finals (333-337), Stay in School (338-344), and Checklists (345-350). The key rookie card in the first series is John Starks. The cards were available in 15-card fin-sealed foil packs that feature four different mail-in offers on the back, or 62-card blister packs that contain two (of four) SkyBox logo cards not available in the 15-card foil packs. As part of a promotion with Cheerios, four SkyBox cards were inserted into specially marked 10-ounce and 15-ounce cereal boxes. These cereal boxes appeared on store shelves in December 1991 and January 1992, and they depicted images of SkyBox cards on the front, back, and side panels.

	MINT	EXC	G-VG
COMPLETE SET (350)	13.00	6.50	1.30
COMMON PLAYER (1-350)	.03	.01	.00
☐ 1 John Battle	.06	.03	.00
☐ 2 Duane Ferrell	.03	.01	.00

1991-92 Sky Box I / 177

☐ 3 Jon Koncak	.03	.01	.00
☐ 4 Moses Malone	.12	.06	.01
☐ 5 Tim McCormick	.03	.01	.00
☐ 6 Sidney Moncrief	.06	.03	.00
☐ 7 Doc Rivers	.06	.03	.00
☐ 8 Rumeal Robinson UER	.06	.03	.00
(Drafted 11th, should say 10th)			
☐ 9 Spud Webb	.06	.03	.00
☐ 10 Dominique Wilkins	.15	.07	.01
☐ 11 Kevin Willis	.08	.04	.01
☐ 12 Larry Bird	.35	.17	.03
☐ 13 Dee Brown	.35	.17	.03
☐ 14 Kevin Gamble	.06	.03	.00
☐ 15 Joe Kleine	.03	.01	.00
☐ 16 Reggie Lewis	.15	.07	.01
☐ 17 Kevin McHale	.10	.05	.01
☐ 18 Robert Parish	.12	.06	.01
☐ 19 Ed Pinckney	.03	.01	.00
☐ 20 Brian Shaw	.06	.03	.00
☐ 21 Michael Smith	.03	.01	.00
☐ 22 Stojko Vrankovic	.12	.06	.01
☐ 23 Muggsy Bogues	.03	.01	.00
☐ 24 Rex Chapman	.06	.03	.00
☐ 25 Dell Curry	.03	.01	.00
☐ 26 Kenny Gattison	.06	.03	.00
☐ 27 Kendall Gill	.90	.45	.09
☐ 28 Mike Gminski	.03	.01	.00
☐ 29 Randolph Keys	.03	.01	.00
☐ 30 Eric Leckner	.03	.01	.00
☐ 31 Johnny Newman	.03	.01	.00
☐ 32 J.R. Reid	.06	.03	.00
☐ 33 Kelly Tripucka	.03	.01	.00
☐ 34 B.J. Armstrong	.15	.07	.01
☐ 35 Bill Cartwright	.06	.03	.00
☐ 36 Horace Grant	.12	.06	.01
☐ 37 Craig Hodges	.03	.01	.00
☐ 38 Dennis Hopson	.06	.03	.00
☐ 39 Michael Jordan	1.25	.60	.12
☐ 40 Stacey King	.06	.03	.00
☐ 41 Cliff Levingston	.03	.01	.00
☐ 42 John Paxson	.08	.04	.01
☐ 43 Will Perdue	.03	.01	.00
☐ 44 Scottie Pippen	.40	.20	.04
☐ 45 Winston Bennett	.03	.01	.00
☐ 46 Chucky Brown	.03	.01	.00
☐ 47 Brad Daugherty	.15	.07	.01
☐ 48 Craig Ehlo	.06	.03	.00
☐ 49 Danny Ferry	.06	.03	.00
☐ 50 Steve Kerr	.03	.01	.00
☐ 51 John Morton	.03	.01	.00
☐ 52 Larry Nance	.08	.04	.01
☐ 53 Mark Price	.15	.07	.01
☐ 54 Darnell Valentine	.03	.01	.00
☐ 55 John Williams	.06	.03	.00
☐ 56 Steve Alford	.06	.03	.00
☐ 57 Rolando Blackman	.06	.03	.00

178 / 1991-92 Sky Box I

☐ 58 Brad Davis	.03	.01	.00
☐ 59 James Donaldson	.03	.01	.00
☐ 60 Derek Harper	.06	.03	.00
☐ 61 Fat Lever	.06	.03	.00
☐ 62 Rodney McCray	.03	.01	.00
☐ 63 Roy Tarpley	.06	.03	.00
☐ 64 Kelvin Upshaw	.03	.01	.00
☐ 65 Randy White	.03	.01	.00
☐ 66 Herb Williams	.03	.01	.00
☐ 67 Michael Adams	.08	.04	.01
☐ 68 Greg Anderson	.03	.01	.00
☐ 69 Anthony Cook	.03	.01	.00
☐ 70 Chris Jackson	.08	.04	.01
☐ 71 Jerome Lane	.03	.01	.00
☐ 72 Marcus Liberty	.25	.12	.02
☐ 73 Todd Lichti	.03	.01	.00
☐ 74 Blair Rasmussen	.03	.01	.00
☐ 75 Reggie Williams	.06	.03	.00
☐ 76 Joe Wolf	.03	.01	.00
☐ 77 Orlando Woolridge	.06	.03	.00
☐ 78 Mark Aguirre	.06	.03	.00
☐ 79 William Bedford	.03	.01	.00
☐ 80 Lance Blanks	.06	.03	.00
☐ 81 Joe Dumars	.12	.06	.01
☐ 82 James Edwards	.03	.01	.00
☐ 83 Scott Hastings	.03	.01	.00
☐ 84 Vinnie Johnson	.03	.01	.00
☐ 85 Bill Laimbeer	.06	.03	.00
☐ 86 Dennis Rodman	.12	.06	.01
☐ 87 John Salley	.06	.03	.00
☐ 88 Isiah Thomas	.15	.07	.01
☐ 89 Mario Elie	.20	.10	.02
☐ 90 Tim Hardaway	.75	.35	.07
☐ 91 Rod Higgins	.03	.01	.00
☐ 92 Tyrone Hill	.10	.05	.01
☐ 93 Les Jepsen	.03	.01	.00
☐ 94 Alton Lister	.03	.01	.00
☐ 95 Sarunas Marciulionis	.20	.10	.02
☐ 96 Chris Mullin	.20	.10	.02
☐ 97 Jim Petersen	.03	.01	.00
☐ 98 Mitch Richmond	.12	.06	.01
☐ 99 Tom Tolbert	.03	.01	.00
☐ 100 Adrian Caldwell	.03	.01	.00
☐ 101 Eric(Sleepy) Floyd	.03	.01	.00
☐ 102 Dave Jamerson	.06	.03	.00
☐ 103 Buck Johnson	.03	.01	.00
☐ 104 Vernon Maxwell	.06	.03	.00
☐ 105 Hakeem Olajuwon	.20	.10	.02
☐ 106 Kenny Smith	.03	.01	.00
☐ 107 Larry Smith	.03	.01	.00
☐ 108 Otis Thorpe	.06	.03	.00
☐ 109 Kennard Winchester	.10	.05	.01
☐ 110 David Wood	.08	.04	.01
☐ 111 Greg Dreiling	.03	.01	.00
☐ 112 Vern Fleming	.03	.01	.00
☐ 113 George McCloud	.06	.03	.00
☐ 114 Reggie Miller	.12	.06	.01

1991-92 Sky Box I / 179

☐	115	Chuck Person	.06	.03	.00
☐	116	Mike Sanders	.06	.03	.00
☐	117	Detlef Schrempf	.06	.03	.00
☐	118	Rik Smits	.06	.03	.00
☐	119	LaSalle Thompson	.03	.01	.00
☐	120	Kenny Williams	.03	.01	.00
☐	121	Micheal Williams	.06	.03	.00
☐	122	Ken Bannister	.03	.01	.00
☐	123	Winston Garland	.03	.01	.00
☐	124	Gary Grant	.03	.01	.00
☐	125	Ron Harper	.06	.03	.00
☐	126	Bo Kimble	.06	.03	.00
☐	127	Danny Manning	.12	.06	.01
☐	128	Jeff Martin	.03	.01	.00
☐	129	Ken Norman	.08	.04	.01
☐	130	Olden Polynice	.03	.01	.00
☐	131	Charles Smith	.10	.05	.01
☐	132	Loy Vaught	.12	.06	.01
☐	133	Elden Campbell	.12	.06	.01
☐	134	Vlade Divac	.15	.07	.01
☐	135	Larry Drew	.12	.06	.01
☐	136	A.C. Green	.03	.01	.00
☐	137	Magic Johnson	.90	.45	.09
☐	138	Sam Perkins	.08	.04	.01
☐	139	Byron Scott	.06	.03	.00
☐	140	Tony Smith	.06	.03	.00
☐	141	Terry Teagle	.03	.01	.00
☐	142	Mychal Thompson	.03	.01	.00
☐	143	James Worthy	.12	.06	.01
☐	144	Willie Burton	.06	.03	.00
☐	145	Bimbo Coles	.12	.06	.01
☐	146	Terry Davis	.06	.03	.00
☐	147	Sherman Douglas	.06	.03	.00
☐	148	Kevin Edwards	.03	.01	.00
☐	149	Alec Kessler	.06	.03	.00
☐	150	Grant Long	.03	.01	.00
☐	151	Glen Rice	.40	.20	.04
☐	152	Rony Seikaly	.12	.06	.01
☐	153	Jon Sundvold	.03	.01	.00
☐	154	Billy Thompson	.03	.01	.00
☐	155	Frank Brickowski	.03	.01	.00
☐	156	Lester Conner	.03	.01	.00
☐	157	Jeff Grayer	.03	.01	.00
☐	158	Jay Humphries	.03	.01	.00
☐	159	Larry Krystkowiak	.03	.01	.00
☐	160	Brad Lohaus	.03	.01	.00
☐	161	Dale Ellis	.06	.03	.00
☐	162	Fred Roberts	.03	.01	.00
☐	163	Alvin Robertson	.06	.03	.00
☐	164	Danny Schayes	.03	.01	.00
☐	165	Jack Sikma	.06	.03	.00
☐	166	Randy Breuer	.03	.01	.00
☐	167	Scott Brooks	.03	.01	.00
☐	168	Tony Campbell	.03	.01	.00
☐	169	Tyrone Corbin	.03	.01	.00
☐	170	Gerald Glass	.15	.07	.01
☐	171	Sam Mitchell	.03	.01	.00

180 / 1991-92 Sky Box I

☐ 172	Tod Murphy	.03	.01	.00
☐ 173	Pooh Richardson	.15	.07	.01
☐ 174	Felton Spencer	.06	.03	.00
☐ 175	Bob Thornton	.06	.03	.00
☐ 176	Doug West	.10	.05	.01
☐ 177	Mookie Blaylock	.06	.03	.00
☐ 178	Sam Bowie	.06	.03	.00
☐ 179	Jud Buechler	.06	.03	.00
☐ 180	Derrick Coleman	.50	.25	.05
☐ 181	Chris Dudley	.03	.01	.00
☐ 182	Tate George	.06	.03	.00
☐ 183	Jack Haley	.03	.01	.00
☐ 184	Terry Mills	.20	.10	.02
☐ 185	Chris Morris	.06	.03	.00
☐ 186	Drazen Petrovic	.25	.12	.02
☐ 187	Reggie Theus	.06	.03	.00
☐ 188	Maurice Cheeks	.06	.03	.00
☐ 189	Patrick Ewing	.25	.12	.02
☐ 190	Mark Jackson	.06	.03	.00
☐ 191	Jerrod Mustaf	.10	.05	.01
☐ 192	Charles Oakley	.06	.03	.00
☐ 193	Brian Quinnett	.03	.01	.00
☐ 194	John Starks	.75	.35	.07
☐ 195	Trent Tucker	.03	.01	.00
☐ 196	Kiki Vandeweghe	.06	.03	.00
☐ 197	Kenny Walker	.03	.01	.00
☐ 198	Gerald Wilkins	.06	.03	.00
☐ 199	Mark Acres	.03	.01	.00
☐ 200	Nick Anderson	.15	.07	.01
☐ 201	Michael Ansley	.06	.03	.00
☐ 202	Terry Catledge	.03	.01	.00
☐ 203	Greg Kite	.03	.01	.00
☐ 204	Jerry Reynolds	.15	.07	.01
☐ 205	Dennis Scott	.06	.03	.00
☐ 206	Scott Skiles	.03	.01	.00
☐ 207	Otis Smith	.03	.01	.00
☐ 208	Jeff Turner	.03	.01	.00
☐ 209	Sam Vincent	.03	.01	.00
☐ 210	Ron Anderson	.03	.01	.00
☐ 211	Charles Barkley	.20	.10	.02
☐ 212	Manute Bol	.03	.01	.00
☐ 213	Johnny Dawkins	.03	.01	.00
☐ 214	Armon Gilliam	.03	.01	.00
☐ 215	Rickey Green	.03	.01	.00
☐ 216	Hersey Hawkins	.10	.05	.01
☐ 217	Rick Mahorn	.06	.03	.00
☐ 218	Brian Oliver	.06	.03	.00
☐ 219	Andre Turner	.08	.04	.01
☐ 220	Jayson Williams	.06	.03	.00
☐ 221	Joe Barry Carroll	.03	.01	.00
☐ 222	Cedric Ceballos	.20	.10	.02
☐ 223	Tom Chambers	.08	.04	.01
☐ 224	Jeff Hornacek	.12	.06	.01
☐ 225	Kevin Johnson	.20	.10	.02
☐ 226	Negele Knight	.10	.05	.01
☐ 227	Andrew Lang	.06	.03	.00
☐ 228	Dan Majerle	.12	.06	.01

1991-92 Sky Box I / 181

☐ 229	Xavier McDaniel	.08	.04	.01
☐ 230	Kurt Rambis	.06	.03	.00
☐ 231	Mark West	.03	.01	.00
☐ 232	Alaa Abdelnaby	.10	.05	.01
☐ 233	Danny Ainge	.08	.04	.01
☐ 234	Mark Bryant	.03	.01	.00
☐ 235	Wayne Cooper	.03	.01	.00
☐ 236	Walter Davis	.06	.03	.00
☐ 237	Clyde Drexler	.30	.15	.03
☐ 238	Kevin Duckworth	.03	.01	.00
☐ 239	Jerome Kersey	.03	.01	.00
☐ 240	Terry Porter	.08	.04	.01
☐ 241	Cliff Robinson	.12	.06	.01
☐ 242	Buck Williams	.20	.10	.02
☐ 243	Anthony Bonner	.10	.05	.01
☐ 244	Antoine Carr	.10	.05	.01
☐ 245	Duane Causwell	.03	.01	.00
☐ 246	Bobby Hansen	.06	.03	.00
☐ 247	Jim Les	.03	.01	.00
☐ 248	Travis Mays	.10	.05	.01
☐ 249	Ralph Sampson	.06	.03	.00
☐ 250	Lionel Simmons	.06	.03	.00
☐ 251	Rory Sparrow	.20	.10	.02
☐ 252	Wayman Tisdale	.03	.01	.00
☐ 253	Bill Wennington	.06	.03	.00
☐ 254	Willie Anderson	.03	.01	.00
☐ 255	Terry Cummings	.06	.03	.00
☐ 256	Sean Elliott	.08	.04	.01
☐ 257	Sidney Green	.15	.07	.01
☐ 258	David Greenwood	.03	.01	.00
☐ 259	Avery Johnson	.03	.01	.00
☐ 260	Paul Pressey	.03	.01	.00
☐ 261	David Robinson	.90	.45	.09
☐ 262	Dwayne Schintzius	.06	.03	.00
☐ 263	Rod Strickland	.06	.03	.00
☐ 264	David Wingate	.03	.01	.00
☐ 265	Dana Barros	.03	.01	.00
☐ 266	Benoit Benjamin	.03	.01	.00
☐ 267	Michael Cage	.03	.01	.00
☐ 268	Quintin Dailey	.03	.01	.00
☐ 269	Ricky Pierce	.06	.03	.00
☐ 270	Eddie Johnson	.06	.03	.00
☐ 271	Shawn Kemp	.75	.35	.07
☐ 272	Derrick McKey	.06	.03	.00
☐ 273	Nate McMillan	.03	.01	.00
☐ 274	Gary Payton	.15	.07	.01
☐ 275	Sedale Threatt	.06	.03	.00
☐ 276	Thurl Bailey	.03	.01	.00
☐ 277	Mike Brown	.03	.01	.00
☐ 278	Tony Brown	.03	.01	.00
☐ 279	Mark Eaton	.03	.01	.00
☐ 280	Blue Edwards	.03	.01	.00
☐ 281	Darrell Griffith	.03	.01	.00
☐ 282	Jeff Malone	.08	.04	.01
☐ 283	Karl Malone	.20	.10	.02
☐ 284	Delaney Rudd	.03	.01	.00
☐ 285	John Stockton	.20	.10	.02

182 / 1991-92 Sky Box I

- ☐ 286 Andy Toolson .... .08 .04 .01
- ☐ 287 Mark Alarie .... .03 .01 .00
- ☐ 288 Ledell Eackles .... .06 .03 .00
- ☐ 289 Pervis Ellison .... .25 .12 .02
- ☐ 290 A.J. English .... .12 .06 .01
- ☐ 291 Harvey Grant .... .06 .03 .00
- ☐ 292 Tom Hammonds .... .06 .03 .00
- ☐ 293 Charles Jones .... .03 .01 .00
- ☐ 294 Bernard King .... .08 .04 .01
- ☐ 295 Darrell Walker .... .03 .01 .00
- ☐ 296 John Williams .... .03 .01 .00
- ☐ 297 Haywoode Workman .... .10 .05 .01
- ☐ 298 Muggsy Bogues .... .03 .01 .00
  Charlotte Hornets
  Assist-to-Turnover
  Ratio Leader
- ☐ 299 Lester Conner .... .03 .01 .00
  Milwaukee Bucks
  Steal-to Turnover
  Ratio Leader
- ☐ 300 Michael Adams .... .06 .03 .00
  Denver Nuggets
  Largest One-Year
  Scoring Improvement
- ☐ 301 Chris Mullin .... .10 .05 .01
  Golden State Warriors
  Most Minutes Per Game
- ☐ 302 Otis Thorpe .... .06 .03 .00
  Houston Rockets
  Most Consecutive
  Games Played
- ☐ 303 Mitch Richmond .... .12 .06 .01
  Chris Mullin
  Tim Hardaway
  Highest Scoring Trio
- ☐ 304 Darrell Walker .... .03 .01 .00
  Washington Bullets
  Top Rebounding Guard
- ☐ 305 Jerome Lane .... .03 .01 .00
  Denver Nuggets
  Rebounds Per 48 Minutes
- ☐ 306 John Stockton .... .10 .05 .01
  Utah Jazz
  Assists Per 48 Minutes
- ☐ 307 Michael Jordan .... .60 .30 .06
  Chicago Bulls
  Points Per 48 Minutes
- ☐ 308 Michael Adams .... .06 .03 .00
  Denver Nuggets
  Best Single Game
  Performance: Points
- ☐ 309 Larry Smith .... .03 .01 .00
  Houston Rockets
  Jerome Lane
  Denver Nuggets
  Best Single Game
  Performance: Rebounds

1991-92 Sky Box I / 183

- [ ] 310 Scott Skiles .... .03 .01 .00
Orlando Magic
Best Single Game
Performance: Assists
- [ ] 311 Hakeem Olajuwon .... .20 .10 .02
David Robinson
Best Single Game
Performance: Blocks
- [ ] 312 Alvin Robertson .... .03 .01 .00
Milwaukee Bucks
Best Single Game
Performance: Steals
- [ ] 313 Stay In School Jam .... .03 .01 .00
- [ ] 314 Craig Hodges .... .03 .01 .00
Chicago Bulls
Three-Point Shootout
- [ ] 315 Dee Brown .... .20 .10 .02
Boston Celtics
Slam-Dunk Championship
- [ ] 316 Charles Barkley .... .10 .05 .01
Philadelphia 76ers
All-Star Game MVP
- [ ] 317 Behind the Scenes .... .06 .03 .00
Charles Barkley
Joe Dumars
Kevin McHale
- [ ] 318 Derrick Coleman ART .... .25 .12 .02
New Jersey Nets
- [ ] 319 Lionel Simmons ART .... .12 .06 .01
Sacramento Kings
- [ ] 320 Dennis Scott ART .... .10 .05 .01
Orlando Magic
- [ ] 321 Kendall Gill ART .... .40 .20 .04
Charlotte Hornets
- [ ] 322 Dee Brown ART .... .15 .07 .01
Boston Celtics
- [ ] 323 Magic Johnson .... .40 .20 .04
GQ All-Star Style Team
- [ ] 324 Hakeem Olajuwon .... .10 .05 .01
GQ All-Star Style Team
- [ ] 325 Kevin Willis .... .15 .07 .01
Dominique Wilkins
GQ All-Star Style Team
- [ ] 326 Kevin Willis .... .15 .07 .01
Dominique Wilkins
GQ All-Star Style Team
- [ ] 327 Gerald Wilkins .... .06 .03 .00
GQ All-Star Style Team
- [ ] 328 1891-1991 Basketball .... .08 .04 .01
Centennial Logo
- [ ] 329 Old-Fashioned Ball .... .03 .01 .00
- [ ] 330 Women Take the Court .... .06 .03 .00
- [ ] 331 The Peach Basket .... .03 .01 .00
- [ ] 332 James A. Naismith .... .15 .07 .01
Founder of Basketball
- [ ] 333 Magic Johnson .... 1.00 .50 .10
and Michael Jordan

184 / 1991-92 Sky Box I

		MINT	EXC	G-VG
	Great Moments from the NBA Finals			
☐ 334	Michael Jordan	.60	.30	.06
	Chicago Bulls Great Moments from the NBA Finals			
☐ 335	Vlade Divac	.08	.04	.01
	Los Angeles Lakers Great Moments from the NBA Finals			
☐ 336	John Paxson	.06	.03	.00
	Chicago Bulls Great Moments from the NBA Finals			
☐ 337	Bulls Starting Five	.15	.07	.01
	Great Moments from the NBA Finals			
☐ 338	Language Arts	.03	.01	.00
	Stay in School			
☐ 339	Mathematics	.03	.01	.00
	Stay in School			
☐ 340	Vocational Education	.03	.01	.00
	Stay in School			
☐ 341	Social Studies	.03	.01	.00
	Stay in School			
☐ 342	Physical Education	.03	.01	.00
	Stay in School			
☐ 343	Art	.03	.01	.00
	Stay in School			
☐ 344	Science	.03	.01	.00
	Stay in School			
☐ 345	Checklist 1 (1-60)	.06	.01	.00
☐ 346	Checklist 2 (61-120)	.06	.01	.00
☐ 347	Checklist 3 (121-180)	.06	.01	.00
☐ 348	Checklist 4 (181-244)	.06	.01	.00
☐ 349	Checklist 5 (245-305)	.06	.01	.00
☐ 350	Checklist 6 (306-350)	.06	.01	.00

1991-92 SkyBox Blister Inserts

The first four inserts were featured in series one blister packs, while the last two were inserted in series two blister packs. The cards measure the standard size (2 1/2" by 3 1/2"). The first four have logos on their front and comments on the back. The last two are double-sided cards and display most valuable players from the same team for two consecutive years. The cards are numbered on the back with Roman numerals.

	MINT	EXC	G-VG
COMPLETE SET (6)	2.00	1.00	.20
COMMON PLAYER (1-4)	.25	.12	.02
COMMON PLAYER (5-6)	.25	.12	.02

1991-92 Sky Box II / 185

☐ 1 USA Basketball (Numbered I)	.25	.12	.02
☐ 2 Stay in School It's Your Best Move (Numbered II)	.25	.12	.02
☐ 3 Orlando All-Star Weekend (Numbered III)	.25	.12	.02
☐ 4 Inside Stuff (Numbered IV)	.25	.12	.02
☐ 5 Magic Johnson and James Worthy Back to Back NBA Finals MVP 1987/1988 (Numbered V)	.75	.35	.07
☐ 6 Joe Dumars and Isiah Thomas Back to Back NBA Finals MVP 1989/1990 (Numbered VI)	.25	.12	.02

1991-92 SkyBox II

The 1991-92 SkyBox II basketball set contains 309 cards, measuring the standard size (2 1/2" by 3 1/2"). An unnumbered gold foil-stamped 1992 USA Basketball Team card was randomly inserted into series II foil packs, while the blister packs featured two-card sets of NBA MVPs from the same team for consecutive years. Also the foil packs carry one of four different direct mail offers. On a white card face, the fronts feature color player photos cut out and superimposed on colorful computer-generated geometric shapes and stars. The cards are numbered on the back

186 / 1991-92 Sky Box II

and checklisted below as follows: Team Logos (351-377), Coaches (378-404), Game Frames (405-431), Sixth Man (432-458), Teamwork (459-485), Rising Stars (486-512), Lottery Picks (513-523), Centennial (524-529), 1992 USA Basketball Team (530-546), 1988 USA Basketball Team (547-556), 1984 USA Basketball Team (557-563), The Magic of SkyBox (564-571), SkyBox Salutes (572-576), Skymasters (577-588), Shooting Stars (589-602), Small School Sensations (603-609), NBA Stay in School (610-614), Player Updates (615-653), and Checklists (654-659). The key rookie cards in this series are Stacey Augmon, Larry Johnson, Dikembe Mutumbo, Billy Owens, and Steve Smith.

	MINT	EXC	G-VG
COMPLETE SET (309)	27.00	13.50	2.70
COMMON PLAYER (351-659)	.03	.01	.00
☐ 351 Atlanta Hawks Team Logo	.03	.01	.00
☐ 352 Boston Celtics Team Logo	.03	.01	.00
☐ 353 Charlotte Hornets Team Logo	.03	.01	.00
☐ 354 Chicago Bulls Team Logo	.03	.01	.00
☐ 355 Cleveland Cavaliers Team Logo	.03	.01	.00
☐ 356 Dallas Mavericks Team Logo	.03	.01	.00
☐ 357 Denver Nuggets Team Logo	.03	.01	.00
☐ 358 Detroit Pistons Team Logo	.03	.01	.00
☐ 359 Golden State Warriors Team Logo	.03	.01	.00
☐ 360 Houston Rockets Team Logo	.03	.01	.00
☐ 361 Indiana Pacers Team Logo	.03	.01	.00

1991-92 Sky Box II / 187

- ☐ 362 Los Angeles Clippers .... .03 .01 .00
  Team Logo
- ☐ 363 Los Angeles Lakers .... .03 .01 .00
  Team Logo
- ☐ 364 Miami Heat .... .03 .01 .00
  Team Logo
- ☐ 365 Milwaukee Bucks .... .03 .01 .00
  Team Logo
- ☐ 366 Minnesota Timberwolves .... .03 .01 .00
  Team Logo
- ☐ 367 New Jersey Nets .... .03 .01 .00
  Team Logo
- ☐ 368 New York Knicks .... .03 .01 .00
  Team Logo
- ☐ 369 Orlando Magic .... .03 .01 .00
  Team Logo
- ☐ 370 Philadelphia 76ers .... .03 .01 .00
  Team Logo
- ☐ 371 Phoenix Suns .... .03 .01 .00
  Team Logo
- ☐ 372 Portland Trail Blazers .... .03 .01 .00
  Team Logo
- ☐ 373 Sacramento Kings .... .03 .01 .00
  Team Logo
- ☐ 374 San Antonio Spurs .... .03 .01 .00
  Team Logo
- ☐ 375 Seattle Supersonics .... .03 .01 .00
  Team Logo
- ☐ 376 Utah Jazz .... .03 .01 .00
  Team Logo
- ☐ 377 Washington Bullets .... .03 .01 .00
  Team Logo
- ☐ 378 Bob Weiss CO .... .03 .01 .00
  Atlanta Hawks
- ☐ 379 Chris Ford CO .... .03 .01 .00
  Boston Celtics
- ☐ 380 Allan Bristow CO .... .03 .01 .00
  Charlotte Hornets
- ☐ 381 Phil Jackson CO .... .03 .01 .00
  Chicago Bulls
- ☐ 382 Lenny Wilkens CO .... .06 .03 .00
  Cleveland Cavaliers
- ☐ 383 Richie Adubato CO .... .03 .01 .00
  Dallas Mavericks
- ☐ 384 Paul Westhead CO .... .03 .01 .00
  Denver Nuggets
- ☐ 385 Chuck Daly CO .... .06 .03 .00
  Detroit Pistons
- ☐ 386 Don Nelson CO .... .03 .01 .00
  Golden State Warriors
- ☐ 387 Don Chaney CO .... .03 .01 .00
  Houston Rockets
- ☐ 388 Bob Hill CO .... .06 .03 .00
  Indiana Pacers
- ☐ 389 Mike Schuler CO .... .03 .01 .00
  Los Angeles Clippers
- ☐ 390 Mike Dunleavy CO .... .03 .01 .00

188 / 1991-92 Sky Box II

Los Angeles Lakers			
☐ 391 Kevin Loughery CO	.03	.01	.00
Miami Heat			
☐ 392 Del Harris CO	.03	.01	.00
Milwaukee Bucks			
☐ 393 Jimmy Rodgers CO	.03	.01	.00
Minnesota Timberwolves			
☐ 394 Bill Fitch CO	.03	.01	.00
New Jersey Nets			
☐ 395 Pat Riley CO	.06	.03	.00
New York Knicks			
☐ 396 Matt Guokas CO	.03	.01	.00
Orlando Magic			
☐ 397 Jim Lynam CO	.03	.01	.00
Philadelphia 76ers			
☐ 398 Cotton Fitzsimmons CO	.03	.01	.00
Phoenix Suns			
☐ 399 Rick Adelman CO	.06	.03	.00
Portland Trail Blazers			
☐ 400 Dick Motta CO	.03	.01	.00
Sacramento Kings			
☐ 401 Larry Brown CO	.03	.01	.00
San Antonio Spurs			
☐ 402 K.C. Jones CO	.03	.01	.00
Seattle Supersonics			
☐ 403 Jerry Sloan CO	.03	.01	.00
Utah Jazz			
☐ 404 Wes Unseld CO	.06	.03	.00
Washington Bullets			
☐ 405 Atlanta Hawks	.03	.01	.00
Game Frame			
(Mo Cheeks drives			
around pick)			
☐ 406 Boston Celtics	.03	.01	.00
Game Frame			
(Dee Brown drives			
and shoots)			
☐ 407 Charlotte Hornets	.03	.01	.00
Game Frame			
(Rex Chapman dunking)			
☐ 408 Chicago Bulls	.08	.04	.01
Game Frame			
(Michael Jordan swipes			
Reggie Lewis)			
☐ 409 Cleveland Cavaliers	.03	.01	.00
Game Frame			
(John Williams ties			
up Eddie Lee Wilkins)			
☐ 410 Dallas Mavericks	.03	.01	.00
Game Frame			
(James Donaldson block)			
☐ 411 Denver Nuggets	.03	.01	.00
Game Frame			
(Dikembe Mutombo blocking			
Kenny Smith)			
☐ 412 Detroit Pistons	.06	.03	.00
Game Frame			

1991-92 Sky Box II / 189

(Isiah Thomas)
- 413 Golden State Warriors .... .08 .04 .01
  Game Frame
  (Tim Hardaway and
  Magic Johnson)
- 414 Houston Rockets .... .03 .01 .00
  Game Frame
  (Hakeem Olajuwon
  sets pick)
- 415 Indiana Pacers .... .03 .01 .00
  Game Frame
  (Detlef Schrempf block)
- 416 Los Angeles Clippers .... .03 .01 .00
  Game Frame
  (Danny Manning
  sets pick)
- 417 Los Angeles Lakers .... .08 .04 .01
  Game Frame
  (Magic Johnson
  no-look pass)
- 418 Miami Heat .... .03 .01 .00
  Game Frame
  (Bimbo Coles rebounds)
- 419 Milwaukee Bucks .... .03 .01 .00
  Game Frame
  (Alvin Robertson
  rebounds)
- 420 Minnesota Timberwolves .... .03 .01 .00
  Game Frame
  (Sam Mitchell drives)
- 421 New Jersey Nets .... .03 .01 .00
  Game Frame
  (Sam Bowie blocking
  Mark Eaton's shot)
- 422 New York Knicks .... .03 .01 .00
  Game Frame
  (Mark Jackson
  dribbles between legs)
- 423 Orlando Magic .... .03 .01 .00
  Game Frame
- 424 Philadelphia 76ers .... .03 .01 .00
  Game Frame
  (Charles Barkley
  in rebounding position)
- 425 Phoenix Suns .... .06 .03 .00
  Game Frame
  (Dan Majerle drives)
- 426 Portland Trail Blazers .... .06 .03 .00
  Game Frame
  (Robert Pack drives)
- 427 Sacramento Kings .... .03 .01 .00
  Game Frame
  (Wayman Tisdale drives)
- 428 San Antonio Spurs .... .06 .03 .00
  Game Frame
  (David Robinson scoop)
- 429 Seattle Supersonics .... .03 .01 .00

190 / 1991-92 Sky Box II

Game Frame
(Nate McMillan
protecting ball)
- ☐ 430 Utah Jazz ... .03 .01 .00
Game Frame
(Karl Malone
blocks out)
- ☐ 431 Washington Bullets ... .03 .01 .00
Game Frame
(Michael Adams drives)
- ☐ 432 Duane Ferrell 6M ... .03 .01 .00
Atlanta Hawks
- ☐ 433 Kevin McHale 6M ... .08 .04 .01
Boston Celtics
- ☐ 434 Dell Curry 6M ... .03 .01 .00
Charlotte Hornets
- ☐ 435 B.J. Armstrong 6M ... .08 .04 .01
Chicago Bulls
- ☐ 436 John Williams 6M ... .06 .03 .00
Cleveland Cavaliers
- ☐ 437 Brad Davis 6M ... .03 .01 .00
Dallas Mavericks
- ☐ 438 Marcus Liberty 6M ... .12 .06 .01
Denver Nuggets
- ☐ 439 Mark Aguirre 6M ... .06 .03 .00
Detroit Pistons
- ☐ 440 Rod Higgins 6M ... .03 .01 .00
Golden State Warriors
- ☐ 441 Eric(Sleepy) Floyd 6M ... .03 .01 .00
Houston Rockets
- ☐ 442 Detlef Schrempf 6M ... .06 .03 .00
Indiana Pacers
- ☐ 443 Loy Vaught 6M ... .08 .04 .01
Los Angeles Clippers
- ☐ 444 Terry Teagle 6M ... .03 .01 .00
Los Angeles Lakers
- ☐ 445 Kevin Edwards 6M ... .03 .01 .00
Miami Heat
- ☐ 446 Dale Ellis 6M ... .06 .03 .00
Milwaukee Bucks
- ☐ 447 Tod Murphy 6M ... .03 .01 .00
Minnesota Timberwolves
- ☐ 448 Chris Dudley 6M ... .03 .01 .00
New Jersey Nets
- ☐ 449 Mark Jackson 6M ... .06 .03 .00
New York Knicks
- ☐ 450 Jerry Reynolds 6M ... .03 .01 .00
Orlando Magic
- ☐ 451 Ron Anderson 6M ... .03 .01 .00
Philadelphia 76ers
- ☐ 452 Dan Majerle 6M ... .08 .04 .01
Phoenix Suns
- ☐ 453 Danny Ainge 6M ... .06 .03 .00
Portland Trail Blazers
- ☐ 454 Jim Les 6M ... .06 .03 .00
Sacramento Kings
- ☐ 455 Paul Pressey 6M ... .03 .01 .00

1991-92 Sky Box II / 191

San Antonio Spurs
- ☐ 456 Ricky Pierce 6M .... .06 .03 .00
Seattle Supersonics
- ☐ 457 Mike Brown 6M .... .03 .01 .00
Utah Jazz
- ☐ 458 Ledell Eackles 6M .... .03 .01 .00
Washington Bullets
- ☐ 459 Atlanta Hawks .... .08 .04 .01
  Teamwork
  (Dominique Wilkins
  and Kevin Willis)
- ☐ 460 Boston Celtics .... .12 .06 .01
  Teamwork
  (Larry Bird and
  Robert Parish)
- ☐ 461 Charlotte Hornets .... .15 .07 .01
  Teamwork
  (Rex Chapman and
  Kendall Gill)
- ☐ 462 Chicago Bulls .... .50 .25 .05
  Teamwork
  (Michael Jordan and
  Scottie Pippen)
- ☐ 463 Cleveland Cavaliers .... .06 .03 .00
  Teamwork
  (Craig Ehlo and
  Mark Price)
- ☐ 464 Dallas Mavericks .... .06 .03 .00
  Teamwork
  (Derek Harper and
  Rolando Blackman)
- ☐ 465 Denver Nuggets .... .06 .03 .00
  Teamwork
  (Reggie Williams and
  Chris Jackson)
- ☐ 466 Detroit Pistons .... .08 .04 .01
  Teamwork
  (Isiah Thomas and
  Bill Laimbeer)
- ☐ 467 Golden State Warriors .... .15 .07 .01
  Teamwork
  (Tim Hardaway and
  Chris Mullin)
- ☐ 468 Houston Rockets .... .03 .01 .00
  Teamwork
  (Vernon Maxwell and
  Kenny Smith)
- ☐ 469 Indiana Pacers .... .06 .03 .00
  Teamwork
  (Detlef Schrempf and
  Reggie Miller)
- ☐ 470 Los Angeles Clippers .... .06 .03 .00
  Teamwork
  (Charles Smith and
  Danny Manning)
- ☐ 471 Los Angeles Lakers .... .25 .12 .02
  Teamwork

192 / 1991-92 Sky Box II

(Magic Johnson and
James Worthy)
- ☐ 472 Miami Heat .... .10 .05 .01
    Teamwork
    (Glen Rice and
    Rony Seikaly)
- ☐ 473 Milwaukee Bucks .... .03 .01 .00
    Teamwork
    (Jay Humphries and
    Alvin Robertson)
- ☐ 474 Minnesota Timberwolves .... .06 .03 .00
    Teamwork
    (Tony Campbell and
    Pooh Richardson)
- ☐ 475 New Jersey Nets .... .12 .06 .01
    Teamwork
    (Derrick Coleman and
    Sam Bowie)
- ☐ 476 New York Knicks .... .10 .05 .01
    Teamwork
    (Patrick Ewing and
    Charles Oakley)
- ☐ 477 Orlando Magic .... .06 .03 .00
    Teamwork
    (Dennis Scott and
    Scott Skiles)
- ☐ 478 Philadelphia 76ers .... .10 .05 .01
    Teamwork
    (Charles Barkley and
    Hersey Hawkins)
- ☐ 479 Phoenix Suns .... .08 .04 .01
    Teamwork
    (Kevin Johnson and
    Tom Chambers)
- ☐ 480 Portland Trail Blazers ...... .15 .07 .01
    Teamwork
    (Clyde Drexler and
    Terry Porter)
- ☐ 481 Sacramento Kings .... .08 .04 .01
    Teamwork
    (Lionel Simmons and
    Wayman Tisdale)
- ☐ 482 San Antonio Spurs .... .06 .03 .00
    Teamwork
    (Terry Cummings and
    Sean Elliott)
- ☐ 483 Seattle Supersonics .... .03 .01 .00
    Teamwork
    (Eddie Johnson and
    Ricky Pierce)
- ☐ 484 Utah Jazz .... .15 .07 .01
    Teamwork
    (Karl Malone and
    John Stockton)
- ☐ 485 Washington Bullets .... .06 .03 .00
    Teamwork
    (Harvey Grant and

1991-92 Sky Box II / 193

Bernard King)
- ☐ 486 Rumeal Robinson RS .... .06 .03 .00
  Atlanta Hawks
- ☐ 487 Dee Brown RS .... .20 .10 .02
  Boston Celtics
- ☐ 488 Kendall Gill RS .... .40 .20 .04
  Charlotte Hornets
- ☐ 489 B.J. Armstrong RS .... .10 .05 .01
  Chicago Bulls
- ☐ 490 Danny Ferry RS .... .06 .03 .00
  Cleveland Cavaliers
- ☐ 491 Randy White RS .... .03 .01 .00
  Dallas Mavericks
- ☐ 492 Chris Jackson RS .... .06 .03 .00
  Denver Nuggets
- ☐ 493 Lance Blanks RS .... .03 .01 .00
  Detroit Pistons
- ☐ 494 Tim Hardaway RS .... .40 .20 .04
  Golden State Warriors
- ☐ 495 Vernon Maxwell RS .... .06 .03 .00
  Houston Rockets
- ☐ 496 Micheal Williams RS .... .06 .03 .00
  Indiana Pacers
- ☐ 497 Charles Smith RS .... .06 .03 .00
  Los Angeles Clippers
- ☐ 498 Vlade Divac RS .... .08 .04 .01
  Los Angeles Lakers
- ☐ 499 Willie Burton RS .... .06 .03 .00
  Miami Heat
- ☐ 500 Jeff Grayer RS .... .03 .01 .00
  Milwaukee Bucks
- ☐ 501 Pooh Richardson RS .... .08 .04 .01
  Minnesota Timberwolves
- ☐ 502 Derrick Coleman RS .... .25 .12 .02
  New Jersey Nets
- ☐ 503 John Starks RS .... .20 .10 .02
  New York Knicks
- ☐ 504 Dennis Scott RS .... .10 .05 .01
  Orlando Magic
- ☐ 505 Hersey Hawkins RS .... .06 .03 .00
  Philadelphia 76ers
- ☐ 506 Negele Knight RS .... .06 .03 .00
  Phoenix Suns
- ☐ 507 Cliff Robinson RS .... .10 .05 .01
  Portland Trail Blazers
- ☐ 508 Lionel Simmons RS .... .12 .06 .01
  Sacramento Kings
- ☐ 509 David Robinson RS .... .40 .20 .04
  San Antonio Spurs
- ☐ 510 Gary Payton RS .... .10 .05 .01
  Seattle Supersonics
- ☐ 511 Blue Edwards RS .... .06 .03 .00
  Utah Jazz
- ☐ 512 Harvey Grant RS .... .06 .03 .00
  Washington Bullets
- ☐ 513 Larry Johnson .... 6.00 3.00 .60
  Charlotte Hornets

194 / 1991-92 Sky Box II

☐ 514 Kenny Anderson	1.00	.50	.10
New Jersey Nets			
☐ 515 Billy Owens	3.50	1.75	.35
Golden State Warriors			
☐ 516 Dikembe Mutombo	3.50	1.75	.35
Denver Nuggets			
☐ 517 Steve Smith	1.25	.60	.12
Miami Heat			
☐ 518 Doug Smith	.40	.20	.04
Dallas Mavericks			
☐ 519 Luc Longley	.20	.10	.02
Minnesota Timberwolves			
☐ 520 Mark Macon	.40	.20	.04
Denver Nuggets			
☐ 521 Stacey Augmon	1.00	.50	.10
Atlanta Hawks			
☐ 522 Brian Williams	.40	.20	.04
Orlando Magic			
☐ 523 Terrell Brandon	.50	.25	.05
Cleveland Cavaliers			
☐ 524 The Ball	.03	.01	.00
☐ 525 The Basket	.03	.01	.00
☐ 526 The 24-second Shot	.03	.01	.00
Clock			
☐ 527 The Game Program	.03	.01	.00
☐ 528 The Championship Gift	.03	.01	.00
☐ 529 The Championship Trophy	.03	.01	.00
☐ 530 Charles Barkley USA	.75	.35	.07
☐ 531 Larry Bird USA	1.00	.50	.10
☐ 532 Patrick Ewing USA	.90	.45	.09
☐ 533 Magic Johnson USA	1.75	.85	.17
☐ 534 Michael Jordan USA	2.50	1.25	.25
☐ 535 Karl Malone USA	.75	.35	.07
☐ 536 Chris Mullin USA	.75	.35	.07
☐ 537 Scottie Pippen USA	1.25	.60	.12
☐ 538 David Robinson USA	1.75	.85	.17
☐ 539 John Stockton USA	.75	.35	.07
☐ 540 Chuck Daly CO USA	.25	.12	.02
☐ 541 P.J. Carlesimo CO USA	.25	.12	.02
☐ 542 Mike Krzyzewski CO USA	.40	.20	.04
☐ 543 Lenny Wilkens CO USA	.20	.10	.02
☐ 544 Team USA Card 1	1.50	.75	.15
☐ 545 Team USA Card 2	1.50	.75	.15
☐ 546 Team USA Card 3	1.50	.75	.15
☐ 547 Willie Anderson USA	.06	.03	.00
☐ 548 Stacey Augmon USA	.75	.35	.07
☐ 549 Bimbo Coles USA	.12	.06	.01
☐ 550 Jeff Grayer USA	.06	.03	.00
☐ 551 Hersey Hawkins USA	.15	.07	.01
☐ 552 Dan Majerle USA	.12	.06	.01
☐ 553 Danny Manning USA	.15	.07	.01
☐ 554 J.R. Reid USA	.06	.03	.00
☐ 555 Mitch Richmond USA	.12	.06	.01
☐ 556 Charles Smith USA	.12	.06	.01
☐ 557 Vern Fleming USA	.06	.03	.00
☐ 558 Joe Kleine USA	.06	.03	.00
☐ 559 Jon Koncak USA	.06	.03	.00

1991-92 Sky Box II / 195

- [ ] 560 Sam Perkins USA .... .12 .06 .01
- [ ] 561 Alvin Robertson USA .... .06 .03 .00
- [ ] 562 Wayman Tisdale USA .... .06 .03 .00
- [ ] 563 Jeff Turner USA .... .06 .03 .00
- [ ] 564 Tony Campbell .... .03 .01 .00
  Minnesota Timberwolves
  Magic of SkyBox
- [ ] 565 Joe Dumars .... .08 .04 .01
  Detroit Pistons
  Magic of SkyBox
- [ ] 566 Horace Grant .... .08 .04 .01
  Chicago Bulls
  Magic of SkyBox
- [ ] 567 Reggie Lewis .... .10 .05 .01
  Boston Celtics
  Magic of SkyBox
- [ ] 568 Hakeem Olajuwon .... .10 .05 .01
  Houston Rockets
  Magic of SkyBox
- [ ] 569 Sam Perkins .... .06 .03 .00
  Los Angeles Lakers
  Magic of SkyBox
- [ ] 570 Chuck Person .... .06 .03 .00
  Indiana Pacers
  Magic of SkyBox
- [ ] 571 Buck Williams .... .08 .04 .01
  Portland Trail Blazers
  Magic of SkyBox
- [ ] 572 Michael Jordan .... .60 .30 .06
  Chicago Bulls
  SkyBox Salutes
- [ ] 573 Bernard King .... .06 .03 .00
  NBA All-Star
  SkyBox Salutes
- [ ] 574 Moses Malone .... .08 .04 .01
  Milwaukee Bucks
  SkyBox Salutes
- [ ] 575 Robert Parish .... .08 .04 .01
  Boston Celtics
  SkyBox Salutes
- [ ] 576 Pat Riley CO .... .06 .03 .00
  Los Angeles Lakers
  SkyBox Salutes
- [ ] 577 Dee Brown .... .15 .07 .01
  Boston Celtics
  SkyMaster
- [ ] 578 Rex Chapman .... .06 .03 .00
  Charlotte Hornets
  SkyMaster
- [ ] 579 Clyde Drexler .... .15 .07 .01
  Portland Trail Blazers
  SkyMaster
- [ ] 580 Blue Edwards .... .03 .01 .00
  Utah Jazz
  SkyMaster
- [ ] 581 Ron Harper .... .06 .03 .00
  Los Angeles Clippers

196 / 1991-92 Sky Box II

☐ 582	SkyMaster Kevin Johnson ....10 Phoenix Suns		.05	.01
☐ 583	SkyMaster Michael Jordan ....60 Chicago Bulls		.30	.06
☐ 584	SkyMaster Shawn Kemp ....30 Seattle Supersonics		.15	.03
☐ 585	SkyMaster Xavier McDaniel ....08 New York Knicks		.04	.01
☐ 586	SkyMaster Scottie Pippen ....25 Chicago Bulls		.12	.02
☐ 587	SkyMaster Kenny Smith ....03 Houston Rockets		.01	.00
☐ 588	SkyMaster Dominique Wilkins ....08 Atlanta Hawks		.04	.01
☐ 589	SkyMaster Michael Adams ....06 Denver Nuggets		.03	.00
☐ 590	Shooting Star Danny Ainge ....06 Denver Nuggets		.03	.00
☐ 591	Shooting Star Larry Bird ....20 Boston Celtics		.10	.02
☐ 592	Shooting Star Dale Ellis ....06 Milwaukee Bucks		.03	.00
☐ 593	Shooting Star Hersey Hawkins ....06 Philadelphia 76ers		.03	.00
☐ 594	Shooting Star Jeff Hornacek ....08 Phoenix Suns		.04	.01
☐ 595	Shooting Star Jeff Malone ....08 Utah Jazz		.04	.01
☐ 596	Shooting Star Reggie Miller ....08 Indiana Pacers		.04	.01
☐ 597	Shooting Star Chris Mullin ....10 Golden State Warriors		.05	.01
☐ 598	Shooting Star John Paxson ....06 Chicago Bulls		.03	.00
☐ 599	Shooting Star Drazen Petrovic ....12 New Jersey Nets		.06	.01
☐ 600	Shooting Star Ricky Pierce ....06 Milwaukee Bucks		.03	.00

1991-92 Sky Box II / 197

	Shooting Star		
☐ 601 Mark Price .08	.04	.01
	Cleveland Cavaliers		
	Shooting Star		
☐ 602 Dennis Scott .08	.04	.01
	Orlando Magic		
	Shooting Star		
☐ 603 Manute Bol .03	.01	.00
	Philadelphia 76ers		
	Small School Sensation		
☐ 604 Jerome Kersey .08	.04	.01
	Portland Trail Blazers		
	Small School Sensation		
☐ 605 Charles Oakley .03	.01	.00
	New York Knicks		
	Small School Sensation		
☐ 606 Scottie Pippen .20	.10	.02
	Chicago Bulls		
	Small School Sensation		
☐ 607 Terry Porter .08	.04	.01
	Portland Trail Blazers		
	Small School Sensation		
☐ 608 Dennis Rodman .08	.04	.01
	Detroit Pistons		
	Small School Sensation		
☐ 609 Sedale Threatt .06	.03	.00
	Los Angeles Lakers		
	Small School Sensation		
☐ 610 Business .03	.01	.00
	Stay in School		
☐ 611 Engineering .03	.01	.00
	Stay in School		
☐ 612 Law .03	.01	.00
	Stay in School		
☐ 613 Liberal Arts .03	.01	.00
	Stay in School		
☐ 614 Medicine .03	.01	.00
	Stay in School		
☐ 615 Maurice Cheeks .06	.03	.00
	Atlanta Hawks		
☐ 616 Travis Mays .06	.03	.00
	Atlanta Hawks		
☐ 617 Blair Rasmussen .03	.01	.00
	Atlanta Hawks		
☐ 618 Alexander Volkov .06	.03	.00
	Atlanta Hawks		
☐ 619 Rickey Green .03	.01	.00
	Boston Celtics		
☐ 620 Bobby Hansen .03	.01	.00
	Chicago Bulls		
☐ 621 John Battle .03	.01	.00
	Cleveland Cavaliers		
☐ 622 Terry Davis .08	.04	.01
	Dallas Mavericks		
☐ 623 Walter Davis .06	.03	.00
	Denver Nuggets		
☐ 624 Winston Garland .03	.01	.00

198 / 1991-92 Sky Box II

Denver Nuggets			
☐ 625 Scott Hastings	.03	.01	.00
Denver Nuggets			
☐ 626 Brad Sellers	.03	.01	.00
Denver Nuggets			
☐ 627 Darrell Walker	.03	.01	.00
Detroit Pistons			
☐ 628 Orlando Woolridge	.06	.03	.00
Detroit Pistons			
☐ 629 Tony Brown	.03	.01	.00
Los Angeles Clippers			
☐ 630 James Edwards	.03	.01	.00
Los Angeles Clippers			
☐ 631 Doc Rivers	.06	.03	.00
Los Angeles Clippers			
☐ 632 Jack Haley	.03	.01	.00
Los Angeles Lakers			
☐ 633 Sedale Threatt	.06	.03	.00
Los Angeles Lakers			
☐ 634 Moses Malone	.12	.06	.01
Milwaukee Bucks			
☐ 635 Thurl Bailey	.03	.01	.00
Minnesota Timberwolves			
☐ 636 Rafael Addison	.15	.07	.01
New Jersey Nets			
☐ 637 Tim McCormick	.03	.01	.00
New York Knicks			
☐ 638 Xavier McDaniel	.08	.04	.01
New York Knicks			
☐ 639 Charles Shackleford	.03	.01	.00
Philadelphia 76ers			
☐ 640 Mitchell Wiggins	.03	.01	.00
Philadelphia 76ers			
☐ 641 Jerrod Mustaf	.08	.04	.01
Phoenix Suns			
☐ 642 Dennis Hopson	.06	.03	.00
Sacramento Kings			
☐ 643 Les Jepsen	.06	.03	.00
Sacramento Kings			
☐ 644 Mitch Richmond	.12	.06	.01
Sacramento Kings			
☐ 645 Dwayne Schintzius	.06	.03	.00
Sacramento Kings			
☐ 646 Spud Webb	.06	.03	.00
Sacramento Kings			
☐ 647 Jud Buechler	.03	.01	.00
San Antonio Spurs			
☐ 648 Antoine Carr	.03	.01	.00
San Antonio Spurs			
☐ 649 Tyrone Corbin	.03	.01	.00
Utah Jazz			
☐ 650 Michael Adams	.08	.04	.01
Washington Bullets			
☐ 651 Ralph Sampson	.06	.03	.00
Washington Bullets			
☐ 652 Andre Turner	.06	.03	.00
Washington Bullets			

1983-84 Star NBA / 199

☐ 653 David Wingate Washington Bullets	.03	.01	.00
☐ 654 Checklist "S" (351-404)	.06	.01	.00
☐ 655 Checklist "K" (405-458)	.06	.01	.00
☐ 656 Checklist "Y" (459-512)	.06	.01	.00
☐ 657 Checklist "B" (513-563)	.06	.01	.00
☐ 658 Checklist "O" (564-614)	.06	.01	.00
☐ 659 Checklist "X" (615-659)	.06	.01	.00
☐ NNO Clyde Drexler USA SP (Send-away)	25.00	12.50	2.50
☐ NNO Team USA Card SP	20.00	10.00	2.00

1983-84 Star NBA

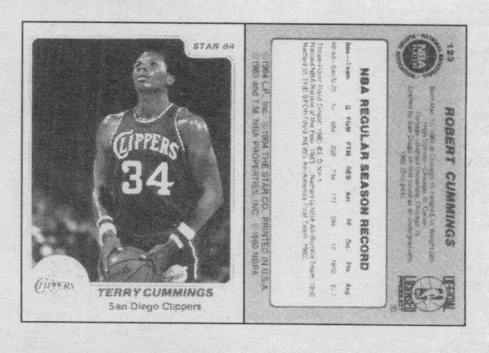

This set of 276 cards was issued in four series during the first six months of 1984. The set features players by team throughout the NBA. Several teams in the first series (1-100) are difficult to obtain due to extensive miscuts (all of which were destroyed according to the company) in the original production process for those teams. Cards measure 2 1/2" by 3 1/2" and have a colored border around the fronts of the cards according to the team with corresponding color printing on the backs. Cards are numbered according to team order, e.g., Philadelphia 76ers (1-12), Los Angeles Lakers (13-25), Boston Celtics (26-37), Milwaukee Bucks (38-48), Dallas Mavericks (49-60), New York Knicks (61-72), Houston Rockets (73-84), Detroit Pistons (85-96), Portland Trail Blazers (97-108), Phoenix Suns (109-120), San Diego Clippers (121-132), Utah Jazz (133-144), New Jersey Nets (145-156), Indiana Pacers (157-168), Chicago Bulls (169-180), Denver

200 / 1983-84 Star NBA

Nuggets (181-192), Seattle Supersonics (193-203), Washington Bullets (204-215), Kansas City Kings (216-227), Cleveland Cavaliers (228-240), San Antonio Spurs (241-251), Golden State Warriors (252-263), and Atlanta Hawks (264-275). The key extended rookie cards in this set are Mark Aguirre, Rolando Blackman, Tom Chambers, Clyde Drexler, Dale Ellis, Derek Harper, Isiah Thomas, Dominique Wilkins, and James Worthy. A promotional card of Sidney Moncrief was produced in limited quantities, but it was numbered 39 rather than 38 as it was in the regular set.

	MINT	EXC	G-VG
COMPLETE SET (276)	2700.00	1250.00	325.00
COMMON 76ER (1-12)	5.00	2.50	.50
COMMON LAKERS (13-25)	3.50	1.75	.35
COMMON CELTICS (26-37)	11.00	5.50	1.10
COMMON BUCKS (38-48)	3.50	1.75	.35
COMMON MAVS (49-60)	30.00	15.00	3.00
COMMON PLAYER (61-275)	1.50	.75	.15
☐ 1 Julius Erving	90.00	45.00	9.00
☐ 2 Maurice Cheeks	14.00	7.00	1.40
☐ 3 Franklin Edwards	5.00	2.50	.50
☐ 4 Marc Iavaroni	5.00	2.50	.50
☐ 5 Clemon Johnson	5.00	2.50	.50
☐ 6 Bobby Jones	7.50	3.75	.75
☐ 7 Moses Malone	35.00	17.50	3.50
☐ 8 Leo Rautins	5.00	2.50	.50
☐ 9 Clint Richardson	5.00	2.50	.50
☐ 10 Sedale Threatt	25.00	12.50	2.50
☐ 11 Andrew Toney	9.00	4.50	.90
☐ 12 Sam Williams	5.00	2.50	.50
☐ 13 Magic Johnson	180.00	90.00	18.00
☐ 14 Kareem Abdul-Jabbar	55.00	27.50	5.50
☐ 15 Michael Cooper	8.00	4.00	.80
☐ 16 Calvin Garrett	3.50	1.75	.35
☐ 17 Mitch Kupchak	3.50	1.75	.35
☐ 18 Bob McAdoo	9.00	4.50	.90
☐ 19 Mike McGee	4.50	2.25	.45
☐ 20 Swen Nater	4.00	2.00	.40
☐ 21 Kurt Rambis	10.00	5.00	1.00
☐ 22 Byron Scott	30.00	15.00	3.00
☐ 23 Larry Spriggs	4.00	2.00	.40
☐ 24 Jamaal Wilkes	5.00	2.50	.50
☐ 25 James Worthy	110.00	55.00	11.00
☐ 26 Larry Bird	150.00	75.00	15.00
☐ 27 Danny Ainge	50.00	25.00	5.00
☐ 28 Quinn Buckner	12.00	6.00	1.20
☐ 29 M.L. Carr	12.00	6.00	1.20
☐ 30 Carlos Clark	11.00	5.50	1.10
☐ 31 Gerald Henderson	11.00	5.50	1.10
☐ 32 Dennis Johnson	15.00	7.50	1.50
☐ 33 Cedric Maxwell	13.50	6.50	1.35
☐ 34 Kevin McHale	45.00	22.50	4.50
☐ 35 Robert Parish	60.00	30.00	6.00
☐ 36 Scott Wedman	12.00	6.00	1.20
☐ 37 Greg Kite	12.00	6.00	1.20
☐ 38 Sidney Moncrief	13.50	6.50	1.35
☐ 39A Sidney Moncrief (Promotional card)	100.00	50.00	10.00
☐ 39B Nate Archibald	13.50	6.50	1.35

1983-84 Star NBA / 201

☐	40 Randy Breuer	5.50	2.75	.55
☐	41 Junior Bridgeman	4.00	2.00	.40
☐	42 Harvey Catchings	3.50	1.75	.35
☐	43 Kevin Grevey	3.50	1.75	.35
☐	44 Marques Johnson	6.00	3.00	.60
☐	45 Bob Lanier	13.50	6.50	1.35
☐	46 Alton Lister	6.00	3.00	.60
☐	47 Paul Mokeski	4.50	2.25	.45
☐	48 Paul Pressey	9.00	4.50	.90
☐	49 Mark Aguirre	75.00	37.50	7.50
☐	50 Rolando Blackman	100.00	50.00	10.00
☐	51 Pat Cummings	35.00	17.50	3.50
☐	52 Brad Davis	40.00	20.00	4.00
☐	53 Dale Ellis	75.00	37.50	7.50
☐	54 Bill Garnett	30.00	15.00	3.00
☐	55 Derek Harper	80.00	40.00	8.00
☐	56 Kurt Nimphius	30.00	15.00	3.00
☐	57 Jim Spanarkel	30.00	15.00	3.00
☐	58 Elston Turner	30.00	15.00	3.00
☐	59 Jay Vincent	35.00	17.50	3.50
☐	60 Mark West	45.00	22.50	4.50
☐	61 Bernard King	12.00	6.00	1.20
☐	62 Bill Cartwright	6.50	3.25	.65
☐	63 Len Elmore	2.50	1.25	.25
☐	64 Eric Fernsten	1.50	.75	.15
☐	65 Ernie Grunfeld	2.50	1.25	.25
☐	66 Louis Orr	1.50	.75	.15
☐	67 Leonard Robinson	2.50	1.25	.25
☐	68 Rory Sparrow	3.50	1.75	.35
☐	69 Trent Tucker	3.00	1.50	.30
☐	70 Darrell Walker	5.00	2.50	.50
☐	71 Marvin Webster	1.50	.75	.15
☐	72 Ray Williams	1.50	.75	.15
☐	73 Ralph Sampson	6.00	3.00	.60
☐	74 James Bailey	1.50	.75	.15
☐	75 Phil Ford	2.00	1.00	.20
☐	76 Elvin Hayes	9.00	4.50	.90
☐	77 Caldwell Jones	2.00	1.00	.20
☐	78 Major Jones	1.50	.75	.15
☐	79 Allen Leavell	1.50	.75	.15
☐	80 Lewis Lloyd	1.50	.75	.15
☐	81 Rodney McCray	7.00	3.50	.70
☐	82 Robert Reid	1.50	.75	.15
☐	83 Terry Teagle	8.00	4.00	.80
☐	84 Wally Walker	1.50	.75	.15
☐	85 Kelly Tripucka	3.50	1.75	.35
☐	86 Kent Benson	2.00	1.00	.20
☐	87 Earl Cureton	2.50	1.25	.25
☐	88 Lionel Hollins	2.00	1.00	.20
☐	89 Vinnie Johnson	4.00	2.00	.40
☐	90 Bill Laimbeer	7.00	3.50	.70
☐	91 Cliff Levingston	8.00	4.00	.80
☐	92 John Long	1.50	.75	.15
☐	93 David Thirdkill	1.50	.75	.15
☐	94 Isiah Thomas	150.00	75.00	15.00
☐	95 Ray Tolbert	2.50	1.25	.25
☐	96 Terry Tyler	1.50	.75	.15

202 / 1983-84 Star NBA

☐ 97 Jim Paxson	2.00	1.00	.20
☐ 98 Kenny Carr	1.50	.75	.15
☐ 99 Wayne Cooper	1.50	.75	.15
☐ 100 Clyde Drexler	350.00	175.00	35.00
☐ 101 Jeff Lamp	2.00	1.00	.20
☐ 102 Lafayette Lever	8.00	4.00	.80
☐ 103 Calvin Natt	2.00	1.00	.20
☐ 104 Audie Norris	1.50	.75	.15
☐ 105 Tom Piotrowski	1.50	.75	.15
☐ 106 Mychal Thompson	3.00	1.50	.30
☐ 107 Darnell Valentine	2.00	1.00	.20
☐ 108 Pete Verhoeven	1.50	.75	.15
☐ 109 Walter Davis	3.00	1.50	.30
☐ 110 Alvan Adams	2.00	1.00	.20
☐ 111 James Edwards	3.00	1.50	.30
☐ 112 Rod Foster	2.00	1.00	.20
☐ 113 Maurice Lucas	3.00	1.50	.30
☐ 114 Kyle Macy	2.00	1.00	.20
☐ 115 Larry Nance	40.00	20.00	4.00
☐ 116 Charles Pittman	1.50	.75	.15
☐ 117 Rick Robey	2.00	1.00	.20
☐ 118 Mike Sanders	4.50	2.25	.45
☐ 119 Alvin Scott	1.50	.75	.15
☐ 120 Paul Westphal	3.00	1.50	.30
☐ 121 Bill Walton	9.00	4.50	.90
☐ 122 Michael Brooks	1.50	.75	.15
☐ 123 Terry Cummings	30.00	15.00	3.00
☐ 124 James Donaldson	3.50	1.75	.35
☐ 125 Craig Hodges	10.00	5.00	1.00
☐ 126 Greg Kelser	2.00	1.00	.20
☐ 127 Hank McDowell	1.50	.75	.15
☐ 128 Billy McKinney	2.00	1.00	.20
☐ 129 Norm Nixon	2.50	1.25	.25
☐ 130 Ricky Pierce	33.00	15.00	3.00
☐ 131 Derek Smith	3.00	1.50	.30
☐ 132 Jerome Whitehead	1.50	.75	.15
☐ 133 Adrian Dantley	5.50	2.75	.55
☐ 134 Mitch Anderson	1.50	.75	.15
☐ 135 Thurl Bailey	7.00	3.50	.70
☐ 136 Tom Boswell	1.50	.75	.15
☐ 137 John Drew	2.00	1.00	.20
☐ 138 Mark Eaton	9.00	4.50	.90
☐ 139 Jerry Eaves	1.50	.75	.15
☐ 140 Rickey Green	3.50	1.75	.35
☐ 141 Darrell Griffith	2.50	1.25	.25
☐ 142 Bobby Hansen	3.50	1.75	.35
☐ 143 Rich Kelley	1.50	.75	.15
☐ 144 Jeff Wilkins	1.50	.75	.15
☐ 145 Buck Williams	40.00	20.00	4.00
☐ 146 Otis Birdsong	2.00	1.00	.20
☐ 147 Darwin Cook	1.50	.75	.15
☐ 148 Darryl Dawkins	3.50	1.75	.35
☐ 149 Mike Gminski	2.50	1.25	.25
☐ 150 Reggie Johnson	1.50	.75	.15
☐ 151 Albert King	2.50	1.25	.25
☐ 152 Mike O'Koren	2.00	1.00	.20
☐ 153 Kelvin Ransey	1.50	.75	.15

1983-84 Star NBA / 203

	#	Player	Price 1	Price 2	Price 3
☐	154	M.R. Richardson	2.00	1.00	.20
☐	155	Clarence Walker	1.50	.75	.15
☐	156	Bill Willoughby	1.50	.75	.15
☐	157	Steve Stipanovich	2.50	1.25	.25
☐	158	Butch Carter	1.50	.75	.15
☐	159	Edwin Leroy Combs	1.50	.75	.15
☐	160	George L. Johnson	1.50	.75	.15
☐	161	Clark Kellogg	3.00	1.50	.30
☐	162	Sidney Lowe	2.50	1.25	.25
☐	163	Kevin McKenna	1.50	.75	.15
☐	164	Jerry Sichting	2.50	1.25	.25
☐	165	Brook Steppe	1.50	.75	.15
☐	166	Jimmy Thomas	1.50	.75	.15
☐	167	Granville Waiters	1.50	.75	.15
☐	168	Herb Williams	7.00	3.50	.70
☐	169	Dave Corzine	1.50	.75	.15
☐	170	Wallace Bryant	1.50	.75	.15
☐	171	Quintin Dailey	2.50	1.25	.25
☐	172	Sidney Green	2.50	1.25	.25
☐	173	David Greenwood	1.50	.75	.15
☐	174	Rod Higgins	3.50	1.75	.35
☐	175	Clarence Johnson	1.50	.75	.15
☐	176	Ronnie Lester	1.50	.75	.15
☐	177	Jawann Oldham	1.50	.75	.15
☐	178	Ennis Whatley	3.00	1.50	.30
☐	179	Mitchell Wiggins	2.50	1.25	.25
☐	180	Orlando Woolridge	20.00	10.00	2.00
☐	181	Kiki Vandeweghe	9.00	4.50	.90
☐	182	Richard Anderson	2.00	1.00	.20
☐	183	Howard Carter	1.50	.75	.15
☐	184	T.R. Dunn	1.50	.75	.15
☐	185	Keith Edmonson	1.50	.75	.15
☐	186	Alex English	9.00	4.50	.90
☐	187	Mike Evans	1.50	.75	.15
☐	188	Bill Hanzlik	3.00	1.50	.30
☐	189	Dan Issel	7.00	3.50	.70
☐	190	Anthony Roberts	1.50	.75	.15
☐	191	Danny Schayes	7.00	3.50	.70
☐	192	Rob Williams	1.50	.75	.15
☐	193	Jack Sikma	3.50	1.75	.35
☐	194	Fred Brown	2.00	1.00	.20
☐	195	Tom Chambers	60.00	30.00	6.00
☐	196	Steve Hawes	1.50	.75	.15
☐	197	Steve Hayes	1.50	.75	.15
☐	198	Reggie King	1.50	.75	.15
☐	199	Scooter McCray	2.00	1.00	.20
☐	200	Jon Sundvold	2.50	1.25	.25
☐	201	Danny Vranes	2.00	1.00	.20
☐	202	Gus Williams	2.00	1.00	.20
☐	203	Al Wood	2.00	1.00	.20
☐	204	Jeff Ruland	3.50	1.75	.35
☐	205	Greg Ballard	1.50	.75	.15
☐	206	Charles Davis	1.50	.75	.15
☐	207	Darren Daye	2.00	1.00	.20
☐	208	Michael Gibson	1.50	.75	.15
☐	209	Frank Johnson	1.50	.75	.15
☐	210	Joe Kopicki	1.50	.75	.15

204 / 1983-84 Star NBA

- ☐ 211 Rick Mahorn ..... 2.50 / 1.25 / .25
- ☐ 212 Jeff Malone ..... 35.00 / 17.50 / 3.50
- ☐ 213 Tom McMillen ..... 4.25 / 2.10 / .42
- ☐ 214 Ricky Sobers ..... 1.50 / .75 / .15
- ☐ 215 Bryan Warrick ..... 1.50 / .75 / .15
- ☐ 216 Billy Knight ..... 1.50 / .75 / .15
- ☐ 217 Don Buse ..... 1.50 / .75 / .15
- ☐ 218 Larry Drew ..... 2.50 / 1.25 / .25
- ☐ 219 Eddie Johnson ..... 17.00 / 8.50 / 1.70
- ☐ 220 Joe Meriweather ..... 1.50 / .75 / .15
- ☐ 221 Larry Micheaux ..... 1.50 / .75 / .15
- ☐ 222 Ed Nealy ..... 3.00 / 1.50 / .30
- ☐ 223 Mark Olberding ..... 1.50 / .75 / .15
- ☐ 224 Dave Robisch ..... 1.50 / .75 / .15
- ☐ 225 Reggie Theus ..... 3.50 / 1.75 / .35
- ☐ 226 LaSalle Thompson ..... 4.00 / 2.00 / .40
- ☐ 227 Mike Woodson ..... 2.00 / 1.00 / .20
- ☐ 228 World B. Free ..... 3.00 / 1.50 / .30
- ☐ 229 John Bagley ..... 9.00 / 4.50 / .90
- ☐ 230 Jeff Cook ..... 1.50 / .75 / .15
- ☐ 231 Geoff Crompton ..... 1.50 / .75 / .15
- ☐ 232 John Garris ..... 1.50 / .75 / .15
- ☐ 233 Stewart Granger ..... 1.50 / .75 / .15
- ☐ 234 Roy Hinson ..... 3.00 / 1.50 / .30
- ☐ 235 Phil Hubbard ..... 1.50 / .75 / .15
- ☐ 236 Geoff Huston ..... 1.50 / .75 / .15
- ☐ 237 Ben Poquette ..... 1.50 / .75 / .15
- ☐ 238 Cliff Robinson ..... 2.00 / 1.00 / .20
- ☐ 239 Lonnie Shelton ..... 1.50 / .75 / .15
- ☐ 240 Paul Thompson ..... 1.50 / .75 / .15
- ☐ 241 George Gervin ..... 8.00 / 4.00 / .80
- ☐ 242 Gene Banks ..... 1.50 / .75 / .15
- ☐ 243 Ron Brewer ..... 1.50 / .75 / .15
- ☐ 244 Artis Gilmore ..... 5.50 / 2.75 / .55
- ☐ 245 Edgar Jones ..... 1.50 / .75 / .15
- ☐ 246 John Lucas ..... 2.50 / 1.25 / .25
- ☐ 247A Mike Mitchell ERR ..... 6.00 / 3.00 / .60
  (Photo actually Mark McNamara)
- ☐ 247B Mike Mitchell COR ..... 2.00 / 1.00 / .20
- ☐ 248A Mark McNamara ERR ..... 6.00 / 3.00 / .60
  (Photo actually Mike Mitchell)
- ☐ 248B Mark McNamara COR ..... 2.00 / 1.00 / .20
- ☐ 249 Johnny Moore ..... 2.00 / 1.00 / .20
- ☐ 250 John Paxson ..... 25.00 / 12.50 / 2.50
- ☐ 251 Fred Roberts ..... 6.00 / 3.00 / .60
- ☐ 252 Joe Barry Carroll ..... 2.00 / 1.00 / .20
- ☐ 253 Mike Bratz ..... 1.50 / .75 / .15
- ☐ 254 Don Collins ..... 1.50 / .75 / .15
- ☐ 255 Lester Conner ..... 1.50 / .75 / .15
- ☐ 256 Chris Engler ..... 1.50 / .75 / .15
- ☐ 257 Sleepy Floyd ..... 7.00 / 3.50 / .70
- ☐ 258 Wallace Johnson ..... 1.50 / .75 / .15
- ☐ 259 Pace Mannion ..... 1.50 / .75 / .15
- ☐ 260 Purvis Short ..... 2.00 / 1.00 / .20
- ☐ 261 Larry Smith ..... 2.00 / 1.00 / .20

1984-85 Star NBA / 205

☐	262 Darren Tillis	1.50	.75	.15
☐	263 Dominique Wilkins	150.00	75.00	15.00
☐	264 Rickey Brown	1.50	.75	.15
☐	265 Johnny Davis	1.50	.75	.15
☐	266 Mike Glenn	1.50	.75	.15
☐	267 Scott Hastings	2.50	1.25	.25
☐	268 Eddie Johnson	1.50	.75	.15
☐	269 Mark Landsberger	1.50	.75	.15
☐	270 Billy Paultz	1.50	.75	.15
☐	271 Doc Rivers	12.00	6.00	1.20
☐	272 Tree Rollins	2.00	1.00	.20
☐	273 Dan Roundfield	2.00	1.00	.20
☐	274 Sly Williams	1.50	.75	.15
☐	275 Randy Wittman	2.50	1.25	.25

1984-85 Star NBA

This set of 288 cards was issued in three series during the first five months of 1985 by the Star Company. The set features players by team throughout the NBA. Cards measure 2 1/2" by 3 1/2" and have a colored border around the fronts of the cards according to the team with corresponding color printing on the backs. Card are organized numerically by team, i.e., Boston Celtics (1-12), Los Angeles Clippers (13-24), New York Knicks (25-37), Phoenix Suns (38-51), Indiana Pacers (52-63), San Antonio Spurs (64-75), Atlanta Hawks (76-87), New Jersey Nets (88-100), Chicago Bulls (101-112), Seattle Supersonics (113-124), Milwaukee Bucks (125-136), Denver Nuggets (137-148), Golden State Warriors (149-160), Portland Trail Blazers (161-171), Los Angeles Lakers (172-184), Washington Bullets (185-194), Philadelphia 76ers (201-212), Cleveland Cavaliers (213-224), Utah Jazz (225-236), Houston Rockets (237-249), Dallas Mavericks (250-260), Detroit Pistons (261-269), and Sacramento Kings (270-280). The set also features a special subseries (195-200) honoring Gold Medal-winning players from the 1984 Olympic basketball competition as well as a subseries of NBA specials (281-288). The key extended rookies cards in this set are Charles Barkley, Michael Jordan, Hakeem Olajuwon and John Stockton.

206 / 1984-85 Star NBA

	MINT	EXC	G-VG
COMPLETE SET (288)	4000.00	1800.00	500.00
COMMON PLAYER (1-288)	1.50	.75	.15

		MINT	EXC	G-VG
☐ 1	Larry Bird	75.00	37.50	7.50
☐ 2	Danny Ainge	8.50	4.25	.85
☐ 3	Quinn Buckner	2.50	1.25	.25
☐ 4	Rick Carlisle	2.00	1.00	.20
☐ 5	M.L. Carr	2.00	1.00	.20
☐ 6	Dennis Johnson	4.50	2.25	.45
☐ 7	Greg Kite	2.00	1.00	.20
☐ 8	Cedric Maxwell	2.50	1.25	.25
☐ 9	Kevin McHale	12.00	6.00	1.20
☐ 10	Robert Parish	15.00	7.50	1.50
☐ 11	Scott Wedman	2.00	1.00	.20
☐ 12	Larry Bird 1983-84 NBA MVP	35.00	17.50	3.50
☐ 13	Marques Johnson	3.00	1.50	.30
☐ 14	Junior Bridgeman	2.00	1.00	.20
☐ 15	Michael Cage	8.00	4.00	.80
☐ 16	Harvey Catchings	1.50	.75	.15
☐ 17	James Donaldson	2.00	1.00	.20
☐ 18	Lancaster Gordon	2.00	1.00	.20
☐ 19	Jay Murphy	1.50	.75	.15
☐ 20	Norm Nixon	2.50	1.25	.25
☐ 21	Derek Smith	2.00	1.00	.20
☐ 22	Bill Walton	7.50	3.75	.75
☐ 23	Bryan Warrick	1.50	.75	.15
☐ 24	Rory White	1.50	.75	.15
☐ 25	Bernard King	7.00	3.50	.70
☐ 26	James Bailey	1.50	.75	.15
☐ 27	Ken Bannister	1.50	.75	.15
☐ 28	Butch Carter	1.50	.75	.15
☐ 29	Bill Cartwright	5.50	2.75	.55
☐ 30	Pat Cummings	2.00	1.00	.20
☐ 31	Ernie Grunfeld	2.00	1.00	.20
☐ 32	Louis Orr	1.50	.75	.15
☐ 33	Leonard Robinson	2.00	1.00	.20
☐ 34	Rory Sparrow	2.00	1.00	.20
☐ 35	Trent Tucker	2.00	1.00	.20
☐ 36	Darrell Walker	2.50	1.25	.25
☐ 37	Eddie Lee Wilkins	2.00	1.00	.20
☐ 38	Alvan Adams	2.00	1.00	.20
☐ 39	Walter Davis	2.50	1.25	.25
☐ 40	James Edwards	2.50	1.25	.25
☐ 41	Rod Foster	1.50	.75	.15
☐ 42	Michael Holton	2.00	1.00	.20
☐ 43	Jay Humphries	8.00	4.00	.80
☐ 44	Charles Jones	1.50	.75	.15
☐ 45	Maurice Lucas	2.50	1.25	.25
☐ 46	Kyle Macy	2.00	1.00	.20
☐ 47	Larry Nance	14.00	7.00	1.40
☐ 48	Charles Pittman	1.50	.75	.15
☐ 49	Rick Robey	2.00	1.00	.20
☐ 50	Mike Sanders	3.00	1.50	.30
☐ 51	Alvin Scott	1.50	.75	.15
☐ 52	Clark Kellogg	2.50	1.25	.25

1984-85 Star NBA / 207

☐ 53	Tony Brown	1.75	.85	.17
☐ 54	Devin Durrant	1.75	.85	.17
☐ 55	Vern Fleming	7.50	3.75	.75
☐ 56	Bill Garnett	1.75	.85	.17
☐ 57	Stuart Gray UER (Photo actually Tony Brown)	2.50	1.25	.25
☐ 58	Jerry Sichting	2.50	1.25	.25
☐ 59	Terence Stansbury	2.50	1.25	.25
☐ 60	Steve Stipanovich	2.50	1.25	.25
☐ 61	Jimmy Thomas	1.75	.85	.17
☐ 62	Granville Waiters	1.75	.85	.17
☐ 63	Herb Williams	3.00	1.50	.30
☐ 64	Artis Gilmore	4.50	2.25	.45
☐ 65	Gene Banks	1.50	.75	.15
☐ 66	Ron Brewer	1.50	.75	.15
☐ 67	George Gervin	6.50	3.25	.65
☐ 68	Edgar Jones	1.50	.75	.15
☐ 69	Ozell Jones	1.50	.75	.15
☐ 70	Mark McNamara	1.50	.75	.15
☐ 71	Mike Mitchell	1.50	.75	.15
☐ 72	Johnny Moore	1.50	.75	.15
☐ 73	John Paxson	10.00	5.00	1.00
☐ 74	Fred Roberts	2.50	1.25	.25
☐ 75	Alvin Robertson	20.00	10.00	2.00
☐ 76	Dominique Wilkins	50.00	25.00	5.00
☐ 77	Rickey Brown	1.50	.75	.15
☐ 78	Antoine Carr	10.00	5.00	1.00
☐ 79	Mike Glenn	1.50	.75	.15
☐ 80	Scott Hastings	2.00	1.00	.20
☐ 81	Eddie Johnson	1.50	.75	.15
☐ 82	Cliff Levingston	3.00	1.50	.30
☐ 83	Leo Rautins	1.50	.75	.15
☐ 84	Doc Rivers	5.00	2.50	.50
☐ 85	Tree Rollins	2.00	1.00	.20
☐ 86	Randy Wittman	1.50	.75	.15
☐ 87	Sly Williams	1.50	.75	.15
☐ 88	Darryl Dawkins	3.00	1.50	.30
☐ 89	Otis Birdsong	2.00	1.00	.20
☐ 90	Darwin Cook	1.50	.75	.15
☐ 91	Mike Gminski	2.00	1.00	.20
☐ 92	George L. Johnson	1.50	.75	.15
☐ 93	Albert King	1.50	.75	.15
☐ 94	Mike O'Koren	1.50	.75	.15
☐ 95	Kelvin Ransey	1.50	.75	.15
☐ 96	M.R. Richardson	2.00	1.00	.20
☐ 97	Wayne Sappleton	1.50	.75	.15
☐ 98	Jeff Turner	2.50	1.25	.25
☐ 99	Buck Williams	16.00	8.00	1.60
☐ 100	Michael Wilson	1.50	.75	.15
☐ 101	Michael Jordan	2000.00	800.00	250.00
☐ 102	Dave Corzine	1.50	.75	.15
☐ 103	Quintin Dailey	1.50	.75	.15
☐ 104	Sidney Green	1.50	.75	.15
☐ 105	David Greenwood	1.50	.75	.15
☐ 106	Rod Higgins	2.00	1.00	.20
☐ 107	Steve Johnson	2.00	1.00	.20

208 / 1984-85 Star NBA

☐ 108	Caldwell Jones	2.00	1.00	.20
☐ 109	Wes Matthews	1.50	.75	.15
☐ 110	Jawann Oldham	1.50	.75	.15
☐ 111	Ennis Whatley	2.50	1.25	.25
☐ 112	Orlando Woolridge	6.50	3.25	.65
☐ 113	Tom Chambers	20.00	10.00	2.00
☐ 114	Cory Blackwell	2.00	1.00	.20
☐ 115	Frank Brickowski	4.50	2.25	.45
☐ 116	Gerald Henderson	1.50	.75	.15
☐ 117	Reggie King	1.50	.75	.15
☐ 118	Tim McCormick	2.50	1.25	.25
☐ 119	John Schweitz	1.50	.75	.15
☐ 120	Jack Sikma	2.50	1.25	.25
☐ 121	Ricky Sobers	1.50	.75	.15
☐ 122	Jon Sundvold	1.50	.75	.15
☐ 123	Danny Vranes	1.50	.75	.15
☐ 124	Al Wood	1.50	.75	.15
☐ 125	Terry Cummings UER (Robert Cummings on card back)	11.00	5.50	1.10
☐ 126	Randy Breuer	2.00	1.00	.20
☐ 127	Charles Davis	1.50	.75	.15
☐ 128	Mike Dunleavy	3.50	1.75	.35
☐ 129	Kenny Fields	2.00	1.00	.20
☐ 130	Kevin Grevey	1.50	.75	.15
☐ 131	Craig Hodges	4.00	2.00	.40
☐ 132	Alton Lister	2.00	1.00	.20
☐ 133	Larry Micheaux	1.50	.75	.15
☐ 134	Paul Mokeski	1.50	.75	.15
☐ 135	Sidney Moncrief	4.00	2.00	.40
☐ 136	Paul Pressey	2.50	1.25	.25
☐ 137	Alex English	6.00	3.00	.60
☐ 138	Wayne Cooper	1.50	.75	.15
☐ 139	T.R. Dunn	1.50	.75	.15
☐ 140	Mike Evans	1.50	.75	.15
☐ 141	Bill Hanzlik	2.00	1.00	.20
☐ 142	Dan Issel	6.00	3.00	.60
☐ 143	Joe Kopicki	1.50	.75	.15
☐ 144	Lafayette Lever	2.50	1.25	.25
☐ 145	Calvin Natt	2.00	1.00	.20
☐ 146	Danny Schayes	2.50	1.25	.25
☐ 147	Elston Turner	1.50	.75	.15
☐ 148	Willie White	1.50	.75	.15
☐ 149	Purvis Short	2.00	1.00	.20
☐ 150	Chuck Aleksinas	1.50	.75	.15
☐ 151	Mike Bratz	1.50	.75	.15
☐ 152	Steve Burtt	1.50	.75	.15
☐ 153	Lester Conner	1.50	.75	.15
☐ 154	Sleepy Floyd	3.00	1.50	.30
☐ 155	Mickey Johnson	1.50	.75	.15
☐ 156	Gary Plummer	1.50	.75	.15
☐ 157	Larry Smith	2.00	1.00	.20
☐ 158	Peter Thibeaux	1.50	.75	.15
☐ 159	Jerome Whitehead	1.50	.75	.15
☐ 160	Othell Wilson	1.50	.75	.15
☐ 161	Kiki Vandeweghe	3.00	1.50	.30
☐ 162	Sam Bowie	11.00	5.50	1.10

1984-85 Star NBA / 209

☐ 163	Kenny Carr	1.50	.75	.15
☐ 164	Steve Colter	2.00	1.00	.20
☐ 165	Clyde Drexler	110.00	55.00	11.00
☐ 166	Audie Norris	1.50	.75	.15
☐ 167	Jim Paxson	1.50	.75	.15
☐ 168	Tom Scheffler	1.50	.75	.15
☐ 169	Bernard Thompson	1.50	.75	.15
☐ 170	Mychal Thompson	2.50	1.25	.25
☐ 171	Darnell Valentine	1.50	.75	.15
☐ 172	Magic Johnson	110.00	55.00	11.00
☐ 173	Kareem Abdul-Jabbar	30.00	15.00	3.00
☐ 174	Michael Cooper	3.00	1.50	.30
☐ 175	Earl Jones	1.50	.75	.15
☐ 176	Mitch Kupchak	2.00	1.00	.20
☐ 177	Ronnie Lester	1.50	.75	.15
☐ 178	Bob McAdoo	4.50	2.25	.45
☐ 179	Mike McGee	1.50	.75	.15
☐ 180	Kurt Rambis	3.25	1.60	.32
☐ 181	Byron Scott	8.00	4.00	.80
☐ 182	Larry Spriggs	1.50	.75	.15
☐ 183	Jamaal Wilkes	2.50	1.25	.25
☐ 184	James Worthy	35.00	17.50	3.50
☐ 185	Gus Williams	2.50	1.25	.25
☐ 186	Greg Ballard	1.50	.75	.15
☐ 187	Dudley Bradley	1.50	.75	.15
☐ 188	Darren Daye	1.50	.75	.15
☐ 189	Frank Johnson	1.50	.75	.15
☐ 190	Charles Jones	1.50	.75	.15
☐ 191	Rick Mahorn	2.00	1.00	.20
☐ 192	Jeff Malone	14.00	7.00	1.40
☐ 193	Tom McMillen	3.50	1.75	.35
☐ 194	Jeff Ruland	2.50	1.25	.25
☐ 195	Michael Jordan	450.00	225.00	45.00
☐ 196	Vern Fleming	3.50	1.75	.35
☐ 197	Sam Perkins	12.00	6.00	1.20
☐ 198	Alvin Robertson	8.00	4.00	.80
☐ 199	Jeff Turner	2.00	1.00	.20
☐ 200	Leon Wood	2.00	1.00	.20
☐ 201	Moses Malone	12.50	6.25	1.25
☐ 202	Charles Barkley	225.00	110.00	22.00
☐ 203	Maurice Cheeks	4.50	2.25	.45
☐ 204	Julius Erving	30.00	15.00	3.00
☐ 205	Clemon Johnson	1.50	.75	.15
☐ 206	George Johnson	1.50	.75	.15
☐ 207	Bobby Jones	2.50	1.25	.25
☐ 208	Clint Richardson	1.50	.75	.15
☐ 209	Sedale Threatt	6.50	3.25	.65
☐ 210	Andrew Toney	2.50	1.25	.25
☐ 211	Sam Williams	1.50	.75	.15
☐ 212	Leon Wood	2.00	1.00	.20
☐ 213	Mel Turpin	2.50	1.25	.25
☐ 214	Ron Anderson	7.50	3.75	.75
☐ 215	John Bagley	2.50	1.25	.25
☐ 216	Johnny Davis	1.50	.75	.15
☐ 217	World B. Free	2.50	1.25	.25
☐ 218	Roy Hinson	2.00	1.00	.20
☐ 219	Phil Hubbard	1.50	.75	.15

210 / 1984-85 Star NBA

☐ 220	Edgar Jones	1.50	.75	.15
☐ 221	Ben Poquette	1.50	.75	.15
☐ 222	Lonnie Shelton	1.50	.75	.15
☐ 223	Mark West	2.50	1.25	.25
☐ 224	Kevin Williams	1.50	.75	.15
☐ 225	Mark Eaton	3.50	1.75	.35
☐ 226	Mitchell Anderson	1.50	.75	.15
☐ 227	Thurl Bailey	2.50	1.25	.25
☐ 228	Adrian Dantley	4.50	2.25	.45
☐ 229	Rickey Green	2.00	1.00	.20
☐ 230	Darrell Griffith	2.50	1.25	.25
☐ 231	Rich Kelley	1.50	.75	.15
☐ 232	Pace Mannion	1.50	.75	.15
☐ 233	Billy Paultz	1.50	.75	.15
☐ 234	Fred Roberts	2.50	1.25	.25
☐ 235	John Stockton	225.00	110.00	22.00
☐ 236	Jeff Wilkins	1.50	.75	.15
☐ 237	Hakeem Olajuwon	160.00	80.00	16.00
☐ 238	Craig Ehlo	18.00	9.00	1.80
☐ 239	Lionel Hollins	1.50	.75	.15
☐ 240	Allen Leavell	1.50	.75	.15
☐ 241	Lewis Lloyd	1.50	.75	.15
☐ 242	John Lucas	2.00	1.00	.20
☐ 243	Rodney McCray	2.50	1.25	.25
☐ 244	Hank McDowell	1.50	.75	.15
☐ 245	Larry Micheaux	1.50	.75	.15
☐ 246	Jim Peterson	3.00	1.50	.30
☐ 247	Robert Reid	1.50	.75	.15
☐ 248	Ralph Sampson	2.50	1.25	.25
☐ 249	Mitchell Wiggins	1.50	.75	.15
☐ 250	Mark Aguirre	6.00	3.00	.60
☐ 251	Rolando Blackman	9.00	4.50	.90
☐ 252	Wallace Bryant	1.50	.75	.15
☐ 253	Brad Davis	2.50	1.25	.25
☐ 254	Dale Ellis	4.50	2.25	.45
☐ 255	Derek Harper	7.00	3.50	.70
☐ 256	Kurt Nimphius	1.50	.75	.15
☐ 257	Sam Perkins	30.00	15.00	3.00
☐ 258	Charlie Sitton	1.50	.75	.15
☐ 259	Tom Sluby	1.50	.75	.15
☐ 260	Jay Vincent	2.00	1.00	.20
☐ 261	Isiah Thomas	50.00	25.00	5.00
☐ 262	Kent Benson	2.00	1.00	.20
☐ 263	Earl Cureton	1.50	.75	.15
☐ 264	Vinnie Johnson	3.00	1.50	.30
☐ 265	Bill Laimbeer	6.00	3.00	.60
☐ 266	John Long	1.50	.75	.15
☐ 267	Dan Roundfield	2.00	1.00	.20
☐ 268	Kelly Tripucka	2.00	1.00	.20
☐ 269	Terry Tyler	1.50	.75	.15
☐ 270	Reggie Theus	2.50	1.25	.25
☐ 271	Don Buse	1.50	.75	.15
☐ 272	Larry Drew	2.00	1.00	.20
☐ 273	Eddie Johnson	6.50	3.25	.65
☐ 274	Billy Knight	1.50	.75	.15
☐ 275	Joe Meriweather	1.50	.75	.15
☐ 276	Mark Olberding	1.50	.75	.15

☐ 277 LaSalle Thompson	2.50	1.25	.25
☐ 278 Otis Thorpe	25.00	12.50	2.50
☐ 279 Pete Verhoeven	1.50	.75	.15
☐ 280 Mike Woodson	2.00	1.00	.20
☐ 281 Julius Erving	20.00	10.00	2.00
☐ 282 Kareem Abdul-Jabbar	20.00	10.00	2.00
☐ 283 Dan Issel	4.00	2.00	.40
☐ 284 Bernard King	4.00	2.00	.40
☐ 285 Moses Malone	6.00	3.00	.60
☐ 286 Mark Eaton	2.50	1.25	.25
☐ 287 Isiah Thomas	22.00	11.00	2.20
☐ 288 Michael Jordan	450.00	225.00	45.00

1985-86 Star NBA

This 172-card set was produced by the Star Company and features players in the NBA. Cards are numbered in team order and measure the standard 2 1/2" by 3 1/2". The team ordering is as follows, Philadelphia 76ers (1-9), Detroit Pistons (10-17), Houston Rockets (18-25), Los Angeles Lakers (26-33), Phoenix Suns (34-41), Atlanta Hawks (42-49), Denver Nuggets (50-57), New Jersey Nets (58-65), Seattle Supersonics (66-73), Sacramento Kings (74-80), Indiana Pacers (81-87), Los Angeles Clippers (88-94), Boston Celtics (95-102), Portland Trail Blazers (103-109), Washington Bullets (110-116), Chicago Bulls (117-123), Milwaukee Bucks (124-130), Golden State Warriors (131-136), Utah Jazz (137-144), San Antonio Spurs (145-151), Cleveland Cavaliers (152-158), Dallas Mavericks (159-165), and New York Knicks (166-172). Players on each team have the same color border on the front. Cards were issued in two series, 1-94 and 95-172. Card backs are very similar to the other Star basketball sets except that the player statistics go up through the 1984-85 season. The key extended rookie cards in this set are Patrick Ewing, Jerome Kersey, and Kevin Willis.

	MINT	EXC	G-VG
COMPLETE SET (172)	1500.00	650.00	175.00
COMMON PLAYER (1-172)	1.50	.75	.15

212 / 1985-86 Star NBA

☐ 1	Maurice Cheeks	3.50	1.75	.35
☐ 2	Charles Barkley	75.00	37.50	7.50
☐ 3	Julius Erving	25.00	12.50	2.50
☐ 4	Clemon Johnson	1.50	.75	.15
☐ 5	Bobby Jones	2.50	1.25	.25
☐ 6	Moses Malone	9.00	4.50	.90
☐ 7	Sedale Threatt	4.50	2.25	.45
☐ 8	Andrew Toney	2.50	1.25	.25
☐ 9	Leon Wood	1.50	.75	.15
☐ 10	Isiah Thomas UER (No Pistons logo on card front)	35.00	17.50	3.50
☐ 11	Kent Benson	2.00	1.00	.20
☐ 12	Earl Cureton	1.50	.75	.15
☐ 13	Vinnie Johnson	2.50	1.25	.25
☐ 14	Bill Laimbeer	4.00	2.00	.40
☐ 15	John Long	1.50	.75	.15
☐ 16	Rick Mahorn	2.00	1.00	.20
☐ 17	Kelly Tripucka	2.00	1.00	.20
☐ 18	Hakeem Olajuwon	50.00	25.00	5.00
☐ 19	Allen Leavell	1.50	.75	.15
☐ 20	Lewis Lloyd	1.50	.75	.15
☐ 21	John Lucas	2.00	1.00	.20
☐ 22	Rodney McCray	2.00	1.00	.20
☐ 23	Robert Reid	1.50	.75	.15
☐ 24	Ralph Sampson	2.50	1.25	.25
☐ 25	Mitchell Wiggins	1.50	.75	.15
☐ 26	Kareem Abdul-Jabbar	30.00	15.00	3.00
☐ 27	Michael Cooper	3.00	1.50	.30
☐ 28	Magic Johnson	120.00	60.00	12.00
☐ 29	Mitch Kupchak	1.75	.85	.17
☐ 30	Maurice Lucas	2.50	1.25	.25
☐ 31	Kurt Rambis	2.75	1.35	.27
☐ 32	Byron Scott	6.00	3.00	.60
☐ 33	James Worthy	30.00	15.00	3.00
☐ 34	Larry Nance	11.00	5.50	1.10
☐ 35	Alvan Adams	2.00	1.00	.20
☐ 36	Walter Davis	2.50	1.25	.25
☐ 37	James Edwards	2.50	1.25	.25
☐ 38	Jay Humphries	3.00	1.50	.30
☐ 39	Charles Pittman	1.50	.75	.15
☐ 40	Rick Robey	2.00	1.00	.20
☐ 41	Mike Sanders	2.50	1.25	.25
☐ 42	Dominique Wilkins	35.00	17.50	3.50
☐ 43	Scott Hastings	2.00	1.00	.20
☐ 44	Eddie Johnson	1.50	.75	.15
☐ 45	Cliff Levingston	2.50	1.25	.25
☐ 46	Tree Rollins	2.00	1.00	.20
☐ 47	Doc Rivers	3.50	1.75	.35
☐ 48	Kevin Willis	27.00	13.50	2.70
☐ 49	Randy Wittman	2.00	1.00	.20
☐ 50	Alex English	4.00	2.00	.40
☐ 51	Wayne Cooper	1.50	.75	.15
☐ 52	T.R. Dunn	1.50	.75	.15
☐ 53	Mike Evans	1.50	.75	.15
☐ 54	Lafayette Lever	2.50	1.25	.25
☐ 55	Calvin Natt	2.00	1.00	.20

1985-86 Star NBA / 213

☐ 56 Danny Schayes	2.00	1.00	.20
☐ 57 Elston Turner	1.50	.75	.15
☐ 58 Buck Williams	12.00	6.00	1.20
☐ 59 Otis Birdsong	1.50	.75	.15
☐ 60 Darwin Cook	1.50	.75	.15
☐ 61 Darryl Dawkins	2.50	1.25	.25
☐ 62 Mike Gminski	2.00	1.00	.20
☐ 63 Mickey Johnson	1.50	.75	.15
☐ 64 Mike O'Koren	1.50	.75	.15
☐ 65 Micheal R. Richardson	2.00	1.00	.20
☐ 66 Tom Chambers	16.00	8.00	1.60
☐ 67 Gerald Henderson	2.00	1.00	.20
☐ 68 Tim McCormick	2.00	1.00	.20
☐ 69 Jack Sikma	2.00	1.00	.20
☐ 70 Ricky Sobers	2.50	1.25	.25
☐ 71 Danny Vranes	1.50	.75	.15
☐ 72 Al Wood	1.50	.75	.15
☐ 73 Danny Young	3.00	1.50	.30
☐ 74 Reggie Theus	2.50	1.25	.25
☐ 75 Larry Drew	2.00	1.00	.20
☐ 76 Eddie Johnson	4.50	2.25	.45
☐ 77 Mark Olberding	1.50	.75	.15
☐ 78 LaSalle Thompson	2.50	1.25	.25
☐ 79 Otis Thorpe	9.00	4.50	.90
☐ 80 Mike Woodson	1.50	.75	.15
☐ 81 Clark Kellogg	2.00	1.00	.20
☐ 82 Quinn Buckner	2.00	1.00	.20
☐ 83 Vern Fleming	2.50	1.25	.25
☐ 84 Bill Garnett	1.50	.75	.15
☐ 85 Terence Stansbury	1.50	.75	.15
☐ 86 Steve Stipanovich	2.00	1.00	.20
☐ 87 Herb Williams	2.50	1.25	.25
☐ 88 Marques Johnson	2.50	1.25	.25
☐ 89 Michael Cage	2.50	1.25	.25
☐ 90 Franklin Edwards	1.50	.75	.15
☐ 91 Cedric Maxwell	2.50	1.25	.25
☐ 92 Derek Smith	2.00	1.00	.20
☐ 93 Rory White	1.50	.75	.15
☐ 94 Jamaal Wilkes	2.50	1.25	.25
☐ 95A Larry Bird (Green border)	55.00	27.50	5.50
☐ 95B Larry Bird (White border)	55.00	27.50	5.50
☐ 96A Danny Ainge (Green border)	7.00	3.50	.70
☐ 96B Danny Ainge (White border)	7.00	3.50	.70
☐ 97A Dennis Johnson (Green border)	3.50	1.75	.35
☐ 97B Dennis Johnson (White border)	3.50	1.75	.35
☐ 98A Kevin McHale (Green border)	10.00	5.00	1.00
☐ 98B Kevin McHale (White border)	10.00	5.00	1.00
☐ 99A Robert Parish ERR (Green border)	12.00	6.00	1.20

214 / 1985-86 Star NBA

(no number on back)			
☐ 99B Robert Parish COR	12.00	6.00	1.20
(White border)			
☐ 100A Jerry Sichting	1.50	.75	.15
(Green border)			
☐ 100B Jerry Sichting	1.50	.75	.15
(White border)			
☐ 101A Bill Walton	6.50	3.25	.65
(Green border)			
☐ 101B Bill Walton	6.50	3.25	.65
(White border)			
☐ 102A Scott Wedman	2.00	1.00	.20
(Green border)			
☐ 102B Scott Wedman	2.00	1.00	.20
(White border)			
☐ 103 Kiki Vandeweghe	2.50	1.25	.25
☐ 104 Sam Bowie	4.00	2.00	.40
☐ 105 Kenny Carr	1.50	.75	.15
☐ 106 Clyde Drexler	90.00	45.00	9.00
☐ 107 Jerome Kersey	36.00	18.00	3.60
☐ 108 Jim Paxson	1.50	.75	.15
☐ 109 Mychal Thompson	2.50	1.25	.25
☐ 110 Gus Williams	2.00	1.00	.20
☐ 111 Darren Daye	1.50	.75	.15
☐ 112 Jeff Malone	11.00	5.50	1.10
☐ 113 Tom McMillen	3.00	1.50	.30
☐ 114 Cliff Robinson	1.50	.75	.15
☐ 115 Dan Roundfield	2.00	1.00	.20
☐ 116 Jeff Ruland	2.50	1.25	.25
☐ 117 Michael Jordan	600.00	300.00	60.00
☐ 118 Gene Banks	1.50	.75	.15
☐ 119 Dave Corzine	1.50	.75	.15
☐ 120 Quintin Dailey	1.50	.75	.15
☐ 121 George Gervin	6.00	3.00	.60
☐ 122 Jawann Oldham	1.50	.75	.15
☐ 123 Orlando Woolridge	4.00	2.00	.40
☐ 124 Terry Cummings	9.00	4.50	.90
☐ 125 Craig Hodges	3.50	1.75	.35
☐ 126 Alton Lister	1.50	.75	.15
☐ 127 Paul Mokeski	1.50	.75	.15
☐ 128 Sidney Moncrief	3.50	1.75	.35
☐ 129 Ricky Pierce	9.00	4.50	.90
☐ 130 Paul Pressey	2.50	1.25	.25
☐ 131 Purvis Short	2.00	1.00	.20
☐ 132 Joe Barry Carroll	2.00	1.00	.20
☐ 133 Lester Conner	1.50	.75	.15
☐ 134 Sleepy Floyd	2.50	1.25	.25
☐ 135 Geoff Huston	1.50	.75	.15
☐ 136 Larry Smith	2.00	1.00	.20
☐ 137 Jerome Whitehead	1.50	.75	.15
☐ 138 Adrian Dantley	3.00	1.50	.30
☐ 139 Mitchell Anderson	1.50	.75	.15
☐ 140 Thurl Bailey	2.00	1.00	.20
☐ 141 Mark Eaton	3.00	1.50	.30
☐ 142 Rickey Green	2.00	1.00	.20
☐ 143 Darrell Griffith	2.50	1.25	.25
☐ 144 John Stockton	75.00	37.50	7.50

			MINT	EXC	G-VG
☐	145	Artis Gilmore	4.00	2.00	.40
☐	146	Marc Iavaroni	1.50	.75	.15
☐	147	Steve Johnson	1.50	.75	.15
☐	148	Mike Mitchell	1.50	.75	.15
☐	149	Johnny Moore	1.50	.75	.15
☐	150	Alvin Robertson	5.00	2.50	.50
☐	151	Jon Sundvold	1.50	.75	.15
☐	152	World B. Free	2.50	1.25	.25
☐	153	John Bagley	2.50	1.25	.25
☐	154	Johnny Davis	1.50	.75	.15
☐	155	Roy Hinson	2.00	1.00	.20
☐	156	Phil Hubbard	1.50	.75	.15
☐	157	Ben Poquette	1.50	.75	.15
☐	158	Mel Turpin	2.00	1.00	.20
☐	159	Rolando Blackman	7.00	3.50	.70
☐	160	Mark Aguirre	4.00	2.00	.40
☐	161	Brad Davis	2.00	1.00	.20
☐	162	Dale Ellis	4.00	2.00	.40
☐	163	Derek Harper	5.00	2.50	.50
☐	164	Sam Perkins	10.00	5.00	1.00
☐	165	Jay Vincent	2.00	1.00	.20
☐	166	Patrick Ewing	240.00	100.00	20.00
☐	167	Bill Cartwright	4.00	2.00	.40
☐	168	Pat Cummings	1.50	.75	.15
☐	169	Ernie Grunfeld	2.00	1.00	.20
☐	170	Rory Sparrow	1.50	.75	.15
☐	171	Trent Tucker	1.50	.75	.15
☐	172	Darrell Walker	2.00	1.00	.20

1990 Star Pics

This premier edition showcases sixty of college basketball's top pro prospects. The cards measure the standard size (2 1/2" by 3 1/2"). The front features a color action player photo, with the player shown in his college uniform. A white border separates the picture from the surrounding "basketball" background. The player's name appears in an aqua box at the bottom. The back has a head shot of the player in the upper left corner and the card number in a red star in the upper right corner. On a tan-colored basketball court design, the back presents biography, accomplishments, and a mini-scouting report that assesses a player's strengths and weaknesses. The more limited "Medallion" edition (supposedly only 25,000 Medallion sets were produced, each with its own serial number) is valued at approximately double the prices listed below. The Medallion cards are distinguished by their more glossy feel and gold metallic print. The Medallion sets did not contain any random autographed cards inserted.

			MINT	EXC	G-VG
	COMPLETE SET (70)		27.00	13.50	2.70
	COMMON PLAYER (1-70)		.05	.02	.00
☐	1	Checklist Card	.05	.02	.00
☐	2	David Robinson (Mr. Robinson)	4.00	2.00	.40
☐	3	Antonio Davis UTEP	.05	.02	.00

216 / 1990 Star Pics

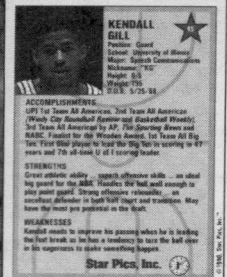

☐	4	Steve Bardo	.12	.06	.01
		Illinois			
☐	5	Jayson Williams	.15	.07	.01
		St. John's			
☐	6	Alaa Abdelnaby	.20	.10	.02
		Duke			
☐	7	Trevor Wilson	.08	.04	.01
		UCLA			
☐	8	Dee Brown	2.50	1.25	.25
		Jacksonville			
☐	9	Dennis Scott	1.25	.60	.12
		Georgia Tech			
☐	10	Danny Ferry	.15	.07	.01
		(Flashback)			
☐	11	Stevie Thompson	.12	.06	.01
		Syracuse			
☐	12	Anthony Bonner	.50	.25	.05
		St. Louis			
☐	13	Keith Robinson	.05	.02	.00
		Notre Dame			
☐	14	Sean Higgins	.35	.17	.03
		Michigan			
☐	15	Bo Kimble	.15	.07	.01
		Loyola Marymount			
☐	16	David Jamerson	.15	.07	.01
		Ohio University			
☐	17	Anthony Pullard	.05	.02	.00
		McNeese State			
☐	18	Phil Henderson	.08	.04	.01
		Duke			
☐	19	Mike Mitchell	.05	.02	.00
		Colorado State			
☐	20	Vanderbilt Team	.05	.02	.00
☐	21	Gary Payton	1.25	.60	.12
		Oregon State			

1990 Star Pics / 217

☐ 22	Tony Massenburg	.15	.07	.01
	Maryland			
☐ 23	Cedric Ceballos	1.00	.50	.10
	Cal State-Fullerton			
☐ 24	Dwayne Schintzius	.12	.06	.01
	Florida			
☐ 25	Bimbo Coles	.60	.30	.06
	Virginia Tech			
☐ 26	Scott Williams	.50	.25	.05
	North Carolina			
☐ 27	Willie Burton	.50	.25	.05
	Minnesota			
☐ 28	Tate George	.15	.07	.01
	U Conn			
☐ 29	Mark Stevenson	.05	.02	.00
	Duquesne			
☐ 30	UNLV Team	1.00	.50	.10
☐ 31	Earl Wise	.05	.02	.00
	Tennessee Tech			
☐ 32	Alec Kessler	.15	.07	.01
	Georgia			
☐ 33	Les Jepsen	.15	.07	.01
	Iowa			
☐ 34	Boo Harvey	.08	.04	.01
	St. John's			
☐ 35	Elden Campbell	.75	.35	.07
	Clemson			
☐ 36	Jud Buechler	.15	.07	.01
	Arizona			
☐ 37	Loy Vaught	.40	.20	.04
	Michigan			
☐ 38	Tyrone Hill	.40	.20	.04
	Xavier			
☐ 39	Toni Kukoc	.75	.35	.07
	Jugoplastika			
☐ 40	Jim Calhoun CO	.08	.04	.01
	U Conn			
☐ 41	Felton Spencer	.35	.17	.03
	Louisville			
☐ 42	Dan Godfread	.05	.02	.00
	Evansville			
☐ 43	Derrick Coleman	5.00	2.50	.50
	Syracuse			
☐ 44	Terry Mills	.50	.25	.05
	Michigan			
☐ 45	Kendall Gill	7.00	3.50	.70
	Illinois			
☐ 46	A.J. English	.50	.25	.05
	Virginia Union			
☐ 47	Duane Causwell	.40	.20	.04
	Temple			
☐ 48	Jerrod Mustaf	.25	.12	.02
	Maryland			
☐ 49	Alan Ogg	.12	.06	.01
	Alabama Birmingham			
☐ 50	Pervis Ellison	1.00	.50	.10
	(Flashback)			

218 / 1990 Star Pics

☐ 51	Matt Bullard Iowa	.25	.12	.02
☐ 52	Melvin Newbern Minnesota	.08	.04	.01
☐ 53	Marcus Liberty Illinois	.60	.30	.06
☐ 54	Walter Palmer Dartmouth	.05	.02	.00
☐ 55	Negele Knight Dayton	.50	.25	.05
☐ 56	Steve Henson Kansas State	.15	.07	.01
☐ 57	Greg Foster UTEP	.12	.06	.01
☐ 58	Brian Oliver Georgia Tech	.12	.06	.01
☐ 59	Travis Mays Texas	.30	.15	.03
☐ 60	All-Rookie Team	.60	.30	.06
☐ 61	Steve Scheffler Purdue	.10	.05	.01
☐ 62	Chris Jackson LSU	.60	.30	.06
☐ 63	Derek Strong Xavier	.10	.05	.01
☐ 64	David Butler UNLV	.08	.04	.01
☐ 65	Kevin Pritchard Kansas	.15	.07	.01
☐ 66	Lionel Simmons LaSalle	1.75	.85	.17
☐ 67	Gerald Glass Mississippi	.50	.25	.05
☐ 68	Tony Harris New Orleans	.10	.05	.01
☐ 69	Lance Blanks Texas	.12	.06	.01
☐ 70	Draft Overview	.05	.02	.00
☐ 71	Medallion special card (Only available as part of Medallion set)	1.00	.50	.10
☐ 72	Medallion special card (Only available as part of Medallion set)	1.00	.50	.10

1991 Star Pics

This 73-card set was produced by Star Pics, subtitled "Pro Prospects," and features 45 of the 54 players picked in the 1991 NBA draft. The cards measure the standard size (2 1/2" by 3 1/2"). The front features a color action photo of player in his college uniform. This picture overlays a black background with a basketball partially in view. The back has a color head shot of the player

1991 Star Pics / 219

in the upper left corner and an orange border. On a two color jersey background, the back presents biographical information, accomplishments, and a mini scouting report assessing the player's strengths and weaknesses. The cards are numbered on the back. The Medallion version of this set is tougher to find than that of the previous year and is valued at triple the prices listed below. The Medallion sets again did not contain any random autographed cards inserted.

	MINT	EXC	G-VG
COMPLETE SET (73)	8.00	4.00	.80
COMMON PLAYER (1-72)	.05	.02	.00
☐ 1 Draft Overview	.05	.02	.00
☐ 2 Derrick Coleman Flashback	.30	.15	.03
☐ 3 Treg Lee Ohio State	.08	.04	.01
☐ 4 Rich King Nebraska	.15	.07	.01
☐ 5 Kenny Anderson Georgia Tech	1.50	.75	.15
☐ 6 John Crotty Virginia	.10	.05	.01
☐ 7 Mark Randall Kansas	.20	.10	.02
☐ 8 Kevin Brooks Southwestern Lousiana	.15	.07	.01
☐ 9 Lamont Strothers Christopher Newport	.10	.05	.01
☐ 10 Tim Hardaway Flashback	.25	.12	.02
☐ 11 Eric Murdock Providence	.30	.15	.03
☐ 12 Melvin Cheatum Alabama	.08	.04	.01
☐ 13 Pete Chilcutt North Carolina	.20	.10	.02

220 / 1991 Star Pics

☐ 14 Zan Tabak Jugoplastika	.12	.06	.01
☐ 15 Greg Anthony UNLV	.40	.20	.04
☐ 16 George Ackles UNLV	.08	.04	.01
☐ 17 Stacey Augmon UNLV	1.25	.60	.12
☐ 18 Larry Johnson UNLV	5.00	2.50	.50
☐ 19 Alvaro Teheran Houston	.05	.02	.00
☐ 20 Reggie Miller Flashback	.12	.06	.01
☐ 21 Steve Smith Michigan State	2.00	1.00	.20
☐ 22 Sean Green Iona	.15	.07	.01
☐ 23 Johnny Pittman Oklahoma State	.08	.04	.01
☐ 24 Anthony Avent Seton Hall	.20	.10	.02
☐ 25 Chris Gatling Old Dominion	.40	.20	.04
☐ 26 Mark Macon Temple	.35	.17	.03
☐ 27 Joey Wright Texas	.08	.04	.01
☐ 28 Von McDade Wisconsin (Milwaukee)	.08	.04	.01
☐ 29 Bobby Phills Southern U	.10	.05	.01
☐ 30 Larry Fleisher HOF and Lawyer (In Memoriam)	.05	.02	.00
☐ 31 Luc Longley New Mexico	.35	.17	.03
☐ 32 Jean Derouillere Kansas State	.05	.02	.00
☐ 33 Doug Smith Missouri	.60	.30	.06
☐ 34 Chad Gallagher Creighton	.08	.04	.01
☐ 35 Marty Dow San Diego State	.08	.04	.01
☐ 36 Tony Farmer Nebraska	.08	.04	.01
☐ 37 John Taft Marshall	.08	.04	.01
☐ 38 Reggie Hanson Kentucky	.08	.04	.01
☐ 39 Terrell Brandon Oregon	.40	.20	.04
☐ 40 Dee Brown Flashback	.20	.10	.02
☐ 41 Doug Overton La Salle	.08	.04	.01

☐ 42	Joe Wylie Miami	.08	.04	.01
☐ 43	Myron Brown Slippery Rock	.10	.05	.01
☐ 44	Steve Hood James Madison	.10	.05	.01
☐ 45	Randy Brown New Mexico State	.15	.07	.01
☐ 46	Chris Corchiani NC State	.15	.07	.01
☐ 47	Kevin Lynch Minnesota	.15	.07	.01
☐ 48	Donald Hodge Temple	.35	.17	.03
☐ 49	LaBradford Smith Louisville	.30	.15	.03
☐ 50	Shawn Kemp Flashback	.25	.12	.02
☐ 51	Brian Shorter Pittsburgh	.08	.04	.01
☐ 52	Gary Waites Alabama	.05	.02	.00
☐ 53	Mike Iuzzolino St. Francis	.35	.17	.03
☐ 54	LeRon Ellis Syracuse	.12	.06	.01
☐ 55	Perry Carter Ohio State	.08	.04	.01
☐ 56	Keith Hughes Rutgers	.08	.04	.01
☐ 57	John Turner Phillips University	.15	.07	.01
☐ 58	Marcus Kennedy Eastern Michigan	.08	.04	.01
☐ 59	Randy Ayers CO Ohio State	.10	.05	.01
☐ 60	All Rookie Team	.35	.17	.03
☐ 61	Jackie Jones Oklahoma	.08	.04	.01
☐ 62	Shaun Vandiver Colorado	.12	.06	.01
☐ 63	Dale Davis Clemson	.35	.17	.03
☐ 64	Jimmy Oliver Purdue	.20	.10	.02
☐ 65	Elliot Perry Memphis State	.15	.07	.01
☐ 66	Jerome Harmon Louisville	.08	.04	.01
☐ 67	Darrin Chancellor Southern Mississippi	.08	.04	.01
☐ 68	Roy Fisher California (Berkeley)	.08	.04	.01
☐ 69	Rick Fox North Carolina	1.00	.50	.10
☐ 70	Kenny Anderson Special Second Card	.50	.25	.05

222 / 1991 Star Pics

☐ 71 Richard Dumas .... .08	.04	.01
Oklahoma State		
☐ 72 Checklist Card .... .05	.02	.00
☐ NNO Salute/American Flag .... .08	.04	.01

1957-58 Topps

The 1957-58 Topps basketball set of 80 cards was Topps first basketball issue. Topps did not release another basketball set until 1969. Cards in the set measure approximately 2 1/2" by 3 1/2". A number of the cards in the set were double printed and hence more plentiful; these are designated DP in the checklist below. In fact there are 49 double prints, 30 single prints, and one quadruple print in the set. Card backs give statistical information from the 1956-57 NBA season. The key rookie cards in this set are Bob Cousy, Tom Heinsohn, Bob Pettit, and Bill Russell. The set contains the only card of Maurice Stokes.

	NRMT	VG-E	GOOD
COMPLETE SET (80)	5000.00	2250.00	600.00
COMMON PLAYER (1-80)	30.00	15.00	3.00
COMMON PLAYER DP	21.00	10.50	2.10
☐ 1 Nat Clifton DP	150.00	35.00	7.00
Detroit Pistons			
☐ 2 George Yardley DP	48.00	24.00	4.80
Detroit Pistons			
☐ 3 Neil Johnston DP	48.00	24.00	4.80
Philadelphia Warriors			
☐ 4 Carl Braun DP	32.00	16.00	3.20
New York Knicks			
☐ 5 Bill Sharman DP	125.00	60.00	12.50
Boston Celtics			
☐ 6 George King DP	32.00	16.00	3.20

1957-58 Topps / 223

	Cincinnati Royals		
☐ 7	Kenny Sears DP 32.00	16.00	3.20
	New York Knicks		
☐ 8	Dick Ricketts DP 27.00	13.50	2.70
	Cincinnati Royals		
☐ 9	Jack Nichols DP 21.00	10.50	2.10
	Boston Celtics		
☐ 10	Paul Arizin DP 65.00	32.50	6.50
	Philadelphia Warriors		
☐ 11	Chuck Noble DP 21.00	10.50	2.10
	Detroit Pistons		
☐ 12	Slater Martin DP 48.00	24.00	4.80
	St. Louis Hawks		
☐ 13	Dolph Schayes DP 85.00	42.50	8.50
	Syracuse Nationals		
☐ 14	Dick Atha DP 21.00	10.50	2.10
	Detroit Pistons		
☐ 15	Frank Ramsey DP 65.00	32.50	6.50
	Boston Celtics		
☐ 16	Dick McGuire DP 40.00	20.00	4.00
	Detroit Pistons		
☐ 17	Bob Cousy DP 375.00	175.00	37.00
	Boston Celtics		
☐ 18	Larry Foust DP 32.00	16.00	3.20
	Minneapolis Lakers		
☐ 19	Tom Heinsohn 200.00	100.00	20.00
	Boston Celtics		
☐ 20	Bill Thieben DP 21.00	10.50	2.10
	Detroit Pistons		
☐ 21	Don Meineke DP 32.00	16.00	3.20
	Cincinnati Royals		
☐ 22	Tom Marshall 30.00	15.00	3.00
	Cincinnati Royals		
☐ 23	Dick Garmaker 30.00	15.00	3.00
	Minneapolis Lakers		
☐ 24	Bob Pettit QP 165.00	75.00	15.00
	St. Louis Hawks		
☐ 25	Jim Krebs DP 32.00	16.00	3.20
	Minneapolis Lakers		
☐ 26	Gene Shue DP 50.00	25.00	5.00
	Detroit Pistons		
☐ 27	Ed Macauley DP 48.00	24.00	4.80
	St. Louis Hawks		
☐ 28	Vern Mikkelsen 42.00	21.00	4.20
	Minneapolis Lakers		
☐ 29	Willie Naulls 42.00	21.00	4.20
	New York Knicks		
☐ 30	Walter Dukes DP 35.00	17.50	3.50
	Detroit Pistons		
☐ 31	Dave Piontek DP 21.00	10.50	2.10
	Cincinnati Royals		
☐ 32	John Kerr 60.00	30.00	6.00
	Syracuse Nationals		
☐ 33	Larry Costello DP 42.00	21.00	4.20
	Syracuse Nationals		
☐ 34	Woody Sauldsberry DP 32.00	16.00	3.20
	Philadelphia Warriors		

224 / 1957-58 Topps

☐ 35	Ray Felix New York Knicks	36.00	18.00	3.60
☐ 36	Ernie Beck Philadelphia Warriors	30.00	15.00	3.00
☐ 37	Cliff Hagan St. Louis Hawks	80.00	40.00	8.00
☐ 38	Guy Sparrow DP New York Knicks	21.00	10.50	2.10
☐ 39	Jim Loscutoff Boston Celtics	45.00	22.50	4.50
☐ 40	Arnie Risen DP Boston Celtics	32.00	16.00	3.20
☐ 41	Joe Graboski Philadelphia Warriors	30.00	15.00	3.00
☐ 42	Maurice Stokes DP UER Cincinnati Royals (Text refers to N.F.L. Record) UER	90.00	45.00	9.00
☐ 43	Rod Hundley DP Minneapolis Lakers	70.00	35.00	7.00
☐ 44	Tom Gola DP Philadelphia Warriors	65.00	32.50	6.50
☐ 45	Med Park St. Louis Hawks	32.00	16.00	3.20
☐ 46	Mel Hutchins DP New York Knicks	21.00	10.50	2.10
☐ 47	Larry Friend DP New York Knicks	21.00	10.50	2.10
☐ 48	Lennie Rosenbluth DP Philadelphia Warriors	40.00	20.00	4.00
☐ 49	Walt Davis Philadelphia Warriors	30.00	15.00	3.00
☐ 50	Richie Regan Cincinnati Royals	32.00	16.00	3.20
☐ 51	Frank Selvy DP St. Louis Hawks	36.00	18.00	3.60
☐ 52	Art Spoelstra DP Minneapolis Lakers	21.00	10.50	2.10
☐ 53	Bob Hopkins Syracuse Nationals	36.00	18.00	3.60
☐ 54	Earl Lloyd Syracuse Nationals	36.00	18.00	3.60
☐ 55	Phil Jordan DP New York Knicks	21.00	10.50	2.10
☐ 56	Bob Houbregs DP Detroit Pistons	36.00	18.00	3.60
☐ 57	Lou Tsioropoulas DP Boston Celtics	21.00	10.50	2.10
☐ 58	Ed Conlin Syracuse Nationals	32.00	16.00	3.20
☐ 59	Al Bianchi Syracuse Nationals	45.00	22.50	4.50
☐ 60	George Dempsey Philadelphia Warriors	32.00	16.00	3.20
☐ 61	Chuck Share St. Louis Hawks	30.00	15.00	3.00
☐ 62	Harry Gallatin DP	45.00	22.50	4.50

1969-70 Topps / 225

			NRMT	VG-E	GOOD
☐	63	Bob Harrison Detroit Pistons	30.00	15.00	3.00
☐	64	Bob Burrow DP Syracuse Nationals	21.00	10.50	2.10
☐	65	Win Wilfong DP Minneapolis Lakers	21.00	10.50	2.10
☐	66	Jack McMahon DP St. Louis Hawks	36.00	18.00	3.60
☐	67	Jack George St. Louis Hawks	30.00	15.00	3.00
☐	68	Charlie Tyra DP Philadelphia Warriors	21.00	10.50	2.10
☐	69	Ron Sobie New York Knicks	30.00	15.00	3.00
☐	70	Jack Coleman New York Knicks	30.00	15.00	3.00
☐	71	Jack Twyman DP St. Louis Hawks	75.00	37.50	7.50
☐	72	Paul Seymour Cincinnati Royals	36.00	18.00	3.60
☐	73	Jim Paxson DP Syracuse Nationals	40.00	20.00	4.00
☐	74	Bob Leonard Cincinnati Royals	36.00	18.00	3.60
☐	75	Andy Phillip Minneapolis Lakers	36.00	18.00	3.60
☐	76	Joe Holup Boston Celtics	30.00	15.00	3.00
☐	77	Bill Russell Syracuse Nationals	2000.00	800.00	250.00
☐	78	Clyde Lovellette DP Boston Celtics	80.00	40.00	8.00
☐	79	Ed Fleming DP Cincinnati Royals	21.00	10.50	2.10
☐	80	Dick Schnittker Minneapolis Lakers	70.00	20.00	4.00

1969-70 Topps

The 1969-70 Topps set of 99 cards was Topps' first basketball issue since 1958. These tall cards measure 2 1/2" by 4 11/16". The cards are much larger than the standard card size, perhaps rather appropriate considering the dimensions of most basketball players. The set features the first card of Lew Alcindor (later Kareem Abdul-Jabbar). Other notable rookie cards in the set are Bill Bradley, Billy Cunningham, Dave DeBusschere, Walt Frazier, John Havlicek, Elvin Hayes, Jerry Lucas, Earl Monroe, Willis Reed, and Wes Unseld. The set was printed on a sheet of 99 cards (nine rows of eleven across) with the checklist card occupying the lower right corner of the sheet.

	NRMT	VG-E	GOOD
COMPLETE SET (99)	2000.00	900.00	225.00
COMMON PLAYER (1-99)	4.00	2.00	.40

226 / 1969-70 Topps

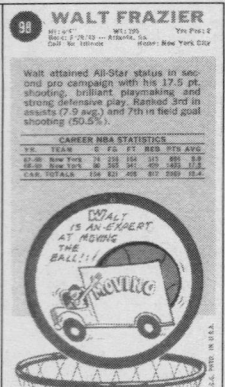

☐ 1 Wilt Chamberlain	225.00	75.00	25.00
Los Angeles Lakers			
☐ 2 Gail Goodrich	21.00	10.50	2.10
Phoenix Suns			
☐ 3 Cazzie Russell	11.00	5.50	1.10
New York Knicks			
☐ 4 Darrall Imhoff	4.50	2.25	.45
Philadelphia 76ers			
☐ 5 Bailey Howell	4.50	2.25	.45
Boston Celtics			
☐ 6 Lucius Allen	7.50	3.75	.75
Seattle Supersonics			
☐ 7 Tom Boerwinkle	5.50	2.75	.55
Chicago Bulls			
☐ 8 Jimmy Walker	5.00	2.50	.50
Detroit Pistons			
☐ 9 John Block	4.50	2.25	.45
San Diego Rockets			
☐ 10 Nate Thurmond	27.00	13.50	2.70
San Francisco Warriors			
☐ 11 Gary Gregor	4.00	2.00	.40
Atlanta Hawks			
☐ 12 Gus Johnson	11.00	5.50	1.10
Baltimore Bullets			
☐ 13 Luther Rackley	4.00	2.00	.40
Cincinnati Royals			
☐ 14 Jon McGlocklin	5.00	2.50	.50
Milwaukee Bucks			
☐ 15 Connie Hawkins	30.00	15.00	3.00

1969-70 Topps / 227

	Phoenix Suns			
☐ 16	Johnny Egan	4.00	2.00	.40
	Los Angeles Lakers			
☐ 17	Jim Washington	4.00	2.00	.40
	Philadelphia 76ers			
☐ 18	Dick Barnett	7.00	3.50	.70
	New York Knicks			
☐ 19	Tom Meschery	4.00	2.00	.40
	Seattle Supersonics			
☐ 20	John Havlicek	165.00	75.00	15.00
	Boston Celtics			
☐ 21	Eddie Miles	4.00	2.00	.40
	Detroit Pistons			
☐ 22	Walt Wesley	4.00	2.00	.40
	Chicago Bulls			
☐ 23	Rick Adelman	12.50	6.25	1.25
	San Diego Rockets			
☐ 24	Al Attles	4.50	2.25	.45
	San Francisco Warriors			
☐ 25	Lew Alcindor	700.00	350.00	70.00
	Milwaukee Bucks			
☐ 26	Jack Marin	5.50	2.75	.55
	Baltimore Bullets			
☐ 27	Walt Hazzard	9.00	4.50	.90
	Atlanta Hawks			
☐ 28	Connie Dierking	4.00	2.00	.40
	Cincinnati Royals			
☐ 29	Keith Erickson	5.50	2.75	.55
	Los Angeles Lakers			
☐ 30	Bob Rule	5.00	2.50	.50
	Seattle Supersonics			
☐ 31	Dick Van Arsdale	5.50	2.75	.55
	Phoenix Suns			
☐ 32	Archie Clark	7.50	3.75	.75
	Philadelphia 76ers			
☐ 33	Terry Dischinger	5.50	2.75	.55
	Detroit Pistons			
☐ 34	Henry Finkel	4.50	2.25	.45
	Boston Celtics			
☐ 35	Elgin Baylor	55.00	27.50	5.50
	Los Angeles Lakers			
☐ 36	Ron Williams	4.50	2.25	.45
	San Francisco Warriors			
☐ 37	Loy Petersen	4.00	2.00	.40
	Chicago Bulls			
☐ 38	Guy Rodgers	4.50	2.25	.45
	Milwaukee Bucks			
☐ 39	Toby Kimball	4.00	2.00	.40
	San Diego Rockets			
☐ 40	Billy Cunningham	45.00	22.50	4.50
	Philadelphia 76ers			
☐ 41	Joe Caldwell	5.00	2.50	.50
	Atlanta Hawks			
☐ 42	Leroy Ellis	5.00	2.50	.50
	Baltimore Bullets			
☐ 43	Bill Bradley	200.00	100.00	20.00
	New York Knicks			

228 / 1969-70 Topps

☐ 44	Len Wilkens UER Seattle Supersonics (Misspelled Wilkins on card back)	16.00	8.00	1.60
☐ 45	Jerry Lucas San Francisco Warriors	45.00	22.50	4.50
☐ 46	Neal Walk Phoenix Suns	4.50	2.25	.45
☐ 47	Emmette Bryant Boston Celtics	4.50	2.25	.45
☐ 48	Bob Kauffman Chicago Bulls	4.50	2.25	.45
☐ 49	Mel Counts Los Angeles Lakers	4.50	2.25	.45
☐ 50	Oscar Robertson Cincinnati Royals	70.00	35.00	7.00
☐ 51	Jim Barnett San Diego Rockets	4.50	2.25	.45
☐ 52	Don Smith Milwaukee Bucks	4.00	2.00	.40
☐ 53	Jim Davis Atlanta Hawks	4.00	2.00	.40
☐ 54	Wally Jones Philadelphia 76ers	4.50	2.25	.45
☐ 55	Dave Bing Detroit Pistons	25.00	12.50	2.50
☐ 56	Wes Unseld Baltimore Bullets	36.00	18.00	3.60
☐ 57	Joe Ellis San Francisco Warriors	4.00	2.00	.40
☐ 58	John Tresvant Seattle Supersonics	4.00	2.00	.40
☐ 59	Larry Siegfried Boston Celtics	5.50	2.75	.55
☐ 60	Willis Reed New York Knicks	45.00	22.50	4.50
☐ 61	Paul Silas Phoenix Suns	11.00	5.50	1.10
☐ 62	Bob Weiss Chicago Bulls	7.00	3.50	.70
☐ 63	Willie McCarter Los Angeles Lakers	4.00	2.00	.40
☐ 64	Don Kojis San Diego Rockets	4.50	2.25	.45
☐ 65	Lou Hudson Atlanta Hawks	11.00	5.50	1.10
☐ 66	Jim King Cincinnati Royals	4.00	2.00	.40
☐ 67	Luke Jackson Philadelphia 76ers	4.50	2.25	.45
☐ 68	Len Chappell Milwaukee Bucks	5.00	2.50	.50
☐ 69	Ray Scott Baltimore Bullets	4.50	2.25	.45
☐ 70	Jeff Mullins San Francisco Warriors	7.00	3.50	.70
☐ 71	Howie Komives	4.50	2.25	.45

1969-70 Topps / 229

	Detroit Pistons			
☐ 72	Tom Sanders	5.50	2.75	.55
	Boston Celtics			
☐ 73	Dick Snyder	4.00	2.00	.40
	Seattle Supersonics			
☐ 74	Dave Stallworth	5.00	2.50	.50
	New York Knicks			
☐ 75	Elvin Hayes	70.00	35.00	7.00
	San Diego Rockets			
☐ 76	Art Harris	4.00	2.00	.40
	Phoenix Suns			
☐ 77	Don Ohl	4.00	2.00	.40
	Atlanta Hawks			
☐ 78	Bob Love	11.00	5.50	1.10
	Chicago Bulls			
☐ 79	Tom Van Arsdale	5.50	2.75	.55
	Cincinnati Royals			
☐ 80	Earl Monroe	45.00	22.50	4.50
	Baltimore Bullets			
☐ 81	Greg Smith	4.00	2.00	.40
	Milwaukee Bucks			
☐ 82	Don Nelson	21.00	10.50	2.10
	Boston Celtics			
☐ 83	Happy Hairston	7.50	3.75	.75
	Detroit Pistons			
☐ 84	Hal Greer	9.00	4.50	.90
	Philadelphia 76ers			
☐ 85	Dave DeBusschere	45.00	22.50	4.50
	New York Knicks			
☐ 86	Bill Bridges	5.50	2.75	.55
	Atlanta Hawks			
☐ 87	Herm Gilliam	4.50	2.25	.45
	Cincinnati Royals			
☐ 88	Jim Fox	4.00	2.00	.40
	Phoenix Suns			
☐ 89	Bob Boozer	4.50	2.25	.45
	Seattle Supersonics			
☐ 90	Jerry West	100.00	50.00	10.00
	Los Angeles Lakers			
☐ 91	Chet Walker	11.00	5.50	1.10
	Chicago Bulls			
☐ 92	Flynn Robinson	4.50	2.25	.45
	Milwaukee Bucks			
☐ 93	Clyde Lee	4.50	2.25	.45
	San Francisco Warriors			
☐ 94	Kevin Loughery	11.00	5.50	1.10
	Baltimore Bullets			
☐ 95	Walt Bellamy	7.00	3.50	.70
	Detroit Pistons			
☐ 96	Art Williams	4.00	2.00	.40
	San Diego Rockets			
☐ 97	Adrian Smith	4.50	2.25	.45
	Cincinnati Royals			
☐ 98	Walt Frazier	75.00	37.50	7.50
	New York Knicks			
☐ 99	Checklist Card	265.00	30.00	6.00

230 / 1970-71 Topps

1970-71 Topps

The 1970-71 Topps basketball card set of 175 full-color cards continued the larger-size card format established the previous year. These tall cards measure approximately 2 1/2" by 4 11/16". Cards numbered 106 to 115 contained the previous season's NBA first and second team All-Star selections. The first six cards in the set (1-6) feature the statistical league leaders from the previous season. The last eight cards in the set (168-175) summarize the results of the previous season's NBA championship playoff series won by the Knicks over the Lakers. The key rookie cards in this set are Pete Maravich, Calvin Murphy, and Pat Riley.

	NRMT	VG-E	GOOD
COMPLETE SET (175)	1200.00	500.00	150.00
COMMON PLAYER (1-110)	2.50	1.25	.25
COMMON PLAYER (111-175)	3.00	1.50	.30
☐ 1 NBA Scoring Leaders Lew Alcindor Jerry West Elvin Hayes	30.00	7.50	1.50
☐ 2 NBA Scoring Average Leaders Jerry West Lew Alcindor Elvin Hayes	18.00	9.00	1.80
☐ 3 NBA FG Pct Leaders Johnny Green Darrall Imhoff	5.00	2.50	.50

1970-71 Topps / 231

	Lou Hudson			
☐ 4	NBA FT Pct Leaders 6.00		3.00	.60
	Flynn Robinson			
	Chet Walker			
	Jeff Mullins			
☐ 5	NBA Rebound Leaders 15.00		7.50	1.50
	Elvin Hayes			
	Wes Unseld			
	Lew Alcindor			
☐ 6	NBA Assist Leaders 6.00		3.00	.60
	Len Wilkens			
	Walt Frazier			
	Clem Haskins			
☐ 7	Bill Bradley 90.00		45.00	9.00
	New York Knicks			
☐ 8	Ron Williams 2.50		1.25	.25
	San Francisco Warriors			
☐ 9	Otto Moore 2.50		1.25	.25
	Detroit Pistons			
☐ 10	John Havlicek 80.00		40.00	8.00
	Boston Celtics			
☐ 11	George Wilson 3.00		1.50	.30
	Buffalo Braves			
☐ 12	John Trapp 2.50		1.25	.25
	San Diego Rockets			
☐ 13	Pat Riley 45.00		22.50	4.50
	Portland Trail Blazers			
☐ 14	Jim Washington 2.50		1.25	.25
	Philadelphia 76ers			
☐ 15	Bob Rule 2.50		1.25	.25
	Seattle Supersonics			
☐ 16	Bob Weiss 3.00		1.50	.30
	Chicago Bulls			
☐ 17	Neil Johnson 2.50		1.25	.25
	Phoenix Suns			
☐ 18	Walt Bellamy 4.50		2.25	.45
	Atlanta Hawks			
☐ 19	McCoy McLemore 2.50		1.25	.25
	Cleveland Cavaliers			
☐ 20	Earl Monroe 15.00		7.50	1.50
	Baltimore Bullets			
☐ 21	Wally Anderzunas 2.50		1.25	.25
	Cincinnati Royals			
☐ 22	Guy Rodgers 3.00		1.50	.30
	Milwaukee Bucks			
☐ 23	Rick Roberson 2.50		1.25	.25
	Los Angeles Lakers			
☐ 24	Checklist 1-110 .... 45.00		4.50	.90
☐ 25	Jimmy Walker 2.50		1.25	.25
	Detroit Pistons			
☐ 26	Mike Riordan 4.00		2.00	.40
	New York Knicks			
☐ 27	Henry Finkel 2.50		1.25	.25
	Boston Celtics			
☐ 28	Joe Ellis 2.50		1.25	.25
	San Francisco Warriors			
☐ 29	Mike Davis 2.50		1.25	.25

232 / 1970-71 Topps

	Buffalo Braves			
☐ 30	Lou Hudson	4.00	2.00	.40
	Atlanta Hawks			
☐ 31	Lucius Allen	3.25	1.60	.32
	Seattle Supersonics			
☐ 32	Toby Kimball	2.50	1.25	.25
	San Diego Rockets			
☐ 33	Luke Jackson	2.50	1.25	.25
	Philadelphia 76ers			
☐ 34	Johnny Egan	2.50	1.25	.25
	Cleveland Cavaliers			
☐ 35	Leroy Ellis	3.00	1.50	.30
	Portland Trail Blazers			
☐ 36	Jack Marin	3.00	1.50	.30
	Baltimore Bullets			
☐ 37	Joe Caldwell	3.00	1.50	.30
	Atlanta Hawks			
☐ 38	Keith Erickson	3.00	1.50	.30
	Los Angeles Lakers			
☐ 39	Don Smith	2.50	1.25	.25
	Milwaukee Bucks			
☐ 40	Flynn Robinson	2.50	1.25	.25
	Cincinnati Royals			
☐ 41	Bob Boozer	2.50	1.25	.25
	Seattle Supersonics			
☐ 42	Howie Komives	2.50	1.25	.25
	Detroit Pistons			
☐ 43	Dick Barnett	3.25	1.60	.32
	New York Knicks			
☐ 44	Stu Lantz	3.00	1.50	.30
	San Diego Rockets			
☐ 45	Dick Van Arsdale	3.00	1.50	.30
	Phoenix Suns			
☐ 46	Jerry Lucas	15.00	7.50	1.50
	San Francisco Warriors			
☐ 47	Don Chaney	7.50	3.75	.75
	Boston Celtics			
☐ 48	Ray Scott	2.50	1.25	.25
	Buffalo Braves			
☐ 49	Dick Cunningham	2.50	1.25	.25
	Milwaukee Bucks			
☐ 50	Wilt Chamberlain	120.00	60.00	12.00
	Los Angeles Lakers			
☐ 51	Kevin Loughery	4.00	2.00	.40
	Baltimore Bullets			
☐ 52	Stan McKenzie	2.50	1.25	.25
	Portland Trail Blazers			
☐ 53	Fred Foster	2.50	1.25	.25
	Cincinnati Royals			
☐ 54	Jim Davis	2.50	1.25	.25
	Atlanta Hawks			
☐ 55	Walt Wesley	2.50	1.25	.25
	Cleveland Cavaliers			
☐ 56	Bill Hewitt	2.50	1.25	.25
	Detroit Pistons			
☐ 57	Darrall Imhoff	2.50	1.25	.25
	Philadelphia 76ers			

1970-71 Topps / 233

☐ 58	John Block San Diego Rockets	2.50	1.25	.25
☐ 59	Al Attles San Francisco Warriors	3.00	1.50	.30
☐ 60	Chet Walker Chicago Bulls	4.25	2.10	.42
☐ 61	Luther Rackley Cleveland Cavaliers	2.50	1.25	.25
☐ 62	Jerry Chambers Atlanta Hawks	3.00	1.50	.30
☐ 63	Bob Dandridge Milwaukee Bucks	7.50	3.75	.75
☐ 64	Dick Snyder Seattle Supersonics	2.50	1.25	.25
☐ 65	Elgin Baylor Los Angeles Lakers	35.00	17.50	3.50
☐ 66	Connie Dierking Cincinnati Royals	2.50	1.25	.25
☐ 67	Steve Kuberski Boston Celtics	3.00	1.50	.30
☐ 68	Tom Boerwinkle Chicago Bulls	2.50	1.25	.25
☐ 69	Paul Silas Phoenix Suns	4.25	2.10	.42
☐ 70	Elvin Hayes San Diego Rockets	28.00	14.00	2.80
☐ 71	Bill Bridges Atlanta Hawks	3.00	1.50	.30
☐ 72	Wes Unseld Baltimore Bullets	10.00	5.00	1.00
☐ 73	Herm Gilliam Buffalo Braves	2.50	1.25	.25
☐ 74	Bobby Smith Cleveland Cavaliers	3.25	1.60	.32
☐ 75	Lew Alcindor Milwaukee Bucks	180.00	90.00	18.00
☐ 76	Jeff Mullins San Francisco Warriors	3.25	1.60	.32
☐ 77	Happy Hairston Los Angeles Lakers	3.25	1.60	.32
☐ 78	Dave Stallworth New York Knicks	3.00	1.50	.30
☐ 79	Fred Hetzel Portland Trail Blazers	2.50	1.25	.25
☐ 80	Len Wilkens Seattle Supersonics	9.00	4.50	.90
☐ 81	Johnny Green Cincinnati Royals	3.25	1.60	.32
☐ 82	Erwin Mueller Detroit Pistons	2.50	1.25	.25
☐ 83	Wally Jones Philadelphia 76ers	2.50	1.25	.25
☐ 84	Bob Love Chicago Bulls	4.25	2.10	.42
☐ 85	Dick Garrett Buffalo Braves	3.00	1.50	.30
☐ 86	Don Nelson	7.50	3.75	.75

234 / 1970-71 Topps

	Boston Celtics		
☐ 87 Neal Walk 2.50	1.25	.25
	Phoenix Suns		
☐ 88 Larry Siegfried 3.00	1.50	.30
	San Diego Rockets		
☐ 89 Gary Gregor 2.50	1.25	.25
	Portland Trail Blazers		
☐ 90 Nate Thurmond 7.50	3.75	.75
	San Francisco Warriors		
☐ 91 John Warren 2.50	1.25	.25
	Cleveland Cavaliers		
☐ 92 Gus Johnson 4.25	2.10	.42
	Baltimore Bullets		
☐ 93 Gail Goodrich 6.00	3.00	.60
	Los Angeles Lakers		
☐ 94 Dorrie Murrey 2.50	1.25	.25
	Portland Trail Blazers		
☐ 95 Cazzie Russell 4.25	2.10	.42
	New York Knicks		
☐ 96 Terry Dischinger 3.00	1.50	.30
	Detroit Pistons		
☐ 97 Norm Van Lier 5.50	2.75	.55
	Cincinnati Royals		
☐ 98 Jim Fox 2.50	1.25	.25
	Chicago Bulls		
☐ 99 Tom Meschery 2.50	1.25	.25
	Seattle Supersonics		
☐ 100 Oscar Robertson 42.00	21.00	4.20
	Milwaukee Bucks		
☐ 101A Checklist 111-175 .... 30.00	3.00	.60
(1970-71 in black)		
☐ 101B Checklist 111-175 .... 30.00	3.00	.60
(1970-71 in white)		
☐ 102 Rich Johnson 2.50	1.25	.25
	Boston Celtics		
☐ 103 Mel Counts 2.50	1.25	.25
	Phoenix Suns		
☐ 104 Bill Hosket 3.00	1.50	.30
	Buffalo Braves		
☐ 105 Archie Clark 3.00	1.50	.30
	Philadelphia 76ers		
☐ 106 Walt Frazier AS 11.00	5.50	1.10
	New York Knicks		
☐ 107 Jerry West AS 28.00	14.00	2.80
	Los Angeles Lakers		
☐ 108 Bill Cunningham AS 6.00	3.00	.60
	Philadelphia 76ers		
☐ 109 Connie Hawkins AS 4.00	2.00	.40
	Phoenix Suns		
☐ 110 Willis Reed AS 7.00	3.50	.70
	New York Knicks		
☐ 111 Nate Thurmond AS 5.00	2.50	.50
	San Francisco Warriors		
☐ 112 John Havlicek AS 27.00	13.50	2.70
	Boston Celtics		
☐ 113 Elgin Baylor AS 16.00	8.00	1.60
	Los Angeles Lakers		

1970-71 Topps / 235

☐ 114 Oscar Robertson AS Milwaukee Bucks	21.00	10.50	2.10
☐ 115 Lou Hudson AS Atlanta Hawks	4.00	2.00	.40
☐ 116 Emmette Bryant Buffalo Braves	3.00	1.50	.30
☐ 117 Greg Howard Phoenix Suns	3.00	1.50	.30
☐ 118 Rick Adelman Portland Trail Blazers	5.00	2.50	.50
☐ 119 Barry Clemens Seattle Supersonics	3.00	1.50	.30
☐ 120 Walt Frazier New York Knicks	30.00	15.00	3.00
☐ 121 Jim Barnes Boston Celtics	3.50	1.75	.35
☐ 122 Bernie Williams San Diego Rockets	3.00	1.50	.30
☐ 123 Pete Maravich Atlanta Hawks	160.00	75.00	15.00
☐ 124 Matt Guokas Philadelphia 76ers	6.00	3.00	.60
☐ 125 Dave Bing Detroit Pistons	8.50	4.25	.85
☐ 126 John Tresvant Los Angeles Lakers	3.00	1.50	.30
☐ 127 Shaler Halimon Chicago Bulls	3.00	1.50	.30
☐ 128 Don Ohl Cleveland Cavaliers	3.00	1.50	.30
☐ 129 Fred Carter Baltimore Bullets	3.50	1.75	.35
☐ 130 Connie Hawkins Phoenix Suns	9.00	4.50	.90
☐ 131 Jim King Cincinnati Royals	3.00	1.50	.30
☐ 132 Ed Manning Portland Trail Blazers	3.50	1.75	.35
☐ 133 Adrian Smith San Francisco Warriors	3.00	1.50	.30
☐ 134 Walt Hazzard Atlanta Hawks	4.50	2.25	.45
☐ 135 Dave DeBusschere New York Knicks	16.50	7.50	1.50
☐ 136 Don Kojis Seattle Supersonics	3.00	1.50	.30
☐ 137 Calvin Murphy San Diego Rockets	25.00	12.50	2.50
☐ 138 Nate Bowman Buffalo Braves	3.00	1.50	.30
☐ 139 Jon McGlocklin Milwaukee Bucks	3.50	1.75	.35
☐ 140 Billy Cunningham Philadelphia 76ers	13.50	6.50	1.25
☐ 141 Willie McCarter Los Angeles Lakers	3.00	1.50	.30
☐ 142 Jim Barnett	3.50	1.75	.35

236 / 1970-71 Topps

	Portland Trail Blazers			
☐ 143	JoJo White	16.00	8.00	1.60
	Boston Celtics			
☐ 144	Clyde Lee	3.00	1.50	.30
	San Francisco Warriors			
☐ 145	Tom Van Arsdale	3.50	1.75	.35
	Cincinnati Royals			
☐ 146	Len Chappell	3.00	1.50	.30
	Cleveland Cavaliers			
☐ 147	Lee Winfield	3.00	1.50	.30
	Seattle Supersonics			
☐ 148	Jerry Sloan	9.00	4.50	.90
	Chicago Bulls			
☐ 149	Art Harris	3.00	1.50	.30
	Phoenix Suns			
☐ 150	Willis Reed	16.50	7.50	1.50
	New York Knicks			
☐ 151	Art Williams	3.00	1.50	.30
	San Diego Rockets			
☐ 152	Don May	3.00	1.50	.30
	Buffalo Braves			
☐ 153	Loy Petersen	3.00	1.50	.30
	Cleveland Cavaliers			
☐ 154	Dave Gambee	3.00	1.50	.30
	San Francisco Warriors			
☐ 155	Hal Greer	5.00	2.50	.50
	Philadelphia 76ers			
☐ 156	Dave Newmark	3.00	1.50	.30
	Atlanta Hawks			
☐ 157	Jimmy Collins	3.50	1.75	.35
	Chicago Bulls			
☐ 158	Bill Turner	3.00	1.50	.30
	Cincinnati Royals			
☐ 159	Eddie Miles	3.00	1.50	.30
	Baltimore Bullets			
☐ 160	Jerry West	65.00	32.50	6.50
	Los Angeles Lakers			
☐ 161	Bob Quick	3.00	1.50	.30
	Detroit Pistons			
☐ 162	Fred Crawford	3.00	1.50	.30
	Buffalo Braves			
☐ 163	Tom Sanders	3.50	1.75	.35
	Boston Celtics			
☐ 164	Dale Schlueter	3.00	1.50	.30
	Portland Trail Blazers			
☐ 165	Clem Haskins	5.00	2.50	.50
	Phoenix Suns			
☐ 166	Greg Smith	3.00	1.50	.30
	Milwaukee Bucks			
☐ 167	Rod Thorn	5.00	2.50	.50
	Seattle Supersonics			
☐ 168	Playoff Game 1 (Willis Reed)	6.00	3.00	.60
☐ 169	Playoff Game 2 (Dick Garrett)	4.50	2.25	.45
☐ 170	Playoff Game 3 (Dave DeBusschere)	6.00	3.00	.60

☐ 171 Playoff Game 4 (Jerry West)	12.00	6.00	1.20
☐ 172 Playoff Game 5 (Bill Bradley)	12.00	6.00	1.20
☐ 173 Playoff Game 6 (Wilt Chamberlain)	14.00	7.00	1.40
☐ 174 Playoff Game 7 (Walt Frazier)	8.00	4.00	.80
☐ 175 Knicks Celebrate (New York Knicks, World Champs)	20.00	5.00	1.00

1971-72 Topps

The 1971-72 Topps basketball set of 233 witnessed a return to the standard-sized card, i.e., 2 1/2" by 3 1/2". National Basketball Association (NBA) players are depicted on cards 1 to 144 and American Basketball Association (ABA) players are depicted on cards 145 to 233. The set was produced on two sheets. The second production sheet contained the ABA players (145-233) as well as 31 double-printed cards (essentially NBA players) from the first sheet. These DP's are indicated in the checklist below. Special subseries within this set include NBA Playoffs (133-137), NBA Statistical Leaders (138-143), and ABA Statistical Leaders (146-151). The key rookie cards in this set are Nate Archibald, Rick Barry, Dave Cowens, Dan Issel, and Bob Lanier.

	NRMT	VG-E	GOOD
COMPLETE SET (233)	850.00	425.00	85.00
COMMON PLAYER (1-144)	1.25	.60	.12
COMMON PLAYER (145-233)	1.50	.75	.15
☐ 1 Oscar Robertson Milwaukee Bucks	50.00	15.00	3.00
☐ 2 Bill Bradley	48.00	24.00	4.80

238 / 1971-72 Topps

New York Knicks			
☐ 3 Jim Fox	1.25	.60	.12
Chicago Bulls			
☐ 4 John Johnson	2.00	1.00	.20
Cleveland Cavaliers			
☐ 5 Luke Jackson	1.25	.60	.12
Philadelphia 76ers			
☐ 6 Don May DP	.90	.45	.09
Atlanta Hawks			
☐ 7 Kevin Loughery	2.50	1.25	.25
Baltimore Bullets			
☐ 8 Terry Dischinger	1.50	.75	.15
Detroit Pistons			
☐ 9 Neal Walk	1.25	.60	.12
Phoenix Suns			
☐ 10 Elgin Baylor	25.00	12.50	2.50
Los Angeles Lakers			
☐ 11 Rick Adelman	3.00	1.50	.30
Portland Trail Blazers			
☐ 12 Clyde Lee	1.25	.60	.12
Golden State Warriors			
☐ 13 Jerry Chambers	1.25	.60	.12
Buffalo Braves			
☐ 14 Fred Carter	1.25	.60	.12
Baltimore Bullets			
☐ 15 Tom Boerwinkle DP	.90	.45	.09
Chicago Bulls			
☐ 16 John Block	1.25	.60	.12
Houston Rockets			
☐ 17 Dick Barnett	1.75	.85	.17
New York Knicks			
☐ 18 Henry Finkel	1.25	.60	.12
Boston Celtics			
☐ 19 Norm Van Lier	1.75	.85	.17
Cincinnati Royals			
☐ 20 Spencer Haywood	10.00	5.00	1.00
Seattle Supersonics			
☐ 21 George Johnson	1.25	.60	.12
Baltimore Bullets			
☐ 22 Bobby Lewis	1.25	.60	.12
Cleveland Cavaliers			
☐ 23 Bill Hewitt	1.25	.60	.12
Detroit Pistons			
☐ 24 Walt Hazzard DP	2.50	1.25	.25
Buffalo Braves			
☐ 25 Happy Hairston	1.75	.85	.17
Los Angeles Lakers			
☐ 26 George Wilson	1.25	.60	.12
Buffalo Braves			
☐ 27 Lucius Allen	1.75	.85	.17
Milwaukee Bucks			
☐ 28 Jim Washington	1.25	.60	.12
Philadelphia 76ers			
☐ 29 Nate Archibald	30.00	15.00	3.00
Cincinnati Royals			
☐ 30 Willis Reed	10.00	5.00	1.00
New York Knicks			

1971-72 Topps / 239

☐ 31	Erwin Mueller Detroit Pistons	1.25	.60	.12
☐ 32	Art Harris Phoenix Suns	1.25	.60	.12
☐ 33	Pete Cross Seattle Supersonics	1.25	.60	.12
☐ 34	Geoff Petrie Portland Trail Blazers	4.50	2.25	.45
☐ 35	John Havlicek Boston Celtics	35.00	17.50	3.50
☐ 36	Larry Siegfried Houston Rockets	1.50	.75	.15
☐ 37	John Tresvant DP Baltimore Bullets	.90	.45	.09
☐ 38	Ron Williams Golden State Warriors	1.25	.60	.12
☐ 39	Lamar Green DP Phoenix Suns	.90	.45	.09
☐ 40	Bob Rule DP Seattle Supersonics	.90	.45	.09
☐ 41	Jim McMillian Los Angeles Lakers	2.50	1.25	.25
☐ 42	Wally Jones Philadelphia 76ers	1.25	.60	.12
☐ 43	Bob Boozer Milwaukee Bucks	1.25	.60	.12
☐ 44	Eddie Miles Baltimore Bullets	1.25	.60	.12
☐ 45	Bob Love DP Chicago Bulls	2.50	1.25	.25
☐ 46	Claude English Portland Trail Blazers	1.25	.60	.12
☐ 47	Dave Cowens Boston Celtics	45.00	22.50	4.50
☐ 48	Emmette Bryant Buffalo Braves	1.25	.60	.12
☐ 49	Dave Stallworth New York Knicks	1.50	.75	.15
☐ 50	Jerry West Los Angeles Lakers	42.00	21.00	4.20
☐ 51	Joe Ellis Golden State Warriors	1.25	.60	.12
☐ 52	Walt Wesley DP Cleveland Cavaliers	.90	.45	.09
☐ 53	Howie Komives Detroit Pistons	1.25	.60	.12
☐ 54	Paul Silas Phoenix Suns	3.00	1.50	.30
☐ 55	Pete Maravich DP Atlanta Hawks	40.00	20.00	4.00
☐ 56	Gary Gregor Portland Trail Blazers	1.25	.60	.12
☐ 57	Sam Lacey Cincinnati Royals	2.00	1.00	.20
☐ 58	Calvin Murphy DP Houston Rockets	5.50	2.75	.55
☐ 59	Bob Dandridge	2.00	1.00	.20

240 / 1971-72 Topps

	Milwaukee Bucks			
☐ 60	Hal Greer	4.00	2.00	.40
	Philadelphia 76ers			
☐ 61	Keith Erickson	1.50	.75	.15
	Los Angeles Lakers			
☐ 62	Joe Cooke	1.25	.60	.12
	Cleveland Cavaliers			
☐ 63	Bob Lanier	35.00	17.50	3.50
	Detroit Pistons			
☐ 64	Don Kojis	1.25	.60	.12
	Seattle Supersonics			
☐ 65	Walt Frazier	15.00	7.50	1.50
	New York Knicks			
☐ 66	Chet Walker DP	2.50	1.25	.25
	Chicago Bulls			
☐ 67	Dick Garrett	1.25	.60	.12
	Buffalo Braves			
☐ 68	John Trapp	1.25	.60	.12
	Houston Rockets			
☐ 69	JoJo White	5.50	2.75	.55
	Boston Celtics			
☐ 70	Wilt Chamberlain	70.00	35.00	7.00
	Los Angeles Lakers			
☐ 71	Dave Sorenson	1.25	.60	.12
	Cleveland Cavaliers			
☐ 72	Jim King	1.25	.60	.12
	Chicago Bulls			
☐ 73	Cazzie Russell	3.00	1.50	.30
	Golden State Warriors			
☐ 74	Jon McGlocklin	1.50	.75	.15
	Milwaukee Bucks			
☐ 75	Tom Van Arsdale	1.50	.75	.15
	Cincinnati Royals			
☐ 76	Dale Schlueter	1.25	.60	.12
	Portland Trail Blazers			
☐ 77	Gus Johnson DP	1.75	.85	.17
	Baltimore Bullets			
☐ 78	Dave Bing	5.50	2.75	.55
	Detroit Pistons			
☐ 79	Billy Cunningham	7.50	3.75	.75
	Philadelphia 76ers			
☐ 80	Len Wilkens	5.50	2.75	.55
	Seattle Supersonics			
☐ 81	Jerry Lucas DP	8.50	4.25	.85
	New York Knicks			
☐ 82	Don Chaney	2.50	1.25	.25
	Boston Celtics			
☐ 83	McCoy McLemore	1.25	.60	.12
	Milwaukee Bucks			
☐ 84	Bob Kauffman DP	.90	.45	.09
	Buffalo Braves			
☐ 85	Dick Van Arsdale	1.50	.75	.15
	Phoenix Suns			
☐ 86	Johnny Green	1.25	.60	.12
	Cincinnati Royals			
☐ 87	Jerry Sloan	3.00	1.50	.30
	Chicago Bulls			

1971-72 Topps / 241

☐ 88 Luther Rackley DP Cleveland Cavaliers	.90	.45	.09
☐ 89 Shaler Halimon Portland Trail Blazers	1.25	.60	.12
☐ 90 Jimmy Walker Detroit Pistons	1.25	.60	.12
☐ 91 Rudy Tomjanovich Houston Rockets	6.00	3.00	.60
☐ 92 Levi Fontaine Golden State Warriors	1.25	.60	.12
☐ 93 Bobby Smith Cleveland Cavaliers	1.50	.75	.15
☐ 94 Bob Arnzen Cincinnati Royals	1.25	.60	.12
☐ 95 Wes Unseld DP Baltimore Bullets	6.00	3.00	.60
☐ 96 Clem Haskins DP Phoenix Suns	1.25	.60	.12
☐ 97 Jim Davis Atlanta Hawks	1.25	.60	.12
☐ 98 Steve Kuberski Boston Celtics	1.25	.60	.12
☐ 99 Mike Davis DP Buffalo Braves	.90	.45	.09
☐ 100 Lew Alcindor Milwaukee Bucks	90.00	45.00	9.00
☐ 101 Willie McCarter Los Angeles Lakers	1.25	.60	.12
☐ 102 Charlie Paulk Chicago Bulls	1.25	.60	.12
☐ 103 Lee Winfield Seattle Supersonics	1.25	.60	.12
☐ 104 Jim Barnett Golden State Warriors	1.50	.75	.15
☐ 105 Connie Hawkins DP Phoenix Suns	6.00	3.00	.60
☐ 106 Archie Clark DP Philadelphia 76ers	1.25	.60	.12
☐ 107 Dave DeBusschere New York Knicks	10.00	5.00	1.00
☐ 108 Stu Lantz DP Houston Rockets	.90	.45	.09
☐ 109 Don Smith Seattle Supersonics	1.25	.60	.12
☐ 110 Lou Hudson Atlanta Hawks	2.50	1.25	.25
☐ 111 Leroy Ellis Portland Trail Blazers	1.25	.60	.12
☐ 112 Jack Marin Baltimore Bullets	1.50	.75	.15
☐ 113 Matt Guokas Cincinnati Royals	2.25	1.10	.22
☐ 114 Don Nelson Boston Celtics	4.50	2.25	.45
☐ 115 Jeff Mullins DP Golden State Warriors	1.50	.75	.15
☐ 116 Walt Bellamy	3.25	1.60	.32

242 / 1971-72 Topps

Atlanta Hawks			
☐ 117 Bob Quick	1.25	.60	.12
Detroit Pistons			
☐ 118 John Warren	1.25	.60	.12
Cleveland Cavaliers			
☐ 119 Barry Clemens	1.25	.60	.12
Seattle Supersonics			
☐ 120 Elvin Hayes DP	14.00	7.00	1.40
Houston Rockets			
☐ 121 Gail Goodrich	2.50	1.25	.25
Los Angeles Lakers			
☐ 122 Ed Manning	1.50	.75	.15
Portland Trail Blazers			
☐ 123 Herm Gilliam DP	.90	.45	.09
Atlanta Hawks			
☐ 124 Dennis Awtrey	1.50	.75	.15
Philadelphia 76ers			
☐ 125 John Hummer DP	.90	.45	.09
Buffalo Braves			
☐ 126 Mike Riordan	1.50	.75	.15
New York Knicks			
☐ 127 Mel Counts	1.25	.60	.12
Phoenix Suns			
☐ 128 Bob Weiss DP	1.50	.75	.15
Chicago Bulls			
☐ 129 Greg Smith DP	.90	.45	.09
Milwaukee Bucks			
☐ 130 Earl Monroe	10.00	5.00	1.00
Baltimore Bullets			
☐ 131 Nate Thurmond DP	5.00	2.50	.50
Golden State Warriors			
☐ 132 Bill Bridges DP	1.25	.60	.12
Atlanta Hawks			
☐ 133 NBA Playoffs G1	9.00	4.50	.90
Alcindor scores 31			
☐ 134 NBA Playoffs G2	2.50	1.25	.25
Bucks make it Two Straight			
☐ 135 NBA Playoffs G3	2.50	1.25	.25
Dandridge makes It Three in a Row			
☐ 136 NBA Playoffs G4	6.50	3.25	.65
A Clean Sweep (Oscar Robertson)			
☐ 137 NBA Champs Celebrate	2.50	1.25	.25
Bucks sweep Bullets			
☐ 138 NBA Scoring Leaders	12.00	6.00	1.20
Lew Alcindor			
Elvin Hayes			
John Havlicek			
☐ 139 NBA Scoring Average	12.00	6.00	1.20
Leaders			
Lew Alcindor			
John Havlicek			
Elvin Hayes			
☐ 140 NBA FG Pct Leaders	10.00	5.00	1.00
Johnny Green			

1971-72 Topps / 243

- [ ] 141 NBA FT Pct Leaders .... 3.50 — 1.75 — .35
  Lew Alcindor
  Wilt Chamberlain
  Chet Walker
  Oscar Robertson
  Ron Williams
- [ ] 142 NBA Rebound Leaders .... 17.00 — 8.50 — 1.70
  Wilt Chamberlain
  Elvin Hayes
  Lew Alcindor
- [ ] 143 NBA Assist Leaders .... 7.00 — 3.50 — .70
  Norm Van Lier
  Oscar Robertson
  Jerry West
- [ ] 144A NBA Checklist 1-144 .... 15.00 — 7.50 — 1.50
  (copyright notation
  extends up to
  card 110)
- [ ] 144B NBA Checklist 1-144 .... 15.00 — 7.50 — 1.50
  (copyright notation
  extends up to
  card 108)
- [ ] 145 ABA Checklist 145-233 .... 15.00 — 7.50 — 1.50
- [ ] 146 ABA Scoring Leaders .... 4.50 — 2.25 — .45
  Dan Issel
  John Brisker
  Charlie Scott
- [ ] 147 ABA Scoring Average .... 9.00 — 4.50 — .90
  Leaders
  Dan Issel
  Rick Barry
  John Brisker
- [ ] 148 ABA 2pt FG Pct Leaders .... 2.75 — 1.35 — .27
  Zelmo Beaty
  Bill Paultz
  Roger Brown
- [ ] 149 ABA FT Pct Leaders .... 8.00 — 4.00 — .80
  Rick Barry
  Darrell Carrier
  Billy Keller
- [ ] 150 ABA Rebound Leaders .... 2.75 — 1.35 — .27
  Mel Daniels
  Julius Keye
  Mike Lewis
- [ ] 151 ABA Assist Leaders .... 2.75 — 1.35 — .27
  Bill Melchionni
  Mack Calvin
  Charlie Scott
- [ ] 152 Larry Brown .... 11.00 — 5.50 — 1.10
  Denver Rockets
- [ ] 153 Bob Bedell .... 1.50 — .75 — .15
  Dallas Chaparrals
- [ ] 154 Merv Jackson .... 1.50 — .75 — .15
  Utah Stars
- [ ] 155 Joe Caldwell .... 2.00 — 1.00 — .20
  Carolina Cougars
- [ ] 156 Billy Paultz .... 2.50 — 1.25 — .25

244 / 1971-72 Topps

New York Nets			
☐ 157 Les Hunter	1.50	.75	.15
Kentucky Colonels			
☐ 158 Charlie Williams	1.50	.75	.15
Memphis Pros			
☐ 159 Stew Johnson	1.50	.75	.15
Pittsburgh Condors			
☐ 160 Mack Calvin	4.50	2.25	.45
Florida Floridians			
☐ 161 Don Sidle	1.50	.75	.15
Indiana Pacers			
☐ 162 Mike Barrett	1.50	.75	.15
Virginia Squires			
☐ 163 Tom Workman	1.50	.75	.15
Denver Rockets			
☐ 164 Joe Hamilton	1.50	.75	.15
Dallas Chaparrals			
☐ 165 Zelmo Beaty	4.00	2.00	.40
Utah Stars			
☐ 166 Dan Hester	1.50	.75	.15
Kentucky Colonels			
☐ 167 Bob Verga	1.50	.75	.15
Carolina Cougars			
☐ 168 Wilbert Jones	1.50	.75	.15
Memphis Pros			
☐ 169 Skeeter Swift	1.50	.75	.15
Pittsburgh Condors			
☐ 170 Rick Barry	75.00	37.50	7.50
New York Nets			
☐ 171 Billy Keller	2.50	1.25	.25
Indiana Pacers			
☐ 172 Ron Franz	1.50	.75	.15
Florida Floridians			
☐ 173 Roland Taylor	2.00	1.00	.20
Virginia Squires			
☐ 174 Julian Hammond	1.50	.75	.15
Denver Rockets			
☐ 175 Steve Jones	3.50	1.75	.35
Dallas Chaparrals			
☐ 176 Gerald Govan	1.50	.75	.15
Memphis Pros			
☐ 177 Darrell Carrier	2.50	1.25	.25
Kentucky Colonels			
☐ 178 Ron Boone	3.00	1.50	.30
Utah Stars			
☐ 179 George Peeples	1.50	.75	.15
Carolina Cougars			
☐ 180 John Brisker	2.00	1.00	.20
Pittsburgh Condors			
☐ 181 Doug Moe	12.50	6.25	1.25
Virginia Squires			
☐ 182 Ollie Taylor	2.00	1.00	.20
New York Nets			
☐ 183 Bob Netolicky	2.00	1.00	.20
Indiana Pacers			
☐ 184 Sam Robinson	1.50	.75	.15
Florida Floridians			

1971-72 Topps / 245

- [ ] 185 James Jones .... 2.00   1.00   .20
      Memphis Pros
- [ ] 186 Julius Keye .... 1.50   .75   .15
      Denver Rockets
- [ ] 187 Wayne Hightower .... 1.50   .75   .15
      Dallas Chaparrals
- [ ] 188 Warren Armstrong .... 2.00   1.00   .20
      Indiana Pacers
- [ ] 189 Mike Lewis .... 2.00   1.00   .20
      Pittsburgh Condors
- [ ] 190 Charlie Scott .... 5.50   2.75   .55
      Virginia Squires
- [ ] 191 Jim Ard .... 1.50   .75   .15
      New York Nets
- [ ] 192 George Lehmann .... 1.50   .75   .15
      Carolina Cougars
- [ ] 193 Ira Harge .... 1.50   .75   .15
      Florida Floridians
- [ ] 194 Willie Wise .... 3.00   1.50   .30
      Utah Stars
- [ ] 195 Mel Daniels .... 6.00   3.00   .60
      Indiana Pacers
- [ ] 196 Larry Cannon .... 1.50   .75   .15
      Denver Rockets
- [ ] 197 Jim Eakins .... 1.50   .75   .15
      Virginia Squires
- [ ] 198 Rich Jones .... 1.50   .75   .15
      Dallas Chaparrals
- [ ] 199 Bill Melchionni .... 2.50   1.25   .25
      New York Nets
- [ ] 200 Dan Issel 36.00   18.00   3.60
      Kentucky Colonels
- [ ] 201 George Stone .... 1.50   .75   .15
      Utah Stars
- [ ] 202 George Thompson .... 1.50   .75   .15
      Pittsburgh Condors
- [ ] 203 Craig Raymond .... 1.50   .75   .15
      Memphis Pros
- [ ] 204 Freddie Lewis .... 2.50   1.25   .25
      Indiana Pacers
- [ ] 205 George Carter .... 1.50   .75   .15
      Virginia Squires
- [ ] 206 Lonnie Wright .... 1.50   .75   .15
      Florida Floridians
- [ ] 207 Cincy Powell .... 1.50   .75   .15
      Kentucky Colonels
- [ ] 208 Larry Miller .... 2.00   1.00   .20
      Carolina Cougars
- [ ] 209 Sonny Dove .... 2.00   1.00   .20
      New York Nets
- [ ] 210 Byron Beck .... 2.00   1.00   .20
      Denver Rockets
- [ ] 211 John Beasley .... 1.50   .75   .15
      Dallas Chaparrals
- [ ] 212 Lee Davis .... 1.50   .75   .15
      Memphis Pros
- [ ] 213 Rick Mount .... 6.00   3.00   .60

246 / 1971-72 Topps

	Indiana Pacers			
☐ 214	Walt Simon	1.50	.75	.15
	Kentucky Colonels			
☐ 215	Glen Combs	2.00	1.00	.20
	Utah Stars			
☐ 216	Neil Johnson	1.50	.75	.15
	Virginia Squires			
☐ 217	Manny Leaks	2.00	1.00	.20
	New York Nets			
☐ 218	Chuck Williams	1.50	.75	.15
	Pittsburgh Condors			
☐ 219	Warren Davis	1.50	.75	.15
	Florida Floridians			
☐ 220	Donnie Freeman	2.50	1.25	.25
	Dallas Chaparrals			
☐ 221	Randy Mahaffey	1.50	.75	.15
	Carolina Cougars			
☐ 222	John Barnhill	1.50	.75	.15
	Denver Rockets			
☐ 223	Al Cueto	1.50	.75	.15
	Memphis Pros			
☐ 224	Louie Dampier	4.25	2.10	.42
	Kentucky Colonels			
☐ 225	Roger Brown	3.00	1.50	.30
	Indiana Pacers			
☐ 226	Joe DePre	1.50	.75	.15
	New York Nets			
☐ 227	Ray Scott	1.50	.75	.15
	Virginia Squires			
☐ 228	Arvesta Kelly	1.50	.75	.15
	Pittsburgh Condors			
☐ 229	Vann Williford	1.50	.75	.15
	Carolina Cougars			
☐ 230	Larry Jones	2.00	1.00	.20
	Florida Floridians			
☐ 231	Gene Moore	1.50	.75	.15
	Dallas Chaparrals			
☐ 232	Ralph Simpson	3.00	1.50	.30
	Denver Rockets			
☐ 233	Red Robbins	2.50	1.00	.20
	Utah Stars			

1972-73 Topps

The 1972-73 Topps set of 264 cards contains NBA players (1-176) and ABA players (177-264). The cards in the set measure standard size, 2 1/2" by 3 1/2". All-Star selections are depicted for the NBA on cards numbered 161 to 170 and for the ABA on cards numbered 249 to 258. Special subseries within this set include NBA Playoffs (154-159), NBA Statistical Leaders (171-176), ABA Playoffs (241-247), and ABA Statistical Leaders (259-264). The key rookie cards in this set are Julius Erving, Artis Gilmore, and Phil Jackson.

1972-73 Topps / 247

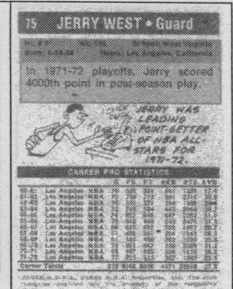

	NRMT	VG-E	GOOD
COMPLETE SET (264)	825.00	375.00	95.00
COMMON PLAYER (1-132)	.80	.40	.08
COMMON PLAYER (133-264)	1.00	.50	.10
☐ 1 Wilt Chamberlain Los Angeles Lakers	75.00	20.00	4.00
☐ 2 Stan Love Baltimore Bullets	.80	.40	.08
☐ 3 Geoff Petrie Portland Trail Blazers	1.00	.50	.10
☐ 4 Curtis Perry Milwaukee Bucks	1.25	.60	.12
☐ 5 Pete Maravich Atlanta Hawks	25.00	12.50	2.50
☐ 6 Gus Johnson Phoenix Suns	1.75	.85	.17
☐ 7 Dave Cowens Boston Celtics	14.00	7.00	1.40
☐ 8 Randy Smith Buffalo Braves	2.00	1.00	.20
☐ 9 Matt Guokas Kansas City-Omaha Kings	1.25	.60	.12
☐ 10 Spencer Haywood Seattle Supersonics	3.00	1.50	.30
☐ 11 Jerry Sloan Chicago Bulls	2.25	1.10	.22
☐ 12 Dave Sorenson Cleveland Cavaliers	.80	.40	.08
☐ 13 Howie Komives Detroit Pistons	.80	.40	.08
☐ 14 Joe Ellis Golden State Warriors	.80	.40	.08
☐ 15 Jerry Lucas	7.00	3.50	.70

248 / 1972-73 Topps

	New York Knicks			
☐ 16	Stu Lantz	.80	.40	.08
	Detroit Pistons			
☐ 17	Bill Bridges	1.00	.50	.10
	Philadelphia 76ers			
☐ 18	Leroy Ellis	.80	.40	.08
	Los Angeles Lakers			
☐ 19	Art Williams	.80	.40	.08
	Boston Celtics			
☐ 20	Sidney Wicks	9.00	4.50	.90
	Portland Trail Blazers			
☐ 21	Wes Unseld	4.50	2.25	.45
	Baltimore Bullets			
☐ 22	Jim Washington	.80	.40	.08
	Atlanta Hawks			
☐ 23	Fred Hilton	.80	.40	.08
	Buffalo Braves			
☐ 24	Curtis Rowe	3.00	1.50	.30
	Detroit Pistons			
☐ 25	Oscar Robertson	20.00	10.00	2.00
	Milwaukee Bucks			
☐ 26	Larry Steele	1.25	.60	.12
	Portland Trail Blazers			
☐ 27	Charlie Davis	.80	.40	.08
	Cleveland Cavaliers			
☐ 28	Nate Thurmond	4.00	2.00	.40
	Golden State Warriors			
☐ 29	Fred Carter	.80	.40	.08
	Philadelphia 76ers			
☐ 30	Connie Hawkins	4.00	2.00	.40
	Phoenix Suns			
☐ 31	Calvin Murphy	3.50	1.75	.35
	Houston Rockets			
☐ 32	Phil Jackson	18.00	9.00	1.80
	New York Knicks			
☐ 33	Lee Winfield	.80	.40	.08
	Seattle Supersonics			
☐ 34	Jim Fox	.80	.40	.08
	Seattle Supersonics			
☐ 35	Dave Bing	4.00	2.00	.40
	Detroit Pistons			
☐ 36	Gary Gregor	.80	.40	.08
	Portland Trail Blazers			
☐ 37	Mike Riordan	1.00	.50	.10
	Baltimore Bullets			
☐ 38	George Trapp	.80	.40	.08
	Atlanta Hawks			
☐ 39	Mike Davis	.80	.40	.08
	Buffalo Braves			
☐ 40	Bob Rule	.80	.40	.08
	Philadelphia 76ers			
☐ 41	John Block	.80	.40	.08
	Philadelphia 76ers			
☐ 42	Bob Dandridge	1.25	.60	.12
	Milwaukee Bucks			
☐ 43	John Johnson	1.00	.50	.10
	Cleveland Cavaliers			

1972-73 Topps / 249

☐ 44	Rick Barry	25.00	12.50	2.50
	Golden State Warriors			
☐ 45	JoJo White	3.00	1.50	.30
	Boston Celtics			
☐ 46	Cliff Meely	.80	.40	.08
	Houston Rockets			
☐ 47	Charlie Scott	1.50	.75	.15
	Phoenix Suns			
☐ 48	Johnny Green	.80	.40	.08
	Kansas City-Omaha Kings			
☐ 49	Pete Cross	.80	.40	.08
	Kansas City-Omaha Kings			
☐ 50	Gail Goodrich	3.00	1.50	.30
	Los Angeles Lakers			
☐ 51	Jim Davis	.80	.40	.08
	Detroit Pistons			
☐ 52	Dick Barnett	1.25	.60	.12
	New York Knicks			
☐ 53	Bob Christian	.80	.40	.08
	Atlanta Hawks			
☐ 54	Jon McGlocklin	1.00	.50	.10
	Milwaukee Bucks			
☐ 55	Paul Silas	2.00	1.00	.20
	Boston Celtics			
☐ 56	Hal Greer	3.00	1.50	.30
	Philadelphia 76ers			
☐ 57	Barry Clemens	.80	.40	.08
	Seattle Supersonics			
☐ 58	Nick Jones	.80	.40	.08
	Golden State Warriors			
☐ 59	Cornell Warner	.80	.40	.08
	Buffalo Braves			
☐ 60	Walt Frazier	10.00	5.00	1.00
	New York Knicks			
☐ 61	Dorrie Murray	.80	.40	.08
	Baltimore Bullets			
☐ 62	Dick Cunningham	.80	.40	.08
	Houston Rockets			
☐ 63	Sam Lacey	1.00	.50	.10
	Kansas City-Omaha Kings			
☐ 64	John Warren	.80	.40	.08
	Cleveland Cavaliers			
☐ 65	Tom Boerwinkle	.80	.40	.08
	Chicago Bulls			
☐ 66	Fred Foster	.80	.40	.08
	Detroit Pistons			
☐ 67	Mel Counts	.80	.40	.08
	Phoenix Suns			
☐ 68	Toby Kimball	.80	.40	.08
	Milwaukee Bucks			
☐ 69	Dale Schlueter	.80	.40	.08
	Portland Trail Blazers			
☐ 70	Jack Marin	1.00	.50	.10
	Houston Rockets			
☐ 71	Jim Barnett	.80	.40	.08
	Golden State Warriors			
☐ 72	Clem Haskins	1.00	.50	.10

250 / 1972-73 Topps

	Phoenix Suns			
☐ 73	Earl Monroe	7.00	3.50	.70
	New York Knicks			
☐ 74	Tom Sanders	1.00	.50	.10
	Boston Celtics			
☐ 75	Jerry West	27.00	13.50	2.70
	Los Angeles Lakers			
☐ 76	Elmore Smith	1.25	.60	.12
	Buffalo Braves			
☐ 77	Don Adams	.80	.40	.08
	Atlanta Hawks			
☐ 78	Wally Jones	.80	.40	.08
	Milwaukee Bucks			
☐ 79	Tom Van Arsdale	1.00	.50	.10
	Kansas City-Omaha Kings			
☐ 80	Bob Lanier	8.50	4.25	.85
	Detroit Pistons			
☐ 81	Len Wilkens	4.00	2.00	.40
	Seattle Supersonics			
☐ 82	Neal Walk	.80	.40	.08
	Phoenix Suns			
☐ 83	Kevin Loughery	2.00	1.00	.20
	Philadelphia 76ers			
☐ 84	Stan McKenzie	.80	.40	.08
	Portland Trail Blazers			
☐ 85	Jeff Mullins	1.00	.50	.10
	Golden State Warriors			
☐ 86	Otto Moore	.80	.40	.08
	Houston Rockets			
☐ 87	John Tresvant	.80	.40	.08
	Baltimore Bullets			
☐ 88	Dean Meminger	1.50	.75	.15
	New York Knicks			
☐ 89	Jim McMillian	1.00	.50	.10
	Los Angeles Lakers			
☐ 90	Austin Carr	5.50	2.75	.55
	Cleveland Cavaliers			
☐ 91	Clifford Ray	2.00	1.00	.20
	Chicago Bulls			
☐ 92	Don Nelson	4.00	2.00	.40
	Boston Celtics			
☐ 93	Mahdi Abdul-Rahman	2.00	1.00	.20
	Buffalo Braves			
	(formerly Walt Hazzard)			
☐ 94	Willie Norwood	.80	.40	.08
	Detroit Pistons			
☐ 95	Dick Van Arsdale	1.00	.50	.10
	Phoenix Suns			
☐ 96	Don May	.80	.40	.08
	Atlanta Hawks			
☐ 97	Walt Bellamy	2.50	1.25	.25
	Atlanta Hawks			
☐ 98	Garfield Heard	2.00	1.00	.20
	Seattle Supersonics			
☐ 99	Dave Wohl	.80	.40	.08
	Philadelphia 76ers			
☐ 100	Kareem Abdul-Jabbar	65.00	32.50	6.50

1972-73 Topps / 251

Milwaukee Bucks			
☐ 101 Ron Knight	.80	.40	.08
Portland Trail Blazers			
☐ 102 Phil Chenier	3.00	1.50	.30
Baltimore Bullets			
☐ 103 Rudy Tomjanovich	2.25	1.10	.22
Houston Rockets			
☐ 104 Flynn Robinson	.80	.40	.08
Los Angeles Lakers			
☐ 105 Dave DeBusschere	7.00	3.50	.70
New York Knicks			
☐ 106 Dennis Layton	1.00	.50	.10
Phoenix Suns			
☐ 107 Bill Hewitt	.80	.40	.08
Detroit Pistons			
☐ 108 Dick Garrett	.80	.40	.08
Buffalo Braves			
☐ 109 Walt Wesley	.80	.40	.08
Cleveland Cavaliers			
☐ 110 John Havlicek	25.00	12.50	2.50
Boston Celtics			
☐ 111 Norm Van Lier	1.50	.75	.15
Chicago Bulls			
☐ 112 Cazzie Russell	2.00	1.00	.20
Golden State Warriors			
☐ 113 Herm Gilliam	.80	.40	.08
Atlanta Hawks			
☐ 114 Greg Smith	.80	.40	.08
Houston Rockets			
☐ 115 Nate Archibald	8.50	4.25	.85
Kansas City-Omaha Kings			
☐ 116 Don Kojis	.80	.40	.08
Kansas City-Omaha Kings			
☐ 117 Rick Adelman	2.25	1.10	.22
Portland Trail Blazers			
☐ 118 Luke Jackson	.80	.40	.08
Philadelphia 76ers			
☐ 119 Lamar Green	.80	.40	.08
Phoenix Suns			
☐ 120 Archie Clark	1.00	.50	.10
Baltimore Bullets			
☐ 121 Happy Hairston	1.25	.60	.12
Los Angeles Lakers			
☐ 122 Bill Bradley	35.00	17.50	3.50
New York Knicks			
☐ 123 Ron Williams	.80	.40	.08
Golden State Warriors			
☐ 124 Jimmy Walker	.80	.40	.08
Houston Rockets			
☐ 125 Bob Kauffman	.80	.40	.08
Buffalo Braves			
☐ 126 Rick Roberson	.80	.40	.08
Cleveland Cavaliers			
☐ 127 Howard Porter	2.00	1.00	.20
Chicago Bulls			
☐ 128 Mike Newlin	1.25	.60	.12
Houston Rockets			

252 / 1972-73 Topps

- [ ] 129 Willis Reed .... 7.00 — 3.50 — .70
  New York Knicks
- [ ] 130 Lou Hudson .... 1.75 — .85 — .17
  Atlanta Hawks
- [ ] 131 Don Chaney .... 2.00 — 1.00 — .20
  Boston Celtics
- [ ] 132 Dave Stallworth .... 1.00 — .50 — .10
  Baltimore Bullets
- [ ] 133 Charlie Yelverton .... 1.00 — .50 — .10
  Portland Trail Blazers
- [ ] 134 Ken Durrett .... 1.00 — .50 — .10
  Kansas City-Omaha Kings
- [ ] 135 John Brisker .... 1.25 — .60 — .12
  Seattle Supersonics
- [ ] 136 Dick Snyder .... 1.00 — .50 — .10
  Seattle Supersonics
- [ ] 137 Jim McDaniels .... 1.25 — .60 — .12
  Seattle Supersonics
- [ ] 138 Clyde Lee .... 1.00 — .50 — .10
  Golden State Warriors
- [ ] 139 Dennis Awtrey UER .... 1.00 — .50 — .10
  Philadelphia 76ers
  (Misspelled Awtry
  on card front)
- [ ] 140 Keith Erickson .... 1.25 — .60 — .12
  Los Angeles Lakers
- [ ] 141 Bob Weiss .... 1.25 — .60 — .12
  Chicago Bulls
- [ ] 142 Butch Beard .... 1.75 — .85 — .17
  Cleveland Cavaliers
- [ ] 143 Terry Dischinger .... 1.25 — .60 — .12
  Portland Trail Blazers
- [ ] 144 Pat Riley .... 10.00 — 5.00 — 1.00
  Los Angeles Lakers
- [ ] 145 Lucius Allen .... 1.25 — .60 — .12
  Milwaukee Bucks
- [ ] 146 John Mengelt .... 1.50 — .75 — .15
  Kansas City-Omaha Kings
- [ ] 147 John Hummer .... 1.00 — .50 — .10
  Buffalo Braves
- [ ] 148 Bob Love .... 2.00 — 1.00 — .20
  Chicago Bulls
- [ ] 149 Bobby Smith .... 1.00 — .50 — .10
  Cleveland Cavaliers
- [ ] 150 Elvin Hayes .... 12.50 — 6.25 — 1.25
  Baltimore Bullets
- [ ] 151 Nate Williams .... 1.00 — .50 — .10
  Kansas City-Omaha Kings
- [ ] 152 Chet Walker .... 2.00 — 1.00 — .20
  Chicago Bulls
- [ ] 153 Steve Kuberski .... 1.00 — .50 — .10
  Boston Celtics
- [ ] 154 NBA Playoffs G1 .... 2.50 — 1.25 — .25
  Knicks win Opener
  (Earl Monroe)
- [ ] 155 NBA Playoffs G2 .... 2.00 — 1.00 — .20
  Lakers Come Back

1972-73 Topps / 253

- [ ] 156 NBA Playoffs G3 .... 2.00   1.00   .20
  Two in a Row
  (under the basket)
- [ ] 157 NBA Playoffs G4 .... 2.00   1.00   .20
  Ellis provides
  bench strength
- [ ] 158 NBA Playoffs G5 .... 5.50   2.75   .55
  Jerry drives in
  (Jerry West)
- [ ] 159 NBA Champs-Lakers .... 6.00   3.00   .60
  (Wilt rebounding)
- [ ] 160 NBA Checklist 1-176 UER .... 12.50   1.50   .30
  (135 Jim King)
- [ ] 161 John Havlicek AS 11.00   5.50   1.10
  Boston Celtics
- [ ] 162 Spencer Haywood AS .... 2.00   1.00   .20
  Seattle Supersonics
- [ ] 163 Kareem Abdul-Jabbar AS 25.00   12.50   2.50
  Milwaukee Bucks
- [ ] 164 Jerry West AS 14.00   7.00   1.40
  Los Angeles Lakers
- [ ] 165 Walt Frazier AS .... 5.50   2.75   .55
  New York Knicks
- [ ] 166 Bob Love AS .... 1.50   .75   .15
  Chicago Bulls
- [ ] 167 Billy Cunningham AS .... 3.00   1.50   .30
  Philadelphia 76ers
- [ ] 168 Wilt Chamberlain AS 25.00   12.50   2.50
  Los Angeles Lakers
- [ ] 169 Nate Archibald AS .... 4.00   2.00   .40
  Kansas City-Omaha Kings
- [ ] 170 Archie Clark AS .... 1.50   .75   .15
  Baltimore Bullets
- [ ] 171 NBA Scoring Leaders .... 9.00   4.50   .90
  Kareem Abdul-Jabbar
  John Havlicek
  Nate Archibald
- [ ] 172 NBA Scoring Average .... 9.00   4.50   .90
  Leaders
  Kareem Abdul-Jabbar
  Nate Archibald
  John Havlicek
- [ ] 173 NBA FG Pct Leaders .... 9.00   4.50   .90
  Wilt Chamberlain
  Kareem Abdul-Jabbar
  Walt Bellamy
- [ ] 174 NBA FT Pct Leaders .... 2.00   1.00   .20
  Jack Marin
  Calvin Murphy
  Gail Goodrich
- [ ] 175 NBA Rebound Leaders 11.00   5.50   1.10
  Wilt Chamberlain
  Kareem Abdul-Jabbar
  Wes Unseld
- [ ] 176 NBA Assist Leaders .... 5.00   2.50   .50
  Len Wilkens

254 / 1972-73 Topps

	Jerry West		
	Nate Archibald		
☐ 177 Roland Taylor 1.00	.50	.10
	Virginia Squires		
☐ 178 Art Becker 1.00	.50	.10
	San Diego Conquistadors		
☐ 179 Mack Calvin 1.75	.85	.17
	Carolina Cougars		
☐ 180 Artis Gilmore 27.00	13.50	2.70
	Kentucky Colonels		
☐ 181 Collis Jones 1.25	.60	.12
	Dallas Chaparrals		
☐ 182 John Roche 1.75	.85	.17
	New York Nets		
☐ 183 George McGinnis 9.00	4.50	.90
	Indiana Pacers		
☐ 184 Johnny Neumann 1.25	.60	.12
	Memphis Tams		
☐ 185 Willie Wise 1.25	.60	.12
	Utah Stars		
☐ 186 Bernie Williams 1.00	.50	.10
	Virginia Squires		
☐ 187 Byron Beck 1.00	.50	.10
	Denver Rockets		
☐ 188 Larry Miller 1.00	.50	.10
	San Diego Conquistadors		
☐ 189 Cincy Powell 1.00	.50	.10
	Kentucky Colonels		
☐ 190 Donnie Freeman 1.25	.60	.12
	Dallas Chaparrals		
☐ 191 John Baum 1.00	.50	.10
	New York Nets		
☐ 192 Billy Keller 1.25	.60	.12
	Indiana Pacers		
☐ 193 Wilbert Jones 1.00	.50	.10
	Memphis Tams		
☐ 194 Glen Combs 1.00	.50	.10
	Utah Stars		
☐ 195 Julius Erving 270.00	125.00	25.00
	Virginia Squires		
	(Forward on front,		
	but Center on back)		
☐ 196 Al Smith 1.00	.50	.10
	Denver Rockets		
☐ 197 George Carter 1.00	.50	.10
	New York Nets		
☐ 198 Louie Dampier 1.75	.85	.17
	Kentucky Colonels		
☐ 199 Rich Jones 1.00	.50	.10
	Dallas Chaparrals		
☐ 200 Mel Daniels 1.75	.85	.17
	Indiana Pacers		
☐ 201 Gene Moore 1.00	.50	.10
	San Diego Conquistadors		
☐ 202 Randy Denton 1.00	.50	.10
	Memphis Tams		
☐ 203 Larry Jones 1.00	.50	.10

1972-73 Topps / 255

Utah Stars			
☐ 204 Jim Ligon 1.00	.50	.10
Virginia Squires			
☐ 205 Warren Jabali 1.25	.60	.12
Denver Rockets			
☐ 206 Joe Caldwell 1.25	.60	.12
Carolina Cougars			
☐ 207 Darrell Carrier 1.25	.60	.12
Kentucky Colonels			
☐ 208 Gene Kennedy 1.25	.60	.12
Dallas Chaparrals			
☐ 209 Ollie Taylor 1.25	.60	.12
San Diego Conquistadors			
☐ 210 Roger Brown 1.25	.60	.12
Indiana Pacers			
☐ 211 George Lehmann 1.00	.50	.10
Memphis Tams			
☐ 212 Red Robbins 1.00	.50	.10
San Diego Conquistadors			
☐ 213 Jim Eakins 1.00	.50	.10
Virginia Squires			
☐ 214 Willie Long 1.00	.50	.10
Denver Rockets			
☐ 215 Billy Cunningham 6.00	3.00	.60
Carolina Cougars			
☐ 216 Steve Jones 1.75	.85	.17
Dallas Chaparrals			
☐ 217 Les Hunter 1.00	.50	.10
San Diego Conquistadors			
☐ 218 Billy Paultz 1.50	.75	.15
New York Nets			
☐ 219 Freddie Lewis 1.25	.60	.12
Indiana Pacers			
☐ 220 Zelmo Beaty 1.75	.85	.17
Utah Stars			
☐ 221 George Thompson 1.00	.50	.10
Memphis Tams			
☐ 222 Neil Johnson 1.00	.50	.10
Virginia Squires			
☐ 223 Dave Robisch 2.00	1.00	.20
Denver Rockets			
☐ 224 Walt Simon 1.00	.50	.10
Kentucky Colonels			
☐ 225 Bill Melchionni 1.25	.60	.12
New York Nets			
☐ 226 Wendell Ladner 1.50	.75	.15
Memphis Tams			
☐ 227 Joe Hamilton 1.00	.50	.10
Dallas Chaparrals			
☐ 228 Bob Netolicky 1.25	.60	.12
Dallas Chaparrals			
☐ 229 James Jones 1.25	.60	.12
Utah Stars			
☐ 230 Dan Issel 10.00	5.00	1.00
Kentucky Colonels			
☐ 231 Charlie Williams 1.00	.50	.10
San Diego Conquistadors			

256 / 1972-73 Topps

☐ 232 Willie Sojourner	1.00	.50	.10
Virginia Squires			
☐ 233 Merv Jackson	1.00	.50	.10
Utah Stars			
☐ 234 Mike Lewis	1.25	.60	.12
Carolina Cougars			
☐ 235 Ralph Simpson	1.50	.75	.15
Denver Rockets			
☐ 236 Darnell Hillman	1.25	.60	.12
Indiana Pacers			
☐ 237 Rick Mount	2.00	1.00	.20
Kentucky Colonels			
☐ 238 Gerald Govan	1.00	.50	.10
Memphis Tams			
☐ 239 Ron Boone	1.25	.60	.12
Utah Stars			
☐ 240 Tom Washington	1.00	.50	.10
New York Nets			
☐ 241 ABA Playoffs G1	1.75	.85	.17
Pacers take lead (under the basket)			
☐ 242 ABA Playoffs G2	3.25	1.60	.32
Barry evens things			
☐ 243 ABA Playoffs G3	2.00	1.00	.20
McGinnis blocks a jumper			
☐ 244 ABA Playoffs G4	3.25	1.60	.32
Rick (Barry) scores on fast break			
☐ 245 ABA Playoffs G5	1.75	.85	.17
Keller becomes Net killer			
☐ 246 ABA Playoffs G6	1.75	.85	.17
Tight Defense			
☐ 247 ABA Champs: Pacers	1.75	.85	.17
☐ 248 ABA Checklist 177-264	12.50	1.50	.30
UER (236 John Brisker)			
☐ 249 Dan Issel AS	4.00	2.00	.40
Kentucky Colonels			
☐ 250 Rick Barry AS	12.50	6.25	1.25
New York Nets			
☐ 251 Artis Gilmore AS	5.00	2.50	.50
Kentucky Colonels			
☐ 252 Donnie Freeman AS	1.25	.60	.12
Dallas Chaparrals			
☐ 253 Bill Melchionni AS	1.25	.60	.12
New York Nets			
☐ 254 Willie Wise AS	1.25	.60	.12
Utah Stars			
☐ 255 Julius Erving AS	65.00	32.50	6.50
Virginia Squires			
☐ 256 Zelmo Beaty AS	1.25	.60	.12
Utah Stars			
☐ 257 Ralph Simpson AS	1.25	.60	.12
Denver Rockets			
☐ 258 Charlie Scott AS	1.25	.60	.12
Virginia Squires			

1973-74 Topps / 257

☐ 259 ABA Scoring Average 2.50		1.25	.25
Leaders			
Charlie Scott			
Rick Barry			
Dan Issel			
☐ 260 ABA 2pt FG Pct. 2.00		1.00	.20
Leaders			
Artis Gilmore			
Tom Washington			
Larry Jones			
☐ 261 ABA 3pt FG Pct. 1.75		.85	.17
Leaders			
Glen Combs			
Louie Dampier			
Warren Jabali			
☐ 262 ABA FT Pct Leaders 2.00		1.00	.20
Rick Barry			
Mack Calvin			
Steve Jones			
☐ 263 ABA Rebound Leaders 11.00		5.50	1.10
Artis Gilmore			
Julius Erving			
Mel Daniels			
☐ 264 ABA Assist Leaders 2.50		1.00	.20
Bill Melchionni			
Larry Brown			
Louie Dampier			

1973-74 Topps

The 1973-74 Topps set of 264 contains NBA players on cards numbered 1 to 176 and ABA players on cards numbered 177 to 264. The cards in the set measure the standard 2 1/2" by 3 1/2". All-Star selections (first and second team) for both leagues are noted on the respective player's regular cards. Card backs are printed in red and green on gray card stock. The backs feature year-by-year ABA and NBA statistics. Subseries within the set include NBA Playoffs (62-68), NBA League Leaders (153-158), ABA Playoffs (202-208), and ABA League Leaders (234-239). The only notable rookie cards in this set are Bob McAdoo and Paul Westphal.

	NRMT	VG-E	GOOD
COMPLETE SET (264)	360.00	165.00	45.00
COMMON PLAYER (1-132)	.50	.25	.05
COMMON PLAYER (133-264)	.50	.25	.05
☐ 1 Nate Archibald AS1	7.50	2.00	.40
Kansas City-Omaha Kings			
☐ 2 Steve Kuberski	.50	.25	.05
Boston Celtics			
☐ 3 John Mengelt	.75	.35	.07
Detroit Pistons			
☐ 4 Jim McMillian	.75	.35	.07
Los Angeles Lakers			

258 / 1973-74 Topps

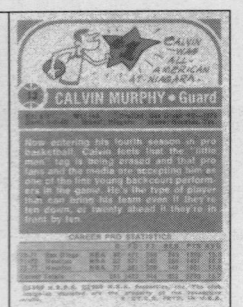

☐ 5 Nate Thurmond	3.00	1.50	.30
Golden State Warriors			
☐ 6 Dave Wohl	.50	.25	.05
Buffalo Braves			
☐ 7 John Brisker	.50	.25	.05
Seattle Supersonics			
☐ 8 Charlie Davis	.50	.25	.05
Portland Trail Blazers			
☐ 9 Lamar Green	.50	.25	.05
Phoenix Suns			
☐ 10 Walt Frazier AS2	8.00	4.00	.80
New York Knicks			
☐ 11 Bob Christian	.50	.25	.05
Atlanta Hawks			
☐ 12 Cornell Warner	.50	.25	.05
Cleveland Cavaliers			
☐ 13 Calvin Murphy	2.50	1.25	.25
Houston Rockets			
☐ 14 Dave Sorenson	.50	.25	.05
Philadelphia 76ers			
☐ 15 Archie Clark	.75	.35	.07
Capital Bullets			
☐ 16 Clifford Ray	.75	.35	.07
Chicago Bulls			
☐ 17 Terry Driscoll	.50	.25	.05
Milwaukee Bucks			
☐ 18 Matt Guokas	.75	.35	.07
Kansas City-Omaha Kings			
☐ 19 Elmore Smith	.75	.35	.07
Buffalo Braves			
☐ 20 John Havlicek AS1	14.00	7.00	1.40
Boston Celtics			
☐ 21 Pat Riley	8.00	4.00	.80
Los Angeles Lakers			
☐ 22 George Trapp	.50	.25	.05

1973-74 Topps / 259

	Detroit Pistons			
☐ 23	Ron Williams	.50	.25	.05
	Golden State Warriors			
☐ 24	Jim Fox	.50	.25	.05
	Seattle Supersonics			
☐ 25	Dick Van Arsdale	.75	.35	.07
	Phoenix Suns			
☐ 26	John Tresvant	.50	.25	.05
	Capital Bullets			
☐ 27	Rick Adelman	1.75	.85	.17
	Portland Trail Blazers			
☐ 28	Eddie Mast	.50	.25	.05
	Atlanta Hawks			
☐ 29	Jim Cleamons	.75	.35	.07
	Cleveland Cavaliers			
☐ 30	Dave DeBusschere AS2	6.00	3.00	.60
	New York Knicks			
☐ 31	Norm Van Lier	.75	.35	.07
	Chicago Bulls			
☐ 32	Stan McKenzie	.50	.25	.05
	Houston Rockets			
☐ 33	Bob Dandridge	.75	.35	.07
	Milwaukee Bucks			
☐ 34	Leroy Ellis	.50	.25	.05
	Philadelphia 76ers			
☐ 35	Mike Riordan	.75	.35	.07
	Capital Bullets			
☐ 36	Fred Hilton	.50	.25	.05
	Buffalo Braves			
☐ 37	Toby Kimball	.50	.25	.05
	Kansas City-Omaha Kings			
☐ 38	Jim Price	.50	.25	.05
	Los Angeles Lakers			
☐ 39	Willie Norwood	.50	.25	.05
	Detroit Pistons			
☐ 40	Dave Cowens AS2	6.00	3.00	.60
	Boston Celtics			
☐ 41	Cazzie Russell	1.25	.60	.12
	Golden State Warriors			
☐ 42	Lee Winfield	.50	.25	.05
	Seattle Supersonics			
☐ 43	Connie Hawkins	3.25	1.60	.32
	Phoenix Suns			
☐ 44	Mike Newlin	.75	.35	.07
	Houston Rockets			
☐ 45	Chet Walker	1.25	.60	.12
	Chicago Bulls			
☐ 46	Walt Bellamy	1.75	.85	.17
	Atlanta Hawks			
☐ 47	John Johnson	.75	.35	.07
	Portland Trail Blazers			
☐ 48	Henry Bibby	1.75	.85	.17
	New York Knicks			
☐ 49	Bobby Smith	.50	.25	.05
	Cleveland Cavaliers			
☐ 50	Kareem Abdul-Jabbar AS1	42.00	21.00	4.20

260 / 1973-74 Topps

☐ 51	Milwaukee Bucks Mike Price .... .50	.25	.05
☐ 52	Philadelphia 76ers John Hummer .... .50	.25	.05
☐ 53	Buffalo Braves Kevin Porter 4.00	2.00	.40
☐ 54	Capital Bullets Nate Williams .... .50	.25	.05
☐ 55	Kansas City-Omaha Kings Gail Goodrich 2.00	1.00	.20
☐ 56	Los Angeles Lakers Fred Foster .... .50	.25	.05
☐ 57	Detroit Pistons Don Chaney 1.25	.60	.12
☐ 58	Boston Celtics Bud Stallworth .... .50	.25	.05
☐ 59	Seattle Supersonics Clem Haskins .... .75	.35	.07
☐ 60	Phoenix Suns Bob Love AS2 .... 1.25	.60	.12
☐ 61	Chicago Bulls Jimmy Walker .... .50	.25	.05
☐ 62	Houston Rockets NBA Eastern Semis .... 1.00 Knicks shoot down Bullets in 5	.50	.10
☐ 63	NBA Eastern Semis .... 1.00 Celts oust Hawks 2nd Straight Year	.50	.10
☐ 64	NBA Western Semis .... 5.00 Lakers outlast Bulls at Wire (W.Chamberlain)	2.50	.50
☐ 65	NBA Western Semis .... 1.00 Warriors over- whelm Milwaukee	.50	.10
☐ 66	NBA Eastern Finals .... 2.50 Knicks stun Celtics at Boston (W.Reed/Finkel)	1.25	.25
☐ 67	NBA Western Finals .... 1.00 Lakers Breeze Past Golden State	.50	.10
☐ 68	NBA Championship .... 3.00 Knicks Do It, Repeat '70 Miracle (W.Frazier/Erickson)	1.50	.30
☐ 69	Larry Steele .... .50	.25	.05
☐ 70	Portland Trail Blazers Oscar Robertson 20.00	10.00	2.00
☐ 71	Milwaukee Bucks Phil Jackson 4.50	2.25	.45
☐ 72	New York Knicks John Wetzel .... .50	.25	.05
☐ 73	Atlanta Hawks Steve Patterson .... 1.00 Cleveland Cavaliers	.50	.10

1973-74 Topps / 261

☐ 74	Manny Leaks Philadelphia 76ers	.50	.25	.05
☐ 75	Jeff Mullins Golden State Warriors	.75	.35	.07
☐ 76	Stan Love Capital Bullets	.50	.25	.05
☐ 77	Dick Garrett Buffalo Braves	.50	.25	.05
☐ 78	Don Nelson Boston Celtics	2.50	1.25	.25
☐ 79	Chris Ford Detroit Pistons	6.00	3.00	.60
☐ 80	Wilt Chamberlain Los Angeles Lakers	45.00	22.50	4.50
☐ 81	Dennis Layton Phoenix Suns	.50	.25	.05
☐ 82	Bill Bradley New York Knicks	21.00	10.50	2.10
☐ 83	Jerry Sloan Chicago Bulls	1.50	.75	.15
☐ 84	Cliff Meely Houston Rockets	.50	.25	.05
☐ 85	Sam Lacey Kansas City-Omaha Kings	.75	.35	.07
☐ 86	Dick Snyder Seattle Supersonics	.50	.25	.05
☐ 87	Jim Washington Atlanta Hawks	.50	.25	.05
☐ 88	Lucius Allen Milwaukee Bucks	.75	.35	.07
☐ 89	LaRue Martin Portland Trail Blazers	.75	.35	.07
☐ 90	Rick Barry Golden State Warriors	15.00	7.50	1.50
☐ 91	Fred Boyd Philadelphia 76ers	.50	.25	.05
☐ 92	Barry Clemens Cleveland Cavaliers	.50	.25	.05
☐ 93	Dean Meminger New York Knicks	.75	.35	.07
☐ 94	Henry Finkel Boston Celtics	.50	.25	.05
☐ 95	Elvin Hayes Capital Bullets	8.00	4.00	.80
☐ 96	Stu Lantz Detroit Pistons	.50	.25	.05
☐ 97	Bill Hewitt Buffalo Braves	.50	.25	.05
☐ 98	Neal Walk Phoenix Suns	.50	.25	.05
☐ 99	Garfield Heard Chicago Bulls	.75	.35	.07
☐ 100	Jerry West AS1 Los Angeles Lakers	24.00	12.00	2.40
☐ 101	Otto Moore Houston Rockets	.50	.25	.05
☐ 102	Don Kojis	.50	.25	.05

262 / 1973-74 Topps

	Kansas City-Omaha Kings		
☐ 103 Fred Brown 4.25	2.10	.42
	Seattle Supersonics		
☐ 104 Dwight Davis .... .75	.35	.07
	Cleveland Cavaliers		
☐ 105 Willis Reed 6.00	3.00	.60
	New York Knicks		
☐ 106 Herm Gilliam .... .50	.25	.05
	Atlanta Hawks		
☐ 107 Mickey Davis .... .75	.35	.07
	Milwaukee Bucks		
☐ 108 Jim Barnett .... .50	.25	.05
	Golden State Warriors		
☐ 109 Ollie Johnson .... .50	.25	.05
	Portland Trail Blazers		
☐ 110 Bob Lanier 6.00	3.00	.60
	Detroit Pistons		
☐ 111 Fred Carter .... .50	.25	.05
	Philadelphia 76ers		
☐ 112 Paul Silas 1.25	.60	.12
	Boston Celtics		
☐ 113 Phil Chenier 1.00	.50	.10
	Capital Bullets		
☐ 114 Dennis Awtrey .... .50	.25	.05
	Chicago Bulls		
☐ 115 Austin Carr 1.00	.50	.10
	Cleveland Cavaliers		
☐ 116 Bob Kauffman .... .50	.25	.05
	Buffalo Braves		
☐ 117 Keith Erickson .... .75	.35	.07
	Los Angeles Lakers		
☐ 118 Walt Wesley .... .50	.25	.05
	Phoenix Suns		
☐ 119 Steve Bracey .... .50	.25	.05
	Atlanta Hawks		
☐ 120 Spencer Haywood AS1 .... 1.75	.85	.17
	Seattle Supersonics		
☐ 121 NBA Checklist 1-176 .... 9.00	.90	.18
☐ 122 Jack Marin .... .75	.35	.07
	Houston Rockets		
☐ 123 Jon McGlocklin .... .75	.35	.07
	Milwaukee Bucks		
☐ 124 Johnny Green .... .50	.25	.05
	Kansas City-Omaha Kings		
☐ 125 Jerry Lucas 5.50	2.75	.55
	New York Knicks		
☐ 126 Paul Westphal 10.00	5.00	1.00
	Boston Celtics		
☐ 127 Curtis Rowe 1.00	.50	.10
	Detroit Pistons		
☐ 128 Mahdi Abdul-Rahman 1.25	.60	.12
	Seattle Supersonics		
	(formerly Walt Hazzard)		
☐ 129 Lloyd Neal 1.25	.60	.12
	Portland Trail Blazers		
☐ 130 Pete Maravich AS1 .... 15.00	7.50	1.50
	Atlanta Hawks		

1973-74 Topps / 263

☐ 131	Don May Philadelphia 76ers	.50	.25	.05
☐ 132	Bob Weiss Chicago Bulls	.75	.35	.07
☐ 133	Dave Stallworth Capital Bullets	.75	.35	.07
☐ 134	Dick Cunningham Milwaukee Bucks	.50	.25	.05
☐ 135	Bob McAdoo Buffalo Braves	15.00	7.50	1.50
☐ 136	Butch Beard Golden State Warriors	.75	.35	.07
☐ 137	Happy Hairston Los Angeles Lakers	.75	.35	.07
☐ 138	Bob Rule Cleveland Cavaliers	.50	.25	.05
☐ 139	Don Adams Detroit Pistons	.50	.25	.05
☐ 140	Charlie Scott Phoenix Suns	1.00	.50	.10
☐ 141	Ron Riley Kansas City-Omaha Kings	.50	.25	.05
☐ 142	Earl Monroe New York Knicks	6.00	3.00	.60
☐ 143	Clyde Lee Golden State Warriors	.50	.25	.05
☐ 144	Rick Roberson Portland Trail Blazers	.50	.25	.05
☐ 145	Rudy Tomjanovich Houston Rockets (Printed without Houston on basket)	1.25	.60	.12
☐ 146	Tom Van Arsdale Philadelphia 76ers	.75	.35	.07
☐ 147	Art Williams Boston Celtics	.50	.25	.05
☐ 148	Curtis Perry Milwaukee Bucks	.50	.25	.05
☐ 149	Rich Rinaldi Capital Bullets	.50	.25	.05
☐ 150	Lou Hudson Atlanta Hawks	1.25	.60	.12
☐ 151	Mel Counts Los Angeles Lakers	.50	.25	.05
☐ 152	Jim McDaniels Seattle Supersonics	.50	.25	.05
☐ 153	NBA Scoring Leaders Nate Archibald Kareem Abdul-Jabbar Spencer Haywood	5.00	2.50	.50
☐ 154	NBA Scoring Average Leaders Nate Archibald Kareem Abdul-Jabbar Spencer Haywood	5.00	2.50	.50
☐ 155	NBA FG Pct Leaders Wilt Chamberlain	6.50	3.25	.65

264 / 1973-74 Topps

	Matt Guokas Kareem Abdul-Jabbar			
☐ 156	NBA FT Pct Leaders	2.00	1.00	.20
	Rick Barry Calvin Murphy Mike Newlin			
☐ 157	NBA Rebound Leaders	5.00	2.50	.50
	Wilt Chamberlain Nate Thurmond Dave Cowens			
☐ 158	NBA Assist Leaders	2.50	1.25	.25
	Nate Archibald Len Wilkens Dave Bing			
☐ 159	Don Smith	.50	.25	.05
	Houston Rockets			
☐ 160	Sidney Wicks	2.00	1.00	.20
	Portland Trail Blazers			
☐ 161	Howie Komives	.50	.25	.05
	Buffalo Braves			
☐ 162	John Gianelli	.50	.25	.05
	New York Knicks			
☐ 163	Jeff Halliburton	.50	.25	.05
	Philadelphia 76ers			
☐ 164	Kennedy McIntosh	.50	.25	.05
	Seattle Supersonics			
☐ 165	Len Wilkens	2.50	1.25	.25
	Cleveland Cavaliers			
☐ 166	Corky Calhoun	.75	.35	.07
	Phoenix Suns			
☐ 167	Howard Porter	.75	.35	.07
	Chicago Bulls			
☐ 168	JoJo White	2.00	1.00	.20
	Boston Celtics			
☐ 169	John Block	.50	.25	.05
	Kansas City-Omaha Kings			
☐ 170	Dave Bing	3.25	1.60	.32
	Detroit Pistons			
☐ 171	Joe Ellis	.50	.25	.05
	Golden State Warriors			
☐ 172	Chuck Terry	.50	.25	.05
	Milwaukee Bucks			
☐ 173	Randy Smith	.75	.35	.07
	Buffalo Braves			
☐ 174	Bill Bridges	.75	.35	.07
	Los Angeles Lakers			
☐ 175	Geoff Petrie	.75	.35	.07
	Portland Trail Blazers			
☐ 176	Wes Unseld	4.50	2.25	.45
	Capital Bullets			
☐ 177	Skeeter Swift	.50	.25	.05
	San Antonio Spurs			
☐ 178	Jim Eakins	.50	.25	.05
	Virginia Squires			
☐ 179	Steve Jones	.75	.35	.07
	Carolina Cougars			
☐ 180	George McGinnis AS1	2.50	1.25	.25

1973-74 Topps / 265

Indiana Pacers
- [ ] 181 Al Smith .... .50 .25 .05
Denver Rockets
- [ ] 182 Tom Washington .... .50 .25 .05
New York Nets
- [ ] 183 Louie Dampier .... .75 .35 .07
Kentucky Colonels
- [ ] 184 Simmie Hill .... .50 .25 .05
San Diego Conquistadors
- [ ] 185 George Thompson .... .50 .25 .05
Memphis Tams
- [ ] 186 Cincy Powell .... .50 .25 .05
Utah Stars
- [ ] 187 Larry Jones .... .50 .25 .05
San Antonio Spurs
- [ ] 188 Neil Johnson .... .50 .25 .05
Virginia Squires
- [ ] 189 Tom Owens .... .75 .35 .07
Carolina Cougars
- [ ] 190 Ralph Simpson AS2 .... .75 .35 .07
Denver Rockets
- [ ] 191 George Carter .... .50 .25 .05
Virginia Squires
- [ ] 192 Rick Mount .... 1.00 .50 .10
Kentucky Colonels
- [ ] 193 Red Robbins .... .50 .25 .05
San Diego Conquistadors
- [ ] 194 George Lehmann .... .50 .25 .05
Memphis Tams
- [ ] 195 Mel Daniels AS2 .... 1.25 .60 .12
Indiana Pacers
- [ ] 196 Bob Warren .... .50 .25 .05
Utah Stars
- [ ] 197 Gene Kennedy .... .50 .25 .05
San Antonio Spurs
- [ ] 198 Mike Barr .... .50 .25 .05
Virginia Squires
- [ ] 199 Dave Robisch .... .75 .35 .07
Denver Rockets
- [ ] 200 Billy Cunningham AS1 .... 5.00 2.50 .50
Carolina Cougars
- [ ] 201 John Roche .... .75 .35 .07
New York Nets
- [ ] 202 ABA Western Semis .... 1.00 .50 .10
Pacers Oust
Injured Rockets
- [ ] 203 ABA Western Semis .... 1.00 .50 .10
Stars sweep Q's
in Four Straight
- [ ] 204 ABA Eastern Semis .... 2.00 1.00 .20
Kentucky overcomes
Squires and Dr. J.
(Issel jump shot)
- [ ] 205 ABA Eastern Semis .... 1.00 .50 .10
Cougars in strong
finish over Nets
- [ ] 206 ABA Western Finals .... 1.00 .50 .10

266 / 1973-74 Topps

☐ 207 ABA Eastern Finals (Pacers nip bitter rival, Stars)	2.00	1.00	.20
☐ 208 ABA Championship (Colonels prevail in grueling Series) (Gilmore shooting)	1.00	.50	.10
☐ 209 Glen Combs (McGinnis leads Pacers to Title) (center jump)	.50	.25	.05
☐ 210 Dan Issel AS2 — Utah Stars	6.00	3.00	.60
☐ 211 Randy Denton — Kentucky Colonels	.50	.25	.05
☐ 212 Freddie Lewis — Memphis Tams	.75	.35	.07
☐ 213 Stew Johnson — Indiana Pacers	.50	.25	.05
☐ 214 Roland Taylor — San Diego Conquistadors	.50	.25	.05
☐ 215 Rich Jones — Virginia Squires	.50	.25	.05
☐ 216 Billy Paultz — San Antonio Spurs	.75	.35	.07
☐ 217 Ron Boone — New York Nets	.75	.35	.07
☐ 218 Walt Simon — Utah Stars	.50	.25	.05
☐ 219 Mike Lewis — Kentucky Colonels	.50	.25	.05
☐ 220 Warren Jabali AS1 — Carolina Cougars	.75	.35	.07
☐ 221 Wilbert Jones — Denver Rockets	.50	.25	.05
☐ 222 Don Buse — Memphis Tams	1.50	.75	.15
☐ 223 Gene Moore — Indiana Pacers	.50	.25	.05
☐ 224 Joe Hamilton — San Diego Conquistadors	.50	.25	.05
☐ 225 Zelmo Beaty — San Antonio Spurs	.75	.35	.07
☐ 226 Brian Taylor — Utah Stars	1.25	.60	.12
☐ 227 Julius Keye — New York Nets	.50	.25	.05
☐ 228 Mike Gale — Denver Rockets	1.00	.50	.10
☐ 229 Warren Davis — Kentucky Colonels	.50	.25	.05
☐ 230 Mack Calvin AS2 — Memphis Tams	1.00	.50	.10
☐ 231 Roger Brown — Carolina Cougars	.75	.35	.07
☐ 232 Chuck Williams — Indiana Pacers	.50	.25	.05

1973-74 Topps / 267

San Diego Conquistadors
- ☐ 233 Gerald Govan .... .50 / .25 / .05

Utah Stars
- ☐ 234 ABA Scoring Average .... 6.00 / 3.00 / .60
  Leaders
  Julius Erving
  George McGinnis
  Dan Issel
- ☐ 235 ABA 2 Pt. Pct. .... 1.00 / .50 / .10
  Leaders
  Artis Gilmore
  Gene Kennedy
  Tom Owens
- ☐ 236 ABA 3 Pt. Pct. .... 1.00 / .50 / .10
  Leaders
  Glen Combs
  Roger Brown
  Louie Dampier
- ☐ 237 ABA F.T. Pct. Leaders .... 1.00 / .50 / .10
  Billy Keller
  Ron Boone
  Bob Warren
- ☐ 238 ABA Rebound Leaders .... 1.00 / .50 / .10
  Artis Gilmore
  Mel Daniels
  Bill Paultz
- ☐ 239 ABA Assist Leaders .... 1.00 / .50 / .10
  Bill Melchionni
  Chuck Williams
  Warren Jabali
- ☐ 240 Julius Erving AS2 .... 75.00 / 37.50 / 7.50
  Virginia Squires
- ☐ 241 Jimmy O'Brien .... .75 / .35 / .07
  Kentucky Colonels
- ☐ 242 ABA Checklist 177-264 .... 9.00 / .90 / .18
- ☐ 243 Johnny Neumann .... .75 / .35 / .07
  Memphis Tams
- ☐ 244 Darnell Hillman .... .75 / .35 / .07
  Indiana Pacers
- ☐ 245 Willie Wise .... .75 / .35 / .07
  Utah Stars
- ☐ 246 Collis Jones .... .50 / .25 / .05
  San Antonio Spurs
- ☐ 247 Ted McClain .... .50 / .25 / .05
  Carolina Cougars
- ☐ 248 George Irvine .... 1.00 / .50 / .10
  Virginia Squires
- ☐ 249 Bill Melchionni .... .75 / .35 / .07
  New York Nets
- ☐ 250 Artis Gilmore AS1 .... 5.50 / 2.75 / .55
  Kentucky Colonels
- ☐ 251 Willie Long .... .50 / .25 / .05
  Denver Rockets
- ☐ 252 Larry Miller .... .75 / .35 / .07
  San Diego Conquistadors
- ☐ 253 Lee Davis .... .50 / .25 / .05
  Memphis Tams

268 / 1973-74 Topps

☐ 254 Donnie Freeman Indiana Pacers	.75	.35	.07
☐ 255 Joe Caldwell Carolina Cougars	.75	.35	.07
☐ 256 Bob Netolicky San Antonio Spurs	.75	.35	.07
☐ 257 Bernie Williams Virginia Squires	.50	.25	.05
☐ 258 Byron Beck Denver Rockets	.50	.25	.05
☐ 259 Jim Chones New York Nets	1.25	.60	.12
☐ 260 James Jones AS1 Utah Stars	.75	.35	.07
☐ 261 Wendell Ladner Kentucky Colonels	.75	.35	.07
☐ 262 Ollie Taylor San Diego Conquistadors	.50	.25	.05
☐ 263 Les Hunter Memphis Tams	.50	.25	.05
☐ 264 Billy Keller Indiana Pacers	.75	.35	.07

1974-75 Topps

The 1974-75 Topps set of 264 cards contains NBA players on cards numbered 1 to 176 and ABA players on cards numbered 177 to 264. For the first time Team Leader (TL) cards are provided for each team. The cards in the set measure the standard 2 1/2" by 3 1/2". All-Star selections (first and second team) for both leagues are noted on the respective player's regular cards. The card backs are printed in blue and red on gray card stock. Subseries within the set include NBA Team Leaders (81-98), NBA Statistical Leaders (144-149), NBA Playoffs (161-164), ABA Statistical

1974-75 Topps / 269

Leaders (207-212), ABA Team Leaders (221-230), and ABA Playoffs (246-249). The key rookie cards in this set are George Gervin and Bill Walton.

	NRMT	VG-E	GOOD
COMPLETE SET (264)	350.00	175.00	35.00
COMMON PLAYER (1-132)	.50	.25	.05
COMMON PLAYER (133-264)	.50	.25	.05
☐ 1 Kareem Abdul-Jabbar AS1 Milwaukee Bucks	40.00	12.50	2.50
☐ 2 Don May Philadelphia 76ers	.50	.25	.05
☐ 3 Bernie Fryer Portland Trail Blazers	.75	.35	.07
☐ 4 Don Adams Detroit Pistons	.50	.25	.05
☐ 5 Herm Gilliam Atlanta Hawks	.50	.25	.05
☐ 6 Jim Chones Cleveland Cavaliers	.75	.35	.07
☐ 7 Rick Adelman Chicago Bulls	1.50	.75	.15
☐ 8 Randy Smith Buffalo Braves	.75	.35	.07
☐ 9 Paul Silas Boston Celtics	1.25	.60	.12
☐ 10 Pete Maravich New Orleans Jazz	12.50	6.25	1.25
☐ 11 Ron Behagen Kansas City-Omaha Kings	.50	.25	.05
☐ 12 Kevin Porter Washington Bullets	1.00	.50	.10
☐ 13 Bill Bridges Los Angeles Lakers (On back team shown as Los And., should be Los Ang.)	.75	.35	.07
☐ 14 Charles Johnson Golden State Warriors	1.00	.50	.10
☐ 15 Bob Love Chicago Bulls	1.25	.60	.12
☐ 16 Henry Bibby New York Knicks	.75	.35	.07
☐ 17 Neal Walk Phoenix Suns	.50	.25	.05
☐ 18 John Brisker Seattle Supersonics	.50	.25	.05
☐ 19 Lucius Allen Milwaukee Bucks	.75	.35	.07
☐ 20 Tom Van Arsdale Philadelphia 76ers	.75	.35	.07
☐ 21 Larry Steele Portland Trail Blazers	.50	.25	.05
☐ 22 Curtis Rowe Detroit Pistons	.75	.35	.07
☐ 23 Dean Meminger	.50	.25	.05

270 / 1974-75 Topps

☐ 24	Atlanta Hawks Steve Patterson	.50	.25	.05
☐ 25	Cleveland Cavaliers Earl Monroe	5.50	2.75	.55
☐ 26	New York Knicks Jack Marin	.50	.25	.05
☐ 27	Buffalo Braves JoJo White	1.75	.85	.17
☐ 28	Boston Celtics Rudy Tomjanovich	1.00	.50	.10
☐ 29	Houston Rockets Otto Moore	.50	.25	.05
☐ 30	Kansas City-Omaha Kings Elvin Hayes AS2	7.00	3.50	.70
☐ 31	Washington Bullets Pat Riley	6.50	3.25	.65
☐ 32	Los Angeles Lakers Clyde Lee	.50	.25	.05
☐ 33	Golden State Warriors Bob Weiss	.75	.35	.07
☐ 34	Chicago Bulls Jim Fox	.50	.25	.05
☐ 35	Seattle Supersonics Charlie Scott	.75	.35	.07
☐ 36	Phoenix Suns Cliff Meely	.50	.25	.05
☐ 37	Houston Rockets Jon McGlocklin	.75	.35	.07
☐ 38	Milwaukee Bucks Jim McMillian	.50	.25	.05
☐ 39	Buffalo Braves Bill Walton	40.00	20.00	4.00
☐ 40	Portland Trail Blazers Dave Bing AS2	3.00	1.50	.30
☐ 41	Detroit Pistons Jim Washington	.50	.25	.05
☐ 42	Atlanta Hawks Jim Cleamons	.50	.25	.05
☐ 43	Cleveland Cavaliers Mel Davis	.50	.25	.05
☐ 44	New York Knicks Garfield Heard	.50	.25	.05
☐ 45	Buffalo Braves Jimmy Walker	.50	.25	.05
☐ 46	Kansas City-Omaha Kings Don Nelson	2.50	1.25	.25
☐ 47	Boston Celtics Jim Barnett	.50	.25	.05
☐ 48	New Orleans Jazz Manny Leaks	.50	.25	.05
☐ 49	Washington Bullets Elmore Smith	.50	.25	.05
☐ 50	Los Angeles Lakers Rick Barry AS1	10.00	5.00	1.00
☐ 51	Golden State Warriors Jerry Sloan Chicago Bulls	1.00	.50	.10

1974-75 Topps / 271

- ☐ 52 John Hummer .... .50 — .25 — .05
  Seattle Supersonics
- ☐ 53 Keith Erickson .... .75 — .35 — .07
  Phoenix Suns
- ☐ 54 George E. Johnson .... .50 — .25 — .05
  Houston Rockets
- ☐ 55 Oscar Robertson .... 16.00 — 8.00 — 1.60
  Milwaukee Bucks
- ☐ 56 Steve Mix .... 1.00 — .50 — .10
  Philadelphia 76ers
- ☐ 57 Rick Roberson .... .50 — .25 — .05
  Portland Trail Blazers
- ☐ 58 John Mengelt .... .50 — .25 — .05
  Detroit Pistons
- ☐ 59 Dwight Jones .... .75 — .35 — .07
  Atlanta Hawks
- ☐ 60 Austin Carr .... .75 — .35 — .07
  Cleveland Cavaliers
- ☐ 61 Nick Weatherspoon .... 1.00 — .50 — .10
  Washington Bullets
- ☐ 62 Clem Haskins .... .75 — .35 — .07
  Phoenix Suns
- ☐ 63 Don Kojis .... .50 — .25 — .05
  Kansas City-Omaha Kings
- ☐ 64 Paul Westphal .... 2.50 — 1.25 — .25
  Boston Celtics
- ☐ 65 Walt Bellamy .... 1.50 — .75 — .15
  New Orleans Jazz
- ☐ 66 John Johnson .... .50 — .25 — .05
  Portland Trail Blazers
- ☐ 67 Butch Beard .... .50 — .25 — .05
  Golden State Warriors
- ☐ 68 Happy Hairston .... .75 — .35 — .07
  Los Angeles Lakers
- ☐ 69 Tom Boerwinkle .... .50 — .25 — .05
  Chicago Bulls
- ☐ 70 Spencer Haywood AS2 .... 1.50 — .75 — .15
  Seattle Supersonics
- ☐ 71 Gary Melchionni .... .50 — .25 — .05
  Phoenix Suns
- ☐ 72 Ed Ratleff .... 1.00 — .50 — .10
  Houston Rockets
- ☐ 73 Mickey Davis .... .50 — .25 — .05
  Milwaukee Bucks
- ☐ 74 Dennis Awtrey .... .50 — .25 — .05
  New Orleans Jazz
- ☐ 75 Fred Carter .... .50 — .25 — .05
  Philadelphia 76ers
- ☐ 76 George Trapp .... .50 — .25 — .05
  Detroit Pistons
- ☐ 77 John Wetzel .... .50 — .25 — .05
  Atlanta Hawks
- ☐ 78 Bobby Smith .... .50 — .25 — .05
  Cleveland Cavaliers
- ☐ 79 John Gianelli .... .50 — .25 — .05
  New York Knicks
- ☐ 80 Bob McAdoo AS2 .... 4.00 — 2.00 — .40

272 / 1974-75 Topps

☐ 81	Atlanta Hawks TL Buffalo Braves Pete Maravich Lou Hudson Walt Bellamy Pete Maravich	2.50	1.25	.25
☐ 82	Boston Celtics TL John Havlicek JoJo White Dave Cowens JoJo White	4.00	2.00	.40
☐ 83	Buffalo Braves TL Bob McAdoo Ernie DiGregorio Bob McAdoo Ernie DiGregorio	1.25	.60	.12
☐ 84	Chicago Bulls TL Bob Love Chet Walker Clifford Ray Norm Van Lier	1.25	.60	.12
☐ 85	Cleveland Cavs TL Austin Carr Austin Carr Dwight Davis Len Wilkens	1.25	.60	.12
☐ 86	Detroit Pistons TL Bob Lanier Stu Lantz Bob Lanier Dave Bing	1.25	.60	.12
☐ 87	Golden State Warriors TL Rick Barry Rick Barry Nate Thurmond Rick Barry	2.50	1.25	.25
☐ 88	Houston Rockets TL Rudy Tomjanovich Calvin Murphy Don Smith Calvin Murphy	1.25	.60	.12
☐ 89	Kansas City Omaha TL Jimmy Walker Jimmy Walker Sam Lacey Jimmy Walker	1.00	.50	.10
☐ 90	Los Angeles Lakers TL Gail Goodrich Gail Goodrich Happy Hairston Gail Goodrich	1.25	.60	.12
☐ 91	Milwaukee Bucks TL Kareem Abdul-Jabbar Oscar Robertson Kareem Abdul-Jabbar Oscar Robertson	7.00	3.50	.70

1974-75 Topps / 273

- [ ] 92 New Orleans Jazz .... 1.00   .50   .10
  Emblem; Expansion
  Draft Picks on Back
- [ ] 93 New York Knicks TL .... 4.25   2.10   .42
  Walt Frazier
  Bill Bradley
  Dave DeBusschere
  Walt Frazier
- [ ] 94 Philadelphia 76ers TL .... 1.00   .50   .10
  Fred Carter
  Tom Van Arsdale
  Leroy Ellis
  Fred Carter
- [ ] 95 Phoenix Suns TL .... 1.00   .50   .10
  Charlie Scott
  Dick Van Arsdale
  Neal Walk
  Neal Walk
- [ ] 96 Portland Trail Blazers TL .... 1.00   .50   .10
  Geoff Petrie
  Geoff Petrie
  Rick Roberson
  Sidney Wicks
- [ ] 97 Seattle Supersonics TL .... 1.00   .50   .10
  Spencer Haywood
  Dick Snyder
  Spencer Haywood
  Fred Brown
- [ ] 98 Capitol Bullets TL .... 1.00   .50   .10
  Phil Chenier
  Phil Chenier
  Elvin Hayes
  Kevin Porter
- [ ] 99 Sam Lacey .... .50   .25   .05
  Kansas City-Omaha Kings
- [ ] 100 John Havlicek AS1 .... 14.00   7.00   1.40
  Boston Celtics
- [ ] 101 Stu Lantz .... .50   .25   .05
  New Orleans Jazz
- [ ] 102 Mike Riordan .... .50   .25   .05
  Washington Bullets
- [ ] 103 Larry Jones .... .50   .25   .05
  Philadelphia 76ers
- [ ] 104 Connie Hawkins .... 3.00   1.50   .30
  Los Angeles Lakers
- [ ] 105 Nate Thurmond .... 3.00   1.50   .30
  Golden State Warriors
- [ ] 106 Dick Gibbs .... .50   .25   .05
  Seattle Supersonics
- [ ] 107 Corky Calhoun .... .50   .25   .05
  Phoenix Suns
- [ ] 108 Dave Wohl .... .50   .25   .05
  Houston Rockets
- [ ] 109 Cornell Warner .... .50   .25   .05
  Milwaukee Bucks
- [ ] 110 Geoff Petrie UER .... .75   .35   .07

274 / 1974-75 Topps

☐ 111 Leroy Ellis	Portland Trail Blazers (Misspelled Patrie on card front) .50	.25	.05
☐ 112 Chris Ford	Philadelphia 76ers 2.00	1.00	.20
☐ 113 Bill Bradley	Detroit Pistons 20.00	10.00	2.00
☐ 114 Clifford Ray	New York Knicks .75	.35	.07
☐ 115 Dick Snyder	Chicago Bulls .50	.25	.05
☐ 116 Nate Williams	Cleveland Cavaliers .50	.25	.05
☐ 117 Matt Guokas	Kansas City-Omaha Kings .75	.35	.07
☐ 118 Henry Finkel	Buffalo Braves .50	.25	.05
☐ 119 Curtis Perry	Boston Celtics .50	.25	.05
☐ 120 Gail Goodrich AS1	New Orleans Jazz 1.75	.85	.17
☐ 121 Wes Unseld	Los Angeles Lakers 3.50	1.75	.35
☐ 122 Howard Porter	Washington Bullets .75	.35	.07
☐ 123 Jeff Mullins	New York Knicks .75	.35	.07
☐ 124 Mike Bantom	Golden State Warriors .75	.35	.07
☐ 125 Fred Brown	Phoenix Suns 1.25	.60	.12
☐ 126 Bob Dandridge	Seattle Supersonics .75	.35	.07
☐ 127 Mike Newlin	Milwaukee Bucks .50	.25	.05
☐ 128 Greg Smith	Houston Rockets .50	.25	.05
☐ 129 Doug Collins	Portland Trail Blazers 9.00	4.50	.90
☐ 130 Lou Hudson	Philadelphia 76ers 1.00	.50	.10
☐ 131 Bob Lanier	Atlanta Hawks 4.00	2.00	.40
☐ 132 Phil Jackson	Detroit Pistons 3.50	1.75	.35
☐ 133 Don Chaney	New York Knicks .75	.35	.07
☐ 134 Jim Brewer	Boston Celtics .75	.35	.07
☐ 135 Ernie DiGregorio	Cleveland Cavaliers 2.00	1.00	.20
☐ 136 Steve Kuberski	Buffalo Braves .50	.25	.05
☐ 137 Jim Price	New Orleans Jazz .50	.25	.05
	Los Angeles Lakers		

1974-75 Topps / 275

☐ 138 Mike D'Antoni	.50	.25	.05
Kansas City-Omaha Kings			
☐ 139 John Brown	.50	.25	.05
Atlanta Hawks			
☐ 140 Norm Van Lier AS2	.75	.35	.07
Chicago Bulls			
☐ 141 NBA Checklist 1-176	8.00	.80	.16
☐ 142 Don(Slick) Watts	1.00	.50	.10
Seattle Supersonics			
☐ 143 Walt Wesley	.50	.25	.05
Washington Bullets			
☐ 144 NBA Scoring Leaders	4.50	2.25	.45
Bob McAdoo			
Kareem Abdul-Jabbar			
Pete Maravich			
☐ 145 NBA Scoring	4.50	2.25	.45
Average Leaders			
Bob McAdoo			
Pete Maravich			
Kareem Abdul-Jabbar			
☐ 146 NBA F.G. Pct. Leaders	3.50	1.75	.35
Bob McAdoo			
Kareem Abdul-Jabbar			
Rudy Tomjanovich			
☐ 147 NBA F.T. Pct. Leaders	1.25	.60	.12
Ernie DiGregorio			
Rick Barry			
Jeff Mullins			
☐ 148 NBA Rebound Leaders	1.75	.85	.17
Elvin Hayes			
Dave Cowens			
Bob McAdoo			
☐ 149 NBA Assist Leaders	1.25	.60	.12
Ernie DiGregorio			
Calvin Murphy			
Len Wilkens			
☐ 150 Walt Frazier AS1	7.00	3.50	.70
New York Knicks			
☐ 151 Cazzie Russell	1.00	.50	.10
Golden State Warriors			
☐ 152 Calvin Murphy	1.75	.85	.17
Houston Rockets			
☐ 153 Bob Kauffman	.50	.25	.05
Atlanta Hawks			
☐ 154 Fred Boyd	.50	.25	.05
Philadelphia 76ers			
☐ 155 Dave Cowens	6.00	3.00	.60
Boston Celtics			
☐ 156 Willie Norwood	.50	.25	.05
Detroit Pistons			
☐ 157 Lee Winfield	.50	.25	.05
Buffalo Braves			
☐ 158 Dwight Davis	.50	.25	.05
Cleveland Cavaliers			
☐ 159 George T. Johnson	.50	.25	.05
Golden State Warriors			
☐ 160 Dick Van Arsdale	.75	.35	.07

276 / 1974-75 Topps

	Phoenix Suns		
☐ 161	NBA Eastern Semis 1.00	.50	.10
	Celts over Braves Knicks edge Bullets		
☐ 162	NBA Western Semis 1.00	.50	.10
	Bucks over Lakers Bulls edge Pistons		
☐ 163	NBA Div. Finals 1.00	.50	.10
	Celts over Knicks Bucks sweep Bulls		
☐ 164	NBA Championship 1.00	.50	.10
	Celtics over Bucks		
☐ 165	Phil Chenier .... .75	.35	.07
	Washington Bullets		
☐ 166	Kermit Washington 1.00	.50	.10
	Los Angeles Lakers		
☐ 167	Dale Schlueter .... .50	.25	.05
	Atlanta Hawks		
☐ 168	John Block .... .50	.25	.05
	New Orleans Jazz		
☐ 169	Don Smith .... .50	.25	.05
	Houston Rockets		
☐ 170	Nate Archibald 4.50	2.25	.45
	Kansas City-Omaha Kings		
☐ 171	Chet Walker 1.25	.60	.12
	Chicago Bulls		
☐ 172	Archie Clark .... .75	.35	.07
	Washington Bullets		
☐ 173	Kennedy McIntosh .... .50	.25	.05
	Seattle Supersonics		
☐ 174	George Thompson .... .50	.25	.05
	Milwaukee Bucks		
☐ 175	Sidney Wicks 1.25	.60	.12
	Portland Trail Blazers		
☐ 176	Jerry West 20.00	10.00	2.00
	Los Angeles Lakers		
☐ 177	Dwight Lamar .... .75	.35	.07
	San Diego Conquistadors		
☐ 178	George Carter .... .50	.25	.05
	Virginia Squires		
☐ 179	Wil Robinson .... .50	.25	.05
	Memphis Sounds		
☐ 180	Artis Gilmore AS1 .... 3.75	1.85	.37
	Kentucky Colonels		
☐ 181	Brian Taylor .... .75	.35	.07
	New York Nets		
☐ 182	Darnell Hillman .... .50	.25	.05
	Indiana Pacers		
☐ 183	Dave Robisch .... .75	.35	.07
	Denver Nuggets		
☐ 184	Gene Littles 1.00	.50	.10
	St. Louis Spirits		
☐ 185	Willie Wise AS2 .... .75	.35	.07
	Utah Stars		
☐ 186	James Silas 1.50	.75	.15
	San Antonio Spurs		
☐ 187	Caldwell Jones 3.00	1.50	.30

1974-75 Topps / 277

San Diego Conquistadors
- ☐ 188 Roland Taylor .... .50 .25 .05
Virginia Squires
- ☐ 189 Randy Denton .... .50 .25 .05
Memphis Sounds
- ☐ 190 Dan Issel AS2 .... 4.50 2.25 .45
Kentucky Colonels
- ☐ 191 Mike Gale .... .50 .25 .05
New York Nets
- ☐ 192 Mel Daniels .... 1.00 .50 .10
Memphis Sounds
- ☐ 193 Steve Jones .... .75 .35 .07
Denver Nuggets
- ☐ 194 Marv Roberts .... .50 .25 .05
St. Louis Spirits
- ☐ 195 Ron Boone AS2 .... .75 .35 .07
Utah Stars
- ☐ 196 George Gervin 36.00 18.00 3.60
San Antonio Spurs
- ☐ 197 Flynn Robinson .... .50 .25 .05
San Diego Conquistadors
- ☐ 198 Cincy Powell .... .50 .25 .05
Virginia Squires
- ☐ 199 Glen Combs .... .50 .25 .05
Memphis Sounds
- ☐ 200 Julius Erving AS1 UER 42.00 21.00 4.20
New York Nets
(Misspelled Irving
on card back)
- ☐ 201 Billy Keller .... .75 .35 .07
Indiana Pacers
- ☐ 202 Willie Long .... .50 .25 .05
Denver Nuggets
- ☐ 203 ABA Checklist 177-264 .... 8.00 .80 .16
- ☐ 204 Joe Caldwell .... .75 .35 .07
St. Louis Spirits
- ☐ 205 Swen Nater AS2 .... 2.00 1.00 .20
San Antonio Spurs
- ☐ 206 Rick Mount .... .75 .35 .07
Utah Stars
- ☐ 207 ABA Scoring .... 4.50 2.25 .45
Avg. Leaders
Julius Erving
George McGinnis
Dan Issel
- ☐ 208 ABA 2 Pt. F.G. Pct. Leaders .... 1.00 .50 .10
Swen Nater
James Jones
Tom Owens
- ☐ 209 ABA 3 Pt. F.G. Pct. Leaders .... 1.00 .50 .10
Louie Dampier
Billy Keller
Roger Brown
- ☐ 210 ABA F.T. Pct. Leaders .... 1.00 .50 .10
James Jones
Mack Calvin

278 / 1974-75 Topps

Ron Boone			
☐ 211 ABA Rebound Leaders	1.00	.50	.10
Artis Gilmore			
George McGinnis			
Caldwell Jones			
☐ 212 ABA Assist Leaders	1.00	.50	.10
Al Smith			
Chuck Williams			
Louie Dampier			
☐ 213 Larry Miller	.75	.35	.07
Virginia Squires			
☐ 214 Stew Johnson	.50	.25	.05
San Diego Conquistadors			
☐ 215 Larry Finch	2.00	1.00	.20
Memphis Sounds			
☐ 216 Larry Kenon	2.00	1.00	.20
New York Nets			
☐ 217 Joe Hamilton	.50	.25	.05
Kentucky Colonels			
☐ 218 Gerald Govan	.50	.25	.05
Utah Stars			
☐ 219 Ralph Simpson	.75	.35	.07
Denver Nuggets			
☐ 220 George McGinnis AS1	1.50	.75	.15
Indiana Pacers			
☐ 221 Carolina Cougars TL	1.25	.60	.12
Billy Cunningham			
Mack Calvin			
Tom Owens			
Joe Caldwell			
☐ 222 Denver Nuggets TL	1.00	.50	.10
Ralph Simpson			
Byron Beck			
Dave Robisch			
Al Smith			
☐ 223 Indiana Pacers TL	1.25	.60	.12
George McGinnis			
Billy Keller			
George McGinnis			
Freddie Lewis			
☐ 224 Kentucky Colonels TL	2.00	1.00	.20
Dan Issel			
Louie Dampier			
Artis Gilmore			
Louie Dampier			
☐ 225 Memphis Sounds TL	1.00	.50	.10
George Thompson			
Larry Finch			
Randy Denton			
George Thompson			
☐ 226 New York Nets TL	5.50	2.75	.55
Julius Erving			
John Roche			
Larry Kenon			
Julius Erving			
☐ 227 San Antonio Spurs TL	4.00	2.00	.40
George Gervin			

1974-75 Topps / 279

    George Gervin
    Swen Nater
    James Silas
☐ 228 San Diego Conq. TL .... 1.00   .50   .10
    Dwight Lamar
    Stew Johnson
    Caldwell Jones
    Chuck Williams
☐ 229 Utah Stars TL .... 1.00   .50   .10
    Willie Wise
    James Jones
    Gerald Govan
    James Jones
☐ 230 Virginia Squires TL .... 1.00   .50   .10
    George Carter
    George Irvine
    Jim Eakins
    Roland Taylor
☐ 231 Bird Averitt .... .75   .35   .07
    Kentucky Colonels
☐ 232 John Roche .... .75   .35   .07
    Kentucky Colonels
☐ 233 George Irvine .... .75   .35   .07
    Virginia Squires
☐ 234 John Williamson .... 1.50   .75   .15
    New York Nets
☐ 235 Billy Cunningham .... 4.00   2.00   .40
    St. Louis Spirits
☐ 236 Jimmy O'Brien .... .50   .25   .05
    San Diego Conquistadors
☐ 237 Wilbert Jones .... .50   .25   .05
    Kentucky Colonels
☐ 238 Johnny Neumann .... .75   .35   .07
    Utah Stars
☐ 239 Al Smith .... .50   .25   .05
    Denver Nuggets
☐ 240 Roger Brown .... .75   .35   .07
    Memphis Sounds
☐ 241 Chuck Williams .... .50   .25   .05
    Kentucky Colonels
☐ 242 Rich Jones .... .50   .25   .05
    San Antonio Spurs
☐ 243 Dave Twardzik .... 1.25   .60   .12
    Virginia Squires
☐ 244 Wendell Ladner .... .50   .25   .05
    New York Nets
☐ 245 Mack Calvin AS1 .... .75   .35   .07
    St. Louis Spirits
☐ 246 ABA Eastern Semis .... 1.00   .50   .10
    Nets over Squires
    Colonels sweep Cougars
☐ 247 ABA Western Semis .... 1.00   .50   .10
    Stars over Conquistadors
    Pacers over Spurs
☐ 248 ABA Div. Finals .... 1.00   .50   .10
    Nets sweep Colonels

280 / 1974-75 Topps

	Stars edge Pacers		
☐ 249 ABA Championship 3.00	1.50	.30
	Nets over Stars (Julius Erving)		
☐ 250 Wilt Chamberlain CO 45.00	22.50	4.50
	San Diego Conquistadors		
☐ 251 Ron Robinson .... .50	.25	.05
	Memphis Sounds		
☐ 252 Zelmo Beaty .... .75	.35	.07
	Utah Stars		
☐ 253 Donnie Freeman .... .75	.35	.07
	Indiana Pacers		
☐ 254 Mike Green .... .50	.25	.05
	Denver Nuggets		
☐ 255 Louie Dampier AS2 .... .75	.35	.07
	Kentucky Colonels		
☐ 256 Tom Owens .... .50	.25	.05
	St. Louis Spirits		
☐ 257 George Karl 3.00	1.50	.30
	San Antonio Spurs		
☐ 258 Jim Eakins .... .50	.25	.05
	Virginia Squires		
☐ 259 Travis Grant .... .75	.35	.07
	San Diego Conquistadors		
☐ 260 James Jones AS1 .... .75	.35	.07
	Utah Stars		
☐ 261 Mike Jackson .... .50	.25	.05
	Memphis Sounds		
☐ 262 Billy Paultz .... .75	.35	.07
	New York Nets		
☐ 263 Freddie Lewis .... .75	.35	.07
	Memphis Sounds		
☐ 264 Byron Beck .... .75	.35	.07
	Denver Nuggets (Back refers to ANA, should be ABA)		

1975-76 Topps

The 1975-76 Topps basketball card set of 330 was the largest basketball set ever produced to that time. NBA players are depicted on cards 1-220 and ABA players on cards 221-330. The cards in the set measure the standard 2 1/2" by 3 1/2". Team Leader (TL) cards are provided for each team on cards 116-133 and 278-287. Other subseries in this set include NBA Statistical Leaders (1-6), NBA Playoffs (188-189), NBA Team Checklists (203-220), ABA Statistical Leaders (221-226), ABA Playoffs (309-310), and ABA Team Checklists (321-330). All-Star selections (first and second team) for both leagues are noted on the respective player's regular cards. Card backs are printed in blue and green on gray card stock. The set is particularly hard to sort numerically, as the small card number on the back is printed in blue on a dark green background. The set was printed on three large sheets each containing 110 different cards. Investigation of the second (series) sheet reveals that 22 of the cards were double printed; they are marked DP in the checklist below. The key rookie card in this set is Moses Malone.

1975-76 Topps / 281

	NRMT	VG-E	GOOD
COMPLETE SET (330)	475.00	225.00	47.00
COMMON PLAYER (1-110)	.50	.25	.05
COMMON PLAYER (111-220)	.50	.25	.05
COMMON PLAYER (221-330)	.75	.35	.07
☐ 1 NBA Scoring Average Leaders	9.00	2.50	.50
Bob McAdoo			
Rick Barry			
Kareem Abdul-Jabbar			
☐ 2 NBA Field Goal Percentage Leaders	1.00	.50	.10
Don Nelson			
Butch Beard			
Rudy Tomjanovich			
☐ 3 NBA Free Throw Percentage Leaders	3.50	1.75	.35
Rick Barry			
Calvin Murphy			
Bill Bradley			
☐ 4 NBA Rebounds Leaders	1.25	.60	.12
Wes Unseld			
Dave Cowens			
Sam Lacey			
☐ 5 NBA Assists Leaders	1.25	.60	.12
Kevin Porter			
Dave Bing			
Nate Archibald			
☐ 6 NBA Steals Leaders	2.00	1.00	.20
Rick Barry			
Walt Frazier			
Larry Steele			
☐ 7 Tom Van Arsdale	.75	.35	.07
Atlanta Hawks			
☐ 8 Paul Silas	1.00	.50	.10

282 / 1975-76 Topps

☐ 9	Boston Celtics Jerry Sloan 1.00	.50	.10
☐ 10	Chicago Bulls Bob McAdoo AS1 .... 3.25	1.60	.32
☐ 11	Buffalo Braves Dwight Davis .... .50	.25	.05
☐ 12	Golden State Warriors John Mengelt .... .50	.25	.05
☐ 13	Detroit Pistons George Johnson .... .50	.25	.05
☐ 14	Golden State Warriors Ed Ratleff .... .75	.35	.07
☐ 15	Houston Rockets Nate Archibald AS1 .... 4.00	2.00	.40
☐ 16	Kansas City Kings Elmore Smith .... .50	.25	.05
☐ 17	Milwaukee Bucks Bob Dandridge .... .75	.35	.07
☐ 18	Milwaukee Bucks Louie Nelson .... .75	.35	.07
☐ 19	New Orleans Jazz Neal Walk .... .50	.25	.05
☐ 20	New York Knicks Billy Cunningham 4.00	2.00	.40
☐ 21	Philadelphia 76ers Gary Melchionni .... .50	.25	.05
☐ 22	Phoenix Suns Barry Clemens .... .50	.25	.05
☐ 23	Portland Trail Blazers Jimmy Jones .... .50	.25	.05
☐ 24	Washington Bullets Tom Burleson 2.00	1.00	.20
☐ 25	Seattle Supersonics Lou Hudson 1.00	.50	.10
☐ 26	Atlanta Hawks Henry Finkel .... .50	.25	.05
☐ 27	Boston Celtics Jim McMillian .... .50	.25	.05
☐ 28	Buffalo Braves Matt Guokas .... .75	.35	.07
☐ 29	Chicago Bulls Fred Foster DP .... .50	.25	.05
☐ 30	Cleveland Cavaliers Bob Lanier 4.00	2.00	.40
☐ 31	Detroit Pistons Jimmy Walker .... .50	.25	.05
☐ 32	Kansas City Kings Cliff Meely .... .50	.25	.05
☐ 33	Houston Rockets Butch Beard .... .50	.25	.05
☐ 34	Cleveland Cavaliers Cazzie Russell 1.00	.50	.10
☐ 35	Los Angeles Lakers Jon McGlocklin .... .75	.35	.07
☐ 36	Milwaukee Bucks Bernie Fryer .... .50 New Orleans Jazz	.25	.05

1975-76 Topps / 283

☐ 37	Bill Bradley New York Knicks	18.00	9.00	1.80
☐ 38	Fred Carter Philadelphia 76ers	.50	.25	.05
☐ 39	Dennis Awtrey DP Phoenix Suns	.50	.25	.05
☐ 40	Sidney Wicks Portland Trail Blazers	1.25	.60	.12
☐ 41	Fred Brown Seattle Supersonics	1.00	.50	.10
☐ 42	Rowland Garrett Chicago Bulls	.50	.25	.05
☐ 43	Herm Gilliam Atlanta Hawks	.50	.25	.05
☐ 44	Don Nelson Boston Celtics	2.50	1.25	.25
☐ 45	Ernie DiGregorio Buffalo Braves	.75	.35	.07
☐ 46	Jim Brewer Cleveland Cavaliers	.50	.25	.05
☐ 47	Chris Ford Detroit Pistons	1.50	.75	.15
☐ 48	Nick Weatherspoon Washington Bullets	.50	.25	.05
☐ 49	Zaid Abdul-Aziz (formerly Don Smith) Houston Rockets	.50	.25	.05
☐ 50	Keith Wilkes Golden State Warriors	8.00	4.00	.80
☐ 51	Ollie Johnson DP Kansas City Kings	.50	.25	.05
☐ 52	Lucius Allen Los Angeles Lakers	.75	.35	.07
☐ 53	Mickey Davis Milwaukee Bucks	.50	.25	.05
☐ 54	Otto Moore New Orleans Jazz	.50	.25	.05
☐ 55	Walt Frazier AS1 New York Knicks	7.00	3.50	.70
☐ 56	Steve Mix Philadelphia 76ers	.50	.25	.05
☐ 57	Nate Hawthorne Phoenix Suns	.50	.25	.05
☐ 58	Lloyd Neal Portland Trail Blazers	.50	.25	.05
☐ 59	Don Watts Seattle Supersonics	.75	.35	.07
☐ 60	Elvin Hayes Washington Bullets	7.00	3.50	.70
☐ 61	Checklist 1-110	7.00	.70	.14
☐ 62	Mike Sojourner Atlanta Hawks	.50	.25	.05
☐ 63	Randy Smith Buffalo Braves	.75	.35	.07
☐ 64	John Block DP Chicago Bulls	.50	.25	.05
☐ 65	Charlie Scott	.75	.35	.07

284 / 1975-76 Topps

☐ 66	Boston Celtics Jim Chones	.50	.25	.05
☐ 67	Cleveland Cavaliers Rick Adelman	1.25	.60	.12
☐ 68	Kansas City Kings Curtis Rowe	.75	.35	.07
☐ 69	Detroit Pistons Derrek Dickey	.75	.35	.07
☐ 70	Golden State Warriors Rudy Tomjanovich	1.00	.50	.10
☐ 71	Houston Rockets Pat Riley	6.50	3.25	.65
☐ 72	Los Angeles Lakers Cornell Warner	.50	.25	.05
☐ 73	Milwaukee Bucks Earl Monroe	5.50	2.75	.55
☐ 74	New York Knicks Allan Bristow	1.75	.85	.17
☐ 75	Philadelphia 76ers Pete Maravich DP	9.00	4.50	.90
☐ 76	New Orleans Jazz Curtis Perry	.50	.25	.05
☐ 77	Phoenix Suns Bill Walton	15.00	7.50	1.50
☐ 78	Portland Trail Blazers Leonard Gray	.50	.25	.05
☐ 79	Seattle Supersonics Kevin Porter	.75	.35	.07
☐ 80	Washington Bullets John Havlicek AS2	15.00	7.50	1.50
☐ 81	Boston Celtics Dwight Jones	.50	.25	.05
☐ 82	Atlanta Hawks Jack Marin	.50	.25	.05
☐ 83	Buffalo Braves Dick Snyder	.50	.25	.05
☐ 84	Cleveland Cavaliers George Trapp	.50	.25	.05
☐ 85	Detroit Pistons Nate Thurmond	2.50	1.25	.25
☐ 86	Chicago Bulls Charles Johnson	.50	.25	.05
☐ 87	Golden State Warriors Ron Riley	.50	.25	.05
☐ 88	Houston Rockets Stu Lantz	.50	.25	.05
☐ 89	Los Angeles Lakers Scott Wedman	1.75	.85	.17
☐ 90	Kansas City Kings Kareem Abdul-Jabbar	40.00	20.00	4.00
☐ 91	Los Angeles Lakers Aaron James	.50	.25	.05
☐ 92	New Orleans Jazz Jim Barnett	.50	.25	.05
☐ 93	New York Knicks Clyde Lee Philadelphia 76ers	.50	.25	.05

1975-76 Topps / 285

☐ 94	Larry Steele Portland Trail Blazers	.50	.25	.05
☐ 95	Mike Riordan Washington Bullets	.50	.25	.05
☐ 96	Archie Clark Seattle Supersonics	.75	.35	.07
☐ 97	Mike Bantom Phoenix Suns	.50	.25	.05
☐ 98	Bob Kauffman Atlanta Hawks	.50	.25	.05
☐ 99	Kevin Stacom Boston Celtics	.75	.35	.07
☐ 100	Rick Barry AS1 Golden State Warriors	10.00	5.00	1.00
☐ 101	Ken Charles Buffalo Braves	.50	.25	.05
☐ 102	Tom Boerwinkle Chicago Bulls	.50	.25	.05
☐ 103	Mike Newlin Houston Rockets	.50	.25	.05
☐ 104	Leroy Ellis Philadelphia 76ers	.50	.25	.05
☐ 105	Austin Carr Cleveland Cavaliers	.75	.35	.07
☐ 106	Ron Behagen New Orleans Jazz	.50	.25	.05
☐ 107	Jim Price Milwaukee Bucks	.50	.25	.05
☐ 108	Bud Stallworth New Orleans Jazz	.50	.25	.05
☐ 109	Earl Williams Detroit Pistons	.50	.25	.05
☐ 110	Gail Goodrich Los Angeles Lakers	1.50	.75	.15
☐ 111	Phil Jackson New York Knicks	3.50	1.75	.35
☐ 112	Rod Derline Seattle Supersonics	.50	.25	.05
☐ 113	Keith Erickson Phoenix Suns	.75	.35	.07
☐ 114	Phil Lumpkin Phoenix Suns	.50	.25	.05
☐ 115	Wes Unseld Washington Bullets	3.50	1.75	.35
☐ 116	Atlanta Hawks TL Lou Hudson Lou Hudson John Drew Dean Meminger	1.00	.50	.10
☐ 117	Boston Celtics TL Dave Cowens Kevin Stacom Paul Silas JoJo White	1.75	.85	.17
☐ 118	Buffalo Braves TL Bob McAdoo Jack Marin	1.00	.50	.10

286 / 1975-76 Topps

    Bob McAdoo
    Randy Smith
☐ 119 Chicago Bulls TL .... 1.25   .60   .12
    Bob Love
    Chet Walker
    Nate Thurmond
    Norm Van Lier
☐ 120 Cleveland Cavs TL .... 1.00   .50   .10
    Bobby Smith
    Dick Snyder
    Jim Chones
    Jim Cleamons
☐ 121 Detroit Pistons TL .... 1.50   .75   .15
    Bob Lanier
    John Mengelt
    Bob Lanier
    Dave Bing
☐ 122 Golden State TL .... 2.00   1.00   .20
    Rick Barry
    Rick Barry
    Clifford Ray
    Rick Barry
☐ 123 Houston Rockets TL .... 1.00   .50   .10
    Rudy Tomjanovich
    Calvin Murphy
    Kevin Kunnert
    Mike Newlin
☐ 124 Kansas City Kings TL UER .... 1.25   .60   .12
    Nate Archibald
    Ollie Johnson
    Sam Lacey
    (Lacy on front)
    Nate Archibald
☐ 125 Los Angeles Lakers TL .... 1.25   .60   .12
    Gail Goodrich
    Cazzie Russell
    Happy Hairston
    Gail Goodrich
☐ 126 Milwaukee Bucks TL .... 4.50   2.25   .45
    Kareem Abdul-Jabbar
    Mickey Davis
    Kareem Abdul-Jabbar
    Kareem Abdul-Jabbar
☐ 127 New Orleans Jazz TL .... 2.00   1.00   .20
    Pete Maravich
    Stu Lantz
    E.C. Coleman
    Pete Maravich
☐ 128 New York Knicks TL DP .... 2.50   1.25   .25
    Walt Frazier
    Bill Bradley
    John Gianelli
    Walt Frazier
☐ 129 Phila. 76ers TL DP .... 1.25   .60   .12
    Fred Carter
    Doug Collins
    Billy Cunningham

1975-76 Topps / 287

Billy Cunningham			
☐ 130 Phoenix Suns TL DP 1.00	.50	.10
Charlie Scott			
Keith Erickson			
Curtis Perry			
Dennis Awtrey			
☐ 131 Portland Blazers TL DP 1.00	.50	.10
Sidney Wicks			
Geoff Petrie			
Sidney Wicks			
Geoff Petrie			
☐ 132 Seattle Sonics TL 1.00	.50	.10
Spencer Haywood			
Archie Clark			
Spencer Haywood			
Don Watts			
☐ 133 Washington Bullets TL 1.50	.75	.15
Elvin Hayes			
Clem Haskins			
Wes Unseld			
Kevin Porter			
☐ 134 John Drew 1.50	.75	.15
Atlanta Hawks			
☐ 135 JoJo White AS2 .... 1.75	.85	.17
Boston Celtics			
☐ 136 Garfield Heard .... .50	.25	.05
Buffalo Braves			
☐ 137 Jim Cleamons .... .50	.25	.05
Cleveland Cavaliers			
☐ 138 Howard Porter .... .50	.25	.05
Detroit Pistons			
☐ 139 Phil Smith 1.00	.50	.10
Golden State Warriors			
☐ 140 Bob Love 1.00	.50	.10
Chicago Bulls			
☐ 141 John Gianelli DP .... .50	.25	.05
New York Knicks			
☐ 142 Larry McNeill .... .75	.35	.07
Kansas City Kings			
☐ 143 Brian Winters 1.50	.75	.15
Milwaukee Bucks			
☐ 144 George Thompson .... .50	.25	.05
Milwaukee Bucks			
☐ 145 Kevin Kunnert .... .50	.25	.05
Houston Rockets			
☐ 146 Henry Bibby .... .75	.35	.07
New Orleans Jazz			
☐ 147 John Johnson .... .50	.25	.05
Portland Trail Blazers			
☐ 148 Doug Collins 3.25	1.60	.32
Philadelphia 76ers			
☐ 149 John Brisker .... .50	.25	.05
Seattle Supersonics			
☐ 150 Dick Van Arsdale .... .75	.35	.07
Phoenix Suns			
☐ 151 Leonard Robinson 2.50	1.25	.25
Washington Bullets			

288 / 1975-76 Topps

☐ 152 Dean Meminger	.50	.25	.05
Atlanta Hawks			
☐ 153 Phil Hankinson	.50	.25	.05
Boston Celtics			
☐ 154 Dale Schlueter	.50	.25	.05
Buffalo Braves			
☐ 155 Norm Van Lier	.75	.35	.07
Chicago Bulls			
☐ 156 Campy Russell	2.00	1.00	.20
Cleveland Cavaliers			
☐ 157 Jeff Mullins	.75	.35	.07
Golden State Warriors			
☐ 158 Sam Lacey	.75	.35	.07
Kansas City Kings			
☐ 159 Happy Hairston	.75	.35	.07
Los Angeles Lakers			
☐ 160 Dave Bing DP	2.00	1.00	.20
Detroit Pistons			
☐ 161 Kevin Restani	.75	.35	.07
Milwaukee Bucks			
☐ 162 Dave Wohl	.50	.25	.05
Houston Rockets			
☐ 163 E.C. Coleman	.50	.25	.05
New Orleans Jazz			
☐ 164 Jim Fox	.50	.25	.05
Seattle Supersonics			
☐ 165 Geoff Petrie	.75	.35	.07
Portland Trail Blazers			
☐ 166 Hawthorne Wingo DP UER	.50	.25	.05
New York Knicks			
(Misspelled Harthorne			
on card front)			
☐ 167 Fred Boyd	.50	.25	.05
Philadelphia 76ers			
☐ 168 Willie Norwood	.50	.25	.05
Phoenix Suns			
☐ 169 Bob Wilson	.50	.25	.05
Chicago Bulls			
☐ 170 Dave Cowens	5.50	2.75	.55
Boston Celtics			
☐ 171 Tom Henderson	.75	.35	.07
Atlanta Hawks			
☐ 172 Jim Washington	.50	.25	.05
Buffalo Braves			
☐ 173 Clem Haskins	.75	.35	.07
Washington Bullets			
☐ 174 Jim Davis	.50	.25	.05
Detroit Pistons			
☐ 175 Bobby Smith DP	.50	.25	.05
Cleveland Cavaliers			
☐ 176 Mike D'Antoni	.50	.25	.05
Kansas City Kings			
☐ 177 Zelmo Beaty	.75	.35	.07
Los Angeles Lakers			
☐ 178 Gary Brokaw	.75	.35	.07
Milwaukee Bucks			
☐ 179 Mel Davis	.50	.25	.05

1975-76 Topps / 289

New York Knicks			
☐ 180 Calvin Murphy 1.50	.75	.15
Houston Rockets			
☐ 181 Checklist 111-220 DP 7.00	.70	.14
☐ 182 Nate Williams .... .50	.25	.05
New Orleans Jazz			
☐ 183 LaRue Martin .... .50	.25	.05
Portland Trail Blazers			
☐ 184 George McGinnis 1.50	.75	.15
Philadelphia 76ers			
☐ 185 Clifford Ray .... .50	.25	.05
Golden State Warriors			
☐ 186 Paul Westphal 2.00	1.00	.20
Phoenix Suns			
☐ 187 Talvin Skinner .... .50	.25	.05
Seattle Supersonics			
☐ 188 NBA Playoff Semis DP 1.00	.50	.10
Warriors edge Bulls			
Bullets over Celts			
☐ 189 NBA Playoff Finals 1.00	.50	.10
Warriors sweep Bullets			
(C.Ray blocks shot)			
☐ 190 Phil Chenier AS2 DP .... .75	.35	.07
Washington Bullets			
☐ 191 John Brown .... .50	.25	.05
Atlanta Hawks			
☐ 192 Lee Winfield .... .50	.25	.05
Buffalo Braves			
☐ 193 Steve Patterson .... .50	.25	.05
Cleveland Cavaliers			
☐ 194 Charles Dudley .... .50	.25	.05
Golden State Warriors			
☐ 195 Connie Hawkins DP 2.00	1.00	.20
Los Angeles Lakers			
☐ 196 Leon Benbow .... .50	.25	.05
Chicago Bulls			
☐ 197 Don Kojis .... .50	.25	.05
Kansas City Kings			
☐ 198 Ron Williams .... .50	.25	.05
Milwaukee Bucks			
☐ 199 Mel Counts .... .50	.25	.05
New Orleans Jazz			
☐ 200 Spencer Haywood AS2 .... 1.50	.75	.15
Seattle Supersonics			
☐ 201 Greg Jackson .... .50	.25	.05
Phoenix Suns			
☐ 202 Tom Kozelko DP .... .50	.25	.05
Washington Bullets			
☐ 203 Atlanta Hawks 1.00	.35	.07
Checklist			
☐ 204 Boston Celtics 1.00	.35	.07
Checklist			
☐ 205 Buffalo Braves 1.00	.35	.07
Checklist			
☐ 206 Chicago Bulls 1.00	.35	.07
Checklist			
☐ 207 Cleveland Cavs 1.00	.35	.07

290 / 1975-76 Topps

☐ 208	Detroit Pistons Checklist	1.00	.35	.07
☐ 209	Golden State Checklist	1.00	.35	.07
☐ 210	Houston Rockets Checklist	1.00	.35	.07
☐ 211	Kansas City Kings DP Checklist	1.00	.35	.07
☐ 212	Los Angeles Lakers DP Checklist	1.00	.35	.07
☐ 213	Milwaukee Bucks Checklist	1.00	.35	.07
☐ 214	New Orleans Jazz Checklist	1.00	.35	.07
☐ 215	New York Knicks Checklist	1.00	.35	.07
☐ 216	Philadelphia 76ers Checklist	1.00	.35	.07
☐ 217	Phoenix Suns DP Checklist	1.00	.35	.07
☐ 218	Portland Blazers Checklist	1.00	.35	.07
☐ 219	Seattle Sonics DP Checklist	1.50	.50	.10
☐ 220	Washington Bullets Checklist	1.00	.35	.07
☐ 221	ABA Scoring Average Leaders George McGinnis Julius Erving Ron Boone	3.50	1.75	.35
☐ 222	ABA 2 Pt. Field Goal Percentage Leaders Bobby Jones Artis Gilmore Moses Malone	5.00	2.50	.50
☐ 223	ABA 3 Pt. Field Goal Percentage Leaders Billy Shepherd Louie Dampier Al Smith	1.00	.50	.10
☐ 224	ABA Free Throw Percentage Leaders Mack Calvin James Silas Dave Robisch	1.00	.50	.10
☐ 225	ABA Rebounds Leaders Swen Nater Artis Gilmore Marvin Barnes	1.00	.50	.10
☐ 226	ABA Assists Leaders Mack Calvin Chuck Williams George McGinnis	1.00	.50	.10
☐ 227	Mack Calvin AS1 Virginia Squires	.75	.35	.07

1975-76 Topps / 291

☐ 228 Billy Knight AS1	1.75	.85	.17
Indiana Pacers			
☐ 229 Bird Averitt	.75	.35	.07
Kentucky Colonels			
☐ 230 George Carter	.75	.35	.07
Memphis Sounds			
☐ 231 Swen Nater AS2	1.00	.50	.10
New York Nets			
☐ 232 Steve Jones	1.00	.50	.10
St. Louis Spirits			
☐ 233 George Gervin	9.00	4.50	.90
San Antonio Spurs			
☐ 234 Lee Davis	.75	.35	.07
San Diego Sails			
☐ 235 Ron Boone AS1	1.00	.50	.10
Utah Stars			
☐ 236 Mike Jackson	.75	.35	.07
Virginia Squires			
☐ 237 Kevin Joyce	1.00	.50	.10
Indiana Pacers			
☐ 238 Marv Roberts	.75	.35	.07
Kentucky Colonels			
☐ 239 Tom Owens	.75	.35	.07
Memphis Sounds			
☐ 240 Ralph Simpson	1.00	.50	.10
Denver Nuggets			
☐ 241 Gus Gerard	.75	.35	.07
St. Louis Spirits			
☐ 242 Brian Taylor AS2	1.00	.50	.10
New York Nets			
☐ 243 Rich Jones	.75	.35	.07
San Antonio Spurs			
☐ 244 John Roche	1.00	.50	.10
Utah Stars			
☐ 245 Travis Grant	.75	.35	.07
San Diego Sails			
☐ 246 Dave Twardzik	1.00	.50	.10
Virginia Squires			
☐ 247 Mike Green	.75	.35	.07
Virginia Squires			
☐ 248 Billy Keller	1.00	.50	.10
Indiana Pacers			
☐ 249 Stew Johnson	.75	.35	.07
Memphis Sounds			
☐ 250 Artis Gilmore AS1	3.50	1.75	.35
Kentucky Colonels			
☐ 251 John Williamson	1.00	.50	.10
New York Nets			
☐ 252 Marvin Barnes AS2	4.25	2.10	.42
St. Louis Spirits			
☐ 253 James Silas AS2	1.00	.50	.10
San Antonio Spurs			
☐ 254 Moses Malone	70.00	35.00	7.00
Utah Stars			
☐ 255 Willie Wise	1.00	.50	.10
Virginia Squires			
☐ 256 Dwight Lamar	.75	.35	.07

292 / 1975-76 Topps

	San Diego Sails		
☐ 257	Checklist 221-330 ... 7.00	.70	.14
☐ 258	Byron Beck ... .75	.35	.07
	Denver Nuggets		
☐ 259	Len Elmore ... 3.00	1.50	.30
	Indiana Pacers		
☐ 260	Dan Issel ... 4.50	2.25	.45
	Kentucky Colonels		
☐ 261	Rick Mount ... 1.25	.60	.12
	Memphis Sounds		
☐ 262	Billy Paultz ... 1.00	.50	.10
	New York Nets		
☐ 263	Donnie Freeman ... 1.00	.50	.10
	San Antonio Spurs		
☐ 264	George Adams ... .75	.35	.07
	San Diego Sails		
☐ 265	Don Chaney ... 1.00	.50	.10
	St. Louis Spirits		
☐ 266	Randy Denton ... .75	.35	.07
	Utah Stars		
☐ 267	Don Washington ... .75	.35	.07
	Denver Nuggets		
☐ 268	Roland Taylor ... .75	.35	.07
	Denver Nuggets		
☐ 269	Charlie Edge ... .75	.35	.07
	Indiana Pacers		
☐ 270	Louie Dampier ... 1.25	.60	.12
	Kentucky Colonels		
☐ 271	Collis Jones ... .75	.35	.07
	Memphis Sounds		
☐ 272	Al Skinner ... .75	.35	.07
	New York Nets		
☐ 273	Coby Dietrick ... .75	.35	.07
	San Antonio Spurs		
☐ 274	Tim Bassett ... .75	.35	.07
	San Diego Sails		
☐ 275	Freddie Lewis ... 1.00	.50	.10
	St. Louis Spirits		
☐ 276	Gerald Govan ... .75	.35	.07
	Utah Stars		
☐ 277	Ron Thomas ... .75	.35	.07
	Kentucky Colonels		
☐ 278	Denver Nuggets TL ... 1.25	.60	.12
	Ralph Simpson		
	Mack Calvin		
	Mike Green		
	Mack Calvin		
☐ 279	Indiana Pacers TL ... 1.25	.60	.12
	George McGinnis		
	Billy Keller		
	George McGinnis		
	George McGinnis		
☐ 280	Kentucky Colonels TL ... 1.50	.75	.15
	Artis Gilmore		
	Louie Dampier		
	Artis Gilmore		
	Louie Dampier		

1975-76 Topps / 293

☐ 281 Memphis Sounds TL George Carter Larry Finch Tom Owens Chuck Williams	1.25	.60	.12
☐ 282 New York Nets TL Julius Erving John Williamson Julius Erving Julius Erving	4.50	2.25	.45
☐ 283 St. Louis Spirits TL Marvin Barnes Freddie Lewis Marvin Barnes Freddie Lewis	1.25	.60	.12
☐ 284 San Antonio Spurs TL George Gervin James Silas Swen Nater James Silas	2.50	1.25	.25
☐ 285 San Diego Sails TL Travis Grant Jimmy O'Brien Caldwell Jones Jimmy O'Brien	1.25	.60	.12
☐ 286 Utah Stars TL Ron Boone Ron Boone Moses Malone Al Smith	7.00	3.50	.70
☐ 287 Virginia Squires TL Willie Wise Red Robbins Dave Vaughn Dave Twardzik	1.25	.60	.12
☐ 288 Claude Terry Denver Nuggets	.75	.35	.07
☐ 289 Wilbert Jones Kentucky Colonels	.75	.35	.07
☐ 290 Darnell Hillman Indiana Pacers	.75	.35	.07
☐ 291 Bill Melchionni New York Nets	1.00	.50	.10
☐ 292 Mel Daniels Memphis Sounds	1.25	.60	.12
☐ 293 Fly Williams St. Louis Spirits	1.25	.60	.12
☐ 294 Larry Kenon San Antonio Spurs	1.00	.50	.10
☐ 295 Red Robbins Virginia Squires	.75	.35	.07
☐ 296 Warren Jabali San Diego Sails	1.00	.50	.10
☐ 297 Jim Eakins Utah Stars	.75	.35	.07
☐ 298 Bobby Jones Denver Nuggets	7.00	3.50	.70

294 / 1975-76 Topps

☐ 299 Don Buse	.75	.35	.07
Indiana Pacers			
☐ 300 Julius Erving AS1	42.00	21.00	4.20
New York Nets			
☐ 301 Billy Shepherd	.75	.35	.07
Memphis Sounds			
☐ 302 Maurice Lucas	7.50	3.75	.75
St. Louis Spirits			
☐ 303 George Karl	1.25	.60	.12
San Antonio Spurs			
☐ 304 Jim Bradley	.75	.35	.07
Kentucky Colonels			
☐ 305 Caldwell Jones	1.25	.60	.12
San Diego Sails			
☐ 306 Al Smith	.75	.35	.07
Utah Stars			
☐ 307 Jan Van Breda Kolff	1.00	.50	.10
Virginia Squires			
☐ 308 Darrell Elston	.75	.35	.07
Virginia Squires			
☐ 309 ABA Playoff Semifinals	1.25	.60	.12
Colonels over Spirits; Pacers edge Nuggets			
☐ 310 ABA Playoff Finals	1.50	.75	.15
Colonels over Pacers (Gilmore hooking)			
☐ 311 Ted McClain	.75	.35	.07
Kentucky Colonels			
☐ 312 Willie Sojourner	.75	.35	.07
New York Nets			
☐ 313 Bob Warren	.75	.35	.07
San Antonio Spurs			
☐ 314 Bob Netolicky	.75	.35	.07
Indiana Pacers			
☐ 315 Chuck Williams	.75	.35	.07
Memphis Sounds			
☐ 316 Gene Kennedy	.75	.35	.07
St. Louis Spirits			
☐ 317 Jimmy O'Brien	.75	.35	.07
San Diego Sails			
☐ 318 Dave Robisch	1.00	.50	.10
Denver Nuggets			
☐ 319 Wali Jones	.75	.35	.07
Utah Stars			
☐ 320 George Irvine	1.00	.50	.10
Denver Nuggets			
☐ 321 Denver Nuggets	1.25	.50	.10
Checklist			
☐ 322 Indiana Pacers	1.25	.50	.10
Checklist			
☐ 323 Kentucky Colonels	1.25	.50	.10
Checklist			
☐ 324 Memphis Sounds	1.25	.50	.10
Checklist			
☐ 325 New York Nets	1.25	.50	.10
Checklist			
☐ 326 St. Louis Spirits	1.25	.50	.10

1976-77 Topps / 295

	Checklist (Spirits of St. Louis on card back)			
☐ 327	San Antonio Spurs Checklist	1.25	.50	.10
☐ 328	San Diego Sails Checklist	1.25	.50	.10
☐ 329	Utah Stars Checklist	1.25	.50	.10
☐ 330	Virginia Squires Checklist	1.50	.50	.10

1976-77 Topps

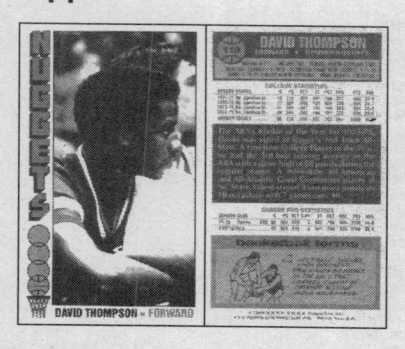

The 144-card 1976-77 Topps set witnesses a return to the larger-sized cards, with each card measuring approximately 3 1/8" by 5 1/4". Cards numbered 126-135 are the previous season's NBA All-Star selections. The cards were printed on two large sheets, each with eight rows and nine columns. The checklist card was located in the lower right corner of the second sheet. The key rookie card in this set is David Thompson.

		NRMT	VG-E	GOOD
COMPLETE SET (144)		200.00	100.00	20.00
COMMON PLAYER (1-144)		.60	.30	.06
☐ 1	Julius Erving New York Nets	40.00	12.50	2.50
☐ 2	Dick Snyder Cleveland Cavaliers	.60	.30	.06
☐ 3	Paul Silas Boston Celtics	1.00	.50	.10
☐ 4	Keith Erickson	.80	.40	.08

296 / 1976-77 Topps

		Phoenix Suns			
☐	5	Wes Unseld	3.50	1.75	.35
		Washington Bullets			
☐	6	Butch Beard	.60	.30	.06
		New York Knicks			
☐	7	Lloyd Neal	.60	.30	.06
		Portland Trail Blazers			
☐	8	Tom Henderson	.60	.30	.06
		Atlanta Hawks			
☐	9	Jim McMillian	.60	.30	.06
		Buffalo Braves			
☐	10	Bob Lanier	3.50	1.75	.35
		Detroit Pistons			
☐	11	Junior Bridgeman	2.00	1.00	.20
		Milwaukee Bucks			
☐	12	Corky Calhoun	.60	.30	.06
		Los Angeles Lakers			
☐	13	Billy Keller	.60	.30	.06
		Indiana Pacers			
☐	14	Mickey Johnson	1.25	.60	.12
		Chicago Bulls			
☐	15	Fred Brown	.80	.40	.08
		Seattle Supersonics			
☐	16	Jamaal Wilkes	2.00	1.00	.20
		Golden State Warriors			
☐	17	Louie Nelson	.60	.30	.06
		New Orleans Jazz			
☐	18	Ed Ratleff	.60	.30	.06
		Houston Rockets			
☐	19	Billy Paultz	.80	.40	.08
		San Antonio Spurs			
☐	20	Nate Archibald	3.50	1.75	.35
		Kansas City Kings			
☐	21	Steve Mix	.60	.30	.06
		Philadelphia 76ers			
☐	22	Ralph Simpson	.60	.30	.06
		Denver Nuggets			
☐	23	Campy Russell	.80	.40	.08
		Cleveland Cavaliers			
☐	24	Charlie Scott	.80	.40	.08
		Boston Celtics			
☐	25	Artis Gilmore	3.00	1.50	.30
		Chicago Bulls			
☐	26	Dick Van Arsdale	.80	.40	.08
		Phoenix Suns			
☐	27	Phil Chenier	.80	.40	.08
		Washington Bullets			
☐	28	Spencer Haywood	1.25	.60	.12
		New York Knicks			
☐	29	Chris Ford	1.25	.60	.12
		Detroit Pistons			
☐	30	Dave Cowens	5.00	2.50	.50
		Boston Celtics			
☐	31	Sidney Wicks	1.25	.60	.12
		Portland Trail Blazers			
☐	32	Jim Price	.60	.30	.06
		Milwaukee Bucks			

1976-77 Topps / 297

☐ 33	Dwight Jones Houston Rockets	.60	.30	.06
☐ 34	Lucius Allen Los Angeles Lakers	.80	.40	.08
☐ 35	Marvin Barnes Detroit Pistons	1.00	.50	.10
☐ 36	Henry Bibby New Orleans Jazz	.80	.40	.08
☐ 37	Joe Meriweather Atlanta Hawks	1.00	.50	.10
☐ 38	Doug Collins Philadelphia 76ers	2.50	1.25	.25
☐ 39	Garfield Heard Phoenix Suns	.60	.30	.06
☐ 40	Randy Smith Buffalo Braves	.80	.40	.08
☐ 41	Tom Burleson Seattle Supersonics	.80	.40	.08
☐ 42	Dave Twardzik Portland Trail Blazers	.80	.40	.08
☐ 43	Bill Bradley New York Knicks	20.00	10.00	2.00
☐ 44	Calvin Murphy Houston Rockets	1.50	.75	.15
☐ 45	Bob Love Chicago Bulls	1.00	.50	.10
☐ 46	Brian Winters Milwaukee Bucks	.80	.40	.08
☐ 47	Glenn McDonald Boston Celtics	.60	.30	.06
☐ 48	Checklist Card	9.00	.90	.18
☐ 49	Bird Averitt Buffalo Braves	.60	.30	.06
☐ 50	Rick Barry Golden State Warriors	8.50	4.25	.85
☐ 51	Ticky Burden New York Knicks	.60	.30	.06
☐ 52	Rich Jones New York Nets	.60	.30	.06
☐ 53	Austin Carr Cleveland Cavaliers	.80	.40	.08
☐ 54	Steve Kuberski Boston Celtics	.60	.30	.06
☐ 55	Paul Westphal Phoenix Suns	1.50	.75	.15
☐ 56	Mike Riordan Washington Bullets	.60	.30	.06
☐ 57	Bill Walton Portland Trail Blazers	11.00	5.50	1.10
☐ 58	Eric Money Detroit Pistons	.80	.40	.08
☐ 59	John Drew Atlanta Hawks	.80	.40	.08
☐ 60	Pete Maravich New Orleans Jazz	9.00	4.50	.90
☐ 61	John Shumate Buffalo Braves	2.50	1.25	.25

298 / 1976-77 Topps

☐ 62	Mack Calvin	.80	.40	.08
	Los Angeles Lakers			
☐ 63	Bruce Seals	.60	.30	.06
	Seattle Supersonics			
☐ 64	Walt Frazier	6.00	3.00	.60
	New York Knicks			
☐ 65	Elmore Smith	.60	.30	.06
	Milwaukee Bucks			
☐ 66	Rudy Tomjanovich	.80	.40	.08
	Houston Rockets			
☐ 67	Sam Lacey	.60	.30	.06
	Kansas City Kings			
☐ 68	George Gervin	8.50	4.25	.85
	San Antonio Spurs			
☐ 69	Gus Williams	6.00	3.00	.60
	Golden State Warriors			
☐ 70	George McGinnis	1.00	.50	.10
	Philadelphia 76ers			
☐ 71	Len Elmore	.80	.40	.08
	Indiana Pacers			
☐ 72	Jack Marin	.60	.30	.06
	Chicago Bulls			
☐ 73	Brian Taylor	.80	.40	.08
	New York Nets			
☐ 74	Jim Brewer	.60	.30	.06
	Cleveland Cavaliers			
☐ 75	Alvan Adams	3.00	1.50	.30
	Phoenix Suns			
☐ 76	Dave Bing	2.50	1.25	.25
	Washington Bullets			
☐ 77	Phil Jackson	3.00	1.50	.30
	New York Knicks			
☐ 78	Geoff Petrie	.80	.40	.08
	Portland Trail Blazers			
☐ 79	Mike Sojourner	.60	.30	.06
	Atlanta Hawks			
☐ 80	James Silas	.80	.40	.08
	San Antonio Spurs			
☐ 81	Bob Dandridge	.80	.40	.08
	Milwaukee Bucks			
☐ 82	Ernie DiGregorio	.80	.40	.08
	Buffalo Braves			
☐ 83	Cazzie Russell	1.00	.50	.10
	Los Angeles Lakers			
☐ 84	Kevin Porter	.80	.40	.08
	Detroit Pistons			
☐ 85	Tom Boerwinkle	.60	.30	.06
	Chicago Bulls			
☐ 86	Darnell Hillman	.60	.30	.06
	Indiana Pacers			
☐ 87	Herm Gilliam	.60	.30	.06
	Seattle Supersonics			
☐ 88	Nate Williams	.60	.30	.06
	New Orleans Jazz			
☐ 89	Phil Smith	.60	.30	.06
	Golden State Warriors			
☐ 90	John Havlicek	10.00	5.00	1.00

1976-77 Topps / 299

	Boston Celtics			
☐ 91	Kevin Kunnert	.60	.30	.06
	Houston Rockets			
☐ 92	Jimmy Walker	.60	.30	.06
	Kansas City Kings			
☐ 93	Billy Cunningham	4.00	2.00	.40
	Philadelphia 76ers			
☐ 94	Dan Issel	3.50	1.75	.35
	Denver Nuggets			
☐ 95	Ron Boone	.80	.40	.08
	Kansas City Kings			
☐ 96	Lou Hudson	1.00	.50	.10
	Atlanta Hawks			
☐ 97	Jim Chones	.60	.30	.06
	Cleveland Cavaliers			
☐ 98	Earl Monroe	4.50	2.25	.45
	New York Knicks			
☐ 99	Tom Van Arsdale	.80	.40	.08
	Buffalo Braves			
☐ 100	Kareem Abdul-Jabbar	27.00	13.50	2.70
	Los Angeles Lakers			
☐ 101	Moses Malone	25.00	12.50	2.50
	Portland Trail Blazers			
☐ 102	Ricky Sobers	1.00	.50	.10
	Phoenix Suns			
☐ 103	Swen Nater	.80	.40	.08
	Milwaukee Bucks			
☐ 104	Leonard Robinson	.80	.40	.08
	Washington Bullets			
☐ 105	Don Watts	.60	.30	.06
	Seattle Supersonics			
☐ 106	Otto Moore	.60	.30	.06
	New Orleans Jazz			
☐ 107	Maurice Lucas	1.50	.75	.15
	Portland Trail Blazers			
☐ 108	Norm Van Lier	.80	.40	.08
	Chicago Bulls			
☐ 109	Clifford Ray	.60	.30	.06
	Golden State Warriors			
☐ 110	David Thompson	17.00	8.50	1.70
	Denver Nuggets			
☐ 111	Fred Carter	.60	.30	.06
	Philadelphia 76ers			
☐ 112	Caldwell Jones	.80	.40	.08
	Philadelphia 76ers			
☐ 113	John Williamson	.80	.40	.08
	New York Nets			
☐ 114	Bobby Smith	.60	.30	.06
	Cleveland Cavaliers			
☐ 115	JoJo White	1.25	.60	.12
	Boston Celtics			
☐ 116	Curtis Perry	.60	.30	.06
	Phoenix Suns			
☐ 117	John Gianelli	.60	.30	.06
	New York Knicks			
☐ 118	Curtis Rowe	.80	.40	.08
	Detroit Pistons			

300 / 1976-77 Topps

- [ ] 119 Lionel Hollins ... 1.75 .85 .17
  Portland Trail Blazers
- [ ] 120 Elvin Hayes ... 6.00 3.00 .60
  Washington Bullets
- [ ] 121 Ken Charles ... .60 .30 .06
  Atlanta Hawks
- [ ] 122 Dave Meyers ... 2.50 1.25 .25
  Milwaukee Bucks
- [ ] 123 Jerry Sloan ... .80 .40 .08
  Chicago Bulls
- [ ] 124 Billy Knight ... .80 .40 .08
  Indiana Pacers
- [ ] 125 Gail Goodrich ... 1.50 .75 .15
  Los Angeles Lakers
- [ ] 126 Kareem Abdul-Jabbar AS ... 14.00 7.00 1.40
  Los Angeles Lakers
- [ ] 127 Julius Erving AS ... 14.00 7.00 1.40
  New York Nets
- [ ] 128 George McGinnis AS ... .80 .40 .08
  Philadelphia 76ers
- [ ] 129 Nate Archibald AS ... 1.50 .75 .15
  Kansas City Kings
- [ ] 130 Pete Maravich AS ... 4.00 2.00 .40
  New Orleans Jazz
- [ ] 131 Dave Cowens AS ... 2.25 1.10 .22
  Boston Celtics
- [ ] 132 Rick Barry AS ... 4.00 2.00 .40
  Golden State Warriors
- [ ] 133 Elvin Hayes AS ... 3.00 1.50 .30
  Washington Bullets
- [ ] 134 James Silas AS ... .80 .40 .08
  San Antonio Spurs
- [ ] 135 Randy Smith AS ... .80 .40 .08
  Buffalo Braves
- [ ] 136 Leonard Gray ... .60 .30 .06
  Seattle Supersonics
- [ ] 137 Charles Johnson ... .60 .30 .06
  Golden State Warriors
- [ ] 138 Ron Behagen ... .60 .30 .06
  New Orleans Jazz
- [ ] 139 Mike Newlin ... .60 .30 .06
  Houston Rockets
- [ ] 140 Bob McAdoo ... 3.00 1.50 .30
  Buffalo Braves
- [ ] 141 Mike Gale ... .60 .30 .06
  San Antonio Spurs
- [ ] 142 Scott Wedman ... .80 .40 .08
  Kansas City Kings
- [ ] 143 Lloyd Free ... 3.50 1.75 .35
  Philadelphia 76ers
- [ ] 144 Bobby Jones ... 3.00 1.00 .20
  Denver Nuggets

1977-78 Topps

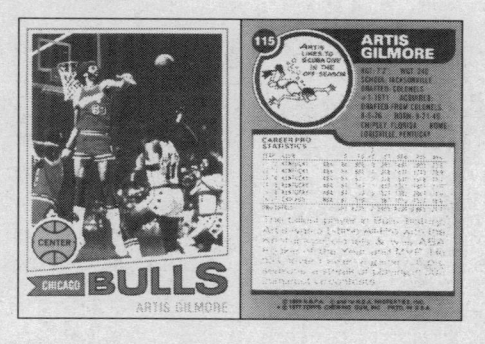

The 1977-78 Topps basketball card set consists of 132 standard-sized (2 1/2" by 3 1/2") cards. Card backs are printed in green and black on either white or gray card stock. The white card stock is considered more desirable by most collectors and may even be a little tougher to find. The key rookie cards in this set are Adrian Dantley and Robert Parish.

	NRMT	VG-E	GOOD
COMPLETE SET (132)	120.00	60.00	12.00
COMMON PLAYER (1-132)	.25	.12	.02
☐ 1 Kareem Abdul-Jabbar	20.00	9.00	1.75
Los Angeles Lakers			
☐ 2 Henry Bibby	.40	.20	.04
Philadelphia 76ers			
☐ 3 Curtis Rowe	.40	.20	.04
Boston Celtics			
☐ 4 Norm Van Lier	.40	.20	.04
Chicago Bulls			
☐ 5 Darnell Hillman	.25	.12	.02
New Jersey Nets			
☐ 6 Earl Monroe	3.00	1.50	.30
New York Knicks			
☐ 7 Leonard Gray	.25	.12	.02
Washington Bullets			
☐ 8 Bird Averitt	.25	.12	.02
Buffalo Braves			
☐ 9 Jim Brewer	.25	.12	.02
Cleveland Cavaliers			
☐ 10 Paul Westphal	.75	.35	.07
Phoenix Suns			
☐ 11 Bob Gross	.60	.30	.06
Portland Trail Blazers			
☐ 12 Phil Smith	.25	.12	.02

302 / 1977-78 Topps

	Golden State Warriors			
☐ 13	Dan Roundfield	1.00	.50	.10
	Indiana Pacers			
☐ 14	Brian Taylor	.40	.20	.04
	Denver Nuggets			
☐ 15	Rudy Tomjanovich	.40	.20	.04
	Houston Rockets			
☐ 16	Kevin Porter	.40	.20	.04
	Detroit Pistons			
☐ 17	Scott Wedman	.40	.20	.04
	Kansas City Kings			
☐ 18	Lloyd Free	.75	.35	.07
	Philadelphia 76ers			
☐ 19	Tom Boswell	.40	.20	.04
	Boston Celtics			
☐ 20	Pete Maravich	6.00	3.00	.60
	New Orleans Jazz			
☐ 21	Cliff Poindexter	.25	.12	.02
	Chicago Bulls			
☐ 22	Bubbles Hawkins	.40	.20	.04
	New Jersey Nets			
☐ 23	Kevin Grevey	.75	.35	.07
	Washington Bullets			
☐ 24	Ken Charles	.25	.12	.02
	Atlanta Hawks			
☐ 25	Bob Dandridge	.40	.20	.04
	Washington Bullets			
☐ 26	Lonnie Shelton	.60	.30	.06
	New York Knicks			
☐ 27	Don Chaney	.40	.20	.04
	Los Angeles Lakers			
☐ 28	Larry Kenon	.40	.20	.04
	San Antonio Spurs			
☐ 29	Checklist Card	3.00	.30	.06
☐ 30	Fred Brown	.40	.20	.04
	Seattle Supersonics			
☐ 31	John Gianelli UER	.25	.12	.02
	Cleveland Cavaliers (Listed as Cavaliers, should be Buffalo Braves)			
☐ 32	Austin Carr	.40	.20	.04
	Cleveland Cavaliers			
☐ 33	Jamaal Wilkes	1.00	.50	.10
	Los Angeles Lakers			
☐ 34	Caldwell Jones	.40	.20	.04
	Philadelphia 76ers			
☐ 35	JoJo White	1.00	.50	.10
	Boston Celtics			
☐ 36	Scott May	1.25	.60	.12
	Chicago Bulls			
☐ 37	Mike Newlin	.25	.12	.02
	Houston Rockets			
☐ 38	Mel Davis	.25	.12	.02
	New Jersey Nets			
☐ 39	Lionel Hollins	.40	.20	.04
	Portland Trail Blazers			
☐ 40	Elvin Hayes	4.00	2.00	.40

1977-78 Topps / 303

	Washington Bullets			
☐ 41	Dan Issel	2.00	1.00	.20
	Denver Nuggets			
☐ 42	Ricky Sobers	.25	.12	.02
	Phoenix Suns			
☐ 43	Don Ford	.25	.12	.02
	Los Angeles Lakers			
☐ 44	John Williamson	.40	.20	.04
	Indiana Pacers			
☐ 45	Bob McAdoo	1.50	.75	.15
	New York Knicks			
☐ 46	Geoff Petrie	.40	.20	.04
	Atlanta Hawks			
☐ 47	M.L. Carr	1.75	.85	.17
	Detroit Pistons			
☐ 48	Brian Winters	.40	.20	.04
	Milwaukee Bucks			
☐ 49	Sam Lacey	.25	.12	.02
	Kansas City Kings			
☐ 50	George McGinnis	.75	.35	.07
	Philadelphia 76ers			
☐ 51	Don Watts	.25	.12	.02
	Seattle Supersonics			
☐ 52	Sidney Wicks	.60	.30	.06
	Boston Celtics			
☐ 53	Wilbur Holland	.25	.12	.02
	Chicago Bulls			
☐ 54	Tim Bassett	.25	.12	.02
	New Jersey Nets			
☐ 55	Phil Chenier	.40	.20	.04
	Washington Bullets			
☐ 56	Adrian Dantley	14.00	7.00	1.40
	Buffalo Braves			
☐ 57	Jim Chones	.25	.12	.02
	Cleveland Cavaliers			
☐ 58	John Lucas	2.50	1.25	.25
	Houston Rockets			
☐ 59	Cazzie Russell	.40	.20	.04
	Los Angeles Lakers			
☐ 60	David Thompson	2.50	1.25	.25
	Denver Nuggets			
☐ 61	Bob Lanier	2.00	1.00	.20
	Detroit Pistons			
☐ 62	Dave Twardzik	.25	.12	.02
	Portland Trail Blazers			
☐ 63	Wilbert Jones	.25	.12	.02
	Indiana Pacers			
☐ 64	Clifford Ray	.25	.12	.02
	Golden State Warriors			
☐ 65	Doug Collins	1.25	.60	.12
	Philadelphia 76ers			
☐ 66	Tom McMillen	4.00	2.00	.40
	New York Knicks			
☐ 67	Rich Kelley	.40	.20	.04
	New Orleans Jazz			
☐ 68	Mike Bantom	.25	.12	.02
	New Jersey Nets			

304 / 1977-78 Topps

☐ 69	Tom Boerwinkle	.25	.12	.02
	Chicago Bulls			
☐ 70	John Havlicek	7.50	3.75	.75
	Boston Celtics			
☐ 71	Marvin Webster	.60	.30	.06
	Seattle Supersonics			
☐ 72	Curtis Perry	.25	.12	.02
	Phoenix Suns			
☐ 73	George Gervin	5.00	2.50	.50
	San Antonio Spurs			
☐ 74	Leonard Robinson	.40	.20	.04
	New Orleans Jazz			
☐ 75	Wes Unseld	1.75	.85	.17
	Washington Bullets			
☐ 76	Dave Meyers	.60	.30	.06
	Milwaukee Bucks			
☐ 77	Gail Goodrich	1.00	.50	.10
	New Orleans Jazz			
☐ 78	Richard Washington	.75	.35	.07
	Kansas City Kings			
☐ 79	Mike Gale	.25	.12	.02
	San Antonio Spurs			
☐ 80	Maurice Lucas	.75	.35	.07
	Portland Trail Blazers			
☐ 81	Harvey Catchings	.40	.20	.04
	Philadelphia 76ers			
☐ 82	Randy Smith	.40	.20	.04
	Buffalo Braves			
☐ 83	Campy Russell	.40	.20	.04
	Cleveland Cavaliers			
☐ 84	Kevin Kunnert	.25	.12	.02
	Houston Rockets			
☐ 85	Lou Hudson	.60	.30	.06
	Atlanta Hawks			
☐ 86	Mickey Johnson	.40	.20	.04
	Chicago Bulls			
☐ 87	Lucius Allen	.40	.20	.04
	Kansas City Kings			
☐ 88	Spencer Haywood	.75	.35	.07
	New York Knicks			
☐ 89	Gus Williams	1.00	.50	.10
	Golden State Warriors			
☐ 90	Dave Cowens	3.25	1.60	.32
	Boston Celtics			
☐ 91	Al Skinner	.25	.12	.02
	New Jersey Nets			
☐ 92	Swen Nater	.40	.20	.04
	Buffalo Braves			
☐ 93	Tom Henderson	.25	.12	.02
	Washington Bullets			
☐ 94	Don Buse	.25	.12	.02
	Indiana Pacers			
☐ 95	Alvan Adams	.60	.30	.06
	Phoenix Suns			
☐ 96	Mack Calvin	.40	.20	.04
	Denver Nuggets			
☐ 97	Tom Burleson	.25	.12	.02

1977-78 Topps / 305

	Kansas City Kings		
☐ 98 John Drew .40	.20	.04
	Atlanta Hawks		
☐ 99 Mike Green .25	.12	.02
	Seattle Supersonics		
☐ 100 Julius Erving 20.00	10.00	2.00
	Philadelphia 76ers		
☐ 101 John Mengelt .25	.12	.02
	Chicago Bulls		
☐ 102 Howard Porter .25	.12	.02
	Detroit Pistons		
☐ 103 Billy Paultz .40	.20	.04
	San Antonio Spurs		
☐ 104 John Shumate .75	.35	.07
	Buffalo Braves		
☐ 105 Calvin Murphy 1.00	.50	.10
	Houston Rockets		
☐ 106 Elmore Smith .25	.12	.02
	Cleveland Cavaliers		
☐ 107 Jim McMillian .25	.12	.02
	New York Knicks		
☐ 108 Kevin Stacom .25	.12	.02
	Boston Celtics		
☐ 109 Jan Van Breda Kolff .25	.12	.02
	New Jersey Nets		
☐ 110 Billy Knight .40	.20	.04
	Indiana Pacers		
☐ 111 Robert Parish 50.00	25.00	5.00
	Golden State Warriors		
☐ 112 Larry Wright .25	.12	.02
	Washington Bullets		
☐ 113 Bruce Seals .25	.12	.02
	Seattle Supersonics		
☐ 114 Junior Bridgeman .40	.20	.04
	Milwaukee Bucks		
☐ 115 Artis Gilmore 1.75	.85	.17
	Chicago Bulls		
☐ 116 Steve Mix .25	.12	.02
	Philadelphia 76ers		
☐ 117 Ron Lee .25	.12	.02
	Phoenix Suns		
☐ 118 Bobby Jones 1.00	.50	.10
	Denver Nuggets		
☐ 119 Ron Boone .25	.12	.02
	Kansas City Kings		
☐ 120 Bill Walton 6.00	3.00	.60
	Portland Trail Blazers		
☐ 121 Chris Ford .75	.35	.07
	Detroit Pistons		
☐ 122 Earl Tatum .25	.12	.02
	Los Angeles Lakers		
☐ 123 E.C. Coleman .25	.12	.02
	New Orleans Jazz		
☐ 124 Moses Malone 10.00	5.00	1.00
	Houston Rockets		
☐ 125 Charlie Scott .40	.20	.04
	Boston Celtics		

306 / 1977-78 Topps

☐ 126 Bobby Smith	.25	.12	.02
Cleveland Cavaliers			
☐ 127 Nate Archibald	2.00	1.00	.20
New Jersey Nets			
☐ 128 Mitch Kupchak	2.25	1.10	.22
Washington Bullets			
☐ 129 Walt Frazier	4.00	2.00	.40
New York Knicks			
☐ 130 Rick Barry	5.00	2.50	.50
Golden State Warriors			
☐ 131 Ernie DiGregorio	.40	.20	.04
Buffalo Braves			
☐ 132 Darryl Dawkins	5.00	1.25	.25
Philadelphia 76ers			

1978-79 Topps

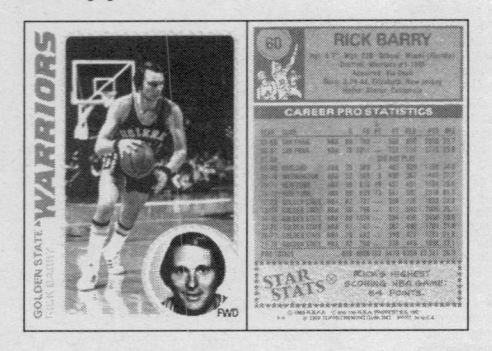

The 1978-79 Topps basketball card set contains 132 cards. The cards in the set measure the standard 2 1/2" by 3 1/2". Card backs are printed in orange and brown on gray card stock. The key rookie cards in this set are Walter Davis, Dennis Johnson, Marques Johnson, Bernard King, and Jack Sikma.

	NRMT	VG-E	GOOD
COMPLETE SET (132)	80.00	40.00	8.00
COMMON PLAYER (1-132)	.20	.10	.02
☐ 1 Bill Walton	9.00	2.50	.50
Portland Trail Blazers			
☐ 2 Doug Collins	.75	.35	.07
Philadelphia 76ers			
☐ 3 Jamaal Wilkes	.60	.30	.06

1978-79 Topps / 307

	Los Angeles Lakers			
☐ 4	Wilbur Holland	.20	.10	.02
	Chicago Bulls			
☐ 5	Bob McAdoo	1.00	.50	.10
	New York Knicks			
☐ 6	Lucius Allen	.35	.17	.03
	Kansas City Kings			
☐ 7	Wes Unseld	1.25	.60	.12
	Washington Bullets			
☐ 8	Dave Meyers	.35	.17	.03
	Milwaukee Bucks			
☐ 9	Austin Carr	.35	.17	.03
	Cleveland Cavaliers			
☐ 10	Walter Davis	5.00	2.50	.50
	Phoenix Suns			
☐ 11	John Williamson	.35	.17	.03
	New Jersey Nets			
☐ 12	E.C. Coleman	.20	.10	.02
	Golden State Warriors			
☐ 13	Calvin Murphy	.75	.35	.07
	Houston Rockets			
☐ 14	Bobby Jones	.60	.30	.06
	Denver Nuggets			
☐ 15	Chris Ford	.75	.35	.07
	Detroit Pistons			
☐ 16	Kermit Washington	.35	.17	.03
	Boston Celtics			
☐ 17	Butch Beard	.20	.10	.02
	New York Knicks			
☐ 18	Steve Mix	.20	.10	.02
	Philadelphia 76ers			
☐ 19	Marvin Webster	.20	.10	.02
	Seattle Supersonics			
☐ 20	George Gervin	3.00	1.50	.30
	San Antonio Spurs			
☐ 21	Steve Hawes	.20	.10	.02
	Atlanta Hawks			
☐ 22	Johnny Davis	.20	.10	.02
	Portland Trail Blazers			
☐ 23	Swen Nater	.35	.17	.03
	San Diego Clippers			
☐ 24	Lou Hudson	.50	.25	.05
	Los Angeles Lakers			
☐ 25	Elvin Hayes	3.50	1.75	.35
	Washington Bullets			
☐ 26	Nate Archibald	1.50	.75	.15
	San Diego Clippers			
☐ 27	James Edwards	3.00	1.50	.30
	Indiana Pacers			
☐ 28	Howard Porter	.20	.10	.02
	New Jersey Nets			
☐ 29	Quinn Buckner	2.00	1.00	.20
	Milwaukee Bucks			
☐ 30	Leonard Robinson	.35	.17	.03
	New Orleans Jazz			
☐ 31	Jim Cleamons	.20	.10	.02
	New York Knicks			

308 / 1978-79 Topps

☐ 32	Campy Russell	.20	.10	.02
	Cleveland Cavaliers			
☐ 33	Phil Smith	.20	.10	.02
	Golden State Warriors			
☐ 34	Darryl Dawkins	1.00	.50	.10
	Philadelphia 76ers			
☐ 35	Don Buse	.20	.10	.02
	Phoenix Suns			
☐ 36	Mickey Johnson	.20	.10	.02
	Chicago Bulls			
☐ 37	Mike Gale	.20	.10	.02
	San Antonio Spurs			
☐ 38	Moses Malone	7.00	3.50	.70
	Houston Rockets			
☐ 39	Gus Williams	.60	.30	.06
	Seattle Supersonics			
☐ 40	Dave Cowens	2.50	1.25	.25
	Boston Celtics			
☐ 41	Bobby Wilkerson	.50	.25	.05
	Denver Nuggets			
☐ 42	Wilbert Jones	.20	.10	.02
	San Diego Clippers			
☐ 43	Charlie Scott	.35	.17	.03
	Los Angeles Lakers			
☐ 44	John Drew	.35	.17	.03
	Atlanta Hawks			
☐ 45	Earl Monroe	2.50	1.25	.25
	New York Knicks			
☐ 46	John Shumate	.35	.17	.03
	Detroit Pistons			
☐ 47	Earl Tatum	.20	.10	.02
	Indiana Pacers			
☐ 48	Mitch Kupchak	.35	.17	.03
	Washington Bullets			
☐ 49	Ron Boone	.20	.10	.02
	Kansas City Kings			
☐ 50	Maurice Lucas	.35	.17	.03
	Portland Trail Blazers			
☐ 51	Louie Dampier	.35	.17	.03
	San Antonio Spurs			
☐ 52	Aaron James	.20	.10	.02
	New Orleans Jazz			
☐ 53	John Mengelt	.20	.10	.02
	Chicago Bulls			
☐ 54	Garfield Heard	.20	.10	.02
	Phoenix Suns			
☐ 55	George Johnson	.20	.10	.02
	New Jersey Nets			
☐ 56	Junior Bridgeman	.35	.17	.03
	Milwaukee Bucks			
☐ 57	Elmore Smith	.20	.10	.02
	Cleveland Cavaliers			
☐ 58	Rudy Tomjanovich	.35	.17	.03
	Houston Rockets			
☐ 59	Fred Brown	.35	.17	.03
	Seattle Supersonics			
☐ 60	Rick Barry UER	4.00	2.00	.40

1978-79 Topps / 309

☐ 61	Golden State Warriors (reversed negative) Dave Bing	1.50	.75	.15
☐ 62	Boston Celtics Anthony Roberts	.20	.10	.02
☐ 63	Denver Nuggets Norm Nixon	2.50	1.25	.25
☐ 64	Los Angeles Lakers Leon Douglas	.35	.17	.03
☐ 65	Detroit Pistons Henry Bibby	.35	.17	.03
☐ 66	Philadelphia 76ers Lonnie Shelton	.35	.17	.03
☐ 67	New York Knicks Checklist Card	2.00	.20	.04
☐ 68	Tom Henderson	.20	.10	.02
☐ 69	Washington Bullets Dan Roundfield	.35	.17	.03
☐ 70	Indiana Pacers Armond Hill	.35	.17	.03
☐ 71	Atlanta Hawks Larry Kenon	.35	.17	.03
☐ 72	San Antonio Spurs Billy Knight	.20	.10	.02
☐ 73	San Diego Clippers Artis Gilmore	1.25	.60	.12
☐ 74	Chicago Bulls Lionel Hollins	.35	.17	.03
☐ 75	Portland Trail Blazers Bernard King	14.00	7.00	1.40
☐ 76	New Jersey Nets Brian Winters	.35	.17	.03
☐ 77	Milwaukee Bucks Alvan Adams	.35	.17	.03
☐ 78	Phoenix Suns Dennis Johnson	8.50	4.25	.85
☐ 79	Seattle Supersonics Scott Wedman	.35	.17	.03
☐ 80	Kansas City Kings Pete Maravich	4.50	2.25	.45
☐ 81	New Orleans Jazz Dan Issel	1.50	.75	.15
☐ 82	Denver Nuggets M.L. Carr	.35	.17	.03
☐ 83	Detroit Pistons Walt Frazier	3.50	1.75	.35
☐ 84	Cleveland Cavaliers Dwight Jones	.20	.10	.02
☐ 85	Houston Rockets JoJo White	.75	.35	.07
☐ 86	Boston Celtics Robert Parish	11.00	5.50	1.10
☐ 87	Golden State Warriors Charlie Criss	.35	.17	.03
☐ 88	Atlanta Hawks Jim McMillian New York Knicks	.20	.10	.02

310 / 1978-79 Topps

☐ 89	Chuck Williams .... San Diego Clippers	.20	.10	.02
☐ 90	George McGinnis .... Philadelphia 76ers	.50	.25	.05
☐ 91	Billy Paultz .... San Antonio Spurs	.20	.10	.02
☐ 92	Bob Dandridge .... Washington Bullets	.35	.17	.03
☐ 93	Ricky Sobers .... Indiana Pacers	.20	.10	.02
☐ 94	Paul Silas .... Seattle Supersonics	.50	.25	.05
☐ 95	Gail Goodrich .... New Orleans Jazz	.75	.35	.07
☐ 96	Tim Bassett .... New Jersey Nets	.20	.10	.02
☐ 97	Ron Lee .... Phoenix Suns	.20	.10	.02
☐ 98	Bob Gross .... Portland Trail Blazers	.20	.10	.02
☐ 99	Sam Lacey .... Kansas City Kings	.20	.10	.02
☐ 100	David Thompson .... Denver Nuggets (College North Carolina, should be NC State)	2.00	1.00	.20
☐ 101	John Gianelli .... Milwaukee Bucks	.20	.10	.02
☐ 102	Norm Van Lier .... Chicago Bulls	.35	.17	.03
☐ 103	Caldwell Jones .... Philadelphia 76ers	.35	.17	.03
☐ 104	Eric Money .... Detroit Pistons	.20	.10	.02
☐ 105	Jim Chones .... Cleveland Cavaliers	.20	.10	.02
☐ 106	John Lucas .... Houston Rockets	.50	.25	.05
☐ 107	Spencer Haywood .... New York Knicks	.50	.25	.05
☐ 108	Eddie Johnson .... Atlanta Hawks	.60	.30	.06
☐ 109	Sidney Wicks .... Boston Celtics	.50	.25	.05
☐ 110	Kareem Abdul-Jabbar .... Los Angeles Lakers	14.00	7.00	1.40
☐ 111	Sonny Parker .... Golden State Warriors	.35	.17	.03
☐ 112	Randy Smith .... San Diego Clippers	.35	.17	.03
☐ 113	Kevin Grevey .... Washington Bullets	.35	.17	.03
☐ 114	Rich Kelley .... New Orleans Jazz	.20	.10	.02
☐ 115	Scott May .... Chicago Bulls	.35	.17	.03
☐ 116	Lloyd Free	.35	.17	.03

	Philadelphia 76ers			
☐ 117	Jack Sikma	7.00	3.50	.70
	Seattle Supersonics			
☐ 118	Kevin Porter	.35	.17	.03
	New Jersey Nets			
☐ 119	Darnell Hillman	.20	.10	.02
	Denver Nuggets			
☐ 120	Paul Westphal	.60	.30	.06
	Phoenix Suns			
☐ 121	Richard Washington	.35	.17	.03
	Kansas City Kings			
☐ 122	Dave Twardzik	.20	.10	.02
	Portland Trail Blazers			
☐ 123	Mike Bantom	.20	.10	.02
	Indiana Pacers			
☐ 124	Mike Newlin	.20	.10	.02
	Houston Rockets			
☐ 125	Bob Lanier	1.50	.75	.15
	Detroit Pistons			
☐ 126	Marques Johnson	3.50	1.75	.35
	Milwaukee Bucks			
☐ 127	Foots Walker	.35	.17	.03
	Cleveland Cavaliers			
☐ 128	Cedric Maxwell	1.50	.75	.15
	Boston Celtics			
☐ 129	Ray Williams	.75	.35	.07
	New York Knicks			
☐ 130	Julius Erving	14.00	7.00	1.40
	Philadelphia 76ers			
☐ 131	Clifford Ray	.20	.10	.02
	Golden State Warriors			
☐ 132	Adrian Dantley	3.00	1.00	.20
	Los Angeles Lakers			

1979-80 Topps

The 1979-80 Topps basketball card set contains 132 cards of NBA players. The cards in the set measure the standard 2 1/2" by 3 1/2". Card backs are printed in red and black on gray card stock. All-Star selections are designated as AS1 for first team selections and AS2 for second team selections and are denoted on the front of the player's regular card. Past U.S Olympic basketball team members are indicated in the checklist below by having the year of their participation followed by an "O" to signify that the player was an Olympic team member. Notable rookie cards in this set include Alex English and Reggie Theus.

	MINT	EXC	G-VG
COMPLETE SET (132)	75.00	37.50	7.50
COMMON PLAYER (1-132)	.15	.07	.01
☐ 1 George Gervin	3.00	1.00	.20
San Antonio Spurs			
☐ 2 Mitch Kupchak	.25	.12	.02

312 / 1979-80 Topps

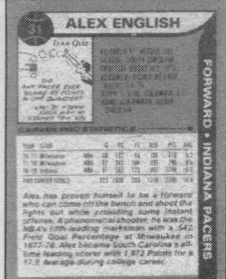

	Washington Bullets		
☐ 3	Henry Bibby .... .25	.12	.02
	Philadelphia 76ers		
☐ 4	Bob Gross .... .15	.07	.01
	Portland Trail Blazers		
☐ 5	Dave Cowens 2.00	1.00	.20
	Boston Celtics		
☐ 6	Dennis Johnson 2.00	1.00	.20
	Seattle Supersonics		
☐ 7	Scott Wedman .... .25	.12	.02
	Kansas City Kings		
☐ 8	Earl Monroe 2.00	1.00	.20
	New York Knicks		
☐ 9	Mike Bantom 720 .... .15	.07	.01
	Indiana Pacers		
☐ 10	Kareem Abdul-Jabbar AS 12.50	6.25	1.25
	Los Angeles Lakers		
☐ 11	JoJo White 680 .... .60	.30	.06
	Golden State Warriors		
☐ 12	Spencer Haywood 680 .... .45	.22	.04
	Utah Jazz		
☐ 13	Kevin Porter .... .25	.12	.02
	Detroit Pistons		
☐ 14	Bernard King 4.00	2.00	.40
	New Jersey Nets		
☐ 15	Mike Newlin .... .15	.07	.01
	Houston Rockets		
☐ 16	Sidney Wicks .... .40	.20	.04
	San Diego Clippers		
☐ 17	Dan Issel 1.25	.60	.12
	Denver Nuggets		
☐ 18	Tom Henderson 720 .... .15	.07	.01
	Washington Bullets		
☐ 19	Jim Chones .... .15	.07	.01
	Cleveland Cavaliers		

1979-80 Topps / 313

☐ 20	Julius Erving	12.50	6.25	1.25
	Philadelphia 76ers			
☐ 21	Brian Winters	.15	.07	.01
	Milwaukee Bucks			
☐ 22	Billy Paultz	.15	.07	.01
	San Antonio Spurs			
☐ 23	Cedric Maxwell	.40	.20	.04
	Boston Celtics			
☐ 24	Eddie Johnson	.25	.12	.02
	Atlanta Hawks			
☐ 25	Artis Gilmore	.75	.35	.07
	Chicago Bulls			
☐ 26	Maurice Lucas	.35	.17	.03
	Portland Trail Blazers			
☐ 27	Gus Williams	.50	.25	.05
	Seattle Supersonics			
☐ 28	Sam Lacey	.15	.07	.01
	Kansas City Kings			
☐ 29	Toby Knight	.15	.07	.01
	New York Knicks			
☐ 30	Paul Westphal AS1	.50	.25	.05
	Phoenix Suns			
☐ 31	Alex English	18.00	9.00	1.80
	Indiana Pacers			
☐ 32	Gail Goodrich	.60	.30	.06
	Utah Jazz			
☐ 33	Caldwell Jones	.25	.12	.02
	Philadelphia 76ers			
☐ 34	Kevin Grevey	.15	.07	.01
	Washington Bullets			
☐ 35	Jamaal Wilkes	.50	.25	.05
	Los Angeles Lakers			
☐ 36	Sonny Parker	.15	.07	.01
	Golden State Warriors			
☐ 37	John Gianelli	.15	.07	.01
	New Jersey Nets			
☐ 38	John Long	.75	.35	.07
	Detroit Pistons			
☐ 39	George Johnson	.15	.07	.01
	New Jersey Nets			
☐ 40	Lloyd Free AS2	.25	.12	.02
	San Diego Clippers			
☐ 41	Rudy Tomjanovich	.35	.17	.03
	Houston Rockets			
☐ 42	Foots Walker	.15	.07	.01
	Cleveland Cavaliers			
☐ 43	Dan Roundfield	.25	.12	.02
	Atlanta Hawks			
☐ 44	Reggie Theus	4.00	2.00	.40
	Chicago Bulls			
☐ 45	Bill Walton	3.50	1.75	.35
	San Diego Clippers			
☐ 46	Fred Brown	.35	.17	.03
	Seattle Supersonics			
☐ 47	Darnell Hillman	.15	.07	.01
	Kansas City Kings			
☐ 48	Ray Williams	.25	.12	.02

314 / 1979-80 Topps

	New York Knicks			
☐ 49	Larry Kenon	.25	.12	.02
	San Antonio Spurs			
☐ 50	David Thompson	1.50	.75	.15
	Denver Nuggets			
☐ 51	Billy Knight	.15	.07	.01
	Indiana Pacers			
☐ 52	Alvan Adams	.25	.12	.02
	Phoenix Suns			
☐ 53	Phil Smith	.15	.07	.01
	Golden State Warriors			
☐ 54	Adrian Dantley 760	1.25	.60	.12
	Los Angeles Lakers			
☐ 55	John Williamson	.25	.12	.02
	New Jersey Nets			
☐ 56	Campy Russell	.15	.07	.01
	Cleveland Cavaliers			
☐ 57	Armond Hill	.15	.07	.01
	Atlanta Hawks			
☐ 58	Bob Lanier	1.25	.60	.12
	Detroit Pistons			
☐ 59	Mickey Johnson	.15	.07	.01
	Chicago Bulls			
☐ 60	Pete Maravich	4.25	2.10	.42
	Utah Jazz			
☐ 61	Nick Weatherspoon	.15	.07	.01
	San Diego Clippers			
☐ 62	Robert Reid	.75	.35	.07
	Houston Rockets			
☐ 63	Mychal Thompson	3.00	1.50	.30
	Portland Trail Blazers			
☐ 64	Doug Collins 720	.50	.25	.05
	Philadelphia 76ers			
☐ 65	Wes Unseld	1.25	.60	.12
	Washington Bullets			
☐ 66	Jack Sikma	1.50	.75	.15
	Seattle Supersonics			
☐ 67	Bobby Wilkerson	.25	.12	.02
	Denver Nuggets			
☐ 68	Bill Robinzine	.25	.12	.02
	Kansas City Kings			
☐ 69	Joe Meriweather	.15	.07	.01
	New York Knicks			
☐ 70	Marques Johnson AS1	.75	.35	.07
	Milwaukee Bucks			
☐ 71	Ricky Sobers	.15	.07	.01
	Indiana Pacers			
☐ 72	Clifford Ray	.15	.07	.01
	Golden State Warriors			
☐ 73	Tim Bassett	.15	.07	.01
	New Jersey Nets			
☐ 74	James Silas	.15	.07	.01
	San Antonio Spurs			
☐ 75	Bob McAdoo	.75	.35	.07
	Boston Celtics			
☐ 76	Austin Carr	.35	.17	.03
	Cleveland Cavaliers			

1979-80 Topps / 315

☐ 77 Don Ford	.15	.07	.01
Los Angeles Lakers			
☐ 78 Steve Hawes	.25	.12	.02
Atlanta Hawks			
☐ 79 Ron Brewer	.35	.17	.03
Portland Trail Blazers			
☐ 80 Walter Davis	1.25	.60	.12
Phoenix Suns			
☐ 81 Calvin Murphy	.75	.35	.07
Houston Rockets			
☐ 82 Tom Boswell	.15	.07	.01
Denver Nuggets			
☐ 83 Lonnie Shelton	.15	.07	.01
Seattle Supersonics			
☐ 84 Terry Tyler	.35	.17	.03
Detroit Pistons			
☐ 85 Randy Smith	.25	.12	.02
San Diego Clippers			
☐ 86 Rich Kelley	.15	.07	.01
Utah Jazz			
☐ 87 Otis Birdsong	.60	.30	.06
Kansas City Kings			
☐ 88 Marvin Webster	.25	.12	.02
New York Knicks			
☐ 89 Eric Money	.15	.07	.01
Philadelphia 76ers			
☐ 90 Elvin Hayes AS1	3.00	1.50	.30
Washington Bullets			
☐ 91 Junior Bridgeman	.25	.12	.02
Milwaukee Bucks			
☐ 92 Johnny Davis	.15	.07	.01
Indiana Pacers			
☐ 93 Robert Parish	7.50	3.75	.75
Golden State Warriors			
☐ 94 Eddie Jordan	.15	.07	.01
New Jersey Nets			
☐ 95 Leonard Robinson	.25	.12	.02
Phoenix Suns			
☐ 96 Rick Robey	.35	.17	.03
Boston Celtics			
☐ 97 Norm Nixon	.60	.30	.06
Los Angeles Lakers			
☐ 98 Mark Olberding	.15	.07	.01
San Antonio Spurs			
☐ 99 Wilbur Holland	.15	.07	.01
Utah Jazz			
☐ 100 Moses Malone AS1	6.00	3.00	.60
Houston Rockets			
☐ 101 Checklist Card	1.75	.15	.03
☐ 102 Tom Owens	.15	.07	.01
Portland Trail Blazers			
☐ 103 Phil Chenier	.25	.12	.02
Washington Bullets			
☐ 104 John Johnson	.25	.12	.02
Seattle Supersonics			
☐ 105 Darryl Dawkins	.75	.35	.07
Philadelphia 76ers			

316 / 1979-80 Topps

- ☐ 106 Charlie Scott 68O .... .25 .12 .02
  Denver Nuggets
- ☐ 107 M.L. Carr .... .25 .12 .02
  Detroit Pistons
- ☐ 108 Phil Ford 76O .... 2.00 1.00 .20
  Kansas City Kings
- ☐ 109 Swen Nater .... .25 .12 .02
  San Diego Clippers
- ☐ 110 Nate Archibald .... 1.25 .60 .12
  Boston Celtics
- ☐ 111 Aaron James .... .15 .07 .01
  Utah Jazz
- ☐ 112 Jim Cleamons .... .15 .07 .01
  New York Knicks
- ☐ 113 James Edwards .... .75 .35 .07
  Indiana Pacers
- ☐ 114 Don Buse .... .15 .07 .01
  Phoenix Suns
- ☐ 115 Steve Mix .... .15 .07 .01
  Philadelphia 76ers
- ☐ 116 Charles Johnson .... .15 .07 .01
  Washington Bullets
- ☐ 117 Elmore Smith .... .15 .07 .01
  Cleveland Cavaliers
- ☐ 118 John Drew .... .25 .12 .02
  Atlanta Hawks
- ☐ 119 Lou Hudson .... .40 .20 .04
  Los Angeles Lakers
- ☐ 120 Rick Barry .... 3.50 1.75 .35
  Houston Rockets
- ☐ 121 Kent Benson .... .50 .25 .05
  Milwaukee Bucks
- ☐ 122 Mike Gale .... .15 .07 .01
  San Antonio Spurs
- ☐ 123 Jan Van Breda Kolff .... .15 .07 .01
  New Jersey Nets
- ☐ 124 Chris Ford .... .45 .22 .04
  Boston Celtics
- ☐ 125 George McGinnis .... .40 .20 .04
  Denver Nuggets
- ☐ 126 Leon Douglas .... .15 .07 .01
  Detroit Pistons
- ☐ 127 John Lucas .... .25 .12 .02
  Golden State Warriors
- ☐ 128 Kermit Washington .... .15 .07 .01
  San Diego Clippers
- ☐ 129 Lionel Hollins .... .25 .12 .02
  Portland Trail Blazers
- ☐ 130 Bob Dandridge AS2 .... .25 .12 .02
  Washington Bullets
- ☐ 131 James McElroy .... .15 .07 .01
  Utah Jazz
- ☐ 132 Bobby Jones 72O .... .50 .20 .04
  Philadelphia 76ers

1980-81 Topps

The 1980-81 Topps basketball card set contains 264 different individual players (1 1/6" by 2 1/2") on 176 different panels of three (2 1/2" by 3 1/2"). The cards come with three individual players per standard card. A perforation line segments each card into three players. In all, there are 176 different complete cards; however, the same player will be on more than one card. The variations stem from the fact that the cards in this set were printed on two separate sheets. In the checklist below, the first 88 cards comprise a complete set of all 264 players. The second 88 cards (89-176) provide a slight rearrangement of players within the card, but still contain the same 264 players. The cards are numbered within each series of 88 by any ordering of the left-hand player's number when the card is viewed from the back. In the checklist below, SD refers to a "Slam Dunk" star card. The letters AS in the checklist refer to an All-Star selection pictured on the front of the checklist card. There are a number of team leader (TL) cards which depict the team's leader in assists scoring or rebounds. Prices given below are for complete panels, as that is the typical way these cards are collected; cards which have been separated into the three parts are relatively valueless. The key card in this set is the combination of Larry Bird, Julius Erving, and Magic Johnson which features both rookie type cards of Bird and Johnson together on the same card. Since this confusing set was issued in three-player panels, there are no single-player rookie cards as the other basketball sets have. However the following players made their first card appearance in this set: James Bailey, Greg Ballard, Larry Bird, Dudley Bradley, Mike Bratz, Joe Bryant, Kenny Carr, Bill Cartwright, Maurice Cheeks, Michael Cooper, Wayne Cooper, David Greenwood, Phil Hubbard, Geoff Huston, Abdul Jeelani, Magic Johnson, Reggie King, Tom LaGarde, Mark Landsberger, Allen Leavell, Sidney Moncrief, Calvin Natt, Roger Phegley, Ben Poquette, Micheal Ray Richardson, Cliff Robinson, Purvis Short, Jerome Whitehead, and Freeman Williams.

	MINT	EXC	G-VG
COMPLETE SET (1-176)	750.00	375.00	75.00
COMMON PANEL	.20	.10	.02
☐ 1 3 Dan Roundfield AS	5.00	2.50	.50
181 Julius Erving			
258 Ron Brewer SD			

318 / 1980-81 Topps

- [ ] 2 7 Moses Malone AS .... 2.00   1.00   .20
       185 Steve Mix
       92 Robert Parish TL
- [ ] 3 12 Gus Williams AS .... .20   .10   .02
       67 Geoff Huston
       5 John Drew AS
- [ ] 4 24 Steve Hawes .... 1.00   .50   .10
       32 Nate Archibald TL
       248 Elvin Hayes
- [ ] 5 29 Dan Roundfield .... .20   .10   .02
       73 Dan Issel TL
       152 Brian Winters
- [ ] 6 34 Larry Bird 500.00   250.00   50.00
       174 Julius Erving TL
       139 Magic Johnson
- [ ] 7 36 Dave Cowens .... .75   .35   .07
       186 Paul Westphal TL
       142 Jamaal Wilkes
- [ ] 8 38 Pete Maravich .... 2.25   1.10   .22
       264 Lloyd Free SD
       194 Dennis Johnson
- [ ] 9 40 Rick Robey .... .30   .15   .03
       234 Ad. Dantley TL
       26 Eddie Johnson
- [ ] 10 47 Scott May .... .20   .10   .02
       196 K. Washington TL
       177 Henry Bibby
- [ ] 11 55 Don Ford .... .20   .10   .02
       145 Quinn Buckner TL
       138 Brad Holland
- [ ] 12 58 Campy Russell .... .20   .10   .02
       247 Kevin Grevey
       52 Dave Robisch TL
- [ ] 13 60 Foots Walker .... .20   .10   .02
       113 Mick. Johnson TL
       130 Bill Robinzine
- [ ] 14 61 Austin Carr .... 2.75   1.35   .27
       8 Kareem Abdul-Jabbar AS
       200 Calvin Natt
- [ ] 15 63 Jim Cleamons .... .20   .10   .02
       256 Robert Reid SD
       22 Charlie Criss
- [ ] 16 69 Tom LaGarde .... .20   .10   .02
       215 Swen Nater TL
       213 James Silas
- [ ] 17 71 Jerome Whitehead .... .30   .15   .03
       259 Artis Gilmore SD
       184 Caldwell Jones
- [ ] 18 74 John Roche TL .... .20   .10   .02
       99 Clifford Ray
       235 Ben Poquette TL
- [ ] 19 75 Alex English .... 2.00   1.00   .20
       2 Marques Johnson AS
       68 Jeff Judkins
- [ ] 20 82 Terry Tyler TL .... .20   .10   .02
       21 Armond Hill TL
       171 M.R. Richardson

1980-81 Topps / 319

- [ ] 21 84 Kent Benson .... .20 .10 .02
  212 John Shumate
  229 Paul Westphal
- [ ] 22 86 Phil Hubbard .... 1.50 .75 .15
  93 Robert Parish TL
  126 Tom Burleson
- [ ] 23 88 John Long .... 2.50 1.25 .25
  1 Julius Erving AS
  49 Ricky Sobers
- [ ] 24 90 Eric Money .... .20 .10 .02
  57 Dave Robisch
  254 Rick Robey SD
- [ ] 25 95 Wayne Cooper .... .20 .10 .02
  226 John Johnson TL
  45 David Greenwood
- [ ] 26 97 Robert Parish .... 3.50 1.75 .35
  187 Leon.Robinson TL
  46 Dwight Jones
- [ ] 27 98 Sonny Parker .... .30 .15 .03
  197 Dave Twardzik TL
  39 Cedric Maxwell
- [ ] 28 105 Rick Barry .... 1.00 .50 .10
  122 Otis Birdsong TL
  48 John Mengelt
- [ ] 29 106 Allen Leavell .... .20 .10 .02
  53 Foots Walker TL
  223 Freeman Williams
- [ ] 30 108 Calvin Murphy .... 1.00 .50 .10
  176 Maur.Cheeks TL
  87 Greg Kelser
- [ ] 31 110 Robert Reid .... .40 .20 .04
  243 Wes Unseld TL
  50 Reggie Theus
- [ ] 32 111 Rudy Tomjanovich .... .20 .10 .02
  13 Eddie Johnson AS
  179 Doug Collins
- [ ] 33 112 Mickey Johnson TL .... .30 .15 .03
  28 Wayne Rollins
  15 M.R.Richardson AS
- [ ] 34 115 Mike Bantom .... .30 .15 .03
  6 Adrian Dantley AS
  227 James Bailey
- [ ] 35 116 Dudley Bradley .... .20 .10 .02
  155 Eddie Jordan TL
  239 Allan Bristow
- [ ] 36 118 James Edwards .... .20 .10 .02
  153 Mike Newlin TL
  182 Lionel Hollins
- [ ] 37 119 Mickey Johnson .... .20 .10 .02
  154 Geo.Johnson TL
  193 Leonard Robinson
- [ ] 38 120 Billy Knight .... .20 .10 .02
  16 Paul Westphal AS
  59 Randy Smith
- [ ] 39 121 George McGinnis .... .20 .10 .02
  83 Eric Money TL
  65 Mike Bratz

320 / 1980-81 Topps

☐ 40	124 Phil Ford TL 101 Phil Smith 224 Gus Williams TL	.20	.10	.02
☐ 41	127 Phil Ford 19 John Drew TL 209 Larry Kenon	.20	.10	.02
☐ 42	131 Scott Wedman 164 B.Cartwright TL 23 John Drew	.20	.10	.02
☐ 43	132 K.Abdul-Jabbar TL 56 Mike Mitchell 81 Terry Tyler TL	2.50	1.25	.25
☐ 44	135 K.Abdul-Jabbar 79 David Thompson 216 Brian Taylor TL	5.00	2.50	.50
☐ 45	137 Michael Cooper 103 Moses Malone TL 148 George Johnson	2.75	1.35	.27
☐ 46	140 Mark Landsberger 10 Bob Lanier AS 222 Bill Walton	1.25	.60	.12
☐ 47	141 Norm Nixon 123 Sam Lacey TL 54 Kenny Carr	.20	.10	.02
☐ 48	143 Marq.Johnson TL 30 Larry Bird TL 232 Jack Sikma	27.00	13.50	2.70
☐ 49	146 Junior Bridgeman 31 Larry Bird TL 198 Ron Brewer	27.00	13.50	2.70
☐ 50	147 Quinn Buckner 133 K.Abdul-Jabbar TL 207 Mike Gale	2.00	1.00	.20
☐ 51	149 Marques Johnson 262 Julius Erving SD 62 Abdul Jeelani	2.00	1.00	.20
☐ 52	151 Sidney Moncrief 260 Lonnie Shelton SD 220 Paul Silas	3.50	1.75	.35
☐ 53	156 George Johnson 9 Bill Cartwright AS 199 Bob Gross	.20	.10	.02
☐ 54	158 Maurice Lucas 261 James Edwards SD 157 Eddie Jordan	.20	.10	.02
☐ 55	159 Mike Newlin 134 Norm Nixon TL 180 Darryl Dawkins	.20	.10	.02
☐ 56	160 Roger Phegley 206 James Silas TL 91 Terry Tyler	.20	.10	.02
☐ 57	161 Cliff Robinson 51 Mike Mitchell TL 80 Bobby Wilkerson	.20	.10	.02
☐ 58	162 Jan V.Breda Kolff 204 George Gervin TL 117 Johnny Davis	.30	.15	.03

1980-81 Topps / 321

☐	59	165 M.R.Richardson TL	.50	.25	.05
		214 Lloyd Free TL			
		44 Artis Gilmore			
☐	60	166 Bill Cartwright	3.00	1.50	.30
		244 Kevin Porter TL			
		25 Armond Hill			
☐	61	168 Toby Knight	.50	.25	.05
		14 Lloyd Free AS			
		240 Adrian Dantley			
☐	62	169 Joe Meriweather	.20	.10	.02
		218 Lloyd Free			
		42 D.Greenwood TL			
☐	63	170 Earl Monroe	.75	.35	.07
		27 James McElroy			
		85 Leon Douglas			
☐	64	172 Marvin Webster	.20	.10	.02
		175 Caldwell Jones TL			
		129 Sam Lacey			
☐	65	173 Ray Williams	.20	.10	.02
		94 John Lucas TL			
		202 Dave Twardzik			
☐	66	178 Maurice Cheeks	45.00	22.50	4.50
		18 Magic Johnson AS			
		237 Ron Boone			
☐	67	183 Bobby Jones	.20	.10	.02
		37 Chris Ford			
		66 Joe Hassett			
☐	68	189 Alvan Adams	.60	.30	.06
		163 B.Cartwright TL			
		76 Dan Issel			
☐	69	190 Don Buse	.30	.15	.03
		242 Elvin Hayes TL			
		35 M.L. Carr			
☐	70	191 Walter Davis	.40	.20	.04
		11 George Gervin AS			
		136 Jim Chones			
☐	71	192 Rich Kelley	1.00	.50	.10
		102 Moses Malone TL			
		64 Winford Boynes			
☐	72	201 Tom Owens	.30	.15	.03
		225 Jack Sikma TL			
		100 Purvis Short			
☐	73	208 George Gervin	1.00	.50	.10
		72 Dan Issel TL			
		249 Mitch Kupchak			
☐	74	217 Joe Bryant	2.50	1.25	.25
		263 Bobby Jones SD			
		107 Moses Malone			
☐	75	219 Swen Nater	.20	.10	.02
		17 Calvin Murphy AS			
		70 Rich.Washington			
☐	76	221 Brian Taylor	.20	.10	.02
		253 John Shumate SD			
		167 Larry Demic			
☐	77	228 Fred Brown	.20	.10	.02
		205 Larry Kenon TL			
		203 Kerm.Washington			

322 / 1980-81 Topps

☐ 78	230 John Johnson 4 Walter Davis AS 33 Nate Archibald	.60	.30	.06
☐ 79	231 Lonnie Shelton 104 Allen Leavell TL 96 John Lucas	.20	.10	.02
☐ 80	233 Gus Williams 20 Dan Roundfield TL 211 Kevin Restani	.20	.10	.02
☐ 81	236 Allan Bristow TL 210 Mark Olberding 255 James Bailey SD	.20	.10	.02
☐ 82	238 Tom Boswell 109 Billy Paultz 150 Bob Lanier	.50	.25	.05
☐ 83	241 Ben Poquette 188 Paul Westphal TL 77 Charlie Scott	.20	.10	.02
☐ 84	245 Greg Ballard 43 Reggie Theus TL 252 John Williamson	.20	.10	.02
☐ 85	246 Bob Dandridge 41 Reggie Theus TL 128 Reggie King	.20	.10	.02
☐ 86	250 Kevin Porter 114 Johnny Davis TL 125 Otis Birdsong	.20	.10	.02
☐ 87	251 Wes Unseld 195 Tom Owens TL 78 John Roche	.50	.25	.05
☐ 88	257 Elvin Hayes SD 144 Marq.Johnson TL 89 Bob McAdoo	.60	.30	.06
☐ 89	3 Dan Roundfield 218 Lloyd Free 42 D.Greenwood TL	.20	.10	.02
☐ 90	7 Moses Malone 247 Kevin Grevey 52 Dave Robisch TL	1.00	.50	.10
☐ 91	12 Gus Williams 210 Mark Olberding 255 James Bailey SD	.20	.10	.02
☐ 92	24 Steve Hawes 226 John Johnson TL 45 David Greenwood	.20	.10	.02
☐ 93	29 Dan Roundfield 113 Mick.Johnson TL 130 Bill Robinzine	.20	.10	.02
☐ 94	34 Larry Bird 164 B.Cartwright TL 23 John Drew	55.00	27.50	5.50
☐ 95	36 Dave Cowens 16 Paul Westphal AS 59 Randy Smith	.75	.35	.07
☐ 96	38 Pete Maravich 187 Leon.Robinson TL 46 Dwight Jones	1.50	.75	.15

1980-81 Topps / 323

☐ 97	40 Rick Robey 37 Chris Ford 66 Joe Hassett	.20	.10	.02
☐ 98	47 Scott May 30 Larry Bird TL 232 Jack Sikma	27.00	13.50	2.70
☐ 99	55 Don Ford 144 Marq.Johnson TL 89 Bob McAdoo	.30	.15	.03
☐ 100	58 Campy Russell 21 Armond Hill TL 171 M.R.Richardson	.20	.10	.02
☐ 101	60 Foots Walker 122 Otis Birdsong TL 48 John Mengelt	.20	.10	.02
☐ 102	61 Austin Carr 56 Mike Mitchell 81 Terry Tyler TL	.20	.10	.02
☐ 103	63 Jim Cleamons 261 James Edwards SD 157 Eddie Jordan	.20	.10	.02
☐ 104	69 Tom LaGarde 109 Billy Paultz 150 Bob Lanier	.50	.25	.05
☐ 105	71 Jerome Whitehead 17 Calvin Murphy AS 70 Rich.Washington	.20	.10	.02
☐ 106	74 John Roche TL 28 Wayne Rollins 15 M.R.Richardson AS	.30	.15	.03
☐ 107	75 Alex English 102 Moses Malone TL 64 Winford Boynes	2.50	1.25	.25
☐ 108	82 Terry Tyler TL 79 David Thompson 216 Brian Taylor TL	.40	.20	.04
☐ 109	84 Kent Benson 259 Artis Gilmore SD 184 Caldwell Jones	.30	.15	.03
☐ 110	86 Phil Hubbard 195 Tom Owens TL 78 John Roche	.20	.10	.02
☐ 111	88 John Long 18 Magic Johnson AS 237 Ron Boone	38.00	15.00	3.00
☐ 112	90 Eric Money 215 Swen Nater TL 213 James Silas	.20	.10	.02
☐ 113	95 Wayne Cooper 154 Geo.Johnson TL 193 Leon.Robinson	.20	.10	.02
☐ 114	97 Robert Parish 103 Moses Malone TL 148 George Johnson	4.00	2.00	.40
☐ 115	98 Sonny Parker 94 John Lucas TL 202 Dave Twardzik	.20	.10	.02

324 / 1980-81 Topps

☐ 116 105 Rick Barry	1.00	.50	.10
123 Sam Lacey TL			
54 Kenny Carr			
☐ 117 106 Allen Leavell	.30	.15	.03
197 Dave Twardzik TL			
39 Cedric Maxwell			
☐ 118 108 Calvin Murphy	.30	.15	.03
51 Mike Mitchell TL			
80 Bobby Wilkerson			
☐ 119 110 Robert Reid	.20	.10	.02
153 Mike Newlin TL			
182 Lionel Hollins			
☐ 120 111 Rudy Tomjanovich	.30	.15	.03
73 Dan Issel TL			
152 Brian Winters			
☐ 121 112 Mick.Johnson TL	.40	.20	.04
264 Lloyd Free SD			
194 Dennis Johnson			
☐ 122 115 Mike Bantom	.30	.15	.03
204 George Gervin TL			
117 Johnny Davis			
☐ 123 116 Dudley Bradley	.20	.10	.02
186 Paul Westphal TL			
142 Jamaal Wilkes			
☐ 124 118 James Edwards	1.00	.50	.10
32 Nate Archibald TL			
248 Elvin Hayes			
☐ 125 119 Mickey Johnson	.30	.15	.03
72 Dan Issel TL			
249 Mitch Kupchak			
☐ 126 120 Billy Knight	.20	.10	.02
104 Allen Leavell TL			
96 John Lucas			
☐ 127 121 George McGinnis	1.00	.50	.10
10 Bob Lanier AS			
222 Bill Walton			
☐ 128 124 Phil Ford TL	.30	.15	.03
234 Adr.Dantley TL			
26 Eddie Johnson			
☐ 129 127 Phil Ford	.20	.10	.02
43 Reggie Theus TL			
252 John Williamson			
☐ 130 131 Scott Wedman	.20	.10	.02
244 Kevin Porter TL			
25 Armond Hill			
☐ 131 132 K.Abdul-Jabbar TL	3.50	1.75	.35
93 Robert Parish TL			
126 Tom Burleson			
☐ 132 135 K.Abdul-Jabbar	5.00	2.50	.50
253 John Shumate SD			
167 Larry Demic			
☐ 133 137 Michael Cooper	1.50	.75	.15
212 John Shumate			
229 Paul Westphal			
☐ 134 140 Mark Landsberger	.50	.25	.05
214 Lloyd Free TL			
44 Artis Gilmore			

1980-81 Topps / 325

- [ ] 135 141 Norm Nixon .... .35   .17   .03
  242 Elvin Hayes TL
  35 M.L. Carr
- [ ] 136 143 Marq.Johnson TL .... .20   .10   .02
  57 Dave Robisch
  254 Rick Robey SD
- [ ] 137 146 Junior Bridgeman .... 2.50 1.25   .25
  1 Julius Erving AS
  49 Ricky Sobers
- [ ] 138 147 Quinn Buckner .... .20   .10   .02
  2 Marques Johnson AS
  68 Jeff Judkins
- [ ] 139 149 Marques Johnson .... .30   .15   .03
  83 Eric Money TL
  65 Mike Bratz
- [ ] 140 151 Sidney Moncrief .... 5.00 2.50   .50
  133 K.Abdul-Jabbar TL
  207 Mike Gale
- [ ] 141 156 George Johnson .... .20   .10   .02
  175 Caldw.Jones TL
  129 Sam Lacey
- [ ] 142 158 Maurice Lucas .... 2.00 1.00   .20
  262 Julius Erving SD
  62 Abdul Jeelani
- [ ] 143 159 Mike Newlin .... .40   .20   .04
  243 Wes Unseld TL
  50 Reggie Theus
- [ ] 144 160 Roger Phegley .... .20   .10   .02
  145 Quinn Buckner TL
  138 Brad Holland
- [ ] 145 161 Cliff Robinson .... .20   .10   .02
  114 Johnny Davis TL
  125 Otis Birdsong
- [ ] 146 162 Jan V.Breda Kolff 100.00 50.00 10.00
  174 Julius Erving TL
  139 Magic Johnson
- [ ] 147 165 M.R.Richardson TL .... 1.25   .60   .12
  185 Steve Mix
  92 Robert Parish TL
- [ ] 148 166 Bill Cartwright .... 3.00 1.50   .30
  13 Eddie Johnson AS
  179 Doug Collins
- [ ] 149 168 Toby Knight .... .20   .10   .02
  188 Paul Westphal TL
  77 Charlie Scott
- [ ] 150 169 Joe Meriweather .... .20   .10   .02
  196 K.Washington TL
  177 Henry Bibby
- [ ] 151 170 Earl Monroe .... .75   .35   .07
  206 James Silas TL
  91 Terry Tyler
- [ ] 152 172 Marvin Webster .... .20   .10   .02
  155 Eddie Jordan TL
  239 Allan Bristow
- [ ] 153 173 Ray Williams .... .30   .15   .03
  225 Jack Sikma TL
  100 Purvis Short

326 / 1980-81 Topps

- [ ] 154   178 Maurice Cheeks .... 4.00   2.00   .40
    11 George Gervin AS
    136 Jim Chones
- [ ] 155   183 Bobby Jones .... .20   .10   .02
    99 Clifford Ray
    235 Ben Poquette TL
- [ ] 156   189 Alvan Adams .... .50   .25   .05
    14 Lloyd Free AS
    240 Adrian Dantley
- [ ] 157 190 Don Buse .... .30   .15   .03
    6 Adrian Dantley AS
    227 James Bailey
- [ ] 158 191 Walter Davis .... .30   .15   .03
    9 Bill Cartwright AS
    199 Bob Gross
- [ ] 159 192 Rich Kelley .... 2.50   1.25   .25
    263 Bobby Jones SD
    107 Moses Malone
- [ ] 160 201 Tom Owens .... .30   .15   .03
    134 Norm Nixon TL
    180 Darryl Dawkins
- [ ] 161 208 George Gervin .... 1.00   .50   .10
    53 Foots Walker TL
    223 Freeman Williams
- [ ] 162 217 Joe Bryant .... 2.50   1.25   .25
    8 K.Abdul-Jabbar AS
    200 Calvin Natt
- [ ] 163 219 Swen Nater .... .20   .10   .02
    101 Phil Smith
    224 Gus Williams TL
- [ ] 164 221 Brian Taylor .... .20   .10   .02
    256 Robert Reid SD
    22 Charlie Criss
- [ ] 165 228 Fred Brown 27.00   13.50   2.70
    31 Larry Bird TL
    198 Ron Brewer
- [ ] 166 230 John Johnson .... .50   .25   .05
    163 B.Cartwright TL
    76 Dan Issel
- [ ] 167 231 Lonnie Shelton .... .20   .10   .02
    205 Larry Kenon TL
    203 Kermit Washington
- [ ] 168 233 Gus Williams .... .20   .10   .02
    41 Reggie Theus TL
    128 Reggie King
- [ ] 169 236 Allan Bristow TL .... .20   .10   .02
    260 Lonnie Shelton SD
    220 Paul Silas
- [ ] 170 238 Tom Boswell .... .20   .10   .02
    27 James McElroy
    85 Leon Douglas
- [ ] 171 241 Ben Poquette .... 1.00   .50   .10
    176 Maurice Cheeks TL
    87 Greg Kelser
- [ ] 172 245 Greg Ballard .... .60   .30   .06
    4 Walter Davis AS
    33 Nate Archibald

☐	173	246 Bob Dandridge	.20	.10	.02
		19 John Drew TL			
		209 Larry Kenon			
☐	174	250 Kevin Porter	.20	.10	.02
		20 Dan Roundfield TL			
		211 Kevin Restani			
☐	175	251 Wes Unseld	.50	.25	.05
		67 Geoff Huston			
		5 John Drew AS			
☐	176	257 Elvin Hayes SD	5.00	2.50	.50
		181 Julius Erving			
		258 Ron Brewer SD			

1981-82 Topps

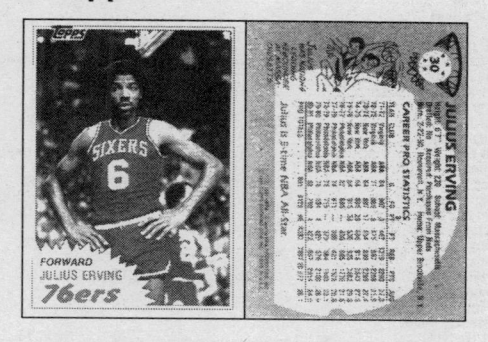

The 1981-82 Topps basketball card set contains a total of 198 cards. The cards in the set measure the standard 2 1/2" by 3 1/2". These cards, however, are numbered depending upon the regional distribution used in the issue. A 66-card national set was issued to all parts of the country; however, subsets of 44 cards each were issued in the east, mid-west, and west. Card numbers over 66 are prefaced on the card by the region in which they were distributed, e.g., East 96. The cards themselves feature the Topps logo in the frame line and a quarter-round sunburst in the lower left-hand corner which lists the name, position, and team of the player depicted. Cards 44-66 are Team Leader (TL) cards picturing each team's statistical leaders. The back, printed in orange and brown on gray stock, features standard Topps biographical data and career statistics. There are a number of Super Action (SA) cards in the set. Rookie Cards included in this set are Joe Barry Carroll, Mike Dunleavy, Mike Gminski, Darrell Griffith, Vinnie Johnson, Bill Laimbeer, Rick Mahorn, Kevin McHale, and Larry Smith. The card numbering sequence is alphabetical within team within series.

	MINT	EXC	G-VG
COMPLETE SET (198)	110.00	55.00	11.00
COMMON CARD (1-43)	.10	.05	.01

328 / 1981-82 Topps

COMMON CARD (44-66)	.15	.07	.01
COMMON CARD (67-110)	.15	.07	.01
☐ 1 John Drew Atlanta Hawks	.20	.10	.02
☐ 2 Dan Roundfield Atlanta Hawks	.10	.05	.01
☐ 3 Nate Archibald Boston Celtics	.75	.35	.07
☐ 4 Larry Bird Boston Celtics	30.00	15.00	3.00
☐ 5 Cedric Maxwell Boston Celtics	.20	.10	.02
☐ 6 Robert Parish Boston Celtics	3.00	1.50	.30
☐ 7 Artis Gilmore Chicago Bulls	.75	.35	.07
☐ 8 Ricky Sobers Chicago Bulls	.10	.05	.01
☐ 9 Mike Mitchell Cleveland Cavaliers	.10	.05	.01
☐ 10 Tom LaGarde Dallas Mavericks	.10	.05	.01
☐ 11 Dan Issel Denver Nuggets	.75	.35	.07
☐ 12 David Thompson Denver Nuggets	.50	.25	.05
☐ 13 Lloyd Free Golden State Warriors	.20	.10	.02
☐ 14 Moses Malone Houston Rockets	2.75	1.35	.27
☐ 15 Calvin Murphy Houston Rockets	.30	.15	.03
☐ 16 Johnny Davis Indiana Pacers	.10	.05	.01
☐ 17 Otis Birdsong Milwaukee Bucks	.10	.05	.01
☐ 18 Phil Ford Kansas City Kings	.25	.12	.02
☐ 19 Scott Wedman Cleveland Cavaliers	.20	.10	.02
☐ 20 Kareem Abdul-Jabbar Los Angeles Lakers	7.00	3.50	.70
☐ 21 Magic Johnson Los Angeles Lakers	45.00	22.50	4.50
☐ 22 Norm Nixon Los Angeles Lakers	.25	.12	.02
☐ 23 Jamaal Wilkes Los Angeles Lakers	.25	.12	.02
☐ 24 Marques Johnson Milwaukee Bucks	.25	.12	.02
☐ 25 Bob Lanier Milwaukee Bucks	.75	.35	.07
☐ 26 Bill Cartwright New York Knicks	1.00	.50	.10
☐ 27 M.R. Richardson New York Knicks	.20	.10	.02

1981-82 Topps / 329

☐ 28	Ray Williams .... .10 New York Knicks	.05	.01
☐ 29	Darryl Dawkins .... .40 Philadelphia 76ers	.20	.04
☐ 30	Julius Erving .... 7.00 Philadelphia 76ers	3.50	.70
☐ 31	Lionel Hollins .... .10 Philadelphia 76ers	.05	.01
☐ 32	Bobby Jones .... .20 Philadelphia 76ers	.10	.02
☐ 33	Walter Davis .... .30 Phoenix Suns	.15	.03
☐ 34	Dennis Johnson .... .60 Phoenix Suns	.30	.06
☐ 35	Leonard Robinson .... .10 Phoenix Suns	.05	.01
☐ 36	Mychal Thompson .... .35 Portland Trail Blazers	.17	.03
☐ 37	George Gervin .... 1.00 San Antonio Spurs	.50	.10
☐ 38	Swen Nater .... .10 San Diego Clippers	.05	.01
☐ 39	Jack Sikma .... .40 Seattle Supersonics	.20	.04
☐ 40	Adrian Dantley .... .75 Utah Jazz	.35	.07
☐ 41	Darrell Griffith .... 1.50 Utah Jazz	.75	.15
☐ 42	Elvin Hayes .... 1.25 Houston Rockets	.60	.12
☐ 43	Fred Brown .... .25 Seattle Supersonics	.12	.02
☐ 44	Atlanta Hawks TL .... .15 John Drew Dan Roundfield Eddie Johnson	.07	.01
☐ 45	Boston Celtics TL .... 1.50 Larry Bird Larry Bird Nate Archibald	.75	.15
☐ 46	Chicago Bulls TL .... .20 Reggie Theus Artis Gilmore Reggie Theus	.10	.02
☐ 47	Cleveland Cavs TL .... .15 Mike Mitchell Kenny Carr Mike Bratz	.07	.01
☐ 48	Dallas Mavericks TL .... .15 Jim Spanarkel Tom LaGarde Brad Davis	.07	.01
☐ 49	Denver Nuggets TL .... .25 David Thompson Dan Issel Kenny Higgs	.12	.02
☐ 50	Detroit Pistons TL .... .15	.07	.01

330 / 1981-82 Topps

	John Long			
	Phil Hubbard			
	Ron Lee			
☐ 51	Golden State TL	.15	.07	.01
	Lloyd Free			
	Larry Smith			
	John Lucas			
☐ 52	Houston Rockets TL	.45	.22	.04
	Moses Malone			
	Moses Malone			
	Allen Leavell			
☐ 53	Indiana Pacers TL	.15	.07	.01
	Billy Knight			
	James Edwards			
	Johnny Davis			
☐ 54	Kansas City Kings TL	.15	.07	.01
	Otis Birdsong			
	Reggie King			
	Phil Ford			
☐ 55	Los Angeles Lakers TL	1.25	.60	.12
	Kareem Abdul-Jabbar			
	Kareem Abdul-Jabbar			
	Norm Nixon			
☐ 56	Milwaukee Bucks TL	.20	.10	.02
	Marques Johnson			
	Mickey Johnson			
	Quinn Buckner			
☐ 57	New Jersey Nets TL	.15	.07	.01
	Mike Newlin			
	Maurice Lucas			
	Mike Newlin			
☐ 58	New York Knicks TL	.20	.10	.02
	Bill Cartwright			
	Bill Cartwright			
	M.R. Richardson			
☐ 59	Philadelphia 76ers TL	1.25	.60	.12
	Julius Erving			
	Caldwell Jones			
	Maurice Cheeks			
☐ 60	Phoenix Suns TL	.20	.10	.02
	Truck Robinson			
	Truck Robinson			
	Alvan Adams			
☐ 61	Portland Blazers TL	.25	.12	.02
	Jim Paxson			
	Mychal Thompson			
	Kermit Washington			
	Kelvin Ransey			
☐ 62	San Antonio Spurs TL	.25	.12	.02
	George Gervin			
	Dave Corzine			
	Johnny Moore			
☐ 63	San Diego Clippers TL	.15	.07	.01
	Freeman Williams			
	Swen Nater			
	Brian Taylor			
☐ 64	Seattle Sonics TL	.25	.12	.02

1981-82 Topps / 331

    Jack Sikma
    Jack Sikma
    Vinnie Johnson
☐ 65 Utah Jazz TL .... .25   .12   .02
    Adrian Dantley
    Ben Poquette
    Allan Bristow
☐ 66 Washington Bullets TL .... .30   .15   .03
    Elvin Hayes
    Elvin Hayes
    Kevin Porter
☐ E67 Charlie Criss .... .15   .07   .01
    Atlanta Hawks
☐ E68 Eddie Johnson .... .15   .07   .01
    Atlanta Hawks
☐ E69 Wes Matthews .... .15   .07   .01
    Atlanta Hawks
☐ E70 Tom McMillen .... .50   .25   .05
    Atlanta Hawks
☐ E71 Tree Rollins .... .25   .12   .02
    Atlanta Hawks
☐ E72 M.L. Carr .... .25   .12   .02
    Boston Celtics
☐ E73 Chris Ford .... .40   .20   .04
    Boston Celtics
☐ E74 Gerald Henderson .... .50   .25   .05
    Boston Celtics
☐ E75 Kevin McHale 14.00   7.00   1.40
    Boston Celtics
☐ E76 Rick Robey .... .15   .07   .01
    Boston Celtics
☐ E77 Darwin Cook .... .30   .15   .03
    Milwaukee Bucks
☐ E78 Mike Gminski .... 1.00   .50   .10
    Milwaukee Bucks
☐ E79 Maurice Lucas .... .25   .12   .02
    Milwaukee Bucks
☐ E80 Mike Newlin .... .15   .07   .01
    New York Knicks
☐ E81 Mike O'Koren .... .35   .17   .03
    Milwaukee Bucks
☐ E82 Steve Hawes .... .15   .07   .01
    Atlanta Hawks
☐ E83 Foots Walker .... .15   .07   .01
    Milwaukee Bucks
☐ E84 Campy Russell .... .15   .07   .01
    New York Knicks
☐ E85 DeWayne Scales .... .15   .07   .01
    New York Knicks
☐ E86 Randy Smith .... .15   .07   .01
    New York Knicks
☐ E87 Marvin Webster .... .15   .07   .01
    New York Knicks
☐ E88 Sly Williams .... .15   .07   .01
    New York Knicks
☐ E89 Mike Woodson .... .40   .20   .04
    Milwaukee Bucks

332 / 1981-82 Topps

☐ E90 Maurice Cheeks	2.00	1.00	.20
Philadelphia 76ers			
☐ E91 Caldwell Jones	.25	.12	.02
Philadelphia 76ers			
☐ E92 Steve Mix	.15	.07	.01
Philadelphia 76ers			
☐ E93A Checklist 1-110 ERR	2.00	.20	.04
(WEST above card number)			
☐ E93B Checklist 1-110 COR	1.00	.10	.02
☐ E94 Greg Ballard	.15	.07	.01
Washington Bullets			
☐ E95 Don Collins	.15	.07	.01
Washington Bullets			
☐ E96 Kevin Grevey	.15	.07	.01
Washington Bullets			
☐ E97 Mitch Kupchak	.15	.07	.01
Washington Bullets			
☐ E98 Rick Mahorn	1.00	.50	.10
Washington Bullets			
☐ E99 Kevin Porter	.15	.07	.01
Washington Bullets			
☐ E100 Nate Archibald SA	.40	.20	.04
Boston Celtics			
☐ E101 Larry Bird SA	9.00	4.50	.90
Boston Celtics			
☐ E102 Bill Cartwright SA	.40	.20	.04
New York Knicks			
☐ E103 Darryl Dawkins SA	.25	.12	.02
Philadelphia 76ers			
☐ E104 Julius Erving SA	4.00	2.00	.40
Philadelphia 76ers			
☐ E105 Kevin Porter SA	.15	.07	.01
Washington Bullets			
☐ E106 Bobby Jones SA	.25	.12	.02
Philadelphia 76ers			
☐ E107 Cedric Maxwell SA	.25	.12	.02
Boston Celtics			
☐ E108 Robert Parish SA	1.50	.75	.15
Boston Celtics			
☐ E109 M.R.Richardson SA	.25	.12	.02
New York Knicks			
☐ E110 Dan Roundfield SA	.25	.12	.02
Atlanta Hawks			
☐ MW67 David Greenwood	.25	.12	.02
Chicago Bulls			
☐ MW68 Dwight Jones	.15	.07	.01
Chicago Bulls			
☐ MW69 Reggie Theus	.25	.12	.02
Chicago Bulls			
☐ MW70 Bobby Wilkerson	.15	.07	.01
Cleveland Cavaliers			
☐ MW71 Mike Bratz	.15	.07	.01
Cleveland Cavaliers			
☐ MW72 Kenny Carr	.15	.07	.01
Cleveland Cavaliers			
☐ MW73 Geoff Huston	.15	.07	.01
Cleveland Cavaliers			

1981-82 Topps / 333

☐ MW74 Bill Laimbeer 6.00	3.00	.60
Cleveland Cavaliers		
☐ MW75 Roger Phegley .... .15	.07	.01
Cleveland Cavaliers		
☐ MW76 Checklist 1-110 .... 1.00	.10	.02
☐ MW77 Abdul Jeelani .... .15	.07	.01
Dallas Mavericks		
☐ MW78 Bill Robinzine .... .15	.07	.01
Dallas Mavericks		
☐ MW79 Jim Spanarkel .... .15	.07	.01
Dallas Mavericks		
☐ MW80 Kent Benson .... .25	.12	.02
Detroit Pistons		
☐ MW81 Keith Herron .... .15	.07	.01
Detroit Pistons		
☐ MW82 Phil Hubbard .... .25	.12	.02
Detroit Pistons		
☐ MW83 John Long .... .15	.07	.01
Detroit Pistons		
☐ MW84 Terry Tyler .... .15	.07	.01
Detroit Pistons		
☐ MW85 Mike Dunleavy 2.50	1.25	.25
Houston Rockets		
☐ MW86 Tom Henderson .... .15	.07	.01
Houston Rockets		
☐ MW87 Billy Paultz .... .15	.07	.01
Houston Rockets		
☐ MW88 Robert Reid .... .15	.07	.01
Houston Rockets		
☐ MW89 Mike Bantom .... .15	.07	.01
Indiana Pacers		
☐ MW90 James Edwards .... .35	.17	.03
Cleveland Cavaliers		
☐ MW91 Billy Knight .... .15	.07	.01
Indiana Pacers		
☐ MW92 George McGinnis .... .30	.15	.03
Indiana Pacers		
☐ MW93 Louis Orr .... .15	.07	.01
Indiana Pacers		
☐ MW94 Ernie Grunfeld .... .60	.30	.06
Kansas City Kings		
☐ MW95 Reggie King .... .15	.07	.01
Kansas City Kings		
☐ MW96 Sam Lacey .... .15	.07	.01
Kansas City Kings		
☐ MW97 Junior Bridgeman .... .25	.12	.02
Milwaukee Bucks		
☐ MW98 Mickey Johnson .... .15	.07	.01
Milwaukee Bucks		
☐ MW99 Sidney Moncrief 1.50	.75	.15
Milwaukee Bucks		
☐ MW100 Brian Winters .... .15	.07	.01
Milwaukee Bucks		
☐ MW101 Dave Corzine .... .35	.17	.03
San Antonio Spurs		
☐ MW102 Paul Griffin .... .15	.07	.01
San Antonio Spurs		

334 / 1981-82 Topps

☐ MW103 Johnny Moore San Antonio Spurs	.30	.15	.03
☐ MW104 Mark Olberding San Antonio Spurs	.15	.07	.01
☐ MW105 James Silas Cleveland Cavaliers	.15	.07	.01
☐ MW106 George Gervin SA San Antonio Spurs	.50	.25	.05
☐ MW107 Artis Gilmore SA Chicago Bulls	.30	.15	.03
☐ MW108 Marq.Johnson SA Milwaukee Bucks	.20	.10	.02
☐ MW109 Bob Lanier SA Milwaukee Bucks	.35	.17	.03
☐ MW110 Moses Malone SA Houston Rockets	1.50	.75	.15
☐ W67 T.R. Dunn Denver Nuggets	.30	.15	.03
☐ W68 Alex English Denver Nuggets	1.75	.85	.17
☐ W69 Billy McKinney Denver Nuggets	.30	.15	.03
☐ W70 Dave Robisch Denver Nuggets	.15	.07	.01
☐ W71 Joe Barry Carroll Golden State Warriors	.60	.30	.06
☐ W72 Bernard King Golden State Warriors	1.50	.75	.15
☐ W73 Sonny Parker Golden State Warriors	.15	.07	.01
☐ W74 Purvis Short Golden State Warriors	.25	.12	.02
☐ W75 Larry Smith Golden State Warriors	.75	.35	.07
☐ W76 Jim Chones Los Angeles Lakers	.15	.07	.01
☐ W77 Michael Cooper Los Angeles Lakers	1.00	.50	.10
☐ W78 Mark Landsberger Los Angeles Lakers	.15	.07	.01
☐ W79 Alvan Adams Phoenix Suns	.25	.12	.02
☐ W80 Jeff Cook Phoenix Suns	.25	.12	.02
☐ W81 Rich Kelley Phoenix Suns	.15	.07	.01
☐ W82 Kyle Macy Phoenix Suns	.35	.17	.03
☐ W83 Billy Ray Bates Portland Trail Blazers	.35	.17	.03
☐ W84 Bob Gross Portland Trail Blazers	.15	.07	.01
☐ W85 Calvin Natt Portland Trail Blazers	.25	.12	.02
☐ W86 Lonnie Shelton Seattle Supersonics	.15	.07	.01
☐ W87 Jim Paxson	.75	.35	.07

	Portland Trail Blazers		
☐ W88 Kelvin Ransey .... .15	.07	.01
	Portland Trail Blazers		
☐ W89 Kermit Washington .... .15	.07	.01
	Portland Trail Blazers		
☐ W90 Henry Bibby .... .15	.07	.01
	San Diego Clippers		
☐ W91 Michael Brooks .... .25	.12	.02
	San Diego Clippers		
☐ W92 Joe Bryant .... .15	.07	.01
	San Diego Clippers		
☐ W93 Phil Smith .... .15	.07	.01
	San Diego Clippers		
☐ W94 Brian Taylor .... .15	.07	.01
	San Diego Clippers		
☐ W95 Freeman Williams .... .25	.12	.02
	San Diego Clippers		
☐ W96 James Bailey .... .15	.07	.01
	Seattle Supersonics		
☐ W97 Checklist 1-110 .... 1.00	.10	.02
☐ W98 John Johnson .... .15	.07	.01
	Seattle Supersonics		
☐ W99 Vinnie Johnson 2.50	1.25	.25
	Seattle Supersonics		
☐ W100 Wally Walker .... .30	.15	.03
	Seattle Supersonics		
☐ W101 Paul Westphal .... .30	.15	.03
	Seattle Supersonics		
☐ W102 Allan Bristow .... .25	.12	.02
	Utah Jazz		
☐ W103 Wayne Cooper .... .25	.12	.02
	Utah Jazz		
☐ W104 Carl Nicks .... .25	.12	.02
	Utah Jazz		
☐ W105 Ben Poquette .... .15	.07	.01
	Utah Jazz		
☐ W106 Kareem Abdul-Jabbar SA 4.00	2.00	.40
	Los Angeles Lakers		
☐ W107 Dan Issel SA .... .40	.20	.04
	Denver Nuggets		
☐ W108 Dennis Johnson SA .... .40	.20	.04
	Phoenix Suns		
☐ W109 Magic Johnson SA 15.00	7.50	1.50
	Los Angeles Lakers		
☐ W110 Jack Sikma SA .... .35	.17	03
	Seattle Supersonics		

1991-92 Upper Deck

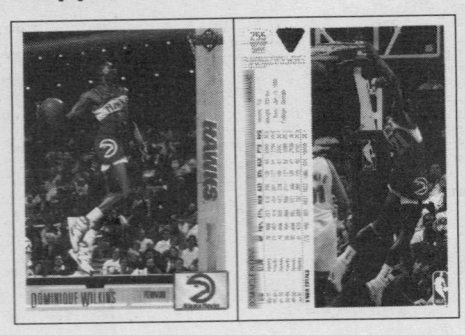

The 1991-92 Upper Deck low series basketball set contains 400 cards, measuring the standard size (2 1/2" by 3 1/2"). Six NBA Award Winner holograms were randomly inserted in high series foil packs. The fronts feature glossy color player photos, bordered below and on the right by a hardwood basketball floor design. The player's name appears beneath the picture, while the team name is printed vertically alongside the picture. The backs display a second color player photo as well as biographical and statistical information. Special subsets featured include Draft Choices (1-21), Classic Confrontations (30-34), All-Rookie Team (35-39), All-Stars (49-72), and Team Checklists (73-99). The key rookie cards in this series are Stacey Augmon, Larry Johnson, Dikembe Mutombo, Steve Smith, and John Starks.

	MINT	EXC	G-VG
COMPLETE SET (400)	23.00	10.00	2.00
COMMON PLAYER (1-400)	.03	.01	.00
☐ 1 Draft Checklist (Stacey Augmon and Rodney Monroe)	.30	.15	.03
☐ 2 Larry Johnson	9.00	4.50	.90
☐ 3 Dikembe Mutombo	5.00	2.50	.50
☐ 4 Steve Smith	2.00	1.00	.20
☐ 5 Stacey Augmon	1.75	.85	.17
☐ 6 Terrell Brandon	.75	.35	.07
☐ 7 Greg Anthony	.75	.35	.07
☐ 8 Rich King	.15	.07	.01
☐ 9 Chris Gatling	.40	.20	.04
☐ 10 Victor Alexander	.30	.15	.03
☐ 11 John Turner	.15	.07	.01
☐ 12 Eric Murdock	.35	.17	.03
☐ 13 Mark Randall	.15	.07	.01
☐ 14 Rodney Monroe	.30	.15	.03
☐ 15 Myron Brown	.10	.05	.01
☐ 16 Mike Iuzzolino	.30	.15	.03

1991-92 Upper Deck / 337

☐	17	Chris Corchiani	.20	.10	.02
☐	18	Elliot Perry	.15	.07	.01
☐	19	Jimmy Oliver	.12	.06	.01
☐	20	Doug Overton	.10	.05	.01
☐	21	Steve Hood UER	.10	.05	.01
		(Card has NBA record, but he's a rookie)			
☐	22	Michael Jordan	.50	.25	.05
		Stay In School			
☐	23	Kevin Johnson	.10	.05	.01
		Stay In School			
☐	24	Kurk Lee	.10	.05	.01
☐	25	Sean Higgins	.15	.07	.01
☐	26	Morlon Wiley	.03	.01	.00
☐	27	Derek Smith	.03	.01	.00
☐	28	Kenny Payne	.03	.01	.00
☐	29	Magic Johnson	1.00	.50	.10
		Assist Record			
☐	30	Larry Bird CC	.20	.10	.02
		and Chuck Person			
☐	31	Karl Malone CC	.20	.10	.02
		and Charles Barkley			
☐	32	Kevin Johnson CC	.20	.10	.02
		and John Stockton			
☐	33	Hakeem Olajuwon CC	.20	.10	.02
		and Patrick Ewing			
☐	34	Magic Johnson CC	1.00	.50	.10
		and Michael Jordan			
☐	35	Derrick Coleman ART	.25	.12	.02
☐	36	Lionel Simmons ART	.15	.07	.01
☐	37	Dee Brown ART	.20	.10	.02
☐	38	Dennis Scott ART	.20	.10	.02
☐	39	Kendall Gill ART	.10	.05	.01
☐	40	Winston Garland	.40	.20	.04
☐	41	Danny Young	.03	.01	.00
☐	42	Rick Mahorn	.03	.01	.00
☐	43	Michael Adams	.06	.03	.00
☐	44	Michael Jordan	1.50	.75	.15
☐	45	Magic Johnson	1.00	.50	.10
☐	46	Doc Rivers	.06	.03	.00
☐	47	Moses Malone	.12	.06	.01
☐	48	Michael Jordan	.60	.30	.06
		All-Star Checklist			
☐	49	James Worthy AS	.08	.04	.01
☐	50	Tim Hardaway AS	.40	.20	.04
☐	51	Karl Malone AS	.12	.06	.01
☐	52	John Stockton AS	.12	.06	.01
☐	53	Clyde Drexler AS	.15	.07	.01
☐	54	Terry Porter AS	.08	.04	.01
☐	55	Kevin Duckworth AS	.03	.01	.00
☐	56	Tom Chambers AS	.06	.03	.00
☐	57	Magic Johnson AS	.50	.25	.05
☐	58	David Robinson AS	.50	.25	.05
☐	59	Kevin Johnson AS	.12	.06	.01
☐	60	Chris Mullin AS	.10	.05	.01
☐	61	Joe Dumars AS	.08	.04	.01
☐	62	Kevin McHale AS	.08	.04	.01

338 / 1991-92 Upper Deck

☐ 63	Brad Daugherty AS	.10	.05	.01
☐ 64	Alvin Robertson AS	.06	.03	.00
☐ 65	Bernard King AS	.06	.03	.00
☐ 66	Dominique Wilkins AS	.10	.05	.01
☐ 67	Ricky Pierce AS	.06	.03	.00
☐ 68	Patrick Ewing AS	.12	.06	.01
☐ 69	Michael Jordan AS	.75	.35	.07
☐ 70	Charles Barkley AS	.12	.06	.01
☐ 71	Hersey Hawkins AS	.06	.03	.00
☐ 72	Robert Parish AS	.08	.04	.01
☐ 73	Alvin Robertson TC	.06	.03	.00
☐ 74	Bernard King TC	.06	.03	.00
☐ 75	Michael Jordan TC	.50	.25	.05
☐ 76	Brad Daugherty TC	.08	.04	.01
☐ 77	Larry Bird TC	.20	.10	.02
☐ 78	Ron Harper TC	.06	.03	.00
☐ 79	Dominique Wilkins TC	.10	.05	.01
☐ 80	Rony Seikaly TC	.06	.03	.00
☐ 81	Rex Chapman TC	.06	.03	.00
☐ 82	Mark Eaton TC	.03	.01	.00
☐ 83	Lionel Simmons TC	.12	.06	.01
☐ 84	Gerald Wilkins TC	.06	.03	.00
☐ 85	James Worthy TC	.08	.04	.01
☐ 86	Scott Skiles TC	.03	.01	.00
☐ 87	Rolando Blackman TC	.06	.03	.00
☐ 88	Derrick Coleman TC	.20	.10	.02
☐ 89	Chris Jackson TC	.06	.03	.00
☐ 90	Reggie Miller TC	.08	.04	.01
☐ 91	Isiah Thomas TC	.10	.05	.01
☐ 92	Hakeem Olajuwon TC	.12	.06	.01
☐ 93	Hersey Hawkins TC	.06	.03	.00
☐ 94	David Robinson TC	.30	.15	.03
☐ 95	Tom Chambers TC	.06	.03	.00
☐ 96	Shawn Kemp TC	.30	.15	.03
☐ 97	Pooh Richardson TC	.08	.04	.01
☐ 98	Clyde Drexler TC	.15	.07	.01
☐ 99	Chris Mullin TC	.12	.06	.01
☐ 100	Checklist 1-100	.06	.01	.00
☐ 101	John Shasky	.03	.01	.00
☐ 102	Dana Barros	.03	.01	.00
☐ 103	Stojko Vrankovic	.15	.07	.01
☐ 104	Larry Drew	.03	.01	.00
☐ 105	Randy White	.03	.01	.00
☐ 106	Dave Corzine	.03	.01	.00
☐ 107	Joe Kleine	.03	.01	.00
☐ 108	Lance Blanks	.06	.03	.00
☐ 109	Rodney McCray	.03	.01	.00
☐ 110	Sedale Threatt	.06	.03	.00
☐ 111	Ken Norman	.06	.03	.00
☐ 112	Rickey Green	.03	.01	.00
☐ 113	Andy Toolson	.10	.05	.01
☐ 114	Bo Kimble	.06	.03	.00
☐ 115	Mark West	.03	.01	.00
☐ 116	Mark Eaton	.03	.01	.00
☐ 117	John Paxson	.06	.03	.00
☐ 118	Mike Brown	.03	.01	.00
☐ 119	Brian Oliver	.06	.03	.00

1991-92 Upper Deck / 339

☐ 120	Will Perdue	.03	.01	.00
☐ 121	Michael Smith	.03	.01	.00
☐ 122	Sherman Douglas	.06	.03	.00
☐ 123	Reggie Lewis	.20	.10	.02
☐ 124	James Donaldson	.03	.01	.00
☐ 125	Scottie Pippen	.50	.25	.05
☐ 126	Elden Campbell	.15	.07	.01
☐ 127	Michael Cage	.03	.01	.00
☐ 128	Tony Smith	.06	.03	.00
☐ 129	Ed Pinckney	.03	.01	.00
☐ 130	Keith Askins	.03	.01	.00
☐ 131	Darrell Griffith	.10	.05	.01
☐ 132	Vinnie Johnson	.03	.01	.00
☐ 133	Ron Harper	.06	.03	.00
☐ 134	Andre Turner	.06	.03	.00
☐ 135	Jeff Hornacek	.10	.05	.01
☐ 136	John Stockton	.12	.06	.01
☐ 137	Derek Harper	.25	.12	.02
☐ 138	Loy Vaught	.06	.03	.00
☐ 139	Thurl Bailey	.12	.06	.01
☐ 140	Olden Polynice	.03	.01	.00
☐ 141	Kevin Edwards	.03	.01	.00
☐ 142	Byron Scott	.03	.01	.00
☐ 143	Dee Brown	.06	.03	.00
☐ 144	Sam Perkins	.40	.20	.04
☐ 145	Rony Seikaly	.08	.04	.01
☐ 146	James Worthy	.12	.06	.01
☐ 147	Glen Rice	.12	.06	.01
☐ 148	Craig Hodges	.50	.25	.05
☐ 149	Bimbo Coles	.03	.01	.00
☐ 150	Mychal Thompson	.12	.06	.01
☐ 151	Xavier McDaniel	.03	.01	.00
☐ 152	Roy Tarpley	.08	.04	.01
☐ 153	Gary Payton	.06	.03	.00
☐ 154	Rolando Blackman	.20	.10	.02
☐ 155	Hersey Hawkins	.06	.03	.00
☐ 156	Ricky Pierce	.12	.06	.01
☐ 157	Fat Lever	.06	.03	.00
☐ 158	Andrew Lang	.06	.03	.00
☐ 159	Benoit Benjamin	.12	.06	.01
☐ 160	Cedric Ceballos	.03	.01	.00
☐ 161	Charles Smith	.20	.10	.02
☐ 162	Jeff Martin	.10	.05	.01
☐ 163	Robert Parish	.03	.01	.00
☐ 164	Danny Manning	.12	.06	.01
☐ 165	Mark Aguirre	.15	.07	.01
☐ 166	Jeff Malone	.06	.03	.00
☐ 167	Bill Laimbeer	.08	.04	.01
☐ 168	Willie Burton	.06	.03	.00
☐ 169	Dennis Hopson	.12	.06	.01
☐ 170	Kevin Gamble	.06	.03	.00
☐ 171	Terry Teagle	.06	.03	.00
☐ 172	Dan Majerle	.03	.01	.00
☐ 173	Shawn Kemp	.12	.06	.01
☐ 174	Tom Chambers	1.00	.50	.10
☐ 175	Vlade Divac	.08	.04	.01
☐ 176	Johnny Dawkins	.12	.06	.01
		.03	.01	.00

340 / 1991-92 Upper Deck

☐ 177 A.C. Green	.06	.03	.00
☐ 178 Manute Bol	.03	.01	.00
☐ 179 Terry Davis	.06	.03	.00
☐ 180 Ron Anderson	.03	.01	.00
☐ 181 Horace Grant	.15	.07	.01
☐ 182 Stacey King	.06	.03	.00
☐ 183 William Bedford	.03	.01	.00
☐ 184 B.J. Armstrong	.20	.10	.02
☐ 185 Dennis Rodman	.15	.07	.01
☐ 186 Nate McMillan	.03	.01	.00
☐ 187 Cliff Levingston	.03	.01	.00
☐ 188 Quintin Dailey	.03	.01	.00
☐ 189 Bill Cartwright	.06	.03	.00
☐ 190 John Salley	.06	.03	.00
☐ 191 Jayson Williams	.06	.03	.00
☐ 192 Grant Long	.03	.01	.00
☐ 193 Negele Knight	.10	.05	.01
☐ 194 Alec Kessler	.03	.01	.00
☐ 195 Gary Grant	.03	.01	.00
☐ 196 Billy Thompson	.03	.01	.00
☐ 197 Delaney Rudd	.03	.01	.00
☐ 198 Alan Ogg	.10	.05	.01
☐ 199 Blue Edwards	.03	.01	.00
☐ 200 Checklist 101-200	.06	.01	.00
☐ 201 Mark Acres	.03	.01	.00
☐ 202 Craig Ehlo	.06	.03	.00
☐ 203 Anthony Cook	.03	.01	.00
☐ 204 Eric Leckner	.03	.01	.00
☐ 205 Terry Catledge	.03	.01	.00
☐ 206 Reggie Williams	.06	.03	.00
☐ 207 Greg Kite	.03	.01	.00
☐ 208 Steve Kerr	.03	.01	.00
☐ 209 Kenny Battle	.03	.01	.00
☐ 210 John Morton	.03	.01	.00
☐ 211 Kenny Williams	.03	.01	.00
☐ 212 Mark Jackson	.06	.03	.00
☐ 213 Alaa Abdelnaby	.10	.05	.01
☐ 214 Rod Strickland	.06	.03	.00
☐ 215 Micheal Williams	.06	.03	.00
☐ 216 Kevin Duckworth	.03	.01	.00
☐ 217 David Wingate	.03	.01	.00
☐ 218 LaSalle Thompson	.03	.01	.00
☐ 219 John Starks	1.00	.50	.10
☐ 220 Cliff Robinson	.20	.10	.02
☐ 221 Jeff Grayer	.06	.03	.00
☐ 222 Marcus Liberty	.30	.15	.03
☐ 223 Larry Nance	.08	.04	.01
☐ 224 Michael Ansley	.06	.03	.00
☐ 225 Kevin McHale	.10	.05	.01
☐ 226 Scott Skiles	.06	.03	.00
☐ 227 Darnell Valentine	.03	.01	.00
☐ 228 Nick Anderson	.20	.10	.02
☐ 229 Brad Davis	.03	.01	.00
☐ 230 Gerald Paddio	.03	.01	.00
☐ 231 Sam Bowie	.06	.03	.00
☐ 232 Sam Vincent	.03	.01	.00
☐ 233 George McCloud	.03	.01	.00

1991-92 Upper Deck / 341

☐ 234 Gerald Wilkins	.06	.03	.00
☐ 235 Mookie Blaylock	.06	.03	.00
☐ 236 Jon Koncak	.03	.01	.00
☐ 237 Danny Ferry	.06	.03	.00
☐ 238 Vern Fleming	.03	.01	.00
☐ 239 Mark Price	.20	.10	.02
☐ 240 Sidney Moncrief	.06	.03	.00
☐ 241 Jay Humphries	.03	.01	.00
☐ 242 Muggsy Bogues	.03	.01	.00
☐ 243 Tim Hardaway	1.00	.50	.10
☐ 244 Alvin Robertson	.06	.03	.00
☐ 245 Chris Mullin	.25	.12	.02
☐ 246 Pooh Richardson	.20	.10	.02
☐ 247 Winston Bennett	.03	.01	.00
☐ 248 Kelvin Upshaw	.03	.01	.00
☐ 249 John Williams	.06	.03	.00
☐ 250 Steve Alford	.06	.03	.00
☐ 251 Spud Webb	.06	.03	.00
☐ 252 Sleepy Floyd	.03	.01	.00
☐ 253 Chuck Person	.06	.03	.00
☐ 254 Hakeem Olajuwon	.25	.12	.02
☐ 255 Dominique Wilkins	.20	.10	.02
☐ 256 Reggie Miller	.15	.07	.01
☐ 257 Dennis Scott	.20	.10	.02
☐ 258 Charles Oakley	.06	.03	.00
☐ 259 Sidney Green	.03	.01	.00
☐ 260 Detlef Schrempf	.06	.03	.00
☐ 261 Rod Higgins	.03	.01	.00
☐ 262 J.R. Reid	.06	.03	.00
☐ 263 Tyrone Hill	.10	.05	.01
☐ 264 Reggie Theus	.06	.03	.00
☐ 265 Mitch Richmond	.15	.07	.01
☐ 266 Dale Ellis	.06	.03	.00
☐ 267 Terry Cummings	.08	.04	.01
☐ 268 Johnny Newman	.06	.03	.00
☐ 269 Doug West	.10	.05	.01
☐ 270 Jim Petersen	.03	.01	.00
☐ 271 Otis Thorpe	.06	.03	.00
☐ 272 John Williams	.06	.03	.00
☐ 273 Kennard Winchester	.08	.04	.01
☐ 274 Duane Ferrell	.03	.01	.00
☐ 275 Vernon Maxwell	.06	.03	.00
☐ 276 Kenny Smith	.06	.03	.00
☐ 277 Jerome Kersey	.06	.03	.00
☐ 278 Kevin Willis	.10	.05	.01
☐ 279 Danny Ainge	.08	.04	.01
☐ 280 Larry Smith	.06	.03	.00
☐ 281 Maurice Cheeks	.03	.01	.00
☐ 282 Willie Anderson	.06	.03	.00
☐ 283 Tom Tolbert	.06	.03	.00
☐ 284 Jerrod Mustaf	.03	.01	.00
☐ 285 Randolph Keys	.08	.04	.01
☐ 286 Jerry Reynolds	.03	.01	.00
☐ 287 Sean Elliott	.03	.01	.00
☐ 288 Otis Smith	.20	.10	.02
☐ 289 Terry Mills	.03	.01	.00
☐ 290 Kelly Tripucka	.20	.10	.02
	.03	.01	.00

342 / 1991-92 Upper Deck

☐	291	Jon Sundvold	.03	.01	.00
☐	292	Rumeal Robinson	.06	.03	.00
☐	293	Fred Roberts	.03	.01	.00
☐	294	Rik Smits	.06	.03	.00
☐	295	Jerome Lane	.03	.01	.00
☐	296	Dave Jamerson	.06	.03	.00
☐	297	Joe Wolf	.03	.01	.00
☐	298	David Wood	.10	.05	.01
☐	299	Todd Lichti	.03	.01	.00
☐	300	Checklist 201-300	.06	.01	.00
☐	301	Randy Breuer	.03	.01	.00
☐	302	Buck Johnson	.03	.01	.00
☐	303	Scott Brooks	.03	.01	.00
☐	304	Jeff Turner	.03	.01	.00
☐	305	Felton Spencer	.08	.04	.01
☐	306	Greg Dreiling	.03	.01	.00
☐	307	Gerald Glass	.12	.06	.01
☐	308	Tony Brown	.03	.01	.00
☐	309	Sam Mitchell	.03	.01	.00
☐	310	Adrian Caldwell	.03	.01	.00
☐	311	Chris Dudley	.03	.01	.00
☐	312	Blair Rasmussen	.03	.01	.00
☐	313	Antoine Carr	.03	.01	.00
☐	314	Greg Anderson	.03	.01	.00
☐	315	Drazen Petrovic	.25	.12	.02
☐	316	Alton Lister	.03	.01	.00
☐	317	Jack Haley	.03	.01	.00
☐	318	Bobby Hansen	.12	.06	.01
☐	319	Chris Jackson	.03	.01	.00
☐	320	Herb Williams	.03	.01	.00
☐	321	Kendall Gill	1.00	.50	.10
☐	322	Tyrone Corbin	.03	.01	.00
☐	323	Kiki Vandeweghe	.06	.03	.00
☐	324	David Robinson	1.25	.60	.12
☐	325	Rex Chapman	.06	.03	.00
☐	326	Tony Campbell	.03	.01	.00
☐	327	Dell Curry	.03	.01	.00
☐	328	Charles Jones	.03	.03	.00
☐	329	Kenny Gattison	.06	.03	.00
☐	330	Haywoode Workman	.10	.05	.01
☐	331	Travis Mays	.06	.03	.00
☐	332	Derrick Coleman	.60	.30	.06
☐	333	Isiah Thomas	.15	.07	.01
☐	334	Jud Buechler	.03	.01	.00
☐	335	Joe Dumars	.12	.06	.01
☐	336	Tate George	.06	.03	.00
☐	337	Mike Sanders	.06	.03	.00
☐	338	James Edwards	.03	.01	.00
☐	339	Chris Morris	.06	.03	.00
☐	340	Scott Hastings	.03	.01	.00
☐	341	Trent Tucker	.03	.01	.00
☐	342	Harvey Grant	.15	.07	.01
☐	343	Patrick Ewing	.30	.15	.03
☐	344	Larry Bird	.40	.20	.04
☐	345	Charles Barkley	.25	.12	.02
☐	346	Brian Shaw	.06	.03	.00
☐	347	Kenny Walker	.03	.01	.00

1991-92 Upper Deck / 343

☐ 348 Danny Schayes	.03	.01	.00
☐ 349 Tom Hammonds	.03	.01	.00
☐ 350 Frank Brickowski	.03	.01	.00
☐ 351 Terry Porter	.15	.07	.01
☐ 352 Orlando Woolridge	.06	.03	.00
☐ 353 Buck Williams	.08	.04	.01
☐ 354 Sarunas Marciulionis	.20	.10	.02
☐ 355 Karl Malone	.25	.12	.02
☐ 356 Kevin Johnson	.25	.12	.02
☐ 357 Clyde Drexler	.30	.15	.03
☐ 358 Duane Causwell	.08	.04	.01
☐ 359 Paul Pressey	.03	.01	.00
☐ 360 Jim Les	.10	.05	.01
☐ 361 Derrick McKey	.06	.03	.00
☐ 362 Scott Williams	.40	.20	.04
☐ 363 Mark Alarie	.03	.01	.00
☐ 364 Brad Daugherty	.20	.10	.02
☐ 365 Bernard King	.06	.03	.00
☐ 366 Steve Henson	.03	.01	.00
☐ 367 Darrell Walker	.03	.01	.00
☐ 368 Larry Krystkowiak	.03	.01	.00
☐ 369 Henry James UER (Scored 20 points versus Pistons, not Jazz)	.10	.05	.01
☐ 370 Jack Sikma	.06	.03	.00
☐ 371 Eddie Johnson	.06	.03	.00
☐ 372 Wayman Tisdale	.06	.03	.00
☐ 373 Joe Barry Carroll	.03	.01	.00
☐ 374 David Greenwood	.03	.01	.00
☐ 375 Lionel Simmons	.25	.12	.02
☐ 376 Dwayne Schintzius	.06	.03	.00
☐ 377 Tod Murphy	.03	.01	.00
☐ 378 Wayne Cooper	.03	.01	.00
☐ 379 Anthony Bonner	.08	.04	.01
☐ 380 Walter Davis	.06	.03	.00
☐ 381 Lester Conner	.03	.01	.00
☐ 382 Ledell Eackles	.03	.01	.00
☐ 383 Brad Lohaus	.03	.01	.00
☐ 384 Derrick Gervin	.03	.01	.00
☐ 385 Pervis Ellison	.30	.15	.03
☐ 386 Tim McCormick	.03	.01	.00
☐ 387 A.J. English	.12	.06	.01
☐ 388 John Battle	.03	.01	.00
☐ 389 Roy Hinson	.03	.01	.00
☐ 390 Armon Gilliam	.03	.01	.00
☐ 391 Kurt Rambis	.06	.03	.00
☐ 392 Mark Bryant	.03	.01	.00
☐ 393 Chucky Brown	.03	.01	.00
☐ 394 Avery Johnson	.03	.01	.00
☐ 395 Rory Sparrow	.03	.01	.00
☐ 396 Mario Elie	.25	.12	.02
☐ 397 Ralph Sampson	.06	.03	.00
☐ 398 Mike Gminski	.03	.01	.00
☐ 399 Bill Wennington	.03	.01	.00
☐ 400 Checklist 301-400	.06	.01	.00

1991-92 Upper Deck Award Winner Holograms

These holograms feature NBA statistical leaders in nine different categories. The first six holograms were random inserts in 1991-92 Upper Deck low series foil and jumbo packs, while the last three were inserted in high series foil and jumbo packs. The standard-size (2 1/2" by 3 1/2") holograms have the player's name and award received in the lower right corner on the front. The back has a color player photo and a summary of the player's performance. The cards are numbered on the back with an AW prefix before the number.

	MINT	EXC	G-VG
COMPLETE SET (9)	10.00	5.00	1.00
COMMON PLAYER (1-9)	.40	.20	.04
☐ 1 Michael Jordan Scoring Leader	3.50	1.75	.35
☐ 2 Alvin Robertson Steals Leader	.40	.20	.04
☐ 3 John Stockton Assists Leader	1.00	.50	.10
☐ 4 Michael Jordan MVP	3.50	1.75	.35
☐ 5 Detlef Schrempf Sixth Man	.40	.20	.04
☐ 6 David Robinson Rebounds Leader	2.50	1.25	.25
☐ 7 Derrick Coleman Rookie-of-the-Year	1.50	.75	.15
☐ 8 Hakeem Olajuwon Blocked Shots Leader	1.00	.50	.10
☐ 9 Dennis Rodman Defensive POY	.75	.35	.07

1991-92 Upper Deck Rookie Standouts

The first 20 cards of this subset were randomly inserted (one per pack) in 1991-92 Upper Deck series one jumbo packs and locker series boxes, while the second 20 cards were offered in the same packaging in the second series. The fronts of the standard-size (2 1/2" by 3 1/2") cards feature color action player photos, bordered on the right and below by a hardwood basketball court and with the "91-92 Rookie Standouts" emblem in the lower right corner. The back features a second color player photo and player profile. The cards are numbered on the back with an R prefix on the card number.

	MINT	EXC	G-VG
COMPLETE SET (40)	35.00	17.50	3.50
COMMON PLAYER (1-20)	.35	.17	.03
COMMON PLAYER (21-40)	.35	.17	.03
☐ 1 Gary Payton Seattle Supersonics	1.00	.50	.10
☐ 2 Dennis Scott Orlando Magic	1.00	.50	.10
☐ 3 Kendall Gill Charlotte Hornets	5.00	2.50	.50
☐ 4 Felton Spencer Minnesota Timberwolves	.35	.17	.03
☐ 5 Bo Kimble Los Angeles Clippers	.35	.17	.03
☐ 6 Willie Burton Miami Heat	.50	.25	.05
☐ 7 Tyrone Hill Golden State Warriors	.50	.25	.05
☐ 8 Loy Vaught Los Angeles Clippers	.35	.17	.03
☐ 9 Travis Mays Sacramento Kings	.35	.17	.03

346 / 1991-92 Upper Deck Rookie Standouts

☐ 10	Derrick Coleman 3.00	1.50	.30
	New Jersey Nets		
☐ 11	Duane Causwell .... .35	.17	.03
	Sacramento Kings		
☐ 12	Dee Brown 1.75	.85	.17
	Boston Celtics		
☐ 13	Gerald Glass .... .50	.25	.05
	Minnesota Timberwolves		
☐ 14	Jayson Williams .... .35	.17	.03
	Philadelphia 76ers		
☐ 15	Elden Campbell .... .60	.30	.06
	Los Angeles Lakers		
☐ 16	Negele Knight .... .35	.17	.03
	Phoenix Suns		
☐ 17	Chris Jackson .... .60	.30	.06
	Denver Nuggets		
☐ 18	Danny Ferry .... .35	.17	.03
	Cleveland Cavaliers		
☐ 19	Tony Smith .... .35	.17	.03
	Los Angeles Lakers		
☐ 20	Cedric Ceballos .... .75	.35	.07
	Phoenix Suns		
☐ 21	Victor Alexander .... .35	.17	.03
	Golden State Warriors		
☐ 22	Terrell Brandon .... .75	.35	.07
	Cleveland Cavaliers		
☐ 23	Rick Fox 1.75	.85	.17
	Boston Celtics		
☐ 24	Stacey Augmon 1.75	.85	.17
	Atlanta Hawks		
☐ 25	Mark Macon .... .60	.30	.06
	Denver Nuggets		
☐ 26	Larry Johnson 9.00	4.50	.90
	Charlotte Hornets		
☐ 27	Paul Graham .... .35	.17	.03
	Atlanta Hawks		
☐ 28	Stanley Roberts UER 1.25	.60	.12
	Orlando Magic		
	(Not the Magic's 1st		
	pick in 1991)		
☐ 29	Dikembe Mutombo 5.00	2.50	.50
	Denver Nuggets		
☐ 30	Robert Pack .... .90	.45	.09
	Portland Trail Blazers		
☐ 31	Doug Smith .... .60	.30	.06
	Dallas Mavericks		
☐ 32	Steve Smith 2.00	1.00	.20
	Miami Heat		
☐ 33	Billy Owens 5.00	2.50	.50
	Golden State Warriors		
☐ 34	David Benoit .... .60	.30	.06
	Utah Jazz		
☐ 35	Brian Williams .... .60	.30	.06
	Orlando Magic		
☐ 36	Kenny Anderson 1.75	.85	.17
	New Jersey Nets		
☐ 37	Greg Anthony .... .75	.35	.07
	New York Knicks		

1991-92 Upper Deck Extended / 347

☐ 38 Dale Davis Indiana Pacers	.50	.25	.05
☐ 39 Larry Stewart Washington Bullets	.50	.25	.05
☐ 40 Mike Iuzzolino Dallas Mavericks	.50	.25	.05

1991-92 Upper Deck Extended

The 1991-92 Upper Deck high series consists of 100 standard-size (2 1/2" by 3 1/2") cards. Three NBA Award Winner holograms were randomly inserted in high series foil packs. Also inserted in the high series are cards of HOFer Jerry West, who is highlighted in a nine-card Basketball Heroes subset. West has signed 2,500 of the set's checklist cards. High series lockers contained seven 12-card packs of cards 1-500 and a special "Rookie Standouts" card. Both low and high series were offered in a 500-card factory set. The fronts feature glossy color player photos, bordered below and on the right by a hardwood basketball floor design. The player's name appears beneath the picture, while the team name is printed vertically alongside the picture. The backs display a second color player photo as well as biographical and statistical information. In addition to rookie and traded players, the high series includes the following topical subsets: Top Prospects (438-448), All-Star Skills (476-484), capturing players who participated in the slam dunk competition as well as the three-point shootout winner, Eastern All-Star Team (449, 451-462), and Western All-Star Team (450, 463-475). The cards are numbered on the back and checklisted below accordingly. The key rookie cards in this series are Kenny Anderson, Rick Fox, and Billy Owens.

	MINT	EXC	G-VG
COMPLETE SET (100)	13.00	6.50	1.30
COMMON PLAYER (401-500)	.03	.01	.00
☐ 401 David Wingate Washington Bullets	.03	.01	.00

348 / 1991-92 Upper Deck Extended

☐ 402 Moses Malone	.12	.06	.01
Milwaukee Bucks			
☐ 403 Darrell Walker	.03	.01	.00
Detroit Pistons			
☐ 404 Antoine Carr	.03	.01	.00
San Antonio Spurs			
☐ 405 Charles Shackleford	.03	.01	.00
Philadelphia 76ers			
☐ 406 Orlando Woolridge	.06	.03	.00
Detroit Pistons			
☐ 407 Robert Pack	.90	.45	.09
Portland Trail Blazers			
☐ 408 Bobby Hansen	.03	.01	.00
Chicago Bulls			
☐ 409 Dale Davis	.35	.17	.03
Indiana Pacers			
☐ 410 Vincent Askew	.15	.07	.01
Golden State Warriors			
☐ 411 Alexander Volkov	.06	.03	.00
Atlanta Hawks			
☐ 412 Dwayne Schintzius	.06	.03	.00
Sacramento Kings			
☐ 413 Tim Perry	.06	.03	.00
Phoenix Suns			
☐ 414 Tyrone Corbin	.03	.01	.00
Utah Jazz			
☐ 415 Pete Chilcutt	.15	.07	.01
Sacramento Kings			
☐ 416 James Edwards	.03	.01	.00
Los Angeles Clippers			
☐ 417 Jerrod Mustaf	.10	.05	.01
Phoenix Suns			
☐ 418 Thurl Bailey	.03	.01	.00
Minnesota Timberwolves			
☐ 419 Spud Webb	.06	.03	.00
Sacramento Kings			
☐ 420 Doc Rivers	.06	.03	.00
Los Angeles Clippers			
☐ 421 Sean Green	.12	.06	.01
Indiana Pacers			
☐ 422 Walter Davis	.06	.03	.00
Denver Nuggets			
☐ 423 Terry Davis	.06	.03	.00
Dallas Mavericks			
☐ 424 John Battle	.03	.01	.00
Cleveland Cavaliers			
☐ 425 Vinnie Johnson	.06	.03	.00
San Antonio Spurs			
☐ 426 Sherman Douglas	.06	.03	.00
Boston Celtics			
☐ 427 Kevin Brooks	.12	.06	.01
Denver Nuggets			
☐ 428 Greg Sutton	.10	.05	.01
San Antonio Spurs			
☐ 429 Rafael Addison	.15	.07	.01
New Jersey Nets			
☐ 430 Anthony Mason	.40	.20	.04

1991-92 Upper Deck Extended / 349

☐ 431 Paul Graham New York Knicks Atlanta Hawks	.35	.17	.03
☐ 432 Anthony Frederick Charlotte Hornets	.15	.07	.01
☐ 433 Dennis Hopson Sacramento Kings	.06	.03	.00
☐ 434 Rory Sparrow Los Angeles Lakers	.03	.01	.00
☐ 435 Michael Adams Washington Bullets	.08	.04	.01
☐ 436 Kevin Lynch Charlotte Hornets	.15	.07	.01
☐ 437 Randy Brown Sacramento Kings	.15	.07	.01
☐ 438 NBA Top Prospects Checklist (Larry Johnson and Billy Owens)	.75	.35	.07
☐ 439 Stacey Augmon TP Atlanta Hawks	.50	.25	.05
☐ 440 Larry Stewart TP Washington Bullets	.50	.25	.05
☐ 441 Terrell Brandon TP Cleveland Cavaliers	.25	.12	.02
☐ 442 Billy Owens TP Golden State Warriors	5.00	2.50	.50
☐ 443 Rick Fox TP Boston Celtics	1.75	.85	.17
☐ 444 Kenny Anderson TP New Jersey Nets	1.75	.85	.17
☐ 445 Larry Johnson TP Charlotte Hornets	3.50	1.75	.35
☐ 446 Dikembe Mutombo TP Denver Nuggets	1.25	.60	.12
☐ 447 Steve Smith TP Miami Heat	.60	.30	.06
☐ 448 Greg Anthony TP New York Knicks	.25	.12	.02
☐ 449 East All-Star Checklist	.12	.02	.00
☐ 450 West All-Star Checklist	.12	.02	.00
☐ 451 Isiah Thomas AS (Magic Johnson also shown)	.20	.10	.02
☐ 452 Michael Jordan AS	.75	.35	.07
☐ 453 Scottie Pippen AS	.30	.15	.03
☐ 454 Charles Barkley AS	.12	.06	.01
☐ 455 Patrick Ewing AS	.15	.07	.01
☐ 456 Michael Adams AS	.06	.03	.00
☐ 457 Dennis Rodman AS	.08	.04	.01
☐ 458 Reggie Lewis AS	.12	.06	.01
☐ 459 Joe Dumars AS	.08	.04	.01
☐ 460 Mark Price AS	.08	.04	.01
☐ 461 Brad Daugherty AS	.10	.05	.01
☐ 462 Kevin Willis AS	.06	.03	.00

350 / 1991-92 Upper Deck Extended

- ☐ 463 Clyde Drexler AS .... .15 .07 .01
- ☐ 464 Magic Johnson AS .... .60 .30 .06
- ☐ 465 Chris Mullin AS .... .10 .05 .01
- ☐ 466 Karl Malone AS .... .12 .06 .01
- ☐ 467 David Robinson AS .... .40 .20 .04
- ☐ 468 Tim Hardaway AS .... .40 .20 .04
- ☐ 469 Jeff Hornacek AS .... .08 .04 .01
- ☐ 470 John Stockton AS .... .12 .06 .01
- ☐ 471 Dikembe Mutombo AS UER ..... .50 .25 .05
  (Drafted in 1992,
  should be 1991)
- ☐ 472 Hakeem Olajuwon AS .... .10 .05 .01
- ☐ 473 James Worthy AS .... .08 .04 .01
- ☐ 474 Otis Thorpe AS .... .06 .03 .00
- ☐ 475 Dan Majerle AS .... .06 .03 .00
- ☐ 476 Cedric Ceballos CL .... .10 .05 .01
  All-Star Skills
- ☐ 477 Nick Anderson SD .... .10 .05 .01
  Orlando Magic
- ☐ 478 Stacey Augmon SD .... .25 .12 .02
  Atlanta Hawks
- ☐ 479 Cedric Ceballos SD .... .10 .05 .01
  Phoenix Suns
- ☐ 480 Larry Johnson SD .... 1.25 .60 .12
  Charlotte Hornets
- ☐ 481 Shawn Kemp SD .... .40 .20 .04
  Seattle Supersonics
- ☐ 482 John Starks SD .... .25 .12 .02
  New York Knicks
- ☐ 483 Doug West SD .... .06 .03 .00
  Minnesota Timberwolves
- ☐ 484 Craig Hodges .... .03 .01 .00
  Long Distance Shoot Out
- ☐ 485 LaBradford Smith .... .20 .10 .02
  Washington Bullets
- ☐ 486 Winston Garland .... .03 .01 .00
  Denver Nuggets
- ☐ 487 David Benoit .... .60 .30 .06
  Utah Jazz
- ☐ 488 John Bagley .... .06 .03 .00
  Boston Celtics
- ☐ 489 Mark Macon .... .60 .30 .06
  Denver Nuggets
- ☐ 490 Mitch Richmond .... .15 .07 .01
  Sacramento Kings
- ☐ 491 Luc Longley .... .30 .15 .03
  Minnesota Timberwolves
- ☐ 492 Sedale Threatt .... .06 .03 .00
  Los Angeles Lakers
- ☐ 493 Doug Smith .... .60 .30 .06
  Dallas Mavericks
- ☐ 494 Travis Mays .... .06 .03 .00
  Atlanta Hawks
- ☐ 495 Xavier McDaniel .... .08 .04 .01
  New York Knicks
- ☐ 496 Brian Shaw .... .06 .03 .00
  Miami Heat

1991-92 Upper Deck Heroes Jerry West / 351

☐ 497 Stanley Roberts	1.25	.60	.12
Orlando Magic			
☐ 498 Blair Rasmussen	.03	.01	.00
Atlanta Hawks			
☐ 499 Brian Williams	.60	.30	.06
Orlando Magic			
☐ 500 Checklist Card	.06	.01	.00

1991-92 Upper Deck Heroes Jerry West

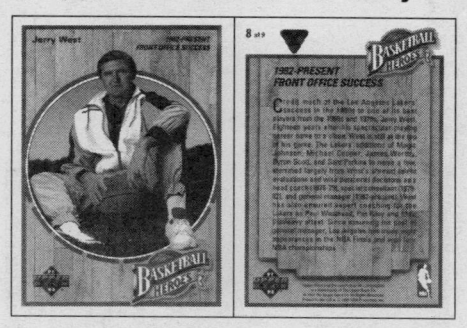

This ten-card insert set was randomly inserted in Upper Deck's high series basketball foil packs. Also included in the packs were 2,500 checklist cards autographed by West. The fronts of the standard-size (2 1/2" by 3 1/2") cards capture memorable moments from his college and professional career. The player photos are cut out and superimposed over a jump ball circle on a hardwood basketball floor design. The card backs present commentary. The cards are numbered on the back.

	MINT	EXC	G-VG
COMPLETE SET (10)	35.00	17.50	3.50
COMMON PLAYER (1-9)	3.00	1.50	.30
☐ 1 Jerry West	3.00	1.50	.30
1959 NCAA Tournament MVP			
☐ 2 Jerry West	3.00	1.50	.30
1960 U.S. Team			
☐ 3 Jerry West	3.00	1.50	.30
1968-69 NBA Playoff MVP			
☐ 4 Jerry West	3.00	1.50	.30
1969-70 NBA Scoring			

352 / 1991-92 Upper Deck Heroes Jerry West

☐ 5	Jerry West .... 1972 NBA World Championship	3.00	1.50	.30
☐ 6	Jerry West .... 1973-74 25,000 Points	3.00	1.50	.30
☐ 7	Jerry West .... 1979 Basketball Hall of Fame	3.00	1.50	.30
☐ 8	Jerry West .... 1982 to the present Front Office Success	3.00	1.50	.30
☐ 9	Jerry West .... Portrait Card	3.00	1.50	.30
☐ NNO	Jerry West .... Cover/Title Card	15.00	7.50	1.50

1991-92 Wild Card Collegiate

The Wild Card Collegiate Basketball set contains 120 cards measuring the standard size (2 1/2" by 3 1/2"). One out of every 100 cards is "Wild", with a numbered stripe to indicate how many cards it can be redeemed for. There are 5, 10, 20, 50, 100, and 1,000 denominations, with the highest numbers the scarcest. Whatever the number, the card can be redeemed for that number of regular cards of the same player, after paying a redemption fee of 4.95 per order. The front design features glossy color action player photos on a black card face, with an orange frame around the picture and different color numbers in the top and right borders. The backs have different shades of purple and a color head shot, biography, and statistics. The cards are numbered on the back. At the San Francisco Card Expo (Aug. 30 to Sept. 2, 1991), promo cards of Kenny Anderson and Larry Johnson were given away. These cards are identical to those inserted in 1991 Wild Card Collegiate football packs, except that they have the San Francisco Expo logo at the lower left corner on the back.

1991-92 Wild Card Collegiate / 353

	MINT	EXC	G-VG
COMPLETE SET (120)	10.00	5.00	1.00
COMMON PLAYER (1-120)	.05	.02	.00

- ☐ 1 Larry Johnson ..... 1.25 — .60 — .12
  First NBA Draft Pick
- ☐ 2 LeRon Ellis ..... .12 — .06 — .01
  Syracuse
- ☐ 3 Alvaro Teheran ..... .05 — .02 — .00
  Houston
- ☐ 4 Eric Murdock ..... .30 — .15 — .03
  Providence
- ☐ 5A Surprise Card 1 ..... 1.00 — .50 — .10
- ☐ 5B Dikembe Mutombo ..... 1.75 — .85 — .17
  Georgetown
- ☐ 6 Anthony Avent ..... .20 — .10 — .02
  Seton Hall
- ☐ 7 Isiah Thomas ..... .15 — .07 — .01
  Indiana
- ☐ 8 Abdul Shamsid-Deen ..... .05 — .02 — .00
  Providence
- ☐ 9 Linton Townes ..... .05 — .02 — .00
  James Madison
- ☐ 10 Joe Wylie ..... .08 — .04 — .01
  Miami
- ☐ 11 Cozell McQueen ..... .08 — .04 — .01
  North Carolina State
- ☐ 12 David Benoit ..... .50 — .25 — .05
  Alabama
- ☐ 13 Chris Mullin ..... .20 — .10 — .02
  St. John's
- ☐ 14 Dale Davis ..... .35 — .17 — .03
  Clemson
- ☐ 15 Patrick Ewing ..... .25 — .12 — .02
  Georgetown
- ☐ 16 Greg Anthony ..... .40 — .20 — .04
  UNLV
- ☐ 17 Robert Pack ..... .75 — .35 — .07
  USC
- ☐ 18 Phil Zevenbergen ..... .05 — .02 — .00
  Washington
- ☐ 19 Rick Fox ..... 1.00 — .50 — .10
  North Carolina
- ☐ 20 Chris Corchiani ..... .15 — .07 — .01
  North Carolina State
- ☐ 21 Elliot Perry ..... .15 — .07 — .01
  Memphis State
- ☐ 22 Kevin Brooks ..... .15 — .07 — .01
  SW Louisiana
- ☐ 23 Mark Macon ..... .35 — .17 — .03
  Temple
- ☐ 24 Larry Johnson ..... 5.00 — 2.50 — .50
  UNLV
- ☐ 25 George Ackles ..... .08 — .04 — .01
  UNLV
- ☐ 26A Surprise Card 5 ..... .75 — .35 — .07
- ☐ 26B Christian Laettner ..... 1.25 — .60 — .12

354 / 1991-92 Wild Card Collegiate

	(Promo) Duke			
☐ 27	Andy Fields	.05	.02	.00
	Cheyney State			
☐ 28	Kevin Lynch	.15	.07	.01
	Minnesota			
☐ 29	Graylin Warner	.05	.02	.00
	SW Louisiana			
☐ 30	James Bullock	.05	.02	.00
	Purdue			
☐ 31	Steve Bucknall	.08	.04	.01
	North Carolina			
☐ 32	Carl Thomas	.08	.04	.01
	Eastern Michigan			
☐ 33	Doug Overton	.08	.04	.01
	La Salle			
☐ 34	Brian Shorter	.08	.04	.01
	Pittsburgh			
☐ 35	Chad Gallagher	.08	.04	.01
	Creighton			
☐ 36	Antonio Davis	.05	.02	.00
	Texas-El Paso			
☐ 37	Sean Green	.15	.07	.01
	Iona			
☐ 38	Randy Brown	.15	.07	.01
	New Mexico State			
☐ 39	Richard Dumas	.08	.04	.01
	Oklahoma State			
☐ 40	Terrell Brandon	.40	.20	.04
	Oregon			
☐ 41	Marty Embry	.05	.02	.00
	DePaul			
☐ 42	Ronald Coleman	.08	.04	.01
	USC			
☐ 43	King Rice	.08	.04	.01
	North Carolina			
☐ 44	Perry Carter	.08	.04	.01
	Ohio State			
☐ 45A	Surprise Card 2	1.00	.50	.10
☐ 45B	Billy Owens	1.75	.85	.17
	Syracuse			
☐ 46A	Surprise Card 3	.60	.30	.06
☐ 46B	Stacey Augmon	1.00	.50	.10
	UNLV			
☐ 47	Andrew Gaze	.05	.02	.00
	Seton Hall			
☐ 48	Jimmy Oliver	.20	.10	.02
	Purdue			
☐ 49	Treg Lee	.08	.04	.01
	Ohio State			
☐ 50	Ricky Winslow	.08	.04	.01
	Houston			
☐ 51	Danny Vranes	.08	.04	.01
	Utah			
☐ 52	Jay Murphy	.08	.04	.01
	Boston College			
☐ 53	Adrian Dantley	.08	.04	.01
	Notre Dame			

1991-92 Wild Card Collegiate / 355

☐ 54	Joe Arlauckas Niagara University	.05	.02	.00
☐ 55	Moses Scurry UNLV	.08	.04	.01
☐ 56	Andy Toolson Brigham Young	.08	.04	.01
☐ 57	Ramon Rivas Temple	.08	.04	.01
☐ 58	Charles Davis Vanderbilt	.05	.02	.00
☐ 59	Butch Wade Michigan	.05	.02	.00
☐ 60	John Pinone Villanova	.05	.02	.00
☐ 61	Bill Wennington St. John's	.08	.04	.01
☐ 62	Walter Berry St. John's	.08	.04	.01
☐ 63	Terry Dozier South Carolina	.05	.02	.00
☐ 64	Mitchell Anderson Bradley	.05	.02	.00
☐ 65	Pace Mannion Utah	.08	.04	.01
☐ 66	Pete Myers Little Rock	.05	.02	.00
☐ 67	Eddie Lee Wilkins Gardner Webb	.08	.04	.01
☐ 68	Mark Hughes Michigan	.05	.02	.00
☐ 69	Darryl Dawkins No College	.08	.04	.01
☐ 70	Jay Vincent Michigan State	.05	.02	.00
☐ 71	Doug Lee Purdue	.12	.06	.01
☐ 72	Russ Schoene Tennessee-Chattanooga	.05	.02	.00
☐ 73	Tim Kempton Notre Dame	.05	.02	.00
☐ 74	Earl Cureton Detroit	.08	.04	.01
☐ 75	Terence Stansbury Temple	.08	.04	.01
☐ 76	Frank Kornet Vanderbilt	.05	.02	.00
☐ 77	Bob McAdoo North Carolina	.08	.04	.01
☐ 78	Haywoode Workman Oral Roberts	.08	.04	.01
☐ 79	Vinny Del Negro North Carolina State	.08	.04	.01
☐ 80	Harold Pressley Villanova	.08	.04	.01
☐ 81	Robert Smith UNLV	.05	.02	.00
☐ 82	Adrian Caldwell Lamar	.05	.02	.00

356 / 1991-92 Wild Card Collegiate

☐ 83	Scottie Pippen Central Arkansas	.30	.15	.03
☐ 84	John Stockton Gonzaga	.20	.10	.02
☐ 85	Elwayne Campbell Henderson State	.05	.02	.00
☐ 86	Chris Gatling Old Dominion	.40	.20	.04
☐ 87	Cedric Henderson Georgia	.05	.02	.00
☐ 88	Mike Iuzzolino St. Francis	.35	.17	.03
☐ 89	Fennis Dembo Wyoming	.08	.04	.01
☐ 90	Darnell Valentine Kansas	.05	.02	.00
☐ 91	Michael Brooks LaSalle	.05	.02	.00
☐ 92	Marty Conlon Providence	.12	.06	.01
☐ 93	Lamont Strothers Christopher Newport	.12	.06	.01
☐ 94	Donald Hodge Temple	.35	.17	.03
☐ 95	Pete Chilcutt North Carolina	.20	.10	.02
☐ 96	Kenny Anderson Georgia Tech	1.50	.75	.15
☐ 97	Ian Lockhart Tennessee	.05	.02	.00
☐ 98A	Surprise Card 4	.90	.45	.09
☐ 98B	Steve Smith Michigan State	1.50	.75	.15
☐ 99	Larry Lawrence Dartmouth	.05	.02	.00
☐ 100	Jerome Mincy Alabama-Birmingham	.08	.04	.01
☐ 101	Ben Coleman Maryland	.08	.04	.01
☐ 102	Tom Copa Marquette	.05	.02	.00
☐ 103	Demetrius Calip Michigan	.12	.06	.01
☐ 104	Myron Brown Slippery Rock	.10	.05	.01
☐ 105	Derrick Pope Montana	.05	.02	.00
☐ 106	Kelvin Upshaw Utah	.08	.04	.01
☐ 107	Andrew Moten Florida	.08	.04	.01
☐ 108	Terry Tyler Detroit	.05	.02	.00
☐ 109	Kevin Magee Cal-Irvine	.05	.02	.00
☐ 110	Tharon Mayes Florida State	.12	.06	.01

1991-92 Wild Card Red Hot Rookies / 357

☐ 111 Perry McDonald Georgetown	.08	.04	.01
☐ 112 Jose Ortiz Oregon State	.08	.04	.01
☐ 113 Rick Mahorn Hampton	.08	.04	.01
☐ 114 David Butler UNLV	.08	.04	.01
☐ 115 Carl Herrera Houston	.20	.10	.02
☐ 116 Darrell Mickens Houston	.05	.02	.00
☐ 117 Steve Bardo Illinois	.08	.04	.01
☐ 118 Checklist 1	.05	.02	.00
☐ 119 Checklist 2	.05	.02	.00
☐ 120 Checklist 3	.05	.02	.00

1991-92 Wild Card Red Hot Rookies

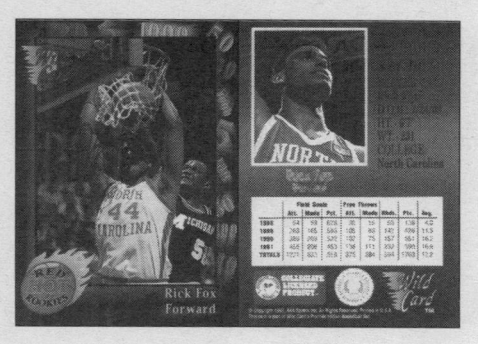

These cards were randomly packed in the Collegiate Basketball foil cases, and they included denomination cards. The cards measure the standard size (2 1/2" by 3 1/2"). The front design features glossy color action player photos on a black card face, with an orange frame around the picture and different color numbers in the top and right borders. The "Red Hot Rookies" emblem in the lower left corner rounds out the card face. The backs have a color close-up photo, biography, and complete college statistics. The cards are numbered on the back.

	MINT	EXC	G-VG
COMPLETE SET (10)	45.00	22.50	4.50
COMMON PLAYER (1-10)	2.00	1.00	.20

358 / 1991-92 Wild Card Red Hot Rookies

☐ 1 Dikembe Mutombo Georgetown	8.00	4.00	.80
☐ 2 Larry Johnson UNLV	15.00	7.50	1.50
☐ 3 Steve Smith Michigan State	6.50	3.25	.65
☐ 4 Billy Owens Syracuse	9.00	4.50	.90
☐ 5 Mark Macon Temple	2.50	1.25	.25
☐ 6 Stacey Augmon UNLV	6.00	3.00	.60
☐ 7 Victor Alexander Iowa State	2.00	1.00	.20
☐ 8 Mike Iuzzolino St. Francis	2.00	1.00	.20
☐ 9 Rick Fox North Carolina	4.00	2.00	.40
☐ 10 Terrell Brandon UER Oregon (Name misspelled Terrel on card front)	3.00	1.50	.30

SMOKEY'S
SPORTSCARDS, INC. · of · Las · Vegas

WORLDWIDE SERVICE

"Simply the Best ... We Guarantee It."

BASKETBALL · BASEBALL · FOOTBALL · HOCKEY
MEMORABILIA · SUPPLIES · WE SHIP WORLDWIDE

to Order call 1-800-SMOKEYS (800-766-5397)
or order by 24-hr. fax (702) 876-1846

**HEADQUARTERS/
WAREHOUSE**
3330 W. Desert Inn Rd.
Las Vegas, NV 89102
702-876-9779
Fax 702-876-1846

SMOKEY'S
Las Vegas

**SPORTSCARD STADIUM
LAS VEGAS "STRIP"**
3734 Las Vegas Blvd. So. · L.V., NV 89109
(Right next to the Boardwalk Hotel & Casino)
702-739-0003
Fax 702-736-8957

1·800·766·5397

AMERICAN SPORTSCARDS
WHOLESALE • RETAIL • BUY • SELL

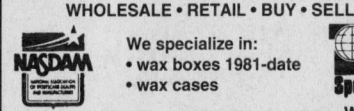

We specialize in:
- wax boxes 1981-date
- wax cases

WA 17

Mon.-Fri. 10-7 • Sat. 10-5 • Sun. 12-5

(509) 326-1729

5527 North Wall
Spokane, WA 99205

BEVERLY HILLS BASEBALL CARD SHOP
OWNER: MATT FEDERGREEN

Specializing in:
- Baseball Cards
- Sports Memorabilia
- Pro Hats & Jerseys

1137 South Robertson
Los Angeles, CA 90035
(1/2 block north of Pico)
(213) 278-GAME
Tue. - Sun. CALL FOR HOURS

BUY/SELL

BILL'S SPORTS COLLECTIBLES

2335 South Broadway
Denver, CO 80210
(303) 733-4878

Baseball, Football and
All Sports Cards
Programs, Books, Autographs
and other Sports Collectibles

Brewart Coins & Stamps

Baseball Cards

We also buy & sell unopened cases & sets.

Mon.-Fri. 9-5:30   Sat. 9-4

403 West Katella - Anaheim, CA 92802

(714) 533-0400

★ Two blocks from Disneyland ★

COLLECTORS WORLD
Buy - Sell - Trade

BASEBALL, FOOTBALL, BASKETBALL, HOCKEY
& NON-SPORTS CARDS · OLD RECORDS · COMICS

Mon. & Sat. 11-6:30
Tues. closed
Wed. & Thur. 2-8
Fri. 11-8
Sun. 11-4

JACK BYRD
612 Quince Orchard Rd.
Gaithersburg, MD 20878
Phone: (301) 840-0520

235 Muddy Branch Rd.
Gaithersburg, MD 20878
Phone: (301) 840-9729

FASTBALL SPORTSCARDS

348 Wilson Avenue
Downsview, Ontario
TORONTO, CANADA M3H 1S9
(416) 398-9400

One of Canada's Largest Basketball Sportscards Stores

Mon.-Fri. 11-7
Sat. 10-5
Sun. 12-4

Steven Panet
Jerry Panet

Buying • Selling
Basketball Baseball
Hockey   Boxing
Football   Non-Sports

COLLECTOR'S STADIUM

BUY - SELL

Baseball Cards
Sports Memorabilia
Posters & Prints
Photographs
Baseball Collecting Supplies

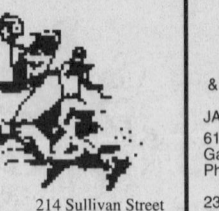

214 Sullivan Street
New York, NY 10012

(212) 353-1531

SPORTS MEMORABILIA INSURANCE
Cornell & Finkelmeier, Inc.

P.O. Box 210
Wapakoneta, OH 45895
(419) 738-3314

THE NATION'S LARGEST INSURER OF SPORTS
MEMORABILIA DEALERS AND COLLECTORS

GARY'S COLLECTABLES
PREMIUM CARDS

Baseball • Football • Basketball • Send Want Lists

GARY ALEXANIAN
P.O. Box 6511
Moraga, CA 94570
(510) 944-1080

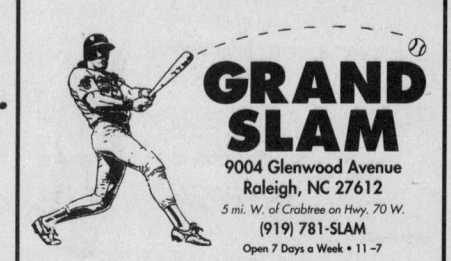

GRAND SLAM

9004 Glenwood Avenue
Raleigh, NC 27612

5 mi. W. of Crabtree on Hwy. 70 W.
(919) 781-SLAM
Open 7 Days a Week • 11-7

Buy, Sell, Trade and Appraise

FIRST BASE
A Sports Nostalgia Shop

216 Webb Chapel Village Shopping Center
(SE Corner of Webb Chapel & Forest)
Dallas, Texas 75229
(214) 243-5271

11-7 Mon.-Sat.
Closed Sun.

Buy • Sell   (312) 594-1925

GRAF BASEBALL CARD CO.

Baseball • Football • Hockey
Basketball • Cases Bought & Sold
"Everything For The Card Collector"

5754 N. Milwaukee Avenue
Chicago, IL 60646

M-F 12-7
Saturday 10:30-6
Sunday 1-5

(818) 700-9537
Fax (818) 700-0573

Hours: Mon.-Sat. 12-5

Mr. B's Basketball Cards

Nationwide Service

Mr. B

20555 Devonshire St.
Chatsworth, CA 91311

Bill Raulerson or Dave Morgan
(818) 585-0464

Mudville

Baseball Cards
Sports Memorabilia

336 N. Allen Avenue
Pasadena, CA 91106

Open:
Mon. – Thurs. & Sat. 10 - 6
Fri. & Sun. Noon - 6

BASKETBALL, FOOTBALL & BASEBALL SPORTS CARDS
BOUGHT & SOLD

WANT LISTS FILLED

Pat's Coins & Cards
3229 WEST 24th ST.
ERIE, PA 16506

(814) 833-0566
OR (814) 838-9703

By Appointment Only
9 a.m. - 9 p.m.
DAILY & SUNDAY

T.J. SCHWARTZ

ROB CHAIN

PORKY'S

M-F 11-8
Sat. 10-7
Sun. 11-5

BASEBALL CARDS & STUFF

Specializing in Pre-1970
Sports Cards Stars & Commons
Football, Basketball,
Hockey, Non-Sports
Autographed Memorabilia
Satellite TV Sports Lounge
Lakers, Kings & Dodgers Tickets

Buy, Sell & Trade
12458 Magnolia Blvd.
N. Hollywood, CA 91607
(818) 760-3800

VISA DISCOVER

Ragtime

Basketball Cards · Hockey Cards
Basketball Cards · Football Cards

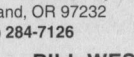

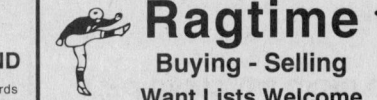

Ragtime
Buying - Selling
Want Lists Welcome

18 Fairfield Ave.
Bridgeport, CT 06604
(203) 331-9944

Bill Rudd
Mon.-Sat. 9-5

San Francisco Card Exchange

MAX & BARRY   (415) 665-TEAM

SAN FRANCISCO CARD EXCHANGE

Baseball Cards · Sports Memorabilia
Collector Supplies

1316 -18th Ave.
Betw. Irving/Judah
94122

Mon.-Fri.: 12-6
Sat.: 10-5
Sun.: Closed

Portland Sports Card Co.

SCA

Dept. BK2
2401 N.E. Broadway
Portland, OR 97232
(503) 284-7126

BILL WESSLUND

- Baseball Cards • Football, Basketball, Hockey & Soccer Cards
- Minor League Sets • Hobby Supplies • Publications • Sports Posters
- Autographs • Non-Sports Cards • Other Sports Collectibles

CALL OR SEND FOR FREE PRICE LIST
We pay top prices for old baseball cards

Roanoke Coin Exchange / Lynchburg Coin & Collectibles

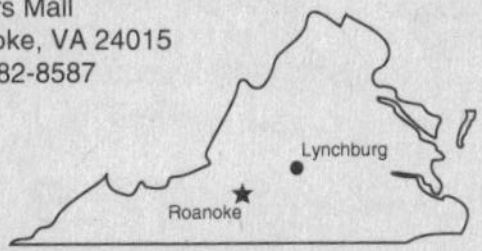

Baseball, Football
Hockey, Basketball
Cards
Mon-Sat 10-6

Coins, Stamps,
Gold, Silver
Bought & Sold Daily.

Roanoke Coin Exchange
Towers Mall
Roanoke, VA 24015
703-982-8587

Lynchburg Coin & Collectibles
218 Wards Road (Hills Plaza)   Catalog of Licensed Products
Lynchburg, VA 24502   Available. Send $1.00 Postage
804-237-2741   & Handling - refundable with 1st order

SPORTS SOURCE

A POWERFUL SOURCE FOR THE FAN

Baseball • Football • Basketball
All Years
(Stars, Sets & Commons)
Plus Souvenirs & Apparel

Mon.-Sat., 10-6
Sun., 12-5

920 N. Hollywood Way
Burbank, CA 91505
(818) 846-4060

STAMPS & CARDS UNLIMITED

SPECIALIZING IN BASKETBALL CARDS

1576 CHEROKEE DR., SALINAS, CA 93906

PREMIUM BASKETBALL, BASEBALL CARDS & SUPPLIES

HERB DALLAS, JR.

TELEPHONE
(408) 443-4533

1957-58, 1969-82 Topps
1961-62 Fleer

Steven Roeglin

specializing in vintage basketball cards

815 North New Street
Kirksville, MO 63501

Mail order, or by appointment
(816) 665-8730

Specializing in
Sportscards
through the mail.

TWO CAPITALS CARD CO.

P.O. Box 920
Williamsburg, VA 23187

Baseball - Football
Basketball - Hockey

Send Your
Want List.

All Inquiries
Promptly Answered.

TOUCHDOWN!

Dr. James Beckett scores again with his national bestseller, *The Official® Price Guide to Football Cards*.

- Comprehensive coverage of all the major series, including Bowman, Topps, Fleer, and Upper Deck
- Valuable tips on buying, selling, and finding cards
- Current market values

BY *THE* LEADING EXPERT!

HOUSE OF COLLECTABLES
201 East 50th Street
New York, New York 10022

Please send me *The Official® 1993 Price Guide to Football Cards*, 12th Ed. . . 0-876-37897-1 . . .$5.99. I am enclosing $_____ (add $2.00 for the first book and 50¢ for each additional book to cover postage and handling). Send check or money order — no cash or C.O.D.'s, please. Prices and numbers are subject to change without notice.

Name _____

Address _____

City _____ State _____ Zip _____

Allow at least 4 weeks for delivery

Want To Get The Most Enjoyment Out Of Card Collecting?...

Make Sure You're Fully Equipped!

Order Your Subscription To *Beckett Basketball Monthly* Today.

Just as a player looks for the right equipment to make him feel comfortable in his game, the sports card collector looks for the right equipment to make him feel comfortable in his hobby. In *Beckett Basketball Monthly*, a collector can find many of the things he's looking for to better equip himself for total enjoyment of the hobby.

- The most up-to-date Price Guide in the hobby.
- Full-color, superstar covers and Hot hobby art suitable for autographs.
- Informative features, punctuated by colorful action photos.
- National rankings to keep you up with who's Hot and who's not.

- Tips on building collections.
- Answers to your hobby questions and insights into what other collectors are thinking.

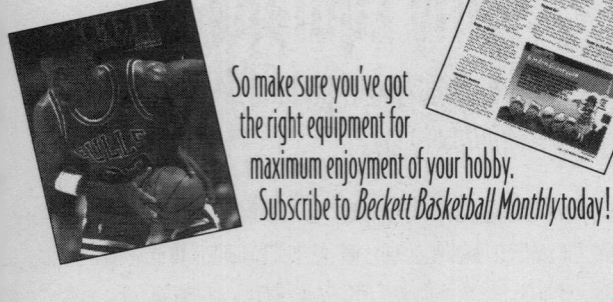

So make sure you've got the right equipment for maximum enjoyment of your hobby. Subscribe to *Beckett Basketball Monthly* today!

Name (Please print) _____ Age _____

Address _____

City _____ State _____ Zip _____

Payment enclosed via: ☐ Check or Money Order ☐ VISA/MasterCard (Please do NOT send cash)

Signature _____ Exp. _____

Name (Print) _____

Credit Card # ☐☐☐☐-☐☐☐☐-☐☐☐☐-☐☐☐☐

Check one please:	Your Price
1 year (a savings of $15.45 for 12 issues)	**$19.95**
2 years (a savings of $34.85 for 24 issues)	**$35.95**

All foreign addresses add $12 per year for postage (includes G.S.T.).
All payments payable in U.S. funds. Please allow 6 to 8 weeks for delivery of your first copy.

Mail to: Beckett Publications, Beckett Basketball Monthly,
P.O. Box 1915, Marion, OH 43305-1915

DKH93

BECKETT BASKETBALL MONTHLY

Like all of our magazines, *Beckett Baseball Card Monthly* features a monthly Price Guide which keeps you current on the values of the most popular cards. Send for your subscription today!

Name (Please print) _____ Age _____

Address _____

City _____ State _____ Zip _____

Payment enclosed via: ☐ Check or Money Order ☐ VISA/MasterCard (Please do NOT send cash)

Signature _____ Exp. _____

Name (Print) _____

Credit Card # ☐☐☐☐-☐☐☐☐-☐☐☐☐-☐☐☐☐

Check one please:

		Your Price
1 year	(a savings of $15.45 for 12 issues)	$19.95
2 years	(a savings of $34.85 for 24 issues)	$35.95

All foreign addresses add $12 per year for postage (includes G.S.T.).
All payments payable in U.S. funds. Please allow 6 to 8 weeks for delivery of your first copy.

Mail to: Beckett Publications, Beckett Baseball Card Monthly,
P.O. Box 2048, Marion, OH 43305-2048

DKH93

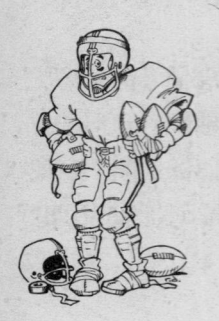

With *Beckett Football Card Monthly*, you can count on the same full-color, superstar covers and Hot hobby art that you'll find in all of our magazines. Don't wait! Subscribe now!

Name (Please print) _____ Age _____

Address _____

City _____ State _____ Zip _____

Payment enclosed via: ☐ Check or Money Order ☐ VISA/MasterCard (Please do NOT send cash)

Signature _____ Exp. _____

Name (Print) _____

Credit Card # ☐☐☐☐-☐☐☐☐-☐☐☐☐-☐☐☐☐

Check one please:

		Your Price
1 year	(a savings of $15.45 for 12 issues)	**$19.95**
2 years	(a savings of $34.85 for 24 issues)	**$35.95**

All foreign addresses add $12 per year for postage (includes G.S.T.).
All payments payable in U.S. funds. Please allow 6 to 8 weeks for delivery of your first copy.

Mail to: Beckett Publications, Beckett Football Card Monthly,
P.O. Box 1915, Marion, OH 43305-1915

DKH93

In every issue of *Beckett Hockey Monthly*, you get informative features, punctuated by colorful action photos, and national rankings that keep you up with who's Hot and who's not. That's something you can expect in all of our magazines. Subscribe today!

Name (Please print) _____ Age ____

Address _____

City _____ State _____ Zip _____

Payment enclosed via: ☐ Check or Money Order   ☐ VISA/MasterCard   (Please do NOT send cash)

Signature _____ Exp. ____

Name (Print) _____

Credit Card # ☐☐☐☐-☐☐☐☐-☐☐☐☐-☐☐☐☐

Check one please:

		Your Price
1 year	(a savings of $15.45 for 12 issues)	$19.95
2 years	(a savings of $34.85 for 24 issues)	$35.95

All foreign addresses add $12 per year for postage (includes G.S.T.).
All payments payable in U.S. funds. Please allow 6 to 8 weeks for delivery of your first copy.

Mail to: Beckett Publications, Beckett Hockey Monthly,
P.O. Box 1915, Marion, OH 43305-1915

BECKETT HOCKEY MONTHLY

DKH93

The monthly multisport magazine concentrating on Hot young prospects, *Beckett Focus on Future Stars* gives you tips on building card collections, answers to your hobby questions and insights into what other collectors are thinking. Plus you get a monthly Price Guide. Send for your subscription today!

Name (Please print) _____ Age _____

Address _____

City _____ State _____ Zip _____

Payment enclosed via: ☐ Check or Money Order   ☐ VISA/MasterCard   (Please do NOT send cash)

Signature _____ Exp. _____

Name (Print) _____

Credit Card # ☐☐☐☐-☐☐☐☐-☐☐☐☐-☐☐☐☐

Check one please:

		Your Price
☐	1 year (a savings of $15.45 for 12 issues)	$19.95
☐	2 years (a savings of $34.85 for 24 issues)	$35.95

All foreign addresses add $12 per year for postage (includes G.S.T.).
All payments payable in U.S. funds. Please allow 6 to 8 weeks for delivery of your first copy.

Mail to: Beckett Publications, Beckett Focus on Future Stars,
P.O. Box 1915, Marion, OH 43305-1915

DKH93